German aesthetic and literary criticism

German aesthetic and literary criticism: Kant, Fichte, Schelling, Schopenhauer, Hegel

*Edited and introduced by
David Simpson*

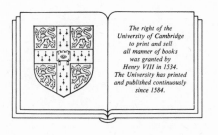

The right of the
University of Cambridge
to print and sell
all manner of books
was granted by
Henry VIII in 1534.
The University has printed
and published continuously
since 1584.

Cambridge University Press

Cambridge
London   New York   New Rochelle
Melbourne   Sydney

Published by the Press Syndicate of the University of Cambridge
The Pitt Building, Trumpington Street, Cambridge CB2 1RP
32 East 57th Street, New York, NY 10022, USA
296 Beaconsfield Parade, Middle Park, Melbourne 3206, Australia

© Cambridge University Press 1984

First published 1984

Printed in Great Britain by the University Press, Cambridge

Library of Congress catalogue card number: 83-15320

British Library Cataloguing in Publication Data
German aesthetic and literary criticism.
1. German literature—18th century—History and
criticism   2. German literature—19th century—History and criticism
I. Simpson, David
830'.9'006   PT311

ISBN 0 521 23630 4 hard covers
ISBN 0 521 28086 9 paperback

Contents

Acknowledgements

The greatest debt, and one that must be felt at all times by anyone undertaking this sort of enterprise, is to the other editors and translators of German Idealist philosophy. Most translations have been slightly modified, and some (e.g. William Smith's of Fichte) have been heavily revised; but in every case it has been clear to me that my own sense of an 'improvement' might not have been possible without other available versions. Of course, as I must declare myself, somewhat nervously, to be responsible for various modifications or initiatives, so I must anticipate that my own decisions will be themselves modified and 'improved'. The task of putting the German Romantics into English must continue to be 'work in progress', and I can only hope that others will experience the same spirit of cooperative sympathy that I have felt at all stages of this work.

I must also thank the following for help in elucidating difficult allusions and references: John Gage, Ronald Martinez, Gezà von Molnàr, Martin Mueller. Versions of the introduction were read and much improved by the careful attentions of three colleagues: Nancy Fraser, Erich Heller, and Herbert Tucker. They will perceive their contributions even as they notice the points on which I have not been persuaded! My thoughts on the whole subject of German Romantic aesthetics were much sharpened by a series of timely discussions with Patricia O'Neill-Cerritos. I owe a special debt of thanks to John Barrell, who was responsible for much of the initial organization of this project.

The production of the final manuscript would have been much less efficient without the considerable assistance of Kathy Beckerman, Estelle Frye, Barbara Seaman, and Marge Weiner. I cannot imagine a more convivial and cooperative editor than Terry Moore, whose personal contribution to the wider English-speaking awareness of German thought and literature I should here like to acknowledge. I must also thank Caroline Murray for some very keen-eyed copy-editing.

Citations and abbreviations

Most references give simply author and date of edition cited, so that the bibliography must be consulted for full details. The index should be consulted for reference to topics, e.g. tragedy, lyric poetry.

The following abbreviations have been used:

CJ	Kant, *Critique of Judgement*
Ak.	*Kants gesammelte Schriften*, 'Akademie' edition
AE	Schiller, *On the Aesthetic Education of Man*
SK	Fichte, *Science of Knowledge (Wissenschaftslehre)*
System	Schelling, *System of Transcendental Idealism*

A note on selections and translations

There are obvious limits to what a single anthology can represent. As I shall show, there was unusually close contact between the philosophers and the poets, critics, and theologians during the Romantic period in Germany, so that any anthology of this sort must risk making philosophy appear much more isolated from its general cultural and political environment than it actually was. Thus I have found myself frequently stressing these connections where I am aware of them. Somewhat in the same spirit, I have at times decided to translate or reprint texts which are not themselves directly about aesthetics, or explicit examples of literary criticism. This decision was taken in the hope that this sequence of writings might give some sense of the whole within which aesthetics was a living part. It cannot of course give a complete sense of this whole, but I hope nevertheless that the importance of, for example, Kant's *What is Enlightenment?* to the general situation out of which specifically aesthetic priorities were generated will be apparent. Even within the specific field of writings on aesthetics, it is of course the case that my selections must themselves constitute some sort of shaping of the available materials. Hard as I have tried to maintain some measure of disinterest, readers will surely notice that some themes and arguments seem to be emphasized at the expense of others. Partly this is a matter of coherence: after establishing Kant's emphasis on the disinterested nature of the aesthetic judgement it seems natural to include Hegel's views on the relation of art and desire, and so forth. Nevertheless, readers who are already well informed are certainly going to argue for sins of omission and sins of inclusion on my part.

The following texts are organized by author rather than by date or by theme. Organization by theme would have been too restrictive and discontinuous, perhaps even impossible where themes themselves come not as single spies but in battalions. It was more tempting to present the texts in order of publication, so that, for example, Fichte in 1805 would follow Schelling in 1800. This would have been closer to the way in which German Idealism actually developed, but I have decided to retain the more traditional arrangement by author, whilst trying to signal the most important connections in the footnotes. These writers are seldom easy to understand, and the task would not be made easier by giving up the thread of biographical continuity.

In translating or in revising or modifying existing translations, my general policy has been to try to achieve the maximum symmetry, wherever it seems appropriate, between the translation of Kant's vocabulary and that of his successors. *The Critique of Judgement* is not only the most sophisticated of all these writings in its rational discrimination of terms, but it is historically, intellectually and philosophically prior to and constitutive of the others. As such it offers the translator the most useful basis for a symmetrical vocabulary. There are of course problems here. This policy works well for a word like *Verstand*, which I have generally made conformable to the Kantian "understanding", because the English word has in this case a similar latitude to the German: it can signify either a very precise philosophical faculty (as it mostly does in Kant) or stand as roughly descriptive of our rational faculties or intelligence in general. Occasions do arise, however, where it is undesirable to use the same English word to translate the same German word at all times. Key terms like *Geist, Bildung, Trieb, Begriff, Anschauung, Vorstellung*, and so forth, operate in German across a wider range of meanings than any compatible English word would do. In the hands of different writers, and even for the same writer at different times (for example in Fichte according to whether one is reading his popular or specialist works), such terms as these can range from absolutely commonplace to highly differentiated significations. Often, indeed, this breadth of potential meanings has an incremental place in the argument, most obviously in Hegel, who had a conscious policy of exposing the philosophical basis or potential of everyday German. Obviously, perfection in this matter is not something a translator may expect to achieve. I have tried to give the German word or phrase in parentheses, or to include a footnote, on occasions where the choice of an English word seems especially unstable or inadequate. Some readers may however find that the vocabulary of Kant's followers has been brought too rigidly into line with that of their great precursor. For example, I have often amended *Anschauung* to read "intuition" rather than "vision", "sight", or "contemplation"; or *Vorstellung* to read "representation" rather than "idea" or "image"; or *Begriff* to read "concept" rather than "notion" or "idea". I have done so at times because the usage has seemed to me much more strictly Kantian than other translators have allowed, and at times because a Kantian word may be used to indicate a qualification of its significance in Kant's own writings: the example of the "intellectual intuition" is perhaps the most famous. Similarly, Hegel's *Begriff* is not Kant's, but we are clearly meant to sense the subversion of Kant, which we cannot do if it is translated as "notion" or "idea".

One feature of the vocabulary of these writers is the frequent use of synonyms, one of German and one of foreign provenance. Sometimes they are discriminated, as *Objekt* and *Gegenstand* seem to be in Kant; sometimes not, as *Poesie* and *Dichtung* in Schelling; and sometimes it is hard to be sure. This is important, given that the initiation of a specifically German philosophical vocabulary was (at times) a priority for both Fichte and Hegel. Again, I have used parentheses and endnotes to explain these points.

The question of 'translation' is perhaps even more anxious at the level of syntax than of vocabulary. English readers have often winced at the long sentences and dizzying use of reflexives that characterize the prose styles of some of these thinkers. I have generally sought to preserve a middle way between the quite inappropriate demands of 'plain English' and the at times bewildering syntax of the German. Generally I have tried to make sure that the reader knows he is reading German, and a particular kind of German at that. This has meant the occasional modification of translations where it has seemed to me that the form of the German is especially important to the sense, so that the general flavour of what follows is perhaps more 'Germanic' than some speakers of English might wish. If it were not so, then we would entirely lose the point of the specific demands made by these writers upon their imme- diate (as well as their latterday) readers, and also of the complaints which so many of their contemporaries (English especially but some Germans also) registered against them!

The translation of Kant's 'An Answer to the Question: What is Enlighten- ment?' is taken from Immanuel Kant, *On History*, translated by L.W. Beck, R. Anchor and E. Fackenheim, copyright © 1957, by The Liberal Arts Press, Inc., 1968 by The Bobbs-Merrill Co., Inc., reprinted by permission of the publisher. Excerpts from *The Critique of Judgement* are taken from *Kant: The Critique of Judgement*, translated by James Creed Meredith (2 vols., 1952), reprinted by permission of Oxford University Press.

The Foreword to Fichte's *The Vocation of Man*, translated by R.M. Chis- holm, copyright © 1956, by the Liberal Arts Press, Inc., is reprinted by permission of the Liberal Arts Press Division of The Bobbs-Merrill Co., Inc.

Schelling's *System of Transcendental Idealism* is reprinted from *The Philosophies of Art and Beauty*, edited by A. Hofstadter and R. Kuhns, by permission of the University of Chicago Press. Selections from 'Concerning the Relations of the Plastics Arts to Nature' are reproduced by permission of Professor Michael Bullock.

Selections from Schopenhauer's *The World as Will and Representation* are reprinted by permission of Dover Publications, Inc.

Excerpts from Hegel's *Aesthetics: Lectures on Fine Art* are taken from *Hegel's Aesthetics*, translated by T.M. Knox (2 vols., 1975), reprinted by permission of Oxford University Press. The excerpt from *The Philosophy of Spirit* is taken from *Hegel's Philosophy of Mind*, translated by William Wallace (1971), re- printed by permission of Oxford University Press.

Introduction

Romanticism and aesthetics

The exponents of the Enlightenment in Germany, and of the Idealism that followed it, demonstrate, together with their European aftermath, an unusually coherent and central interest in the psychology of aesthetic response and in the exemplary significance of works of fine art. But philosophers have not always been interested in aesthetics. With the exception of some philosophers today, in fact, the situation now is much as it was when Ogden and Richards wrote, in 1923, that

Many intelligent people indeed have given up aesthetic speculation and take no interest in discussions about the nature or object of Art, because they feel that there is little likelihood of arriving at any definite conclusion. Authorities appear to differ so widely in their judgments as to which things are beautiful, and when they do agree there is no means of knowing *what* they are agreeing about.   Ogden and Richards (1949), p. 139

Much of this turning away from aesthetics was of course a reaction to a tradition of Idealism, associated chiefly with the interpreters of Hegel. Since this was written, the discipline of literary criticism has come into being, and it has occupied much of the territory that a philosophical aesthetics might have sought to explore. It is however at least arguable, and some would say self-evident, that literary criticism has not constituted itself as a philosophical method; that it does not ask the same questions or go about its concerns in the way that such a method would have to. Of the thinkers represented in this anthology, Schelling, Schopenhauer and Hegel at least are pursuing the sort of inquiry which might appear to modern philosophers and literary critics as a sort of middle way, neither one thing nor the other, whereas Kant and Fichte might well seem not to be writing explicitly about literature at all. Thus much of what follows may seem at first sight naively irrelevant and out of date to philosophers, and incomprehensibly obscure and theoretical to literary critics.

Those who are, however, motivated by the desire to come to a deeper understanding of Romanticism will not give way to either of these reactions, for they will already have sensed, not only that the division of disciplines within which we now operate did not exist in the same way for the writers and thinkers of the early nineteenth century, but that the particular arguments put forward by Kant, Fichte, Schelling, Schopenhauer and Hegel were of great importance, both in Europe and in America. This is the case both theoretically and historically: theoretically, because in the transition from the *Critique of Judgement* to Hegel's *Aesthetics* one can trace already a move from rational philosophy to something approaching what we now recognize as 'literary criticism'; and historically, because these thinkers exerted a definite influence on nineteenth-century thought, offering as some of them did a philosophical rationale for the newer movements in political theory, sociology, and the study of history and literature, as well as more technical initiatives in epistemology or in the philosophy of science.

In the particular context of German Romanticism it seems almost impossible to overestimate the influence of Kant and his successors on the artists, writers and critics of the time. There was a continual and creative interchange between the poets and the philosophers, to a degree that may be impossible for us to imagine now. As Ernst Cassirer has put it, in a passage which itself incorporates the organicist assumptions of Romantic theory and serves thereby to remind us how familiar they have become:

Windelband said of Kant's *Critique of Judgment* that it constructs, as it were, *a priori* the concept of Goethe's poetry, and that what the latter presents as achievement and act is founded and demanded in the former by the pure necessity of philosophical thought. This unity of demand and act, of artistic form and reflective contemplation, is not sought after or artificially induced in German intellectual history of the eighteenth century; it results directly from the dynamic interplay of its fundamental formative forces.   E. Cassirer (1951), p. 278

Thus, as the most important artists of the period were busy reading their philosophy – Goethe's and Schiller's reactions to Kant would be just two examples – so the philosophers insisted on an important role in their systems for the theory and practice of art or for the aesthetic response. For the early Schelling, in fact, art has the highest possible role as the pinnacle of philosophical self-consciousness. Art is the visibly embodied and therefore communicable union of the Idea in nature with that in humanity. Thus it is a "necessary, integral part of a state founded on Ideas", and it is a "disgrace in those who have a direct or indirect part in governing the state not to have familiarity with or receptivity to art" (Schelling 1966, p. 151). This argument, and others like it, constitute one of the high points in the western tradition's various answers to Plato's originary banishing of (some kinds of) artists from the ideal state. It is also a part of the historical context in which, for example, Wordsworth's preface to *Lyrical Ballads* and Shelley's *A Defence of Poetry* came into being.

One of the reasons making it hard for the reader brought up in the culture of the English language to appreciate the importance of philosophy to the German Romantics is simply that there has not been a period in English or American literature in which the contacts between art and philosophy have been so close and vital. The transcendentalist movement in nineteenth-century America perhaps comes closest, but here the *major* philosophers involved were foreign ones – precisely the likes of Fichte and Schelling. In English literature one would have to look very hard indeed for a comparison. Science and philosophy are at the heart of much didactic poetry of the eighteenth century, but this poetry has never been allowed into our construction of the major 'canon'. Often we have tended to admire our great writers to the precise degree that they can be made subversive of any relation to or assimilation of other disciplines or systems of thought: Shakespeare would be a prime case. Even looking to the literature of the Middle Ages or the Renaissance, say to Chaucer's Boethius or Spenser's Platonism, one recognizes the importance of formal systems of thought without being able to follow the pattern of a constantly evolving personal relation between a poet and a living philosopher.

In Germany during the Romantic period we have to bear in mind the close personal contacts and intellectual exchanges between Fichte, Schelling, the Schlegels, Schleiermacher, Schiller, Tieck, Novalis, Goethe and so forth. Schleiermacher authored some of the entries among Friedrich Schlegel's *Athenaeum Fragments* and appears as a 'character' in the latter's novel *Lucinde*. Kant's brief comments on the "beautiful soul" receive an expanded reincarnation in Schiller's *On Grace and Dignity*, appearing again in the fictional forum of Goethe's *Wilhelm Meister* and in the denser text of Hegel's *Phenomenology of Spirit*. Everyone, it seems, knew or knew of everyone else, and perhaps only Goethe was a more unavoidable presence to his contemporaries than was the Kantian philosophy. With some credibility Friedrich Schlegel could announce that "The French Revolution, Fichte's philosophy, and Goethe's *Meister* are the greatest tendencies of the age" (1971, p. 190).

Schlegel's sense of the essential connection between politics, philosophy and literature seems to declare almost spontaneously the centrality of aesthetics. (Schlegel's criticism is represented in Volume 3 of this series.) The very word *aesthetics*, it is usually agreed, was reactivated from the Greek by Alexander Baumgarten (1714–62). Baumgarten actually preserves much of the breadth of reference contained in the Greek root, for he means by it the whole science of such knowledge as it is gained through the senses: *cognitionis sensitivae*.[1] As he puts it elsewhere, logic deals with things "known" and aesthetics with things "perceived": see Baumgarten (1974), p. 78. But he did write particularly about art, and though I am not qualified to engage in any definitive speculations about ultimate origins, it is clear that there is much in his thought which anticipates later preoccupations: not only the whole argument about the scientific or unscientific status of aesthetic response (in the narrow sense), but more precise formulations of e.g. the poetic efficiency of "confused complex concepts" (1964, p. 47), which can be read as a scholastically phrased precursor of remarks by Kant and Fichte (and Coleridge) about the effect of imagination consisting in its oversupply of images to concepts.

For our purposes and within our declared limits, it is Kant who inaugurates the tradition of philosophical aesthetics. It was only toward the end of his career, in fact, that he came to see the subject as having serious philosophical implications. As late as the second edition of the *Critique of Pure Reason* (1787) he wrote that

The Germans are the only people who currently make use of the word 'aesthetic' in order to signify what others call the critique of taste. This usage originated in the abortive attempt made by Baumgarten, that admirable analytical thinker, to bring the critical treatment of the beautiful under rational principles, and to raise its rules to the rank of a science. But such efforts are fruitless.   B 36; Kant (1933), p. 66

Thus far Kant would seem to be at one with those described by Ogden and Richards; but by 1790 he had devised a way of doing exactly this, or rather, of demonstrating rationally and scientifically the ways in which it could and could not be done.

Germany and its language

Before passing on to an account of some of the major themes in the aesthetic speculations of Kant and his followers, it is necessary to make a few obvious remarks about the state of affairs in Germany at the time, and to make clear from the start that no such entity as 'Germany' existed. What we now think of as Germany, i.e. before 1945, came into being only in the middle of the nineteenth century. Political power before the unification under Bismarck's Prussia was divided up among numerous small principalities, each governing itself and deriving its models of taste and behaviour as much from England, France and Austria as from any coherent notion of a 'German' identity. Thus Goethe in his autobiography:

Each one of the German universities has a particular character; for, as no universal cultivation can pervade our fatherland, every place adheres to its own fashion, and carries out, even to the last, its own characteristic peculiarities: exactly the same thing holds good of the universities.   Goethe (1974), I, 270

Prussia under the Hohenzollerns was the strongest among these states, and the period in which Kant and his followers were writing was one preceded by what historians call the 'rise of Prussia'. Throughout the Napoleonic years, moreover, the whole of western and central Europe was engaged in a variously intense struggle against France. These facts are of the greatest importance, though we should resist going so far as to assert that the politically incoherent nature of life in 'Germany' was in some simple sense responsible for the introspective tendencies of philosophical idealism, or to claim that the entire and extraordinary creation of a German literary and philosophical identity was the result of a massive reaction against a taste and literature imported largely from abroad.[2]

Equally relevant to an understanding of some of the texts that follow is the fact that during the eighteenth century the German language itself was in the process of coming into being – not, of course, as a means of basic communication between people, but as a medium for serious and precisely discriminated theoretical speculation. Before the middle of the century the philosopher would have been inclined to write in French, as Leibniz did, or in Latin. Goethe again is eloquent about the linguistic state of affairs into which he was born:

even for objects already known, people were induced to make use of foreign expressions and turns of speech. The German, having run wild for nearly two hundred years in an unhappy tumultuary state, went to school with the French to learn manners, and with the Romans in order to express his thoughts with propriety.   Goethe (1974), I, 278

It is Christian Wolff who is usually credited with initiating a truly philosophical German style.[3] As Descartes, in 1636, had written the *Discourse on Method* in French partly because of the freedom to originate afforded him by that as yet philosophically 'innocent' language, so a similar exuberance can be found in the language of a Fichte or a Hegel. Of course, this move towards the achieving of a sophisticated technical language as good as ensured that German philosophy would be ignored or misunderstood by other European readers for whom even basic German was not a familiar language. This more than anything, apart perhaps from the difficulty of contact brought about by the wars against France, accounts for the gap between the Germans and their potential English-speaking audience, one that could not in this sense match the internationalism of the Germans themselves, brought up as they were to read English and French books either in the original languages or in the almost instantly available translations into German. And it helps to explain the difficulties faced by the first generation of English Romantics, for example Wordsworth and Coleridge, who with the best and most serious of intentions were faced with learning a language still actively taking shape. Wordsworth wrote defiantly of his ambitions in a letter of February 1799:

I mean by learning the language not merely the knowing that "Liebe" is German for "love", and "darum" for "therefore" &c. but the having your mind in such a state that the several German idioms and phrases without any act of thought or consideration shall immediately excite feelings analogous to those which are excited in the breasts of the natives. Unless our minds *are* in this state, what we call knowledge of languages is a wretched self-delusion; words are a mere dead letter in the mind.
                                                        Wordsworth (1967), pp. 249–50

Small wonder that he abandoned his project, and wrote later in the same month that "I do not consider myself as knowing *any* thing of the German language" (p. 255).

Manner and matter in philosophical aesthetics

In fact, had he confronted any of the texts in this volume, Wordsworth would have found a language explicitly inciting him to acts of thought or consideration, reflections upon the mind's own workings, though not always admittedly its linguistic operations. This anticipates a problem which the modern reader

will be likely to feel, especially a reader confronting these arguments for the
first time. Such a reader might express surprise at the way in which the thorny
arguments of the *Critique of Judgement* are almost unadorned by examples, and
at the apparent abstractness of Schelling's *System of Transcendental Idealism*,
even as it establishes the fine arts as the keystone of its argument. Many of
these writings make demands of an extreme sort upon the average reader, and
they always have done. Henry Crabb Robinson was not simply an insular
Englishman in half-complaining about Schelling's "most profound abstraction & enthusiastick mysticism". Not that Schelling himself was unaware of
national propensities in the reception of ideas, as Robinson's account of the
Philosophy of Art lectures makes clear:

I shall hear again Burke and Horne & the 'thick-skinned' Johnson & the 'shallow'
Priestley briefly dispatched And hear it intimated that it is absurd to expect the *science*
of beauty in a country that values the Mathematics only as it helps to make Spinning
Jennies & Stocking-weav^g machines and beauty only as it recommends their Manufac-
tories abroad. I shall sigh & say too true!   Robinson (1929), pp. 117–18

But at the same time, as we shall see, there is no more damning indictment of
obscurity than that delivered by Schopenhauer against his own countrymen,
and against Hegel in particular.

   This matter of difficulty and obscurity of style and content was, as it happens, quite consciously in the minds of those thus accused. Fichte deliberately
set out to produce popular versions of his philosophy, knowing that the *Wissenschaftslehre* (*Science of Knowledge*) would only ever reach a small number of
readers. Kant's way of writing changes according to the kind of argument he
is putting forth; according to whether it belongs to the "critical" philosophy
or not. In no. 14 of the *Reflexions* on the *Critique of Pure Reason*, he writes:

I have adopted the scholastic method and preferred it to the free play of mind and wit,
although I indeed found, since I wanted every thoughtful mind to share in this investigation, that the aridity of this method would frighten off readers of the kind who seek a
direct connection with the practical. Even if I had the utmost command of wit and
literary charm, I would want to exclude them from this, for it is very important to me
not to leave the slightest suspicion that I wanted to beguile the reader and gain his
assent that way, but rather I had to anticipate no concurrence whatsoever from him
except from the sheer force of my insight. The method actually was the result of
deliberation on my part.   E. Cassirer (1981), p. 140

This explanation of the difficulties of the argument is well worth pondering.
We may note the fear of popular prejudices, of lazy habits of reading, and of
the power of words and images to beguile or deceive their reader into an
improper compliance, one based on mystification rather than reason. All these
ideas relate very closely to the spirit of some among the British Romantic poets
in their attempts to make their readers examine their own minds without the
mediation of debased forms of language. Wordsworth's attack on poetic diction would be the exemplary case, and Wordsworth shares with Kant a strong
Protestant suspicion of the dangers of ornament and image, in language as in

political and social life. Of course, Wordsworth is writing for a different sort of reader, and aiming at stimulating a new self-consciousness about universal feelings rather than philosophical propositions. He seeks precisely a "direct connection with the practical". But even if his method cannot be thought of as an arid one, his aspirations are comparable with those of Kant. There is the same desire to purify the medium into a state of universal availability and commonality, and the same distrust of images and superficial charms as distracting functions. Again, the ambiguities of Keats' 'The Eve of St. Agnes', which make us question the degree to which Madeline's imagination might be beguiled by a heightened physical and spiritual atmosphere, whilst seeming to suspend judgement on this process, can also be located within the spectrum of problems raised by Kant's declaration. Indeed, Keats seems to achieve also the beguiling of his reader, in order that the lesson might be proven on the pulses.

Kant's conscious election of difficulty of style is also at one with the intended subject of the critical philosophy. The whole enterprise of transcendental idealism is built upon the investigation of the conditions that must be thought to determine, in an *a priori* way, the limits of possible knowledge for the (normative) human mind. Despite the undoubted popular awareness of the writings of Kant and others, this was not nor could it ever be a commonplace concern. One might compare perhaps the modern popular consciousness of Freud, or Marx, or Darwin, who are 'known' often without being read, and thus frequently misrepresented. This specialized focus also helps to explain the difficulties Coleridge experienced in finding an audience for his *Biographia Literaria* (and some say also in the writing of it), for this book too is conceived in the transcendental mode, whose emphasis on the *a priori* element in experience, whether it be the deduction of the categories of the understanding, of the moral laws, or of the assumed universality of the judgement of taste, cannot be stressed enough. It explains why Kant's critical writings in general, and specifically the *Critique of Judgement*, are almost entirely devoid of *examples* (which Coleridge tries harder to provide). Given Kant's aims, any excessive concentration on examples, consisting as they must in empirically embodied *things* such as statues or paintings, must tend to induce us to believe that he is establishing some sort of canon of beautiful *objects*. In this he shares with many other Romantics the conviction that we are all too prone to mistake as themselves active the things *through which* we must recognize our own active and creative powers. Thus the almost total absence of examples from the *Critique of Judgement* is meant to alert us continually to its concentration upon acts of mind rather than upon already created objects.

In fact, a movement away from the rigour of the *Critique*'s analysis of the assumptions implicit in the aesthetic response of the normative mind is apparent very soon in the writings of Kant's successors. There emerges a curiosity about the creative mind of the artist himself, and about the history of art, and the various implications of its different forms at different times: topics which had a very low priority indeed in Kant's argument, belonging more to what he would have called "anthropology" than to the transcendental method. This movement in aesthetics is symmetrical with the general tendency observable in the history of philosophy between Kant and Hegel or Schopenhauer, roughly speaking a movement from an emphasis on knowledge to an emphasis on will. As we shall see, Kant was perceived by all of his followers, starting with Fichte, to have preserved the philosophy of exemplary subjectivity – by which I mean the analysis of a universal mind dealing in a timeless and normative way with the classical problems of epistemology or ethics – only by opening up a series of regrettable divisions within the mind and between the mind and its experience. Kant became a sort of Urizen figure, to invoke Blake's mythological vocabulary: the repressive high priest of Enlightenment rationalism and the prescriber of impossible laws, pronounced also with the Urizenic tears emanating from a self-induced stoical isolation. Just as Blake and Shelley cast themselves in opposition to the crippling dualisms they saw perpetrated by Wordsworth and by the traditions and interests for which he spoke, so Kant's successors (with rather more homage to their ancestor) saw as their task the closing of the gaps he had created: between nature and freedom, phenomena and noumena (things as they appear and as they must be thought to be in themselves), the empirical and the moral, the realm of appetite and the realm of practical reason, and ultimately between the exemplary self and its wider community. In closing these gaps, they often claimed the authority of an absolute, the knowledge of an essential or "noumenal" identity about which Kant himself had been objectively hypothetical. And, in arguing away the various dualisms at the heart of Kant's thought, his successors were also obliged to reopen the very questions he had meant to avoid by relegating them to the non-critical writings. If there is once again a unified subjectivity, and a wholeness or continuum in the philosophical explanation of experience, what single principle or force then becomes the mainspring? Despite all the saving gestures – often indeed relying upon reference to art – made by Fichte, Schelling, Schopenhauer and Hegel in the cause of justifying a rational pattern to experience, and one that all minds must share, it nevertheless seems undeniable that their philosophies more and more admit, even as they qualify, what we may call a philosophy of will – by which I mean one more and more explicitly founded upon the modifications enacted upon subjectivity by interest and appetite, by history or ideology, by the unconscious. The subject can no longer be simply maintained as the timeless and self-evidently efficient entity that it is in Kant's *Critiques*. It is on the way to becoming the more problematic concept that we tend to regard as normal in the modern age.

Much of the fascination of German Idealism and many of the dramas of its theoretical strategies lie in the way in which this gradual recognition of the forces of methodological chaos (for it is arguable that the very terms of a philosophy of will pre-empt the clear solution of the questions it foregrounds) is yet contained, more or less, within models of mind and history that remain at some level rational, normative, scientific. In fact, one can find many of these questions anticipated in the non-critical writings of Kant himself – the writings he chose *not* to make the centre of his philosophy. In the *Anthropology* of 1797, a late publication of the contents of one of his lecture courses, he speaks of the mind in a way which displays precisely the energy of what is kept out of the *Critiques*:

> In man (and so in beasts too) there is an immense field of sensuous intuitions and sensations we are not conscious of, though we can conclude with certainty that we have them. In other words, the field of our *obscure* representations [Vorstellungen] is immeasureable, while our clear ones are only the infinitesimally few points on this map that lie open to consciousness: our mind is like an immense map with only a few places *illuminated*.   Kant (1974), p. 16; *Ak.* VII, 135

Those few places must therefore be illuminated all the more sharply, since they represent our only hopes of agreement, rational consensus and normality. The following Schopenhauer-like insight actually comes from the author of the categorical imperative:

> From the day a human being begins to speak in terms of *Ich* he brings forth his beloved self wherever he can, and egoism progresses incessantly. He may not show it (for the egoism of others checks him); but it progresses secretly, at least, so that his apparent self-abnegation and specious modesty will give him a better chance of being highly esteemed by others.   Kant (1974), p. 10; *Ak.* VII, 128

Of course, we can trace the presence of theories of unconscious self-interest well before Kant. It is not a case of his 'discovering' something. Rather, what is of interest is the play between the *Anthropology*, e.g., and the scrupulously limiting arguments of the *Critiques*. Kant is one version of the man of the Enlightenment in his belief that the passions, whether the physical passions or the passions for honour, domination, possession and so forth, are the things which open us most dangerously to the possibility of being *used* by others, as reason never does. For it is the passions that give others "the power to use a man through his own inclinations" (1974, p. 139). In terms of this tension or division between the *Anthropology* and the *Critiques*, it can be argued that the *Critique of Judgement* performs a very special function. The peculiar status of the aesthetic judgement as somewhere 'between' a mere "inclination" and an activity governed rationally by concepts makes its exact articulation crucial in further specifying the division between the empirical ego (the subject of the *Anthropology*) and the transcendental ego (the subject of the first two *Critiques*, in the realms of epistemology and ethics). The aesthetic judgement is the one that seems to partake of both extremes: it can never be proven to be universal (hence governed by concepts), but in enacting it we are somehow compelled to assume that it is so. Subjectively, in other words, we refuse to accept its status as merely an inclination.

This is as far as Kant will take the transcendental method into the sphere of inclination, and we can now see how the decision to adopt and maintain a severe and unadorned style is related to the deepest preoccupations in Kant's thought, and is implicated in his sense of the importance of rational freedom of thought and of judging for oneself, in the way that his essay *What is Enlightenment?* explains. The unconscious, and the things which appeal to it, can have no place in the critical philosophy, whose very purpose is indeed the clarification of superstition and not the exploitation of it. The transcendental method is above all designed to explain and maintain those (few and limited) areas of experience upon which we may establish and preserve a rational consensus. The following passage goes a long way toward explaining why the third *Critique* might seem so little interested in the psychology of the creative artist:

To observe in ourselves the various acts of the representative power *when we call them forth* merits our reflection; it is necessary and useful for logic and metaphysics. – But to try to eavesdrop on ourselves when they occur in our mind *unbidden* and spontaneously (as happens through the play of the imagination when it inverts images unintentionally) is to overturn the natural order of the cognitive powers, because then the principles of thinking do not come first (as they should), but instead follow after. If it is not already a form of mental illness (hypochondria), it leads to this and to the lunatic asylum.   Kant (1974), p. 15

When the principles of thinking do come first, they lead to the essential, transcendental self-consciousness; the alternative would be the after-the-fact passive assemblage of random data, perhaps no more than phantasies – a complete subversion of the mind's intelligibility to itself, as well as (let us not forget) a loss of political and civic responsibility as Kant sees it. This is tied directly to lazy and commonplace habits of reading, just as it was to be by Wordsworth:

Reading novels has the result, along with many other mental disorders, of making distraction habitual. It is true that a novel, by sketching (though with some exaggeration) characters really to be found among men, gives thoughts the same *coherence* as in a true history, which must always be reported in a certain *systematic* way. Still, it permits our mind to interpolate digressions while we are reading it (namely, to interpolate other happenings we invent), and the course of our thought becomes *fragmentary*, in such a way that we let ideas of one and the same object play in our minds in a scattered way instead of as combined in accordance with the unity of understanding.
                                                                 Kant (1974), p. 79

Kant is emphatic about this (compare *CJ*, I, 125–6, not included in the selections below), just as he is about the necessary priority of understanding or taste over mere genius in *CJ* §50:

Taste, like judgement in general, is the discipline (or corrective) of genius. It severely clips its wings, and makes it orderly or polished; but at the same time it gives it guidance . . . and in so doing gives stability to the ideas, and qualifies them at once for permanent and universal approval, for being followed by others . . .   *CJ*, I, 183

What holds together both these passages is their concern for the maintenance of *consensus*. This is what the understanding achieves in ordinary experience, and what the phantasies evoked by undisciplined reading render impossible. It is thus one of the goals of a rigorous style and subject matter.

Rational consensus: for and against

However forcefully Kant's philosophical followers differ from their master – and we shall see that they do so differ – they yet remain solidly with him in the case against phantasy, against the unconscious when it is not disciplined by reference to the understanding. This tends to be expressed as a common cause against *Schwärmerei*, a term which may be translated as 'fanaticism' or 'irrational enthusiasm', whether in reading, writing, or social life. Kant calls this "a deep-seated, brooding passion" and an "undermining disease" (*CJ*, remark following §29), and again he relates it to our susceptibility to manipulation by others, "by way of the confusion caused by alleged inspiration from on high and powers flowing into us, by none of our doing, from some unknown source" (1974, pp. 14–15). Fichte, in the lecture version of *On the Spirit and the Letter* (not translated here) speaks of an arbitrary imagination which is a "product of blind natural force", which must be distinguished from the true *Geist* or "spirit" and which, instead of introducing order into nature, merely destroys that which is already there (Fichte, 1964–, II, 3, p. 324). In the *Characteristics of the Present Age* his account of the present as the third of five epochs of history involves recognizing in it the function of *Schwärmerei*, of a "blind, natural thinking-power" searching for "certain mysterious and hitherto inconceivable properties in the principles of nature" (Fichte, 1849, pp. 126ff.). It seems clear that Fichte has Schelling in mind on this particular occasion, for the manifestation of this fanaticism is *Naturphilosophie*, wherein sensuous instinct surreptitiously rules thought. But the same general polemic can be found throughout the philosophical writings in the period, for example in Hegel's remarks on "feeling" in the *Aesthetics* (see below). Goethe's young Werther was often cited as the exemplary *Schwärmer*, and any residual symptom of the *Sturm und Drang* or "Storm and Stress" movement would have been open to the same criticism. But there were two particular tendencies in the life and thought of turn-of-the-century Germany which were not entirely disconnected and which may be usefully discussed in terms of the way they challenged the philosophical ideal of rational consensus by emphasizing gestures of feeling or of self-reflection: Pietism and Romantic irony.

As Methodism in eighteenth-century Britain had functioned to remove the experience of illumination from the control of the established church, stressing the spontaneous and individual authentication of faith, so Pietism in Germany worked to personalize the act of faith and to make it more dependent upon feeling than upon reason. The philosophers of the late eighteenth century who drew most strongly upon this tradition – such as Hamann and Jacobi – are not represented in this volume (though Hamann appears in Volume 1), and they are often in implicit opposition to the Kantians. A particularly important figure in the bringing together of the various common problems of philosophy, theology, and what we now call literary criticism, was Schleiermacher, also unfortunately absent from the following selections.

Friedrich E.D. Schleiermacher (1768–1834) is mostly read today as a theologian, though he has received some recent attention as a theorist of hermeneutics. In his own generation he was a popular and eclectic writer who seemed to touch on all the major issues of the time. A friend of Novalis and Friedrich Schlegel, and a contributor to the important journal of the Schlegel circle, the *Athenaeum*, his work of 1799, *On Religion: Speeches to its Cultured Despisers*, soon became very influential as a declaration of the privacy of all essential religious experience:

I ask, therefore, that you turn from everything usually reckoned religion, and fix your regard on the inward emotions and dispositions, as all utterances and acts of inspired men direct.   Schleiermacher (1958), p. 18

The privacy here recommended was not of the Kantian sort, a stoical policy of rational self-discipline, but something much more enthusiastic. Schleiermacher's idea of the imagination as the central human faculty, working through the "free generation of thoughts" and giving rise to "the feeling of omnipotence" (p. 98) could all too easily be turned to support a cultivation of the irrational. There are overlaps between Schleiermacher's ideas and some of the arguments in Fichte, especially in the popular works and the even more popular misinterpretations of them, but the other-worldliness of remarks such as the following, from the *Soliloquies* of 1810, would have incensed Fichte as a philosopher of action:

I, for my part, am a stranger to the life and thought of this present generation, I am a prophet-citizen of a later world, drawn thither by a vital imagination and strong faith; to it belong my every word and deed. What the present world is doing and undergoing leaves me unmoved; far below me it appears insignificant, and I can at a glance survey the confused course of its great revolutions. Through every revolution whether in the field of science or of action it returns ever to the same point, and presenting ever the same features clearly reveals its limitations and the narrow scope of its endeavours.
                                                          Schleiermacher (1926), p. 62

This posture of the self as the unmoved centre of a turning world must have seemed to the rational theologians and the philosophers to be of the very essence of *Schwärmerei*. Kant and his more rigorous successors had consistently emphasized the rationality of reflection about subjectivity within the transcendental method. For them, interest in the *a priori* structure and potential of the mind had nothing to do with cheapening or ignoring the empirical or the commonplace; Kant's theory of knowledge is indeed intended to explain the fact of agreement within ordinary experience.

It is true that Kant's thought as a whole does depend upon a sense that the empirical world will always prove unsatisfying or frustrating, but there is a great deal of difference between the stoical self-dependence to which this drives him (as it did Dr Johnson) and the nervous other-worldliness of the passage from Schleiermacher. The point is well made by Coleridge in his definition of the word *transcendental* as

exclusively the domain of PURE philosophy, . . . in order to discriminate it at once, both from mere reflection and *re*-presentation on the one hand, and on the other from those flights of lawless speculation which, abandoned by *all* distinct consciousness, because transgressing the bounds and purposes of our intellectual faculties, are justly condemned, as *transcendent*.   Coleridge (1954), I, 164

There is much more to Schleiermacher's thought than this brief summary might imply, though I can give it only the briefest of notices here. Perhaps his greatest contribution was to the developing discipline of Bible criticism, or 'hermeneutics', and thus to the theory of interpretation. Throughout the eighteenth century, and above all in Germany, a whole tradition of inquiry had developed around the question of the authenticity of various parts of the Scriptures (see Frei, 1974). The Enlightenment attack on all forms of superstition had called into question the status of all inherited dogma. In Germany this questioning mood was supported by the strong Lutheran insistence on the individual's direct relationship to the holy writings, which not unnaturally gave rise to an urgency about what might be most essential in them. Schleiermacher was very important in this tradition, carried on later by Dilthey and others. He formulates, for example, the problem of the "hermeneutic circle", still a living issue in modern literary theory:

One must already know a man in order to understand what he says, and yet one first becomes acquainted with him by what he says . . .

The understanding of a particular is always conditioned by an understanding of the whole.   Schleiermacher (1977), pp. 56, 59

Specifically, he takes on the philosophers for their lack of interest in hermeneutics – "The philosopher seldom works at understanding, because he believes that it occurs by necessity" (p. 96) – and thereby joins in the challenge to Kant's assumption of certain sorts of objectivity in the mind's operations. His great work, *The Christian Faith* (1821–2; second edition 1831–2), is full of implications for the study of literature and should be consulted as part of any full assessment of Romantic theories of interpretation: see Schleiermacher (1928). Briefly, he there posits a core of poetic and figurative insight and expression at the centre of the Scriptures, which is closest of all to the life and spirit of Christ. According as explanations or textual elaborations do or do not illuminate this core, they are to be judged as true or false (see pp. 84–8). The reader must himself bring faith to the text, he cannot expect to deduce faith from it (p. 591), but within certain limits the Scriptures must be treated as any other book would be (p. 600). Although the true believer is always alone with his Bible, Schleiermacher like Coleridge accepts the role of the clerisy, without whom it would be "impossible to avoid a confusing uncertainty, leading to a fruitless and self-consuming waste of varied forces" (p. 616).[4]

Despite the range and complexity of Schleiermacher's thought, there is no doubt that his early pronouncements on the Kantians and his affiliation with Friedrich Schlegel mark him out as a defender of feeling against the claims of reason. And, while he is not dismissive of the problems of excessive or exclusive advocacy of subjective inspiration in its relation to consensus, his arguments do tend in a direction overtly threatening to the cause of rational verification. Johnson feared the effects of Methodism for precisely this reason, as Boswell reports:

Speaking of the *inward light*, to which some methodists pretended, he said, it was a principle utterly incompatible with social or civil security. "If a man (said he) pretends to a principle of action of which I can know nothing, nay, not so much as that he has it, but only that he pretends to it; how can I tell what that person may be prompted to do? When a person professes to be governed by a written ascertained law, I can then know where to find him."   Boswell (1970), p. 443

Another version of self-reflection that the philosophers almost to a man regarded as dangerous to their enterprise was that which goes by the name of Romantic irony. Its sources and elements have been well documented – see Prang (1972) and Strohschneider-Kohrs (1960) – and for our purposes here it is enough to see it as a secular application of the principles of subjective freedom that Pietism had helped to popularize. As we have seen, Friedrich Schlegel, who was its major proponent, took Fichte's philosophy as his ally in publicizing the gesture of infinite self-reflection that was at the centre of the spirit of Romantic irony. Remarking favourably on the *Wissenschaftslehre* as "always simultaneously philosophy and philosophy of philosophy" (1971, p. 202), he does indeed reflect the emphasis on self-consciousness central to Kant and to his followers. But the sort of self-reflection he himself encouraged was often intended to go no further, and to remove the individual from all relationship to contingent experience, as Fichte was to complain (see below). The achievement of the ironic perspective, with its consciousness of the limits of all identifiable and contingent relations to the world, was often thought to introduce into aesthetics what Schleiermacher had introduced into religion: a tendency toward unaccountability and a determination to stand outside consensus. At the same time, his conflation of the highest philosophy with poetry and with the dynamic forces of life (see 1971, p. 205), involving as it does an approval of the synthetic ambitions of Schelling, connects him with the popular versions of the *Naturphilosophie* and their interest in an aesthetics of organicism.

Kant's remarks on organicism are to be found in the second part of the *Critique of Judgement*, the "Critique of Teleological Judgement". Here, as we shall see, he is careful to insist that the organic model be restricted to our estimates of nature according to teleological assumptions. When we look at a plant or some other organism or natural process, it is convenient to assume (for example in the articulation of the natural sciences) that nature behaves and develops with an *end* in view. Seed produces plant, plant produces fruit. This logic should not, however, according to Kant, be applied to the productions of human intelligence or ingenuity. Works of art are not like plants or flowers; they do not evolve dynamically according to their own laws. Nevertheless, there was a widespread tendency among some of Kant's successors to conflate the two parts of the *Critique*, bringing together aesthetics and teleology in the search for an organic theory of art. In the "Critique of Aesthetic Judgement" Kant seldom shows any interest in the psychology of creation; he is much more concerned with the psychology of response. His followers were often much more interested in the nature of the creative process, and in the connections between mind and nature that organicist theories could be used to support. Goethe saw in them a way of synthesizing his own preoccupations in the fine arts and in natural science into some kind of unified field theory.[5] In the same spirit, A.W. Schlegel's 1801 lectures include an exposition of Kant's third *Critique*, complaining that it is insufficiently organical (see 1962–74, II, 60–99). The transcendental method is said here to teach us that body and soul are essentially and originally one, that "organization" is merely the outward manifestation of *Geist* (p. 72). Kant himself is regarded as having stopped half way in the essential argument (p. 80), and it is Schelling who continues it, following the direction indicated by the work of Karl Philipp Moritz. Things are in a state of eternal becoming, and we recognize this by our own participation in the process. The artist dramatizes this most precisely of all, discovering nature in the very centre of his being: art is the spiritual intuition and revelation of concentrated nature (pp. 90–2).

This bringing together of art and nature is not at all true to the spirit of Kant, any more than the theories and models of social organization which it was to generate in the nineteenth century are true to his views of the nature of civil society. Kant directs the individual always to act as if he *were* prescribing a law for universal human behaviour (this is the fascination of the aesthetic judgement, as it is the imperative of the moral faculty), but his writings on history make it clear that he did not foresee such prescription as ever being empirically effective. The essence of the judgement consists indeed in its being delivered in despite of this fact. Organicist theories, on the other hand, whether of art or society, tend to place the individual in the role of an achieved universality, an empirical synthesis of the one and the many. Divisions of interest are here either ignored or harmoniously reconciled; discordant qualities are balanced and reconciled also, as they are in Coleridge's model of the operations of the imagination.

We can now see that in their various ways Pietism, Romantic irony, and even the *Naturphilosophie* as its organicist aspirations were applied to aesthetics, all tended either to challenge or to qualify (even beyond recognition) the basic account offered by Kant of the prospects for rational consensus, and the limited spheres in which it may be assumed or prescribed. By the time we reach Schelling's argument for fine art as the exemplary public form of philosophical consciousness (1800), we have quite left behind the drama of Kant's

rehabilitation of aesthetics from the limbo of mere fashion or personal preference, where it had remained for him throughout the greater part of his career.
In the *Critique of Judgement* taste finally comes within the orbit of rational
inquiry; the aesthetic judgement satisfies the conditions of intersubjectivity
and consensus not as a fact but as a matter of necessary assumption and
aspiration. In Schelling, these necessary assumptions come to be spoken of as
matters of fact, and the union of mind and nature in art becomes unambigu-
ously affirmative.

The status of aesthetics in relation to issues of sociability and consensus
cannot be sufficiently stressed if we are to understand what Kant is doing in
the third *Critique*. Addison, Shaftesbury, Hume and others had all argued for
some degree of agreement or consensus about what is thought of as beautiful,
but a gentlemanly agreement rather than a rational necessity was the strongest argument available to explain it, one enforced of course by the pressures of
habit and fashion but never a universal judgement. Universality could always
of course be prescribed by invoking a Platonic idea, but Kant is equally
determined to stay away from such an objective metaphysics, locating as it
does what is most important in things rather than in states of mind. As an
alternative to both of these arguments Kant offers a rational psychology: in
declaring something beautiful we assume the necessary agreement of all other
beholders, and are compelled to do so, even though no empirical consensus or
proven universal agreement need ever come about. For Kant, this is the root
of the connection between aesthetics and morality, one of the most important
and difficult questions raised by any reading of the *Critique*. For in the moral
judgement we similarly find ourselves legislating over our actions as if they
were universal, and in despite of actual confirmation or disproof by others. In
neither case does such confirmation or disproof have anything to do with the
essential nature of the judgement; other people never do and never should
change our minds, either about what is beautiful or about what is right.

The relation between the aesthetic and the moral, if any, is a constant
preoccupation in Idealist aesthetics, and will be pursued at various points in
the following extracts. In the context of the specific question of consensus, it
should be noted that Kant apparently makes a much closer connection between the sublime and the moral than he does between the beautiful and the
moral. It is as if we are intimidated into recognition of the moral law within
by the experience of the sublime – one might compare Shelley's attributing to
Mont Blanc a voice that can repeal "Large codes of fraud and woe" (1977,
p. 91), or Wordsworth's ongoing analysis of the quickening effects of the
sublime in *The Prelude*. In *CJ* §29 Kant relates the *less secure* assumption of
universality in the experience of the sublime (as compared to the beautiful)
more closely to the moral sense. Because it is a cultivated taste – that which
seems sublime to those trained to appreciate it is merely frightening to others –
we are less likely to assume its necessary universality than we are in the case of
the beautiful. So much is this the case, indeed, that (Kant says) it is only

through prior cultivation of the moral faculty, which also functions by setting our empirical satisfactions against more powerful demands which may in fact extinguish them (this is what we feel in the face of the mighty forces of nature e.g.), that we can expect to achieve the full experience of the sublime. Thus we get here a weak statement of the relation of the sublime to the possibility of consensus – we assume it but only by recognizing the stringent limits – and a strong statement of its relation to morality. In the case of judgements of the beautiful the opposite formulation obtains: there is a strong and immediate assumption of universality but a more tentative relation to the moral faculty. This is in tune with the stringent and stoical nature of Kant's ethics. Whereas the beautiful is merely independent of all interest, the sublime is positively in opposition to the interests of sense and of empirical well-being. The beautiful "represents freedom rather as in *play* than as exercising a law-ordained *function*, which is the genuine characteristic of human morality, where reason has to impose its dominion upon sensibility" (*CJ*, I, 120). Correspondingly the sublime imposes respect where the beautiful draws forth love, just as "human nature does not of its own proper motion accord with the good, but only by virtue of the dominion which reason exercises over sensibility" (p. 124). This distinction between the sublime and the beautiful in the context of ethics is behind the various attempts among Kant's successors (not unfortunately well represented in the following selections) to narrow the gap between the two, at least when arguments for the moral effects of the beautiful are being pursued.

Formalism and free play

If we now go on to ask what it might be in the object that leads to or incites the necessary assumption of universality in aesthetic judgements of taste, then we come up against the question of formalism. It is a widely held view that Kant is 'responsible for' a formalist method, and it would be hard to challenge this in any extreme way. It is, however, worth trying to explain the place and function of the formalist argument in Kant's terms. As we shall see, it is the emphasis on the *disinterestedness* of the aesthetic judgement that allows for the assumption of agreement: because we do not seek to convert the representation into an actual object for some form of empirical consumption, then its presentation is not subject to the things which commonly divide us from other individuals – empirical wants and needs.[6] Appetite and desire have no place in the aesthetic, and they are the things which divide us from our better selves and from others, as has been said above.

This capacity of art to pre-empt or mitigate desire was an important element in Romantic aesthetics at large, and I think it explains the formalist aspect of Kant's argument in particular. Because we are left strictly with representations, and because they must by definition please without any reference to contingent experience, it must be thought that it is their forms, or combinations of their represented parts, that cause pleasure. The insistence that it is the form alone that is the essence of the beautiful (i.e. is so judged) would then seem to be the strongest possible statement of the identification of the beautiful with disinterestedness, and this is a claim that Kant does seem to make:

> In painting, sculpture, and in fact in all the visual [bildenden] arts, in architecture and horticulture so far as they are fine arts, the *design* [*Zeichnung*] is what is essential. Here it is not what gratifies in sensation but merely what pleases by its form, that is the fundamental prerequisite for taste.   *CJ* §14; *Ak*. V, 225

Once again, it is the need to establish what may be the substance of a consensus that makes necessary the formalist argument. In no sense does this determine that other aspects of the art-work might not cause pleasure in some people; it is simply that in Kant's terms such pleasure would not meet the definition of the aesthetic judgement of taste.[7]

Another aspect of Kant's exposition was to be of considerable importance to other aesthetic theorists from Schiller onwards, and that is the idea of aesthetic response as free play. In *CJ* §54, as an appendix to his consignment of music to the lowest rank among the fine arts, by virtue of its comparatively greater reliance upon sensation, Kant expands upon the nature of such gratification. Sensation belongs within the sphere of the agreeable, which by definition cannot demand the agreement of everyone. Here, although Kant is explicitly not talking about the dominant features of the fine arts, he does sketch out what such a sensation-based or physiological theory of aesthetic appreciation might be, and indeed largely is in the particular case of music. Here, the "changing free play of sensations" is itself gratifying "because it promotes the feeling of health" (*CJ*, I, 197). Lively after-dinner conversations – totally engrossing at the time though later forgotten – and jokes have exactly the same effect, bringing about "an equilibrium of the vital forces of the body" (p. 199). Our mental reactions are sympathetic to our bodies, and "may involve a corresponding and reciprocal straining and slackening of the elastic parts" (p. 201) conducive to eventual physical repose.

Although this case is a subordinate part of Kant's argument, and is indeed expounded as lying outside the principal evidence for the fine arts as they relate to the beautiful rather than the agreeable, the reader of Schiller's *Aesthetic Education* will note their presence there, and these parts of the *Critique* stand as an important legacy of Enlightenment materialism and a prefiguring of other physiologically based theories of art to come. Kant's placing of music here lends a new purpose to Schopenhauer's making music precisely the highest of the fine arts because it represents the supersession of concrete form and exists through the outpouring of pure will, freed from any binding relation to representation. We may also note in passing the availability of this physiological argument for the developing nineteenth-century criticisms of the debilitating effects of industrial labour, developing only parts of the body, stunting or redirecting growth, disturbing the equilibrium of the parts, and so forth. These were also, of course, formalized versions of the ideal of free play, putting it back into an objective context by way of the traditional Platonizing formulae of the *discordia concors* or the *Eins im Vielen*, the balance or reconciliation of opposite or discordant qualities. All of these arguments relate to and draw upon the ground covered by Kant, without (usually) being especially scrupulous about respecting the limitations of his argument. This is not just a matter of perversity; it is rather that, in drawing upon the organicist passages of the second part of the *Critique* or in taking the agreeable as if it were the beautiful, other thinkers were responding to what they needed in Kant to assist the articulation of their own priorities. This is indeed the nature of all worthwhile inspiration, and such complexities of transmission should serve to caution us against any monolithic characterizations of the relations between Idealist and subsequent theories. The Romantic period in general can be thought of as embracing more theoretical options than it can produce into complete coherence, and I have discussed above the relation of Kant's critical and non-critical writings as a spectacular example of this. We can indeed observe general trends: from reason to imagination, scepticism to Christianity; from a psychology of response to one of creation; from classicism to mediaevalism, and so forth. But the period is full of counter-currents, and significant exceptions to the rule. It is common wisdom that, for example, the German romantics are frequently engaged in a philosophical or aesthetic legitimation of Christianity against the challenges of scepticism or paganism. But this same Christianity was seen to be premissed on an inwardness and individuality itself threatening to various forms of social or intellectual solidarity. In *The Social Contract*, Rousseau had spoken of the divisive effects of Christianity on the social order:

Christianity is a spiritual religion, relative only to celestial objects: the Christian's inheritance is not of this world. He performs his duty, it is true, but this he does with a profound indifference for the good or ill success of his endeavours . . . If the state be in a flourishing situation, he can hardly venture to rejoice in the public felicity, lest he should be puffed up with the inordinate pride of his country's glory; if the state decline he blesses the hand of God that humbles his people to the dust.

Rousseau (1767), V, 179

So, when we find A.W. Schlegel applauding the receptiveness of the Germanic people to the spirit of Christianity, as he does in the first of his lectures *On Dramatic Art and Literature*, we must be aware also of the tension between this endorsement of inwardness (frequently connected to the demands of the northern climate!) and the more 'classical' desire for rational sociability, which also preoccupies Romantic theory in its suspicion of the extremes of subjective enthusiasm of *Schwärmerei*. This tension indeed lends particular urgency to Hegel's project for a rational Christianity, and helps to explain the paradoxical nature of his affection for the Greeks (which I discuss later in this volume).

Similarly, as the Horatian *sapere aude* comes to require the inclusion of the Socratic "know thyself", the strains which Kant had sought to alleviate by establishing two independent modes or genres of writing come more and more into play within the mainstream of philosophical inquiry. Hegel, for example, certainly produced conclusions and sought to reason toward them in some definitive fashion. But his continued availability to theorists in various disciplines and of both left and right has less to do with these conclusions than with the tensions and ambiguities necessarily apparent in any nineteenth-century system with such total aspirations. It is even part of his theory that, whilst the evolution of *Geist* may indeed be received as a synthesis of reason and faith, it is yet obliged to reveal within itself all the traces of the forms of thought it purports to transcend. Such inclusiveness is the very essence of sublimation and remembrance, *Aufhebung* and *Erinnerung*, and the drama of their testing out is therefore much more than a mere theoretical inelegance or residual superfluity. That is why there is a Romantic art, and one acting out the necessity of its own disappearance, dramatizing in style and content the passage of art into the prose of pure thought.

The question of influences: a guide to further reading

Apart from the obvious case of the influence of the following philosophers on each other, which I have dealt with specifically in the endnotes, there are other points to be made about the general subject of influence. Neither space nor the editor's competence permits any analysis of the relation of the great Idealists to subsequent explorations in strictly philosophical aesthetics: Croce, Nietzsche, the Scottish Hegelians, Bradley, Dewey and so forth. The very close relations subsisting between the philosophers and their friends and contemporaries in German Romantic literature have been indicated already. The major interest of the English-speaking reader must lie, I assume, in the influence of Kant and his successors upon the literature of Britain and America.

This is a difficult and complicated subject, and apart from describing a few of the less obvious cases much of what I shall have to say will consist of referring the reader to work already available. The contribution of German thought to the growth of the transcendentalist movement in nineteenth-century America is well known, and substantial efforts have been made in recovering the details of its incorporation: see Vogel (1955), Pochmann (1957), and Wellek (1965). In the case of English literature the presence or absence of direct connections has been much harder to assess. The easy cases are signalled by direct reference or translation, but in the crucial case of Coleridge, for example, the whole question of the exact degree and kind of assimilation of German thought remains an open one. We do not yet have reliable modern editions of all the major works, and the task of producing them is not made easier by Coleridge's tendency to avoid mention of his specific sources, a fact which itself has sparked off famous controversies over whether or not we should consider him a 'plagiarist'. Moreover, in the first three decades of the nineteenth century Coleridge is struggling to come to grips with a mode of thought hardly 'familiar' to an English speaker, much less popular. The general attitude to German philosophy before about 1830 seems to have been one of vaguely hostile curiosity. Curiosity, because many people had a sense that something important might be going on, but hostile because it was going on in an unstable and unfamiliar language, and because such of its apparent conclusions as did 'translate' were often felt to be at odds with British tastes.

Generally it is safe to assume that, with the exception of the well-known cases, such influence as did pass over from Germany before 1830 was relatively indirect or coincidental. The reader familiar with English Romantic writing will quite commonly find in what follows ideas or arguments teasingly close to those discovered in English literature at the time; take, for example, the similarity of some among Schelling's arguments and even his images and metaphors to those evident in Shelley's *A Defence of Poetry*. Shelley did read Black's translation of A.W. Schlegel's lectures, and Schlegel learned much from Schelling; and of course we may refer these connections to the *Zeitgeist* or "spirit of the age", a phrase Hazlitt and Shelley themselves used in explaining the relations of art and history. But in this period the spirit of the age in Germany had been significantly formed by a wholesale incorporation, through almost immediate translation, of all the important eighteenth-century British treatises on aesthetics, ethics, political theory, and philosophy at large (see Price 1934, 1955), as well as most of the significant novels and journals. Kant and his successors thus quite literally stand in the tradition of Hume, Shaftesbury, Addison, Hutcheson and so on, just as do the English Romantic writers. This adds to the difficulty of estimating exactly how much someone like Coleridge might have taken directly from the Germans, rather than from his own reading of the likes of Locke, Cudworth, and Berkeley, as well as of the enduring sources available to both cultures: Plato, Aristotle, Plotinus, Augustine and so forth. Perhaps the most probable general hypothesis would imagine a Coleridge who was already primed by his own readings to receive the maximum value from the arguments he found in the Germans, recognizing them as derived from and contributing to a common tradition. This would help explain why Coleridge might have seen the German influence as less significant than many of his later critics have argued it to be, and why he might have estimated its proponents in a surprising way, as when Crabb Robinson reports as follows:

He adheres to Kant, notwithstanding all Schelling has written, and maintains that from the latter he has gained no new ideas. All Schelling has said, Coleridge has either thought himself, or found in Jacob Boehme.   Robinson (1869), I, 388

Not that the originality of the German tradition should be slighted. It was a definite originality, and the gradual recognition of it was among the reasons

for the increasing excitement about all things German noticeable in the later
nineteenth century; or at least, some things German, as they suited the needs
of the time. The most difficult period for the literary historian is the period of
partial or possible assimilation, before German thought becomes unarguably
fashionable and unashamedly celebrated. There is a considerable literature to
help us through this period. Studies of Coleridge in particular have come
more and more to recognize the question of the German influence: see Orsini
(1969), McFarland (1969), Shaffer (1975), Wheeler (1980), among others.
Even Shelley has received attention in this context: see Klapper (1975).
Hirsch (1960) has written of a deliberately 'indirect' common ground between
Wordsworth and Schelling, and there are a number of general books on the
relation of German to English thought: see Wellek (1931 and 1965), Stokoe
(1926), and Ashton (1980). The two books by Abrams (1953 and 1971) are
indispensable in coming to an understanding of the range of connections and
common preoccupations, and Engell (1981) should also be consulted.

There were several contemporary accounts of developments in German philosophy: Drummond (1805) speaks scathingly of a popular vogue for Kant among
those who "know metaphysics *a priori*, who possess an intuitive faculty, who see
visions of pure reason, and who carried the whole science of geometry in their
heads, before they even looked into Euclid" (p. 358). He seems to be working
largely with a French defence of Kant written by Villar rather than with Kant
himself, and finds his disciples "unable to convey any clear idea of the meaning
of their master" (p. 367). Dugald Stewart, writing in the next decade, continues
to rely largely on French accounts of Kant, though he has seen enough German
by 1827 to suggest that its convoluted structures might be responsible for the
confusions in Kant's thoughts: see Stewart (1854), IV, 53. In 1815 Stewart had
claimed to be able to make nothing of Fichte, and to find in Schelling only a
"transcendental mysticism" (I, 418–19). Even where glimpses of the authentic
Kant do emerge in the English language before 1830 or so, they are not much
concerned with aesthetics, and it is safest to assume that any parallels between
the English and German traditions in this respect are a result of the common
tradition explained above. Stokoe (1926) argues that there was a greater
popular awareness of German literature in the 1790s than one might have
expected, but with the protracted state of war between Britain and the conti-
nent such contacts could not have been easily maintained, and anyway Wellek
(1931) makes clear that they did not involve much cognisance of the critical
philosophy. The translation from the French of Madame de Staël's *Germany*, in
1813, provided something of a ready-reference guide to the subject, but few
readers could have been converted by the following summary of Kant's
thoughts:

Kant wished to establish primitive truths and spontaneous activity in the soul, conscience in morals, and the *ideal* in the arts.   (III, 73)

There follows a quite extraordinary reading of the argument of the third *Critique*:

Kant maintains, that there are in poetry, and in the arts which are capable, as poetry is, of painting sentiments by images, two kinds of beauty: one which may be referred to time and to this life; the other, to eternity and infinity.   (III, 89)

This second sort of beauty is "the realization of that image which is constantly present to the soul" (p. 89), and its universality is ensured by virtue of all men having in their souls "sentiments of celestial origin, which beauty awakens, and of which it excites the enjoyment" (pp. 90–1). Fichte and Schelling fare a little better in their summarized identities, and, in fact, Madame de Staël's account is intended to be a positive one. She regards it as "infinitely better for the literature of a country, that its poetical system should be founded upon philosophical notions, even if they are a little abstract, than upon simple external rules" (p. 143). At the same time, she has to regret that such philosophical speculations "only place the ignorant and the enlightened at too great a distance from each other. There are too many new, and not enough common, ideas circulating in Germany, for the knowledge of men and things" (pp. 169–70).

In estimating the reaction to German thought in England, we must of course remember that we are faced with what is even more fundamentally a reaction to Germanically inclined Englishmen, like Peacock's Mr Flosky (Coleridge) in *Nightmare Abbey* (1818). Hazlitt, for example, never had much time for Kant and his kind, but he rises to heights of vituperation when the time comes to review Coleridge's *Biographia Literaria*, accusing Kant of publishing "the most wilful and monstrous absurdity that was ever invented": see Hazlitt (1930–4), XVI, 123. De Quincey, who himself translated Kant, offers a more reasoned view of the situation:

everything yet published on the subject of Kant in the English language errs by one of two defects. Either it is mere nonsense, in a degree possible only to utter and determined ignorance of the German language; or it is so close a translation of the *ipsissima verba* of Kant as to offer no sort of assistance to an uninitiated student, to say nothing of the barbarous effect produced by a German structure of sentence and a terminology altogether new.   De Quincey (1889–90), VIII, 87

This was written in 1830, by which time some of the wisdom of hindsight had come to be available. De Quincey details his own struggles with the Germans in the *Autobiography*, reporting how he found the "negative" spirit of the first *Critique* so hard to take (II, 86); like most readers of his generation he wanted more than sound Enlightenment advice about what *not* to believe. But he found positive things too: the harmony of philosophy with mathematics, the doctrine of the categories, and the account of the functions of practical reason (II, 106); and by 1823 he is blaming Coleridge for obfuscating doctrines that are much clearer in their original Kantian formulations (X, 77). De Quincey's later writings already reveal an interest in German Idealism for its potential availability in criticizing the condition of England, as he refers to "the unpopularity of *all* speculative philosophy whatsoever, no matter how treated, in a country where the structure and tendency of society impress upon the whole activities of the nation a direction almost exclusively practical" (IV, 324–5). Here, the very mysteries that had perplexed and were to continue to perplex even sympathetic readers are focussed as a criticism of utilitarian society, and German philosophy has entered the public debate in nineteenth-century Britain. When Morris speaks of the capacities of art to heal the disastrous psychic effects of the division of labour, and Arnold speaks of the "free play of the mind" at its healthiest moments (as Leavis was to do after him), neither of them sees any need to invoke Schiller, or Kant, or Fichte. The process of naturalization has already taken place, partly through the efforts of Carlyle and Coleridge (among others), partly because the terms of German Idealist aesthetics have been brought fully into the mainstream as a challenge to the spirit of the age in Victorian England.

Part 1

Kant

Immanuel Kant

(1724–1804)

Kant is quite simply one of the half dozen or so most important figures in the history of philosophy. Although brought up in a Pietist household, his earliest preoccupations were in the natural sciences, and much of the point of the great *Critique of Pure Reason* (1781; second edition 1787) can be said to depend upon its inquiry into how the apparently original discoveries of the scientific method are both possible and intelligible.

The first *Critique* is Kant's most famous work, and is the founding text for the whole of what came to be known as the "critical" or "transcendental" philosophy. Roughly speaking, it is an investigation of the *a priori* element implicit though usually unnoticed in all empirical perception, which is governed by what Kant defines as the "understanding" [Verstand]. The model of the transcendental synthesis of apperception, which explains the conjunction of that which is in the mind (*a priori*) with that which is in the world, and their regular synthesis into habitual and communicable experience, is in fact a going behind and beyond the various versions of materialism and idealism Kant had inherited from his predecessors: it puts together elements of both approaches and explains the synthesis as the only reasonable explanation of experience. Thus experience must be thought of as a synthesis of concept [Begriff] and intuition [Anschauung], neither being open to self-consciousness without the assumption of the other. Without the concepts of the understanding, sense data would make no sense; and without the reception of such data, the concepts would never be deducible. This synthesis is operative all the time in ordinary experience – or, more strictly speaking, it is what must be supposed if the self-evident coherence of experience is to be explained.

Obviously I cannot try to do justice to the sophistications of the arguments of the first *Critique*, and various ones have exercised various kinds of readers. The distinction between analytic and synthetic judgements, for example, has been a popular stalking horse for philosophers but does not (as far as I can see) much impinge upon Kant's aesthetics. We should, however, register here Kant's use of the distinction between phenomena and noumena, things as they appear to us in experience and things as they must be thought to be in themselves. This was in itself controversial among Kant's immediate readers, and the dichotomy it introduces into epistemology is also crucial in the explanation of the nature and function of reason [Vernunft]. The understanding is the faculty governing our relations to the empirical world, and in fact the *Critique of Pure Reason* is mostly about the understanding. But behind it, and properly speaking the keystone of the whole transcendental philosophy, is reason, whose fuller articulation comes in the *Critique of Practical Reason* (1788) and whose operations are in the sphere of freedom and the moral law. Ethical behaviour, for Kant, depends on its very divorce from contingent (empirical) experience; no reference to such experience is called for in its validation. The laws of reason are self-imposed and self-subsisting.

The third of the great critical works, the *Critique of Judgement* (1790), was intended to mediate between the other two, and this explains in part the eagerness with which many of Kant's successors seized upon aesthetics (which is one of its two main subjects, along with teleology) as a way of healing what they thought to be a mind divided tragically between the independent realms of reason and understanding. This is discussed at greater length below.

As soon as there was Kant, there were myths of Kant. The most enduring among them project Kant the silent ascetic, by whose habits one could set one's watch. Herder set going a corrective myth of the enlivening Kant, the ideal host – polymath, raconteur, a perpetually diversifying intelligence. It is indeed the case that attention to the three great *Critiques* alone gives a very incomplete view of the range of Kant's opinions and approaches. I have discussed this, and the reasons for it, in the Introduction; suffice it to say here, once again, that to read the *Anthropology* or peruse the writings on history and civil society is to gain a very different sense of his total intellectual profile, and to recognize his engagement with many more ideas and problems than those with which he is most famously associated.

Further reading

There are many books on Kant. For general introductions and summaries see, among others, Ernst Cassirer (1981), Stephan Körner (1955), and Copleston (1964b). More specialized but very readable accounts and formulations, mostly of the epistemological arguments, may be found in Bennett (1966 and 1974) and Strawson (1966). Studies of the aesthetics include the commentary by H.W. Cassirer (1938), and books by Coleman (1974), Crawford (1974), Guyer (1979) and Shaper (1979). On the English reception of Kant, Wellek (1931) is basic; see also the relevant sections of Orsini (1969), Stokoe (1926), Ashton (1980), among others. Finally, those interested in the deeper and more creative continuities might consult Gadamer (1975) and Ernst Cassirer (1953–7).

An Answer to the Question: What is Enlightenment?
[Beantwortung der Frage: Was ist Aufklärung?]

1784

The following translation is a modified reprint of that by Lewis White Beck, in his *Kant on History* (1963), pp. 3–10.

The German text may be found in *Kants gesammelte Schriften*, published by the Königlich Preussische Akademie der Wissenschaften, 22 vols. (Berlin, 1900–42), VIII, 33–42.

Introductory note

I have explained in the general Introduction the reasons behind the apparent perversity of including in this anthology essays or extracts which do not comment directly on art or aesthetics. The ramifications of this essay of Kant's are not always traceable in the letter – as they certainly are, for example, in Fichte's lectures *On the Nature of the Scholar* or in his analysis of his own generation in the *Characteristics of the Present Age* – but in the spirit they are all-pervasive. In as much as what follows is an exemplary summary of what one of the greatest of thinkers understood by the term 'enlightenment', and stands also as a statement of the principal insights of the philosophers who constituted *the* Enlightenment, the importance of this piece seems self-evident. Readers familiar with the British Romantic writers will perceive many points of comparison and contrast in terms of the implications and responsibilities of a writer's relation to his public: one thinks of Blake's assertive declaration of independence from the systems of other men; of Coleridge's meditations on the paradoxes of authority – how he can persuade or *guide* his reader to the exercise of *independent* judgement; and of Wordsworth's plea to his ideal reader as one who would "decide by his own feelings genuinely, and not by reflection upon what will probably be the judgement of others" (1974, I, 154).

Much of what Kant has to say here marks him out as a man of the Enlightenment rather than as a Romantic, though any extreme version of this historian's dichotomy must inhibit our understanding of the period. Here, the emphasis on the possibility of clear and rational thinking and its salutary effects on society at large is presented with only hints of the darker forces working to complicate the establishment or dissemination of truth. Or perhaps we should say, as we would have to say of William Godwin, that the negative forces are recognized in the argument at the same time as a faith in the possibility of their disappearance is preserved. But for the most part in what follows, superstition and prejudice are external enemies rather than inward ones who may sometimes masquerade as friends.

Enlightenment is man's release from his self-incurred tutelage. Tutelage [Unmündigkeit] is man's inability to make use of his understanding [Verstand] without direction from another. It is self-incurred when its cause lies not in lack of understanding but in lack of resolution and courage to use it without direction from another. *Sapere aude!* "Have courage to exercise your own understanding!" – that is the motto of enlightenment.[1]

Laziness and cowardice are the reasons why so great a portion of mankind, after nature has long since discharged them from external direction (*naturaliter maiorennes*), nevertheless remain under lifelong tutelage, and why it is so easy for others to set themselves up as their guardians. It is so easy not to be of age. If I have a book which understands for me, a pastor who has a conscience for me, a physician who decides my diet, and so forth, I need not trouble myself. I need not think, if I can only pay – others will readily undertake the irksome work for me.

That the initiative towards independence and majority [Mündigkeit] is held to be very dangerous by the far greater portion of mankind (and by the entire fair sex) – quite apart from its being arduous – is seen to by those guardians who have so kindly assumed superintendence over them. After the guardians have first made their domestic cattle dumb and have made sure that these placid creatures will not dare take a single step without the harness of the cart to which they are tethered, the guardians then show them the danger which threatens if they try to go alone. Actually, however, this danger is not so great, for by falling a few times they would finally learn to walk alone. But an example of this failure makes them timid and ordinarily frightens them away from all further trials.

For any single individual to work himself out of the life under tutelage which has become almost his nature is very difficult. He has come to be fond of this state, and he is for the present really incapable of making use of his understanding, for no one has ever let him try it out. Statutes and formulas, those mechanical tools of the rational employment or rather mis-employment of his natural gifts, are the fetters of an everlasting tutelage. Whoever throws them off makes only an uncertain leap over the narrowest ditch because he is not accustomed to that kind of free motion. Therefore, there are few who have succeeded by their own exercise of mind and spirit [Geist] both in freeing themselves from tutelage and in achieving a steady pace.

But that the public should enlighten itself is more possible; indeed, if only freedom is granted, enlightenment is almost sure to follow. For there will always be some independent thinkers, even among the established guardians of the great masses, who, after throwing off the yoke of tutelage from their own shoulders, will disseminate the spirit of the rational appreciation of both their own worth and every man's vocation for thinking for himself. But be it noted that the public, which has first been brought under this yoke by their guardians, forces the guardians themselves to remain bound when it is later incited to do so by those among these guardians who are themselves incapable of all enlightenment[2] – so harmful is it to implant prejudices, for in the end they take vengeance on their cultivators or on their descendants. Thus the public can only slowly attain enlightenment. Perhaps a decrease in personal despotism and of avaricious or tyrannical oppression may be accomplished by revolution, but never a true reform in ways of thinking. Rather, new prejudices will serve as well as old ones to harness the great thoughtless masses.[3]

For this enlightenment, however, nothing is required but freedom, and freedom of the most harmless sort among its various definitions: freedom to make public use of one's reason [Vernunft][4] at every point. But I hear on all sides, "Do not argue!" The officer says: "Do not argue but drill!" The tax collector: "Do not argue but pay!" The cleric: "Do not argue but believe!" Only one prince in the world says, "Argue as much as you will, and about what you will, but obey!" Everywhere there is restriction on freedom.[5]

Which restriction is an obstacle to enlightenment, and which is not an obstacle but a promoter of it? I answer: The public use of one's reason must always be free, and it alone can bring about enlightenment among men. The private use of reason, on the other hand, may often be very narrowly restricted without particularly hindering the progress of enlightenment. By the public use of one's reason I understand the use which a person makes of it as a scholar before the reading public. Private use I call that which one may make of it in a particular civil post or office which is entrusted to him. Many affairs which are conducted in the interest of the community require a certain mechanism through which some members of the community must passively conduct themselves with an artificial unanimity, so that the government may direct them to public ends, or at least prevent them from destroying those ends. Here argument is certainly not allowed – one must obey. But so far as a part of the mechanism regards himself at the same time as a member of the whole community or of a society of world citizens, and thus in the role of a scholar who addresses the public (in the proper sense of the word) through his writings, he certainly can argue without hurting the affairs for which he is in part responsible as a passive member. Thus it would be ruinous for an officer in service to debate about the suitability or utility of a command given to him by his superior; he must obey. But the right to make remarks on errors in the military service and to lay them before the public for judgement cannot equitably be refused him as a scholar. The citizen cannot refuse to pay the taxes imposed on him; indeed, an impudent complaint at those levied on him can be punished as a scandal (as it could occasion general refractoriness). But the same person nevertheless does not act contrary to his duty as a citizen when, as a scholar, he publicly expresses his thoughts on the inappropriateness or even the injustice of these levies. Similarly a clergyman is obligated to make his sermon to his pupils in catechism and his congregation conform to the symbol of the church which he serves, for he has been accepted on this condition. But as a scholar he has complete freedom, even the calling, to communicate to the public all his carefully tested and well-meaning thoughts on that which is erroneous in the symbol and to make suggestions for the better organization of the religious body and church. In doing this there is nothing that could be laid as a burden on his conscience. For what he teaches as a consequence of his office as a representative of the church, this he considers something about which he has no freedom to teach according to his own lights; it is something which he is appointed to propound at the dictation of and in the name of another. He will say, "Our church teaches this or that; those are the proofs which it adduces." He thus extracts all practical uses for his congregation from statutes to which he himself would not subscribe with full conviction but to the enunciation of which he can very well pledge himself because it is not impossible that truth lies hidden in them, and, in any case, there is at least nothing in them contradictory to inner religion. For if he believed he had found such in them, he could not conscientiously discharge the duties of his office; he would have to give it up. The use, therefore, which an appointed teacher makes of his reason before his congregation is merely private, because this congregation is only a domestic one (even if it be a large gathering); with respect to it, as a priest, he is not free, nor can he be free, because he carries out the orders of another. But as a scholar, whose writings speak to his true public, the world, the clergyman in the public use of his reason enjoys an unlimited freedom to use his own reason and to speak in his own person. That the guardians of the people (in spiritual things) should themselves be incompetent is an absurdity which amounts to the eternalization of absurdities.[6]

But would not a society of clergymen, perhaps a church conference or a venerable classis (as they call themselves among the Dutch), be justified in obligating itself by oath to a certain unchangeable symbol in order to enjoy an unceasing guardianship over each of its members and thereby over the people [das Volk] as a whole, and even to make it eternal? I answer that this is altogether impossible. Such a contract, made to shut off all further enlightenment from the human race, is absolutely null and void even if confirmed by the supreme power, by parliaments, and by the most ceremonious of peace treaties. An age cannot bind itself and ordain to put the succeeding one into such a condition that it cannot extend its (at best very occasional) knowledge, purify itself of errors, and progress in general enlightenment. That would be a crime against human nature, the proper destination of which lies precisely in this progress; and the descendants would be fully justified in rejecting those decrees as having been made in an unwarranted and malicious manner.

The touchstone of everything that can be concluded as a law for a people lies in the question whether the people could have imposed such a law on itself. Now such a religious compact might be possible for a short and definitely limited time, as it were, in expectation of a better. One might let every citizen, and especially the clergyman, in the role of scholar, make his comments freely and publicly, i.e., through writing, on the erroneous aspects of the present institution. The newly introduced order might last until insight into the nature of these things had become so general and widely approved that through uniting their voices (even if not unanimously) they could bring a proposal to the throne to take those congregations under protection which had united into a changed religious organization according to their better ideas, without, however, hindering others who wish to remain in the old order. But to unite in a permanent religious institution which is not to be subject to doubt before the public even in the lifetime of one man, and thereby to make a period of time fruitless in the progress of mankind toward improvement, thus working to the disadvantage of posterity – that is absolutely forbidden. For himself (and only for a short time) a man may postpone enlightenment in what he ought to know, but to renounce it for himself and even more to renounce it for posterity is to injure and trample on the rights of mankind.

And what a people may not decree for itself can even less be decreed for them by a monarch, for his law-giving authority rests on his uniting the general public will in his own. If he only sees to it that all true or alleged improvement stands together with civil order, he can leave it to his subjects to do what they find necessary for their spiritual welfare. This is not his concern, though it is incumbent on him to prevent one of them from violently hindering another in determining and promoting this welfare to the best of his ability. To meddle in these matters lowers his own majesty, since by the writings in which his subjects seek to present their views he may evaluate his own governance. He can do this when, with deepest understanding, he lays upon himself the reproach, *Caesar non est supra grammaticos.*[7] Far more does he injure his own majesty when he degrades his supreme power by supporting the ecclesiastical despotism of some tyrants in his state over his other subjects.

If we are asked, "Do we now live in an *enlightened* age?" the answer is, "No", but we do live in an age of *enlightenment.*[8] As things now stand, much is lacking which prevents men from being, or easily becoming, capable of correctly using their own understandings in religious matters with assurance and free from outside direction. But, on the other hand, we have clear indications that the field has now been opened wherein men may freely deal with these things and that the obstacles to general enlightenment or the release from self-imposed tutelage are gradually being reduced. In this respect, this is the age of enlightenment, or the century of Frederick.

A prince who does not find it unworthy of himself to say that he holds it to be his duty to prescribe nothing to men in religious matters but to give them complete freedom while renouncing the haughty name of *tolerance*, is himself enlightened and deserves to be esteemed by the grateful world and posterity as the first, at least from the side of government, who divested the human race of its tutelage and left each man free to make use of his reason in matters of conscience. Under him venerable ecclesiastics are allowed, in the role of scholars, and without infringing on their official duties, freely to submit for public testing their judgements and views which here and there diverge from the established symbol. And an even greater freedom is enjoyed by those who are restricted by no official duties. This spirit of freedom spreads beyond this land, even to those in which it must struggle with external obstacles erected by a government which misunderstands its own interest. For an example gives evidence to such a government that in freedom there is not the least cause for concern about public peace and the stability of the community. Men work themselves gradually out of barbarity if only intentional artifices are not made to hold them in it.

I have placed the main point of enlightenment – the escape of men from their self-incurred tutelage – chiefly in matters of religion because our rulers have no interest in playing the guardian with respect to the arts and sciences and also because religious incompetence is not only the most harmful but also the most degrading of all. But the manner of thinking of the head of a state who favours religious enlightenment goes further, and he sees that there is no danger in his law-giving in allowing his subjects to make public use of their reason and to publish their thoughts on a better formulation of his legislation and even their open-minded criticisms of the laws already made. Of this we have a shining example wherein no monarch is superior to him whom we honour.[9]

But only one who is himself enlightened, is not afraid of shadows, and who has a numerous and well-disciplined army to assure public peace, can say: "Argue as much as you will, and about what you will, only obey!" A republic could not dare say such a thing. Here is shown a strange and unexpected trend in human affairs in which almost everything, looked at in the large, is paradoxical. A greater degree of civil freedom appears advantageous to the freedom of mind of the people, and yet it places inescapable limitations upon it; a lower degree of civil freedom, on the contrary, provides the mind with room for each man to extend himself to his full capacity. As nature has uncovered from under this hard shell the seed for which she most tenderly cares – the propensity and vocation to free thinking – this gradually works back upon the character of the people, who thereby gradually become capable of managing freedom; finally, it affects the principles of government, which finds it to its advantage to treat men, who are now more than machines, in accordance with their dignity.[10]

Selections from
The Critique of Judgement
[Kritik der Urtheilskraft]

1790

Excerpts from the translation by James Creed Meredith, slightly modified.

German text in *Ak*. V, 167ff.

Introductory Note

Kant famously said of Hume that reading the Scottish philosopher had taken possession of him as if with a giant's hand and woken him from his slumbers. As a description of Kant's own effect on his immediate generation in Germany this might almost seem too modest. As the first two *Critiques* established the terms of the debates in epistemology and ethics for years to come, so the *Critique of Judgement* is the immediate inspiration and reference point for almost everything written by philosophers on aesthetics during the following half century. It was read eagerly though not always accurately by writers and critics – Goethe, Schiller and the Schlegel brothers among them – and Fichte, Schelling and Schopenhauer all saw themselves as in some sense true to the spirit of Kant even as they differed among themselves. In fact there are few arguments in Romantic aesthetics which cannot either be traced back directly to the *CJ* or intelligibly related to it in thematic terms, whether to its major arguments or to the hints and observations that arise with them or qualify them.

Kant was sixty-six when the *CJ* was published in 1790. It was not his first pronouncement on the subject of aesthetics. His early work of 1764, the *Observations on the Feeling of the Beautiful and Sublime* (see Kant, 1960), is of a very different character. It does indeed anticipate some of the concerns of the *Critique*, but as remarks rather than as methodical formulations. Thus there are comments on the relation of taste to virtue, and on the incompatibility of taste and interest, but the general assumption of the book is that no philosophically exact aesthetic theory is possible. This seems to have been Kant's conviction for much of his career.

There is an early draft of the introduction to *CJ*, translated under a different title by Humayun Kabir (see Kant, 1935), but this need not concern us here; readers interested in following up possible significant shifts of position between the early draft and the finished work should consult Crawford (1974), pp. 3–28.

The third of the great *Critiques*, which might more exactly be rendered into English as that of the "power of judging" [Urtheilskraft] and of the "faculty for making estimations" [Beurtheilungsvermögen], describes this power of judging as the "middle term between understanding and reason" (*CJ*, I, 4). Thus it complements and mediates the conclusions of the two earlier parts of the critical philosophy in epistemology (understanding) and ethics (reason). Understanding and reason coexist in the human subject but neither can interfere with the other; it is judgement that provides "the mediating concept between concepts of nature and concepts of freedom" (I, 13). As

35

such, judgement is the "faculty of thinking the particular as contained under the universal" (I, 18), and it operates on transcendental principles, prescribing laws in an *a priori* fashion. Its estimations are however always only referable to subjective assumptions, albeit necessary ones. Thus, as applied to the two parts of the inquiry in *CJ*, aesthetics and teleology, we are compelled to assume that judgements about the beautiful are as universal *as if they were* containable under a concept (for Kant the guarantee of intersubjective experience), and that nature demonstrates a purposiveness, *as if it were* aiming at an end. But in each case there is strictly speaking only "a finality in respect of the subject's faculty of cognition" (I, 25).

Whilst aesthetic and teleological judgements are the exclusive subjects of the *CJ*, judgement properly speaking enters into every perception. However in ordinary experience the subsumption of intuitions under concepts is so habitual that we no longer distinguish the parts of the process (I, 27–8), and seldom therefore experience any feeling of pleasure or any other incentive to self-consciousness. It is in aesthetic experience and in teleological estimates of objects of nature that we most readily achieve such self-consciousness, because the pleasure is experienced independently of any confirmation of successful subsumption of intuition under concept: we react as if this had taken place at the same time as knowing that it cannot. There are no objective verifications of beauty, or of an end in nature, but we are somehow compelled to behave as if there were.

The second part of the *CJ*, the 'Critique of Teleological Judgement', is not very fully represented in the selections that follow, though it would have been possible to produce an anthology more heavily weighted toward theories of organic form based on longer extracts from this second part. Exemplary passages have been included, but most of what follows has been excerpted from the 'Critique of Aesthetic Judgement'. Even here, as might be expected, no complete coverage is possible, and certain important arguments simply cannot be followed through completely without reference to parts of the book not here reprinted. This is unavoidable given the demands of space, and I have tried to indicate important parallels or qualifications in the endnotes. Perhaps most regrettably, the whole of the dialectic of aesthetic judgement (§§55–60), which refines on the relation between judgements of taste and concepts, has been omitted; hence also the important §59, central as it is to any proper grasp of Kant's view of the relation of beauty to morality. It is here that the notion of beauty as the "symbol" of the moral is explored, along with the strong claim that this is our sole source of pleasure in the assumption of its communicability.

There is a more 'public' and less specialized exposition of some of the main points of *CJ* in the later *Anthropology*, and this too should be consulted (Kant, 1974, pp. 108–16; *Ak.* VII, 239–49). Here, for example, the relation of aesthetic and moral experience appears in a different form:

Ideal taste has a tendency to promote morality in an external way. Making a man *well-mannered* as a social being falls short of forming a *morally good* man, but it still prepares him for it by the effort he makes, in society, to please others (to make them love or admire him). (Kant, 1974, pp. 111–12)

The *Anthropology*, it might be thought, can afford to explore the unconscious relation of uncontingent self-legislation to social approbation in a way that the critical philosophy cannot.

For detailed exposition and commentary, the reader should consult H.W. Cassirer (1938); and Meredith (1911) is especially useful for its comprehensive evidence of Kant's possible borrowings from British eighteenth-century writers on aesthetics.

Part I   Critique of Aesthetic Judgement

FIRST BOOK
ANALYTIC OF THE BEAUTIFUL

§2

The delight which determines the judgement of taste is independent of all interest

The delight which we connect with the representation of the real existence of an object is called interest. Such a delight, therefore, always involves a reference to the faculty of desire [Begehrungsvermögen][1], either as its determining ground, or else as necessarily implicated with its determining ground. Now, where the question is whether something is beautiful, we do not want to know whether we or anyone else are, or even could be, concerned in the real existence of the thing, but rather what estimate we form of it on mere contemplation [Betrachtung] (intuition or reflection) . . . All one wants to know is whether the mere representation [bloße Vorstellung] of the object is to my liking, no matter how indifferent I may be to the real existence of the object of this representation. It is quite plain that in order to say that the object *is beautiful*, and to show that I have taste [Geschmack], everything turns on the meaning which I can give to this representation, and not on any factor which makes me dependent on the real existence of the object. Every one must allow that a judgement on the beautiful which is tinged with the slightest interest, is very partial and not a pure judgement of taste. One must not be in the least prepossessed of the real existence of the thing, but must preserve complete indifference in this respect, in order to play the part of judge in matters of taste.

[Kant goes on to distinguish "the beautiful" from two other forms of the relation of representations to pleasure and displeasure, the "agreeable" and the "good". Unlike the "beautiful" they are dependent upon interest, and on a concern for the real existence of the object. This interest pre-empts freedom: "All interest presupposes a want, or calls one forth; and, being a ground determining approval, deprives the judgement on the object of its freedom" (§5).]

DEFINITION OF THE BEAUTIFUL DERIVED FROM THE FIRST
MOMENT

Taste is the faculty of estimating an object or a mode of representation by means of a delight or aversion *apart from any interest*. The object of such a delight is called *beautiful*.

SECOND MOMENT OF THE JUDGEMENT OF TASTE: MOMENT OF QUANTITY

§6

The beautiful is that which, apart from concepts, is represented as the Object[2] of a
UNIVERSAL *delight*

This definition of the beautiful is deducible from the foregoing definition of it
as an object of delight apart from any interest. For where any one is conscious
that his delight in an object is with him independent of interest, it is inevitable
that he should look on the object as one containing a ground of delight for all
men. For, since the delight is not based on any inclination of the subject (or on
any other deliberate interest), but the subject feels himself completely *free* in
respect of the liking which he accords to the object, he can find as reason for
his delight no personal conditions to which his own subjective self might alone
be party. Hence he must regard it as resting on what he may also presuppose
in every other person; and therefore he must believe that he has reason for
demanding a similar delight from every one. Accordingly he will speak of the
beautiful as if beauty were a quality of the object and the judgement logical
(forming a cognition of the Object by concepts of it); although it is only
aesthetic, and contains merely a reference of the representation of the object to
the subject; because it still bears this resemblance to the logical judgement,
that it may be presupposed to be valid for all men. But this universality cannot
spring from concepts. For from concepts there is no transition to the feeling of
pleasure or displeasure (save in the case of pure practical laws, which, however, carry an interest with them; and such an interest does not attach to the
pure judgement of taste).[3] The result is that the judgement of taste, with its
attendant consciousness of detachment from all interest, must involve a claim
to validity for all men, and must do so apart from universality attached to
Objects, i.e. there must be coupled with it a claim to subjective universality.

§7

*Comparison of the beautiful with the agreeable and the good by means of the above
characteristic*

As regards the *agreeable* [*Angenehmen*] every one concedes that his judgement,
which he bases on a private feeling, and in which he declares that an object
pleases him, is restricted merely to himself personally. Thus he does not take it
amiss if, when he says that Canary-wine is agreeable, another corrects the
expression and reminds him that he ought to say: It is agreeable *to me*. This
applies not only to the taste of the tongue, the palate, and the throat, but to

what may with any one be agreeable to eye or ear. A violet colour is to one soft and lovely: to another dull and faded. One man likes the tone of wind instruments, another prefers that of string instruments. To quarrel over such points with the idea of condemning another's judgement as incorrect when it differs from our own, as if the opposition between the two judgements were logical, would be folly. With the agreeable, therefore, the axiom holds good: *Every one has his own taste* (that of sense).

The beautiful stands on quite a different footing. It would, on the contrary, be ridiculous if any one who plumed himself on his taste were to think of justifying himself by saying: This object (the building we see, the dress that person has on, the concert we hear, the poem submitted to our criticism) is beautiful *for me*. For if it merely pleases *him*, he must not call it *beautiful*. Many things may for him possess charm and agreeableness – no one cares about that; but when he puts a thing on a pedestal and calls it beautiful, he demands the same delight from others. He judges not merely for himself, but for all men, and then speaks of beauty as if it were a property of things. Thus he says the *thing* is beautiful; and it is not as if he counted on others agreeing in his judgement of liking owing to his having found them in such agreement on a number of occasions, but he *demands* this agreement of them. He blames them if they judge differently, and denies them taste, which he still requires of them as something they ought to have; and to this extent it is not open to men to say: Every one has his own taste. This would be equivalent to saying that there is no such thing at all as taste, i.e. no aesthetic judgement capable of making a rightful claim upon the assent of all men.

Yet even in the case of the agreeable we find that the estimates men form do betray a prevalent agreement among them, which leads to our crediting some with taste and denying it to others, and that, too, not as an organic sense but as a critical faculty in respect of the agreeable generally. So of one who knows how to entertain his guests with pleasures (of enjoyment through all the senses) in such a way that one and all are pleased, we say that he has taste. But the universality here is only understood in a comparative sense; and the rules that apply are, like all empirical rules, *general* [*generale*] only, not *universal* [*universale*] – the latter being what the judgement of taste upon the beautiful deals or claims to deal in. It is a judgement in respect of sociability so far as resting on empirical rules.[4] In respect of the good it is true that judgements also rightly assert a claim to validity for every one; but the good is only represented as an Object of universal delight *by means of a concept*, which is the case neither with the agreeable nor the beautiful.

§8

... When one forms an estimate [beurtheilt] of Objects merely from concepts, all representation of beauty goes by the board. There can, therefore, be no rule according to which any one is to be compelled to recognize anything as beautiful. Whether a dress, a house, or a flower is beautiful is a matter upon which one declines to allow one's judgement to be swayed by any reasons or principles. We want to get a look at the Object with our own eyes, just as if our delight depended on sensation. And yet, if upon so doing, we call the object beautiful, we believe ourselves to be speaking with a universal voice, and lay claim to the concurrence of every one, whereas one private sensation would be decisive except for the observer alone and *his* liking.

Here, now, we may perceive that nothing is postulated in the judgement of taste but such a *universal* [*allgemeine*] *voice* in respect of delight that is not mediated by concepts; consequently, only the *possibility* of an aesthetic judgement capable of being at the same time deemed valid for every one. The judgement of taste itself does not *postulate* the agreement of every one (for it is only competent for a logically universal judgement to do this, in that it is able to bring forward reasons); it only *imputes* this agreement to every one, as an instance of the rule in respect of which it looks for confirmation, not from concepts, but from the concurrence of others. The universal voice is, therefore, only an idea – resting upon grounds the investigation of which is here postponed.[5] It may be a matter of uncertainty whether a person who thinks he is laying down a judgement of taste is, in fact, judging in conformity with that idea; but that this idea is what is contemplated in his judgement, and that, consequently, it is meant to be a judgement of taste, is proclaimed by his use of the expression 'beauty'. For himself he can be certain on the point from his mere consciousness of the separation of everything belonging to the agreeable and the good from the delight remaining to him; and this is all for which he promises himself the agreement of every one – a claim which, under these conditions, he would also be warranted in making, were it not that he frequently sinned against them, and thus passed an erroneous judgement of taste.

§9

Investigation of the question of the relative priority in a judgement of taste of the feeling of pleasure and the estimating of [Beurtheilung] the object

The solution of this problem is the key to the critique of taste, and so is worthy of all attention.

Were the pleasure in a given object to be the antecedent, and were the universal communicability of this pleasure to be all that the judgement of taste is meant to allow to the representation of the object, such a sequence would be self-contradictory. For a pleasure of that kind would be nothing but the feeling of mere agreeableness to the senses, and so, from its very nature, would possess no more than private validity, seeing that it would be immediately dependent on the representation through which the object *is given*.

Hence it is the universal capacity for being communicated incident to the mental state in the given representation which, as the subjective condition of the judgement of taste, must be fundamental, with the pleasure in the object as its consequent. Nothing, however, is capable of being universally communicated but cognition [Erkenntniß] and representation [Vorstellung], so far as appurtenant to cognition. For it is only as thus appurtenant that the representation is objective, and it is this alone that gives it a universal point of reference with which the power of representation of every one is obliged to harmonize. If, then, the determining ground of the judgement as to this universal communicability of the representation is to be merely subjective, that is to say, is to be conceived independently of any concept of the object, it can be nothing else than the mental state that presents itself in the mutual relation of the powers of representation so far as they refer a given representation *to cognition in general*.

The cognitive powers brought into play by this representation are here engaged in a free play, since no definite concept restricts them to a particular rule of cognition. Hence the mental state in this representation must be one of a feeling of the free play of the powers of representation in a given representation for a cognition in general. Now a representation, whereby an object is given, involves, in order that it may become a source of cognition at all, *imagination* [*Einbildungskraft*] for bringing together the manifold of intuition, and *understanding* [*Verstand*] for the unity of the concept uniting the representations. This state of *free play* of the cognitive faculties attending a representation by which an object is given must admit of universal communication: because cognition, as a definition of the Object with which given representations (in any subject whatever) are to accord, is the one and only mode of representation which is valid for every one.[6]

As the subjective universal communicability of the mode of representation in a judgement of taste is to subsist apart from the presupposition of any definite concept, it can be nothing else than the mental state present in the free play of imagination and understanding (so far as these are in mutual accord, as is requisite for *cognition in general*): for we are conscious that this subjective relation suitable for a cognition in general must be just as valid for every one, and consequently as universally communicable, as is any determinate cognition, which always rests upon that relation as its subjective condition.

Now this purely subjective (aesthetic) estimating of the object, or of the representation through which it is given, is antecedent to the pleasure in it, and is the basis of this pleasure in the harmony of the cognitive faculties. Again, the above-described universality of the subjective conditions of estimating objects forms the sole foundation of this universal subjective validity of the delight which we connect with the representation of the object that we call beautiful.[7]

That an ability to communicate one's mental state, even though it be only in respect of our cognitive faculties, is attended with a pleasure, is a fact which might easily be demonstrated from the natural propensity of mankind to social life, i.e. empirically and psychologically. But what we have here in view calls for something more than this. In a judgement of taste the pleasure felt by

us is exacted from every one else as necessary, just as if, when we call something beautiful, beauty was to be regarded as a quality of the object forming
part of its inherent determination according to concepts; although beauty is
for itself, apart from any reference to the feeling of the subject, nothing. But
the discussion of this question must be reserved until we have answered the
further one of whether, and how, aesthetic judgements are possible *a priori*.

At present we are exercised with the lesser question of the way in which we
become conscious, in a judgement of taste, of a reciprocal subjective common
accord of the powers of cognition. Is it aesthetically by sensation and our mere
internal sense? Or is it intellectually by consciousness of our intentional activity in bringing these powers into play?

Now if the given representation occasioning the judgement of taste were a
concept which united understanding and imagination in the estimate of the
object so as to give a cognition of the Object, the consciousness of this relation
would be intellectual (as in the objective schematism of judgement dealt with in
the Critique).[8] But, then, in that case the judgement would not be laid down
with respect to pleasure and displeasure, and so would not be a judgement of
taste. But, now, the judgement of taste determines the object, independently of
concepts, in respect of delight and of the predicate of beauty. There is, therefore,
no other way for the subjective unity of the relation in question to make itself
known than by sensation. The quickening of both faculties (imagination and
understanding) to an indefinite, but yet, thanks to the given representation,
harmonious activity, such as belongs to cognition generally, is the sensation
whose universal communicability is postulated by the judgement of taste. An
objective relation can, of course, only be thought, yet in so far as, in respect of its
conditions, it is subjective, it may be felt in its effect upon the mind, and, in the
case of a relation (like that of the powers of representation to a faculty of
cognition generally) which does not rest on any concept, no other consciousness
of it is possible beyond that through sensation of its effect upon the mind – an
effect consisting in the more facilitated play of both mental powers (imagination and understanding) as quickened by their mutual accord. A representation
which is singular and independent of comparison with other representations,
and, being such, yet accords with the conditions of the universality that is the
general concern of understanding, is one that brings the cognitive faculties into
that proportionate accord which we require for all cognition and which we
therefore deem valid for every one who is so constituted as to judge by means of
understanding and sense conjointly (i.e. for every man).

DEFINITION OF THE BEAUTIFUL DRAWN FROM THE SECOND MOMENT

The *beautiful* is that which, apart from a concept, pleases universally.

[After further remarks on the pure judgement of taste, which has nothing to do with
"empirical delight" (§14), Kant goes on to distinguish between "free" and "depen-

dent" beauty (§16). The latter does presuppose a concept of what the object should be, and goes beyond the appreciation of pure form to consider ends and purposes. It is therefore not the "pure judgement of taste", though it may be combined with it to produce a harmony in the whole faculty of "representative power" (Vorstellungskraft).]

§17

The ideal of beauty

There can be no objective rule of taste by which what is beautiful may be defined by means of concepts. For every judgement from that source is aesthetic, i.e. its determining ground is the feeling of the subject, and not any concept of an Object. It is only throwing away labour to look for a principle of taste that affords a universal criterion of the beautiful by definite concepts; because what is sought is a thing impossible and inherently contradictory. But in the universal communicability of the sensation (of delight or aversion) – a communicability, too, that exists apart from any concept – in the accord, so far as possible, of all ages and nations as to this feeling in the representation of certain objects, we have the empirical criterion, weak indeed and scarce sufficient to raise a presumption, of the derivation of a taste, thus conformed by examples, from grounds deep-seated and shared alike by all men, underlying their agreement in estimating the forms under which objects are given to them.[9]

For this reason some products of taste are looked on as *exemplary* – not meaning thereby that by imitating others taste may be acquired. For taste must be an original faculty; whereas one who imitates a model, while showing skill commensurate with his success, only displays taste as himself a critic of this model.[10] Hence it follows that the highest model, the archetype of taste, is a mere idea, which each person must beget in his own consciousness, and according to which he must form his estimate of everything that is an Object of taste, or that is an example of critical taste, and even of universal taste itself. Properly speaking, an *idea* signifies a concept of reason, and an *ideal* the representation of an individual existence as adequate to an idea. Hence this archetype of taste – which rests, indeed, upon reason's indeterminate idea of a maximum, but is not, however, capable of being represented by means of concepts, but only in an individual presentation – may more appropriately be called the ideal of the beautiful. While not having this ideal in our possession, we still strive to beget it within us. But it is bound to be merely an ideal of the imagination, seeing that it rests, not upon concepts, but upon the presentation – the faculty of presentation being the imagination. Now how do we arrive at such an ideal of beauty? Is it *a priori* or empirically? Further, what species of the beautiful admits of an ideal?

First of all, we do well to observe that the beauty for which an ideal has to be sought cannot be a beauty that is *free and at large*, but must be one *fixed* by a concept of objective finality. Hence it cannot belong to the Object of an altogether pure judgement of taste, but must attach to one that is partly intellectual. In other words, where an ideal is to have place among the grounds upon which any estimate is formed, then beneath grounds of that kind there must lie some idea of reason according to determinate concepts, by which the end underlying the internal possibility of the object is determined *a priori*. An ideal of beautiful flowers, of a beautiful suite of furniture, or of a beautiful view, is unthinkable. But, it may also be impossible to represent an ideal of a beauty dependent on definite ends, e.g. a beautiful residence, a beautiful tree, a beautiful garden, &c., presumably because their ends are not sufficiently defined and fixed by their concept, with the result that their finality is nearly as free as with beauty that is quite *at large*. Only what has in itself the end of its real existence – only *man* that is able himself to determine his ends by reason, or, where he has to derive them from external perception, can still compare them with essential and universal ends, and then further pronounce aesthetically upon their accord with such ends, only he, among all objects in the world, admits, therefore, of an ideal of *beauty*, just as humanity in his person, as intelligence, alone admits of the ideal of *perfection*.

Two factors are here involved. *First*, there is the aesthetic *normal idea* [*Normalidee*], which is an individual intuition (of the imagination). This represents the norm by which we judge of a man as a member of a particular animal species. *Secondly*, there is the *rational idea* [*Vernunftidee*]. This deals with the ends of humanity so far as incapable of sensuous representation, and converts them into a principle for estimating its outward form, through which these ends are revealed in their phenomenal effect. The normal idea must draw from experience the constituents which it requires for the form of an animal of a particular kind. But the greatest finality in the construction of this form – that which would serve as a universal norm for forming an estimate of each individual of the species in question – the image that, as it were, forms an intentional basis underlying the technic of nature, to which no separate individual, but only the race as a whole, is adequate, has its seat merely in the idea of the judging subject. Yet it is, with all its proportions, an aesthetic idea, and, as such, capable of being fully presented *in concreto* in a model image. Now, how is this effected? In order to render the process to some extent intelligible (for who can wrest nature's whole secret from her?), let us attempt a psychological explanation.

[This "normal idea" is constructed in the imagination by the intuitive standardization of separate mental images into a normative image, of course variable according to whether we are Europeans, Chinamen, etc. But this is only a pre-condition and not a definition of the archetype (Urbild) of beauty. The ideal of the beautiful, to be sought only in the human figure, must involve a perception of the moral.]

... The visible expression of moral [sittlich] ideas[11] that govern men inwardly can, of course, only be drawn from experience; but their combination with all that our reason connects with the morally good in the idea of the highest finality – benevolence, purity, strength, or equanimity, &c. – may be made, as it were, visible in bodily manifestation (as effect of what is internal), and this embodiment involves a union of pure ideas of reason and great imaginative power, in one who would even form an estimate of it, not to speak of being the author of its presentation. The correctness of such an ideal of beauty is evidenced by its not permitting any sensuous charm [Sinnenreiz] to mingle with the delight in its Object, in which it still allows us to take a great interest. This fact in turn shows that an estimate formed according to such a standard can never be purely aesthetic, and that one formed according to an ideal of beauty cannot be a simple judgement of taste.

DEFINITION OF THE BEAUTIFUL DERIVED FROM THIS THIRD MOMENT

Beauty is the form of *finality* in an object, so far as perceived in it *apart from the representation of an end* [12]

FOURTH MOMENT
OF THE JUDGEMENT OF TASTE: MOMENT OF THE MODALITY OF THE DELIGHT IN THE OBJECT

§18

Nature of the modality in a judgement of taste

I may assert in the case of every representation that the synthesis of a pleasure with the representation (as a cognition) is at least *possible*. Of what I call *agreeable* I assert that it *actually* causes pleasure in me. But what we have in mind in the case of the *beautiful* is a *necessary* reference on its part to delight. However, this necessity is of a special kind. It is not a theoretical objective necessity – such as would let us cognize *a priori* that every one *will feel* this delight in the object that is called beautiful by me. Nor yet is it a practical necessity, in which case, thanks to concepts of a pure rational will in which free agents are supplied with a rule, this delight is the necessary consequence of an objective law, and simply means that one ought absolutely (without ulterior purpose) to act in a certain way. Rather, being such a necessity as is thought in an aesthetic judgement, it can only be termed *exemplary*. In other words it is a necessity of the assent of *all* to a judgement regarded as exemplifying a universal rule incapable of formulation. Since an aesthetic judgement is not an objective or cognitive judgement, this necessity is not derivable from definite concepts, and so is not apodictic. Much less is it inferable from universality of experience (of a thorough-going agreement of judgements about the beauty of a certain object). For, apart from the fact that experience would hardly furnish evidences sufficiently numerous for this purpose, empirical judgements do not afford any foundation for a concept of the necessity of these judgements.

[There follows (§§19–22) a description of "common sense" (Gemeinsinn), the assumption of which underlies the *supposition* of universality in judgements of taste. This is to be distinguished from the *sensus communis* which governs the operation of the understanding, which judges by concepts and not by feeling (Gefühl). In a general remark on the first book, the free imagination involved in the judgement of taste is defined as "productive . . . as originator of arbitrary forms of possible intuitions", rather than merely "reproductive".]

GENERAL REMARK ON THE FIRST SECTION OF THE ANALYTIC

. . . All stiff regularity (such as borders on mathematical regularity) is inherently repugnant to taste, in that the contemplation of it affords us no lasting entertainment. Indeed, where it has neither cognition nor some definite practical end expressly in view, we get heartily tired of it. On the other hand, anything that gives the imagination scope for unstudied and final play is always fresh to us. We do not grow to hate the very sight of it. *Marsden* in his description of Sumatra observes that the free beauties of nature so surround the beholder on all sides that they cease to have much attraction for him.[13] On the other hand he found a pepper garden full of charm, on coming across it in mid-forest with its rows of parallel stakes on which the plant twines itself. From all this he infers that wild, and in its appearance quite irregular beauty, is only pleasing as a change to one whose eyes have become surfeited with regular beauty. But he need only have made the experiment of passing one day in his pepper garden to realize that once the regularity has enabled the understanding to put itself in accord with the order that is its constant requirement, instead of the object diverting him any longer, it imposes an irksome constraint upon the imagination: whereas nature subject to no constraint of artificial rules, and lavish, as it there is, in its luxuriant variety can supply constant food for his taste. – Even a bird's song, which we can reduce to no musical rule, seems to have more freedom in it, and thus to be richer for taste, than the human voice singing in accordance with all the rules that the art of music prescribes; for we grow tired much sooner of frequent and lengthy repetitions of the latter. Yet here most likely our sympathy with the mirth of a dear little creature is confused with the beauty of its song, for if exactly imitated by man (as has been sometimes done with the notes of the nightingale) it would strike our ear as wholly destitute of taste.[14] . . .

SECOND BOOK
ANALYTIC OF THE SUBLIME [DAS ERHABENE]

§23

Transition from the faculty of estimating the beautiful to that of estimating the sublime

The beautiful and the sublime agree on the point of pleasing on their own account. Further they agree in not presupposing either a judgement of sense or one logically determinant, but one of reflection. Hence it follows that the delight does not depend upon a sensation, as with the agreeable, nor upon a definite concept, as does the delight in the good, although it has, for all that, an indeterminate reference to concepts. Consequently the delight is connected with the mere presentation or faculty of presentation, and is thus taken to express the accord, in a given intuition, of the faculty of presentation, or the imagination, with the *faculty of concepts* that belongs to understanding or reason, in the sense of the former assisting the latter. Hence both kinds of judgements are *singular*, and yet such as profess to be universally valid in respect of every subject, despite the fact that their claims are directed merely to the feeling of pleasure and not to any knowledge of the object.

There are, however, also important and striking differences between the two. The beautiful in nature is a question of the form of the object, and this consists in limitation, whereas the sublime is to be found in an object even devoid of form, so far as it immediately involves, or else by its presence provokes a representation of *limitlessness*, yet with a super-added thought of its totality. Accordingly the beautiful seems to be regarded as a presentation of an indeterminate concept of understanding, the sublime as a presentation of an indeterminate concept of reason. Hence the delight is in the former case coupled with the representation of *Quality*, but in this case with that of *Quantity*. Moreover, the former delight is very different from the latter in kind. For the beautiful is directly attended with a feeling of the furtherance of life, and is thus compatible with charms and a playful imagination.[15] On the other hand, the feeling of the sublime is a pleasure that only arises indirectly, being brought about by the feeling of a momentary check to the vital forces followed at once by a discharge all the more powerful, and so it is an emotion that seems to be no sport, but dead earnest in the affairs of the imagination. Hence it is irreconcilable with charms [Reizen]; and, since the mind is not simply attracted by the object, but is also alternately repelled thereby, the delight in the sublime does not so much involve positive pleasure as admiration or respect, i.e. merits the name of a negative pleasure.

But the most important and vital distinction between the sublime and the beautiful is certainly this: that if, as is allowable, we here confine our attention in the first instance to the sublime of Objects of nature (that of art being always restricted by the conditions of an agreement with nature), we observe that whereas natural beauty (such as is self-subsisting) conveys a finality in its form making the object appear, as it were, preadapted to our power of judgement, so that it thus forms of itself an object of our delight; that which, without our indulging in any refinements of thought, but, simply in our apprehension of it, excites the feeling of the sublime, may appear, indeed, in point of form to contravene the ends of our power of judgement, to be ill-adapted to our faculty of presentation, and to be, as it were, an outrage on the imagination, and yet it is judged all the more sublime on that account.

From this it may be seen at once that we express ourselves on the whole inaccurately if we term any *object of nature* sublime, although we may with perfect propriety call many such objects beautiful. For how can that which is apprehended as inherently contra-final be noted with an expression of approval? All that we can say is that the object lends itself to the presentation of a sublimity discoverable in the mind. For the sublime, in the strict sense of the word, cannot be contained in any sensuous form, but rather concerns ideas of reason, which, although no adequate presentation of them is possible, may be excited and called into the mind by that very inadequacy itself which does admit of sensuous presentation. Thus the broad ocean agitated by storms cannot be called sublime. Its aspect is horrible, and one must have stored one's mind in advance with a rich stock of ideas, if such an intuition is to raise it to the pitch of a feeling which is itself sublime – sublime because the mind has been incited to abandon sensibility, and employ itself upon ideas involving higher finality.

Self-subsisting natural beauty reveals to us a technic of nature which shows it in the light of a system ordered in accordance with laws the principle of which is not to be found within the range of our entire faculty of understanding. This principle is that of a finality relative to the employment of judgement in respect of phenomena which have thus to be assigned, not merely to nature regarded as aimless mechanism, but also to nature regarded after the analogy of art. Hence it gives a veritable extension, not, of course, to our knowledge of Objects of nature, but to our conception of nature itself – nature as mere mechanism being enlarged to the conception of nature as art – an extension inviting profound inquiries as to the possibility of such a form. But in what we are wont to call sublime in nature there is such an absence of anything leading to particular objective principles and corresponding forms of nature, that it is rather in its chaos, or in its wildest and most irregular disorder and desolation, provided it gives signs of magnitude and power, that nature chiefly excites the ideas of the sublime. Hence we see that the concept of the sublime in nature is far less important and rich in consequences than that of its beauty. It gives on the whole no indication of anything final in nature itself, but only in the possible *employment* of our intuitions of it in inducing a feeling in our own selves of a finality quite independent of nature. For the beautiful in nature we must seek a ground external to ourselves, but

for the sublime one merely in ourselves and the attitude of mind that introduces sublimity into the representation of nature. This is a very needful preliminary remark. It entirely separates the ideas of the sublime from that of a
finality of *nature*, and makes the theory of the sublime a mere appendage to the
aesthetic estimate of the finality of nature, because it does not give a representation of any particular form in nature, but involves no more than the development of a final employment by the imagination of its own representation.[16]

[There is a division in the analysis of the sublime, "namely one into the *mathematically*
and the *dynamically* sublime" (§24). Unlike the restful contemplation characterizing the
aesthetic, the sublime involves a mental movement, which may be referred either to
the faculty of cognition or to that of desire, always bearing in mind that such reference
to finality can involve no end or interest. Accordingly it is either mathematical or
dynamical. There follows an elucidation of the mathematically sublime.]

§26

. . . Nature, therefore, is sublime in such of its phenomena as in their intuition
convey the idea of their infinity. But this can only occur through the
inadequacy of even the greatest effort of our imagination in the estimation of
the magnitude of an object. But, now, in the case of the mathematical estimation of magnitude imagination is quite competent to supply a measure equal
to the requirements of any object. For the numerical concepts of the understanding can by progressive synthesis make any measure adequate to any
given magnitude in which we get at once a feeling of the effort towards a
comprehension that exceeds the faculty of imagination for mentally grasping
the progressive apprehension in a whole of intuition, and, with it, a perception
of the inadequacy of this faculty, which has no bounds to its progress, for
taking in and using for the estimation of magnitude a fundamental measure
that understanding could turn to account without the least trouble. Now the
proper unchangeable fundamental measure of nature is its absolute whole,
which, with it, regarded as a phenomenon, means infinity comprehended.
But, since this fundamental measure is a self-contradictory concept (owing to
the impossibility of the absolute totality of an endless progression), it follows
that where the size of a natural Object is such that the imagination spends its
whole faculty of comprehension upon it in vain, it must carry our concept of
nature to a supersensible substrate (underlying both nature and our faculty of
thought) which is great beyond every standard of sense. Thus, instead of the
object, it is rather the cast of the mind in appreciating it that we have to
estimate as *sublime*.

Therefore, just as the aesthetic judgement in its estimate of the beautiful
refers the imagination in its free play to the *understanding*, to bring out its
agreement with the *concepts* of the latter in general (apart from their determination): so in its estimate of a thing as sublime it refers that faculty to *reason* to
bring out its subjective accord with *ideas* of reason (indeterminately indi-

cated), i.e. to induce a temper of mind conformable to that which the influence of definite (practical) ideas would produce upon feeling, and in common accord with it.

This makes it evident that true sublimity must be sought only in the mind of the judging subject, and not in the Object of nature that occasions this attitude by the estimate formed of it. Who would apply the term 'sublime' even to shapeless mountain masses towering one above the other in wild disorder, with their pyramids of ice, or to the dark tempestuous ocean or such like things? But in the contemplation of them, without any regard to their form, the mind abandons itself to the imagination and to a reason placed, though quite apart from any definite end, in conjunction therewith, and merely broadening its view, and it feels itself elevated in its own estimate of itself on finding all the might of imagination still unequal to its ideas.

We get examples of the mathematically sublime of nature in mere intuition in all those instances where our imagination is afforded, not so much a greater numerical concept as a large unit as measure (for shortening the numerical series). A tree judged by the height of man gives, at all events, a standard for a mountain; and, supposing this is, say, a mile high, it can serve as unit for the number expressing the earth's diameter, so as to make it intuitable; similarly the earth's diameter for the known planetary system; this again for the system of the Milky Way; and the immeasurable host of such systems, which go by the name of nebulae, and most likely in turn themselves form such a system, holds out no prospect of a limit. Now in the aesthetic estimate of such an immeasurable whole, the sublime does not lie so much in the greatness of the number, as in the fact that in our onward advance we always arrive at proportionately greater units. The systematic division of the cosmos conduces to this result. For it represents all that is great in nature as in turn becoming little; or, to be more exact, it represents our imagination in all its boundlessness, and with it nature, as sinking into insignificance before the ideas of reason, once their adequate presentation is attempted.[17]

§27

Quality of the delight in our estimate [Beurtheilung] of the sublime

The feeling of our incapacity to attain to an idea *that is a law for us*, is RESPECT [ACHTUNG]. Now the idea of the comprehension of any phenomenon whatever, that may be given us, in a whole of intuition, is an idea imposed upon us by a law of reason, which recognizes no definite, universally valid and unchangeable measure except the absolute whole. But our imagination, even when taxing itself to the uttermost on the score of this required comprehension of a given object in a whole of intuition (and so with a view to the presentation of the idea of reason), betrays its limits and its inadequacy, but still, at the same time, its proper vocation of making itself adequate to the same as a law. Therefore the feeling of the sublime in nature is respect for our own vocation, which we attribute to an Object of nature by a certain subreption [Subreption] (substitution of a respect for the Object in place of one for the idea of humanity in our own self – the subject); and this feeling renders, as it were, intuitable the supremacy of our cognitive faculties on the rational side over the greatest faculty of sensibility.[18]

The feeling of the sublime is, therefore, at once a feeling of displeasure, arising from the inadequacy of imagination in the aesthetic estimation of magnitude to attain to its estimation by reason, and a simultaneously awakened pleasure, arising from this very judgement of the inadequacy of the greatest faculty of sense being in accord with ideas of reason, so far as the effort to attain to these is for us a law. It is, in other words, for us a law (of reason), which goes to make us what we are, that we should esteem as small in comparison with ideas of reason everything which for us is great in nature as an object of sense; and that which makes us alive to the feeling of this supersensible disposition [Bestimmung] of our being harmonizes with that law. Now the greatest effort of the imagination in the presentation of the unit for the estimation of magnitude involves in itself a reference to something *absolutely great*, consequently a reference also to the law of reason that this alone is to be adopted as the supreme measure of what is great. Therefore the inner perception of the inadequacy of every standard of sense to serve for the rational estimation of magnitude is a coming into accord with reason's laws, and a displeasure that makes us alive to the feeling of the supersensible disposition of our being, according to which it is final, and consequently a pleasure, to find every standard of sensibility falling short of the ideas of reason.

The mind feels itself *set in motion* [*bewegt*] in the representation of the sublime in nature; whereas in the aesthetic judgement upon what is beautiful therein it is *restful* contemplation. This movement, especially in its inception, may be compared with a vibration, i.e. with a rapidly alternating repulsion and attraction produced by one and the same Object. The point of excess for the imagination (towards which it is driven in the apprehension of the intuition) is like an abyss in which it fears to lose itself; yet again for the rational idea of the supersensible it is not excessive, but conformable to law, and directed to drawing out such an effort on the part of the imagination: and so in turn as much a source of attraction as it was repellent to mere sensibility. But the judgement itself all the while steadfastly preserves its aesthetic character, because it represents, without being grounded on any definite concept of the Object, merely the subjective play of the mental powers (imagination and reason) as harmonious by virtue of their very contrast. For just as in the estimate of the beautiful, imagination and *understanding* by their concert generate subjective finality of the mental faculties, so imagination and *reason* do so here by their conflict – that is to say they induce a feeling of our possessing a pure and self-sufficient reason, or a faculty for the estimation of magnitude, whose pre-eminence can only be made intuitively evident by the inadequacy of that faculty which in the presentation of magnitudes (of objects of sense) is itself unbounded.[19]

Measurement of a space (as apprehension) is at the same time a description of it, and so an objective movement in the imagination and a progression. On the other hand the comprehension of the manifold in the unity, not of thought, but of intuition, and consequently the comprehension of the successively apprehended parts at one glance, is a retrogression that removes the time-condition in the progression of the imagination, and renders *coexistence* intuitable. Therefore, since the time-series is a condition of the internal sense and of an intuition, it is a subjective movement of the imagination by which it does violence to the internal sense – a violence which must be proportionately more striking the greater the quantum which the imagination comprehends in one intuition. The effort, therefore, to receive in a single intuition a measure for magnitudes which it takes an appreciable time to apprehend, is a mode of representation which, subjectively considered, is contra-final, but, objectively, is requisite for the estimation of magnitude, and is consequently final. Here the very same violence that is wrought on the subject through the imagination is estimated as final *for the whole province* [*Bestimmung*] of the mind.

The *quality* of the feeling of the sublime consists in its being, in respect of the faculty of forming aesthetic estimates, a feeling of displeasure at an object, which yet, at the same time, is represented as being final – a representation which derives its possibility from the fact that the subject's very incapacity betrays the consciousness of an unlimited faculty of the same subject, and that the mind can only form an aesthetic estimate of the latter faculty by means of that incapacity.

In the case of the logical estimation of magnitude the impossibility of ever arriving at absolute totality by the progressive measurement of things of the sensible world in time and space was cognized as an objective impossibility, i.e. one of *thinking* the infinite as given, and not as simply subjective, i.e. an incapacity for *grasping* it; for nothing turns there on the amount of the comprehension in one intuition, as measure, but everything depends on a numerical concept. But in an aesthetic estimation of magnitude the numerical concept must drop out of count or undergo a change. The only thing that is final for such estimation is the comprehension on the part of imagination in respect of the unit of measure (the concept of a law of the successive production of the concept of magnitude being consequently avoided). If, now, a magnitude begins to tax the utmost stretch of our faculty of comprehension in an intuition, and still numerical magnitudes – in respect of which we are conscious of the boundlessness of our faculty – call upon the imagination for aesthetic comprehension in a greater unit, the mind then gets a feeling of being aesthetically confined within bounds. Nevertheless, with a view to the extension of imagination necessary for adequacy with what is unbounded in our faculty of reason, namely the idea of the absolute whole, the attendant displeasure, and, consequently, the want of finality in our faculty of imagination, is still represented as final for ideas of reason and their animation. But in this very way the aesthetic judgement itself is subjectively final for reason as source of ideas, i.e. of such an intellectual comprehension as makes all aesthetic comprehension small, and the object is received as sublime with a pleasure that is only possible through the mediation of a displeasure.

B. THE DYNAMICALLY SUBLIME IN NATURE

§28

Nature as Might [*Macht*]

Might is a power which is superior to great hindrances. It is termed *dominion* [*Gewalt*] if it is also superior to the resistance of that which itself possesses might. Nature considered in an aesthetic judgement as might that has no dominion over us, is *dynamically sublime*.

[Nature is an object of fear, in the sublime, but yet we are not afraid of it.]

One who is in a state of fear can no more play the part of a judge of the sublime of nature than one captivated by inclination and appetite can of the beautiful. He flees from the sight of an object filling him with dread; and it is impossible to take delight in terror that is seriously entertained . . .

. . . Bold, overhanging, and, as it were, threatening rocks, thunder clouds piled up to the vault of heaven, borne along with flashes and peals, volcanoes in all their violence of destruction, hurricanes leaving desolation in their track, the boundless ocean rising with rebellious force, the high waterfall of some mighty river, and the like, make our power of resistance of trifling moment in comparison with their might. But provided our own position is secure, their aspect is all the more attractive for its fearfulness; and we readily call these objects sublime, because they raise the forces of the soul above the height of vulgar commonplace, and discover within us a power of resistance of quite another kind, which gives us courage to be able to measure ourselves against the seeming omnipotence of nature.

In the immeasurableness of nature and the incompetence of our faculty for adopting a standard proportionate to the aesthetic estimation of the magnitude of its *realm*, we found our own limitation. But with this we also found in our rational faculty another non-sensuous standard, one which has that infinity itself under it as unit, and in comparison with which everything in nature is small, and so found in our minds a pre-eminence over nature even in its immeasurability.[20] Now in just the same way the irresistibility of the might of nature forces upon us the recognition of our physical helplessness as beings of nature, but at the same time reveals a faculty of estimating ourselves as independent of nature, and discovers a pre-eminence above nature that is the foundation of a self-preservation of quite another kind from that which may be assailed and brought into danger by external nature. This saves humanity in our own person from humiliation, even though as mortal men we have to submit to external violence. In this way external nature is not estimated in our aesthetic judgement as sublime as far as exciting fear, but rather because it challenges our power (one not of nature) to regard as small those things of which we are wont to be solicitous (worldly goods, health, and life), and hence to regard its might (to which in these matters we are no doubt subject) as exercising over us and our personality no such rude dominion that we should bow down before it, once the question becomes one of our highest principles and of our asserting or forsaking them. Therefore nature is here called sublime merely because it raises the imagination to a presentation of those cases in which the mind can make itself sensible of the appropriate sublimity of the sphere of its own being, even above nature.

This estimation of ourselves loses nothing by the fact that we must see ourselves safe in order to feel this soul-stirring delight – a fact from which it might be plausibly argued that, as there is no seriousness in the danger, so there is just as little seriousness in the sublimity of our faculty of spirit [Geistesvermögens]. For here the delight only concerns the *province* [*Bestimmung*] of our faculty disclosed in such a case, so far as this faculty has its root in our nature; notwithstanding that its development and exercise is left to ourselves and remains an obligation. Here indeed there is truth – no matter how conscious a man, when he stretches his reflection so far abroad, may be of his actual present helplessness.

[§29 pursues the connection of the sublime with the moral idea. Kant says quite explicitly that the development of the moral idea is the element in culture [Cultur] necessary for the experience of the sublime. Without it, such experience would be simply terrifying and not at all uplifting. Though preparatory culture is necessary for the appreciation of the sublime, it cannot yet *produce* it. The requisite faculty must be thought to be latent in the human mind "in that which, at once with common understanding, we may expect every one to possess and may require of him, namely, a native capacity for the feeling for (practical) ideas, i.e. for moral feeling" (*CJ*, I, 116). Thus it is a part of transcendental philosophy rather than of empirical psychology. In the "General Remark upon the Exposition of Aesthetic Reflective Judgements", Kant pursues the relation between the aesthetic and the moral (see my introduction for a discussion of this). In the following passage, he explains away any concern we might have about locating the sublime beyond sensuous representation.]

. . . We have no reason to fear that the feeling of the sublime will suffer from an abstract mode of presentation like this, which is altogether negative as to what is sensuous. For though the imagination, no doubt, finds nothing beyond the sensible world to which it can lay hold, still this thrusting aside of the sensible barriers gives it a feeling of being unbounded; and that removal is thus a presentation of the infinite. As such it can never be anything more than a negative presentation – but still it expands the soul. Perhaps there is no more sublime passage in the Jewish Law than the commandment: Thou shalt not make unto thee any graven image, or any likeness of anything that is in heaven or on earth, or under the earth, &c. This commandment can alone explain the enthusiasm which the Jewish people, in their moral period, felt for their religion when comparing themselves with others, or the pride inspired by Mohammedanism. The very same holds good of our representation of the moral law and of our native capacity for morality. The fear that, if we divest this representation of everything that can commend it to the senses, it will thereupon be attended only with a cold and lifeless approbation and not with any moving force or emotion, is wholly unwarranted. The very reverse is the truth. For when nothing any longer meets the eye of sense, and the unmistakable and ineffaceable idea of morality [Moralität] is left in possession of the field, there would be need rather of tempering the ardour of an unbounded imagination to prevent it rising to enthusiasm, than of seeking to lend these ideas the aid of images and childish devices for fear of their being wanting in potency. For this reason governments have gladly let religion be fully equipped with these accessories, seeking in this way to relieve their subjects of the exertion, but to deprive them, at the same time, of the ability, required for expanding their spiritual powers beyond the limits arbitrarily laid down for them, and which facilitate their being treated as though they were merely passive.[21]

This pure, elevating, merely negative presentation of morality [Sittlichkeit] involves, on the other hand, no fear of *fanaticism* [*Schwärmerei*], which is a *delusion* that would *will some* VISION *beyond all the bounds of sensibility*; i.e. would dream according to principles (rational raving). The safeguard is the purely negative character of the presentation. For *the inscrutability of the idea of freedom* precludes all positive presentation. The moral law, however, is a sufficient and original source of determination within us: so it does not for a moment permit us to cast about for a ground of determination external to itself. If enthusiasm [Enthusiasm] is comparable to *delirium*, fanaticism may be compared to *mania*. Of these the latter is least of all compatible with the sublime, for it is *profoundly* ridiculous. In enthusiasm, as an affection, the imagination is unbridled; in fanaticism, as a deep-seated, brooding passion, it is anomalous [regellos]. The first is a transitory accident to which the healthiest understanding is liable to become at times the victim; the second is an undermining disease.[22]

Simplicity (artless finality) is, as it were, the style adopted by nature in the sublime. It is also that of morality. The latter is a second (supersensible) nature, whose laws alone we know, without being able to attain to an intuition of the supersensible faculty within us – that which contains the ground of this legislation.

One further remark. The delight in the sublime, no less than in the beautiful, by reason of its universal *communicability* not only is plainly distinguished from other aesthetic judgements, but also from this same property acquires an interest in society (in which it admits of such communication). Yet, despite this, we have to note the fact that *isolation from all society* is looked upon as something sublime, provided it rests upon ideas which disregard all sensible interest. To be self-sufficing, and so not to stand in need of society, yet without being unsociable, i.e. without shunning it, is something approaching the sublime – a remark applicable to all superiority to wants. On the other hand, to shun our fellow men from *misanthropy*, because of enmity towards them, or from *anthropophobia*, because we imagine the hand of every man is against us, is partly odious, partly contemptible. There is, however, a misanthropy (most improperly so called), the tendency towards which is to be found with advancing years in many right-minded men, that, as far as *good will* goes, is, no doubt, philanthropic enough, but as the result of long and sad experience, is widely removed from *delight* in mankind. We see evidences of this in the propensity to reclusiveness, in the fanciful desire for a retired country seat, or else (with the young) in the dream of the happiness of being able to spend one's life with a little family on an island unknown to the rest of the world – material of which novelists or writers of Robinsonades know how to make such good use. Falsehood, ingratitude, injustice, the puerility of the ends which we ourselves look upon as great and momentous, and to compass which man inflicts upon his brother man all imaginable evils – these all so contradict the idea of what men might be if they only would, and are so at variance with our active wish to see them better, that to avoid hating where we cannot love, it seems but a slight sacrifice to forego all the joys of fellowship with our kind.[23]

[Kant goes on to compare his own transcendental interest in the sublime and the beautiful with that of Burke, which for him is limited to the psychological and physiological sphere and therefore belongs to "anthropology". As such, it can never resolve the question of why it is that agreement about such responses is assumed by all subjects without empirical reference to what others think, which is the primary focus of Kant's interest. Only the transcendental method can address this question, by reference to the transcendental, *a priori* principles which Kant goes on to deduce (§§ 30–9), stressing once again that the very absence of proofs or objective principles in the determination of judgements of taste makes the presence of an inherited body of culture and art, a 'tradition', all the more important (cf. §§17–22). The job of the critic is not however to draw up a list of items for inclusion in such a canon, but to investigate the faculties which themselves make possible such judgements. In §34 Kant makes this the distinction between "art" (Kunst) and "science" (Wissenschaft), identifying himself firmly with the latter. The question of the deduction of judgements of taste belongs within the general problematic of the transcendental philosophy, already broached in the earlier *Critiques*: how are synthetic *a priori* judgements possible? §39 is an important restatement of the issues surrounding the assumption of universality in aesthetic judgements. It should be consulted, though it is not included here.]

§40

Taste as a kind of sensus communis

The name of sense [Sinn] is often given to judgement where what attracts attention is not so much its reflective act [Reflexion] as merely its result. So we speak of a sense of truth, of a sense of propriety, or of justice, &c. And yet, of course, we know, or at least ought well enough to know, that a sense cannot be the true abode of these concepts, not to speak of its being incompetent, even in the slightest degree, to pronounce universal rules. On the contrary, we recognize that a representation of this kind, be it of truth, propriety, beauty, or justice, could never enter our thoughts were we not able to raise ourselves above the level of the senses to that of higher faculties of cognition. *Common human understanding* which, as merely reliable (not yet cultivated) understanding, is looked upon as the least we can expect from any one claiming the name of man, has therefore the doubtful honour of having the name of common sense [Gemeinsinn] (*sensus communis*) bestowed upon it; and bestowed, too, in an acceptation of the word *common* (not merely in our own language, where it actually has a double meaning, but also in many others) which makes it amount to what is *vulgar* – what is everywhere to be met with – a quality which by no means confers credit or distinction upon its possessor.

However, by the name *sensus communis* is to be understood the idea of a *public* sense, i.e. a faculty of making estimations [Beurtheilungsvermögen] which in its reflection on the mode of representation has regard in thought (*a priori*) to all others, in order, *as it were*, to weigh its judgement with the collective reason of mankind, and thereby avoid the illusion arising from subjective and personal conditions which could readily be taken for objective, an illusion that would exert a prejudicial influence upon its judgement. This is accomplished by weighing the judgement, not so much with actual, as rather with the merely possible, judgements of others, and by putting ourselves in the position of every one else, as the result of a mere abstraction from the limitations which contingently affect our own estimate. This, in turn, is effected by so far as possible letting go the element of matter, i.e. sensation, in our general state of representative activity, and confining attention to the formal peculiarities of our representation or general state of representative activity. Now it may seem that this operation of reflection is too artificial to be attributed to the faculty which we call *common* sense. But this is an appearance due only to its expression in abstract formulae. In itself nothing is more natural than to abstract from charm and emotion where one is looking for a judgement intended to serve as a universal rule.

While the following maxims of common human understanding do not properly come in here as constituent parts of the critique of taste, they may still serve to elucidate its fundamental propositions. They are these: (1) to think for oneself; (2) to think from the standpoint of every one else; (3) always to think consistently. The first is the maxim of *unprejudiced* thought, the second that of *enlarged* thought, the third that of *consistent* thought. The first is the maxim of a never-*passive* reason. To be given to such passivity, consequently to heteronomy of reason, is called *prejudice* [*Vorurtheil*]; and the greatest of all prejudices is that of fancying nature not to be subject to rules which the understanding by virtue of its own essential law lays at its basis: i.e. *superstition* [*Aberglaube*].[24]

Emancipation from superstition is called *enlightenment*;[25] for although this term applies also to emancipation from prejudices generally, still superstition deserves pre-eminently (*in sensu eminenti*) to be called a prejudice. For the condition of blindness into which superstition puts one, which it as much as demands from one as an obligation, makes the need of being led by others, and consequently the passive state of the reason, pre-eminently conspicuous. As the second maxim belonging to our habits of thought, we have quite got into the way of calling a man narrow (*narrow*, as opposed to being *of enlarged mind*) whose talents fall short of what is required for employment upon work of any magnitude (especially that involving intensity). But the question here is not one of the faculty of cognition, but of the *mental habit* of making a final use of it. This, however small the range and degree to which a man's natural endowments extend, still indicates a man of *enlarged mind*: if he detaches himself from the subjective personal conditions of his judgement, which cramp the minds of so many others, and reflects upon his own judgement from a *universal standpoint* (which he can only determine by shifting his ground to the standpoint of others). The third maxim – that, namely, of *consistent* thought – is the hardest of attainment, and is only attainable by the union of both the former, and after constant attention to them has made one at home in their observance. We may say: the first of these is the maxim of understanding, the second that of judgement, the third that of reason.[26]

[Though no interest can be the determining ground of a judgement of taste, interest can subsequently be combined with such a judgement in a secondary or tributary way (§41). "Empirical" interests of this sort are related to sociability, and to man's natural desire to communicate with others: there is a pleasure in communicability itself, though not one essential to judgements of taste since, after all, the assumption of universality does *not* determine that people *will* actually agree. There is also an "intellectual interest" in the beautiful, which Kant proceeds to relate to the moral faculty through a distinction between art and nature.]

§42

... Now I willingly admit that the interest in the *beautiful of art* (including under this heading the artificial use of natural beauties for personal adornment, and so from vanity) gives no evidence at all of a habit of mind attached to the morally good, or even inclined that way. But, on the other hand, I do maintain that to take an *immediate interest* in the beauty of *nature* (not merely to have taste in estimating it) is always a mark of a good soul; and that, where this interest is habitual, it is at least indicative of a temper of mind favourable to the moral feeling that it should readily associate itself with the *contemplation* [*Beschauung*] *of nature*. It must, however, be borne in mind that I mean to refer strictly to the beautiful *forms* [*Formen*] of nature, and to put to one side the *charms* [*Reize*] which she is wont so lavishly to combine with them; because, though the interest in these is no doubt immediate, it is nevertheless empirical.

[Kant goes on to assert that our preference for the forms made by nature over those made by artifice or imitation, and for the pure properties of art rather than those appealing to social vanity, is the true mark of the "beautiful soul" (schöne Seele) and similarly accordant with the moral feeling. He expands on this analogy below.]

. . . We have a faculty of judgement which is merely aesthetic – a faculty of judging of forms without the aid of concepts, and of finding, in the mere estimate of them, a delight that we at the same time make into a rule for every one, without this judgement being founded on an interest, or yet producing one. – On the other hand we have also a faculty of intellectual judgement for the mere forms of practical maxims (so far as they are of themselves qualified for universal legislation) – a faculty of determining an *a priori* delight, which we make into a law for every one, without our judgement being founded on any interest, *though here it produces one*. The pleasure or displeasure in the former judgement is called that of taste; the latter is called that of the moral feeling.

But, now, reason is further interested in ideas (for which in our moral feeling it brings about an immediate interest), having also objective reality. That is to say, it is of interest to reason that nature should at least show a trace or give a hint that it contains in itself some ground or other for assuming a uniform accordance of its products with our wholly disinterested delight (a delight which we cognize *a priori* as a law for every one without being able to ground it upon proofs). That being so, reason must take an interest in every manifestation on the part of nature of some such accordance. Hence the mind cannot reflect on the beauty of *nature* without at the same time finding its interest engaged. But this interest is akin to the moral. One, then, who takes such an interest in the beautiful in nature can only do so in so far as he has previously set his interest deep in the foundations of the morally good. On these grounds we have reason for presuming the presence of at least the germ of a good moral disposition in the case of a man to whom the beauty of nature is a matter of immediate interest.[27]

[The interest in the beautiful in nature is not, for Kant, commonly found, but tends to be most possible for those who are already trained to an admiration of the good. To afford the fullest delight, the beautiful must properly inhere in nature: imitations are quite differently received. Whereas the imitation – Kant gives the example of a boy blowing a whistle in perfect replication of the song of the nightingale – derives its appeal from its proximity to nature, that of the truly natural demands relation to the sense of finality which we carry within ourselves, i.e. to the moral faculty. Art, that is, appeals most strongly when it has the appearance of nature. It must therefore not display the labour enacted in its creation.[28] Nature gives rules to art through what we call 'genius', whose products must be original and exemplary, and beyond the conscious control of the artist: "where an author owes a product to his genius, he does not himself know how the *ideas* for it have entered into his head, nor has he it in his power to invent the like at pleasure, or methodically, and communicate the same to others in such precepts as would put them in a position to produce similar products" (§46).[29] Though taste is responsible for the estimation of the products of genius (§48), in a sort of secondary way, it must coexist *with* genius in the true artist, as that which enables him to

[give form to his creations, and to turn them into something exemplary. One could have genius without taste: not all who have it are artists in the proper sense of the word. §49 continues with an analysis of "spirit".]

. . . *Spirit* [*Geist*] in an aesthetical sense, signifies the animating principle in the mind. But that whereby this principle animates the soul [Seele] – the material which it employs for that purpose – is that which sets the mental powers into a swing that is final, i.e. into a play which is self-maintaining and which strengthens those powers for such activity.[30]

Now my proposition is that this principle is nothing else than the faculty of presenting *aesthetic ideas*. But, by an aesthetic idea I mean that representation of the imagination which induces much thought, yet without the possibility of any definite thought whatever, i.e. *concept*, being adequate to it, and which language, consequently, can never get quite on level terms with or render completely intelligible. It is easily seen, that an aesthetic idea is the counterpart (pendant) of a *rational idea*, which, conversely, is a concept to which no *intuition* (representation of the imagination) can be adequate.

The imagination (as a productive faculty of cognition) is a powerful agent for creating, as it were, a second nature out of the material supplied to it by actual nature. It affords us entertainment where experience proves too commonplace; and we even use it to remodel experience, always following, no doubt, laws that are based on analogy, but still also following principles which have a higher seat in reason (and which are every whit as natural to us as those followed by the understanding in laying hold of empirical nature). By this means we get a sense of our freedom from the law of association (which attaches to the empirical employment of the imagination), with the result that the material can be borrowed by us from nature in accordance with that law, but be worked up by us into something else – namely, what surpasses nature.

Such representations of the imagination may be termed *ideas*. This is partly because they at least strain after something lying out beyond the confines of experience, and so seek to approximate to a presentation of rational concepts (i.e. intellectual ideas), thus giving to these concepts the semblance of an objective reality. But, on the other hand, there is this most important reason, that no concept can be wholly adequate to them as internal intuitions. The poet essays the task of interpreting to sense the rational ideas of invisible beings, the kingdom of the blessed, hell, eternity, creation, &c. Or, again, as to things of which examples occur in experience, e.g. death, envy, and all vices, as also love, fame, and the like, transgressing the limits of experience he attempts with the aid of an imagination which emulates the display of reason in its attainment of a maximum, to body them forth to sense with a completeness of which nature affords no parallel; and it is in fact precisely in the poetic art that the faculty of aesthetic ideas can show itself to full advantage. This faculty, however, regarded solely on its own account, is properly no more than a talent [Talent] (of the imagination).[31]

If, now, we attach to a concept a representation of the imagination belonging to its presentation, but inducing solely on its own account such a wealth of thought as would never admit of comprehension in a definite concept, and, as a consequence, giving aesthetically an unbounded expansion to the concept itself, then the imagination here displays a creative activity, and it puts the faculty of intellectual ideas (reason) into motion – a motion, at the instance of a representation, towards an extension of thought, that, while germane, no doubt, to the concept of the object, exceeds what can be laid hold of in that representation or clearly expressed.

... In a word, the aesthetic idea is a representation of the imagination, annexed to a given concept, with which, in the free employment of imagination, such a multiplicity of partial representations is bound up, that no expression indicating a definite concept can be found for it – one which on that account allows a concept to be supplemented in thought by much that is indefinable in words, and the feeling of which quickens the cognitive faculties and with language, as a mere thing of the letter, binds up the spirit also.[32]

The mental powers whose union in a certain relation constitutes *genius* [*Genie*] are imagination and understanding. Now, since the imagination, in its employment on behalf of cognition, is subjected to the constraint of the understanding and the restriction of having to be conformable to the concept belonging thereto, whereas aesthetically it is free to furnish of its own accord, over and above that agreement with the concept, a wealth of undeveloped material for the understanding, to which the latter paid no regard in its concept, but which it can make use of, not so much objectively for cognition, as subjectively for quickening the cognitive faculties, and hence also indirectly for cognitions, it may be seen that genius properly consists in the happy relation, which science cannot teach nor industry learn, enabling one to find out ideas for a given concept, and, besides, to hit upon the *expression* for them – the expression by means of which the subjective mental condition induced by the ideas as the concomitant of a concept may be communicated to others. This latter talent is properly that which is termed spirit [Geist]. For to get an expression for what is indefinable in the mental state accompanying a particular representation and to make it universally communicable – be the expression in language or painting or statuary – is a thing requiring a faculty for laying hold of the rapid and transient play of the imagination, and for unifying it in a concept (which for that very reason is original, and reveals a new rule which could not have been inferred from any preceding principles or examples) that admits of communication without any constraint of rules.[33]

§50

... Taste, like judgement in general, is the discipline (or corrective) of genius. It severely clips its wings, and makes it orderly or polished; but at the same time it gives it guidance, directing and controlling its flight, so that it may preserve its character of finality. It introduces a clearness and order into the plenitude of thought, and in so doing gives stability to the ideas, and qualifies them at once for permanent and universal approval, for being followed by others, and for a continually progressive culture [Cultur]. And so, where the interests of both these qualities clash in a product, and there has to be a sacrifice of something, then it should rather be on the side of genius; and judgement, which in matters of fine art bases its decision on its own proper principles, will more readily endure an abatement of the freedom and wealth of the imagination, than that the understanding should be compromised.[34]

[§§51–52 explore the division of the fine arts, which are then evaluated, with poetry at the top.]

§53

Comparative estimate of the aesthetic worth of the fine arts

Poetry [*Dichtkunst*] (which owes its origin almost entirely to genius and is least willing to be led by precepts or example) holds the first rank among all the arts. It expands the mind by giving freedom to the imagination and by offering, from among the boundless multiplicity of possible forms accordant with a given concept to whose bounds it is restricted, that one which couples with the presentation of the concept a wealth of thought to which no verbal expression is completely adequate, and thus raises itself aesthetically to ideas. It invigorates the mind by letting it feel its faculty – free, spontaneous, and independent of determination by nature – of regarding and estimating nature as phenomenon in the light of aspects which nature of itself does not afford us in experience, either for sense or understanding, and of employing it accordingly in behalf of, and as a sort of schema for, the supersensible. It plays with semblance [Schein], which it produces at will, but not as an instrument of deception; for its avowed pursuit is merely one of play [Spiel], which, however, understanding may turn to good account and employ for its own purpose.[35]

Part II   Critique of Teleological Judgement

[The second part of Kant's third *Critique* is less relevant to aesthetics than the first, being concerned with finality in nature, and the logical status of judgements of purposive phenomena. The following extract discusses what we have come to call 'organic form'. Kant is not here talking about art, except in so far as it provides a *partial* analogy for what must be supposed in nature, i.e. a finality providing a credible basis for natural science to estimate its own processes according to ends. But in what he says about reciprocal cause and effect, and about the relation of part to whole, Kant is employing a model which was to be applied to works of art (as a standard of excellence), and also to subsequent models of methodological and social organization (Coleridge's notion of the 'symbol' being a case in point). In insisting that "the organization of nature has nothing analogous to any causality known to us", Kant may once

again be meaning to pre-empt the tendency of speculative theology toward an argument from design, in which God becomes the "artist" of our world. As always, Kant's
emphasis is on the articulation of our subjective capacity to estimate finality.]

§4 (65)

Things considered as physical ends are organisms [*organisierte Wesen*]

Where a thing is a product of nature and yet, so regarded, has to be cognized
as possible only as a physical end, it must, from its character as set out in the
preceding section, stand to itself reciprocally in the relation of cause and
effect. This is, however, a somewhat inexact and indeterminate expression
that needs derivation from a definite conception.

In so far as the causal connection is thought merely by means of understanding it is a nexus constituting a series, namely of causes and effects, that is
invariably progressive. The things that as effects presuppose others as their
causes cannot themselves in turn be also causes of the latter. This causal
connexion is termed that of efficient causes (*nexus effectivus*). On the other
hand, however, we are also able to think a causal connexion according to a
rational concept, that of ends, which, if regarded as a series, would involve
regressive as well as progressive dependency. It would be one in which the
thing that for the moment is designated effect deserves none the less, if we take
the series regressively, to be called the cause of the thing of which it was said to
be the effect. In the domain of practical matters, namely in art, we readily
find examples of a nexus of this kind.[36] Thus a house is certainly the cause of
the money that is received as rent, but yet, conversely, the representation of
this possible income was the cause of the building of the house. A causal nexus
of this kind is termed that of final causes (*nexus finalis*). The former might,
perhaps, more appropriately be called the nexus of real, and the latter the
nexus of ideal causes, because with this use of terms it would be understood at
once that there cannot be more than these two kinds of causality.

Now the *first* requisite of a thing, considered as a physical end, is that its
parts, as to both their existence and form, are only possible by their relation to
the whole. For the thing is itself an end, and is, therefore, comprehended
under a conception or an idea that must determine *a priori* all that is to be
contained in it. But so far as the possibility of a thing is only thought in this
way, it is simply a work of art. It is the product, in other words, of an
intelligent cause, distinct from the matter, or parts, of the thing, and of one
whose causality, in bringing together and combining the parts, is determined
by its idea of a whole made possible through that idea, and consequently, not
by external nature.

But if a thing is a product of nature, and in this character is notwithstanding to contain intrinsically and in its inner possibility a relation to ends, in
other words, is to be possible only as a physical end and independently of the
causality of the conceptions of external rational agents, then this *second* requi-

site is involved, namely, that the parts of the thing combine of themselves into
the unity of a whole by being reciprocally cause and effect of their form. For
this is the only way in which it is possible that the idea of the whole may
conversely, or reciprocally, determine in its turn the form and combination of
all the parts, not as cause – for that would make it an art-product – but as the
epistemological basis upon which the systematic unity of the form and combination of all the manifold contained in the given matter becomes cognizable
for the person estimating it.

What we require, therefore, in the case of a body which in its intrinsic
nature and inner possibility has to be estimated as a physical end, is as follows.
Its parts must in their collective unity reciprocally produce one another alike
as to form and combination, and thus by their own causality produce a whole,
the conception of which, conversely – in a being possessing the causality
according to conceptions that is adequate for such a product – could in turn
be the cause of the whole according to a principle, so that, consequently, the
nexus of *efficient causes* might be no less estimated as an *operation brought about by
final* causes.

In such a natural product as this every part is thought as *owing* its presence
to the *agency* of all the remaining parts, and also as existing *for the sake of the
others* and of the whole, that is as an instrument, or organ. But this is not
enough – for it might be an instrument of art, and thus have no more than its
general possibility referred to an end. On the contrary the part must be an
organ *producing* the other parts – each, consequently, reciprocally producing
the others.³⁷ No instrument of art can answer to this description, but only the
instrument of that nature from whose resources the materials of every instrument are drawn – even the materials for instruments of art. Only under these
conditions and upon these terms can such a product be an *organized* and *self-
organized being*, and, as such, be called a *physical end*.

In a watch one part is the instrument by which the movement of the others
is effected, but one wheel is not the efficient cause of the production of the
other. One part is certainly present for the sake of another, but it does not owe
its presence to the agency of that other. For this reason, also, the producing
cause of the watch and its form is not contained in the nature of this material,
but lies outside the watch in a being that can act according to ideas of a whole
which its causality makes possible. Hence one wheel in the watch does not
produce the other, and, still less, does one watch produce other watches, by
utilizing, or organizing, foreign material; hence it does not of itself replace
parts of which it has been deprived, nor, if these are absent in the original
construction, does it make good the deficiency by the subvention of the rest;
nor does it, so to speak, repair its own casual disorders. But these are all things
which we are justified in expecting from organized nature. An organized
being is, therefore, not a mere machine. For a machine has solely *motive power*,
whereas an organized being possesses inherent *formative power* [*bildende Kraft*],
and such, moreover, as it can impart to material devoid of it – material which

it organizes. This, therefore, is a self-propagating formative power, which cannot be explained by the capacity of movement alone, that is to say, to mechanism.

We do not say half enough of nature and her capacity in organized products when we speak of this capacity as being the *analogue of art*. For what is here present to our minds is an artist – a rational being – working from without. But nature, on the contrary, organizes itself, and does so in each species of its organized products – following a single pattern, certainly, as to general features, but nevertheless admitting deviations calculated to secure self-preservation under particular circumstances. We might perhaps come nearer to the description of this impenetrable property if we were to call it an *analogue of life*. But then either we should have to endow matter as mere matter with a property (hylozoism) that contradicts its essential nature; or else we should have to associate with it a foreign principle standing in community with it (a soul). But, if such a product is to be a natural product, then we have to adopt one or other of two courses in order to bring in a soul. Either we must presuppose organized matter as the instrument of such a soul, which makes organized matter no whit more intelligible, or else we must make the soul the artificer of this structure, in which case we must withdraw the product from (corporeal) nature. Strictly speaking, therefore, the organization of nature has nothing analogous to any causality known to us.[38] Natural beauty may justly be termed the analogue of art, for it is only ascribed to the objects in respect of reflection upon the *external* intuition of them and, therefore, only on account of their superficial form. But *intrinsic natural perfection*, as possessed by things that are only possible as *physical ends*, and that are therefore called organisms, is unthinkable and inexplicable on any analogy to any known physical, or natural, agency, not even excepting – since we ourselves are part of nature in the widest sense – the suggestion of any strictly apt analogy to human art.[39]

The concept of a thing as intrinsically a physical end is, therefore, not a constitutive conception either of understanding or of reason, but yet it may be used by reflective judgement as a regulative conception for guiding our investigation of objects of this kind by a remote analogy with our own causality according to ends generally, and as a basis of reflection upon their supreme source. But in the latter connexion it cannot be used to promote our knowledge either of nature or of such original source of those objects, but must on the contrary be confined to the service of just the same practical faculty of reason in analogy with which we considered the cause of the finality in question.

Organisms are, therefore, the only beings in nature that, considered in their separate existence and apart from any relation to other things, cannot be thought possible except as ends of nature. It is they, then, that first afford objective reality to the conception of an *end* that is an end *of nature* and not a practical end.[40] Thus they supply natural science with the basis for a teleology, or, in other words, a mode of estimating its Objects on a special principle

that it would otherwise be absolutely unjustifiable to introduce into that
science – seeing that we are quite unable to perceive *a priori* the possibility of
such a kind of causality.

[§22 (83) exposes the stoical side of Kant's thought about man's place in the world. Not
only is he not an 'end' of physical nature: his own inner disposition also produces
conflict. Culture (Cultur), or the *aptitude* for setting ends before *himself*, is the only final
end of nature in man. Because its manifestation in 'skill' (Geschicklichkeit) is un-
equally distributed, Kant offers a somewhat gloomy analysis of the vocation of the
human race.]

... external nature is far from having made a particular favourite of man or
from having preferred him to all other animals as the object of its beneficence.
For we see that in its destructive operations – plague, famine, flood, cold,
attacks from animals great and small, and all such things – it has as little
spared him as any other animal. But, besides all this, the discord of inner
natural tendencies betrays him into further misfortunes of his own invention, and
reduces other members of his species, through the oppression of lordly power,
the barbarism of wars, and the like, to such misery, while he himself does all he
can to work ruin to his race, that, even with the utmost goodwill on the part of
external nature, its end, supposing it were directed to the happiness of our
species, would never be attained in a system of terrestrial nature, because our
own nature is not capable of it. Man, therefore, is ever but a link in the chain
of physical ends. True, he is a principle in respect of many ends to which
nature seems to have predetermined him, seeing that he makes himself so; but,
nevertheless, he is also a means towards the preservation of the finality in the
mechanism of the remaining members. As the single being upon earth that
possesses understanding, and, consequently, a capacity for setting before himself ends of his deliberate choice, he is certainly titular lord of nature, and,
supposing we regard nature as a teleological system, he is born to be its
ultimate end. But this is always on the terms that he has the intelligence and
the will to give to it and to himself such a reference to ends as can be self-
sufficing independently of nature, and, consequently, a final end. Such an
end, however, must not be sought in nature.

... Skill can hardly be developed in the human race otherwise than by means
of inequality among men. For the majority, in a mechanical kind of way that
calls for no special art, provide the necessaries of life for the ease and conve-
nience of others who apply themselves to the less necessary branches of culture
in science and art. These keep the masses in a state of oppression, with hard
work and little enjoyment, though in the course of time much of the culture of
the higher classes spreads to them also. But with the advance of this culture –
the culminating point of which, where devotion to what is superfluous begins
to be prejudicial to what is indispensable, is called luxury – misfortunes in-
crease equally on both sides. With the lower classes they arise by force of
domination from without, with the upper from seeds of discontent within. Yet
this splendid misery is connected with the development of natural tendencies

in the human race, and the end pursued by nature itself, though it be not our end, is thereby attained.[41] The formal condition under which nature can alone attain this its real end is the existence of a constitution so regulating the mutual relations of men that the abuse of freedom by individuals striving one against another is opposed by a lawful authority centred in a whole, called a *civil community*. For it is only in such a constitution that the greatest development of natural tendencies can take place. In addition to this we should also need a *cosmopolitan* whole – had men but the ingenuity to discover such a constitution and the wisdom voluntarily to submit themselves to its constraint. It would be a system of all states that are in danger of acting injuriously to one another. In its absence, and with the obstacles that ambition, love of power, and avarice, especially on the part of those who hold the reins of authority, put in the way even of the possibility of such a scheme, *war* is inevitable. Sometimes this results in states splitting up and resolving themselves into lesser states, sometimes one state absorbs other smaller states and endeavours to build up a larger unit. But if on the part of men war is a thoughtless undertaking, being stirred up by unbridled passions, it is nevertheless a deep-seated, maybe far-seeing, attempt on the part of supreme wisdom, if not to found, yet to prepare the way for a rule of law governing the freedom of states, and thus bring about their unity in a system established on a moral basis. And, in spite of the terrible calamities which it inflicts on the human race, and the hardships, perhaps even greater, imposed by the constant preparation for it in time of peace, yet – as the prospect of the dawn of an abiding reign of national happiness keeps ever retreating farther into the distance – it is one further spur for developing to the highest pitch all the talents that minister to culture.

Part 2

Fichte

Johann Gottlieb Fichte

(1762–1814)

Along with Schelling, Fichte is among the great German Idealists the least known to the English-speaking world. After the conventional training in theology, he was inspired by Lessing and Spinoza, and above all by Kant, to turn to philosophy, and his first publication, the *Critique of All Revelation* (1792), was by virtue of its anonymous authorship widely mistaken for Kant's fourth critique.

In 1794 he took up a chair at Jena, which he abandoned in 1799 as a result of the notorious accusations of atheism directed at him: for an account of the controversy see Edwards (1967), article *Atheismusstreit*. He held a chair at Erlangen before moving to Berlin in 1809, dying of a fever five years later.

There are myths of Fichte just as there are myths of Kant. Lewes (1857) paints the picture of a meditative and solitary child, a transcendentalist *Wunderkind*: "He stands for hours, gazing into the far distance, or in mournful yearning at the silent sky overarching him" (p. 566). His popular lectures on the Germanic identity and on the moral obligation to freedom and resistance have often been taken as evidence of his political importance in the struggle against the French, but this too has been disputed: see Fichte (1968), p. xxvii. Perhaps most significantly of all, he was widely known as the leading spirit of the *Ichphilosophie* or ego-philosophy, itself mistakenly understood as a rationale for various forms of self-indulgence or self-obsession. Such a view quite misrepresents the scrupulous arguments of his great *Wissenschaftslehre* or *Science of Knowledge*, but it was supported by Goethe's and Schiller's habit of describing him as "the great *Ich* from Osmannstedt", and by the young Friedrich Schlegel's invocation of his system as a philosophical analogue of Romantic irony. As early as the 1798 *Sittenlehre (Science of Ethics)* Fichte differentiates himself from any affiliation with what was popularly recognized as irony, which he regarded simply as an elaborate self-protection and an avoidance of *action*, one of the most important obligations of enlightenment. Self-reflection is absolutely necessary to the personality caught up in the transcendental method, and it must indeed be continual, but it should never remain merely speculative. When it does, then such a man has

acquired an excellent knowledge of all the rules of that play of thoughts . . . but he does so only for the purpose of thereby producing another play in his mind. He causes good and noble sentiments and thoughts to arise in his mind; but merely in order to make these sentiments themselves an object of his enjoyment, and to amuse himself at the appearance of harmony . . . But he is and remains corrupt; for the whole interests him for his own enjoyment's sake; he has no serious interest in it, no interest lying beyond himself. Fichte (1907), p. 397

In the *Characteristics of the Present Age* (1804–5) Fichte does admit that a period of unsettled hovering [freie Schweben] between "authority and mere emptiness" is and has been a necessary step in the progress of the race, but it is only usefully so when it impels us toward determinate knowledge: see Fichte (1849), p. 82.

Throughout his career Fichte was emphatic about the need to convert the insights of the transcendental philosophy into action, and social action at that. In this ambition he had to face certain difficulties in the Kantian inheritance. Much of what Kant had to say about philosophy strictly conceived, and almost everything he had said about ethics and aesthetics, was premissed on the absence of an element of contingent interest in the highest states of mind. Fichte's task was thus to preserve the basic spirit and technique of Kant's arguments whilst somehow turning them into some form of social interventionism. Only through acting "in and for society" does man do his duty – see Fichte (1845), IV, 235 – and this generates the need for a community of scholars or learned men, in order that the freedom that each man has for himself "to question everything and to inquire freely and independently" shall be represented in some external and institutional form (IV, 248). Any healthily evolving society will have to throw aside the authority of merely received judgements; it thus becomes all the more important that there be a learned class to preserve some sense of direction, and one based on authenticated truth, even as this class must never be constrained in the subjects and conclusions of its inquiries.

Thus Fichte sought to establish the necessity of institutions based on freedom (Coleridge's ideas about the place of an enlightened clerisy might be compared here); a way of distributing through society the positive results of detached and interest-free individual speculations. His revision of Kant's method had of course much more technical manifestations, and they may be traced through the various versions of the *Wissenschaftslehre* appearing after 1794. Here Fichte sets going the gestures followed by so many others in his generation, aiming at closing the gaps or divisions in the mind argued for by Kant himself. He seeks to establish the grounds for a self-consciousness much more dynamic and exploratory, knowing itself not in the apparently timeless deploying of the categories of the understanding in repetitive ways, but in an ongoing positing of self and other through the biographical passage of time. This is to overstate the case somewhat, but it is worth doing to make clear the extent to which Fichte anticipates Hegel in this respect. Crudely put, the self becomes a more restless and aspiring entity, and it becomes so *for itself*, i.e. in its most important movements of self-recognition (as opposed to having these unstable elements excluded from critical attention, as they were by Kant). Interest and inclination, with a blurring of the divisions between the higher and lower faculties of desire, are readmitted in the cause of reuniting the activities of understanding and reason into a coherent personality. Thus, for Fichte, an aesthetic element is fundamental in all perception, and empirical inclinations are made continuous with our higher faculties of freedom and morality. Religion also reappears in places from which it had been carefully excluded by Kant.

In Fichte we can also see the awareness of a problem of audience, and he went perhaps further than any of his contemporaries in the search for popular epitomes of the critical philosophy. The wide range of his writings is not well represented in English translations, although the recent translation of the *Wissenschaftslehre* is an important step in the task of making his most important arguments available to a new audience: see Fichte (1970). Other major works available in English tend to exist only in somewhat outdated nineteenth-century translations: see Fichte (1889), (1907). Revised or recent translations do exist of the *Addresses to the German Nation, The Vocation of Man*, and the *Critique of all Revelation*: see Fichte (1968), (1956), (1978).

Further reading

Again, apart from the accounts in the standard histories, e.g. Copleston (1965a), there is very little expository or interpretive work on Fichte in English. Exceptions are Engelbrecht (1933) and Seidel (1976). Two standard works in French should be mentioned: those of Léon (1922–7) and Guéroult (1930). See also the bibliography by Baumgartner & Jacobs (1968).

On the Spirit and the Letter in Philosophy
[*Über Geist und Buchstab in der Philosophie*]

In a series of Letters, 1794

Translated by Elizabeth Rubenstein.

German text in *Johann Gottlieb Fichtes sämmtliche Werke* (1845), VIII, 270–300.

Introductory note

This hitherto untranslated work is one of three attempts at exploring the topic of the title, all dating from Fichte's Jena period (1794–5) and written at about the same time as the early versions of the great *Wissenschaftslehre*. One of the other attempts is but a short manuscript fragment; the other a more substantial sequence of three lectures, first transcribed by Siegfried Berger in 1924. These lectures differ from the letters which follow in that they do not deal with aesthetics, but seem rather to be an attempt to incorporate some of the specialized concepts of the *Wissenschaftslehre* into a public or exoteric form: they are a statement for the lay student of what the transcendental philosophy can and must mean for his personal and social development. Both the short fragment and the public lectures have been recently edited and reprinted in the ongoing *Gesamtausgabe*: see Fichte (1964–), II, 3, pp. 293–342.

The three letters on the subject of the spirit and the letter declare themselves as an incomplete sequence, and the history of their non-appearance in *Die Hören* is perhaps the most famous of all cases of a journal editor (Schiller) rejecting a distinguished contribution. Fichte's letters were written in implicit response to Schiller's own epistolary work, *On the Aesthetic Education of Man*, and they represent his most detailed treatment of the aesthetic drive and its place in the constitution of the psyche. An account of the quarrel between the two men, which cooled relations between them for about ten years, can be found in Léon (1922), I, 339–62; in Schiller, *AE*, pp. cxii–cxxi; and in Fichte (1964–), I, 6, pp. 316–31, whose editors include citations of the substantial correspondence on this matter between June and August 1795. See also Fichte (1967), I, 466–501. Léon gives French translations of the important passages.

Close consideration of the two works tends to make the differences between them appear less radical than they must have seemed to their respective authors, and there are paradoxes in each man's position. Schiller appears to have thought of Fichte as an abstract and cold-blooded philosopher, but Fichte might have countered that his own argument was fundamentally more democratic than Schiller's; that the pure abstract idea was in fact more universally available than an unrealistic reliance on the aesthetic (and the fine arts) in an age in which it seemed least likely to be cultivated or generated anew. But this too is part of Schiller's case, if it is not the precise tenor of every part of the argument, and it must often seem that the quarrel has as much to do with the crossing of boundaries as with any ultimately irreconcilable differences. Schiller was trying to be a philosopher, and Fichte was taking on the problem of aesthetic creation and response as it applies to the artist. Thus Schiller complains, in a letter of 24 June 1795, that Fichte writes about the fine arts instead of about philosophy, as he promises to do, and that the same version of *Geist* will not do for both. He found Fichte's explanation of the 'drives' arbitrary and impure, and complained of a disharmony between concept and image in the style of the letters. Fichte responded by declaring that the various manifestations of *Geist* are just different species of the same genus, by defending his account of the drives, and by attacking Schiller's own conflation of concept and image: "I have to translate everything of yours before I can understand it." See Fichte (1967), 1, 467–8, 470, 473.

There is a brief discussion of the role of aesthetics in the *Sittenlehre*, and this should be consulted: see Fichte (1907), pp. 367–70. See also the discussion of the German language in *Addresses to the German Nation*: Fichte (1968), pp. 49ff.

First Letter[1]

You have not yet given up the expectations you have of philosophy, my dear friend. You continue to take an interest in our endeavours, and still spend part of your leisure in philosophical reading. But you were, you tell me, somewhat disturbed when a neighbour brought forward a fresh hazard. He is dubious about the distinction made by one or two modern writers between the spirit and the letter in philosophy generally, and particularly in a certain philosophy and certain philosophical works. Where might this lead to, and what might become of the most assiduous study if any Tom, Dick, or Harry were to be allowed, in a fit of over-enthusiasm, to discount the knowledge so painstakingly gathered on the pretext that it is only of the letter and not of the spirit?[2] Your neighbour is looking for certainty and you want a clear insight into the reasons for feeling a calmness which has been thus far only an undefined feeling. You have noticed that I too am in favour of this distinction, and you ask me for a thorough and intelligible explanation of what is meant by the spirit *of* philosophy and the spirit *in* philosophy, and how it differs from the letter as such and from the merely literal.

I hope that your request for thoroughness will not make demands I cannot meet, and that you do not expect more than that I should, to the best of my knowledge and conscience, derive this distinction from my own perception of the fundamental problem. If I could assume all that is presupposed by an immediate answer to your question then my exposition would not take long. But since this does not seem to be what you require, in that you ask for an explanation intelligible to all, I must take you a longer way round. I hope it will never seem to you to be a detour. You ought to proceed slowly along this path, and to rest from time to time and survey the view; but with a little forbearance I hope to be able to guide you to your destination and relieve your concern. As far as instructing your neighbour is concerned – well, the experience you will gain will be informative at least for yourself.[3]

Before I can make clear to you what I mean by spirit [Geist] in philosophy, we must agree on what we call spirit in general.

You remember the complaints you made when you were reading a certain book, highly acclaimed by some. You could not read yourself into it. You had it in front of you, and your eyes were firmly fixed on it, but you found that every time you began thinking about yourself you were miles away from the book. Each of your attempts to get to grips with the content and the action failed, and every time you thought you had neared grasping the unyielding spirit of the text, it slipped out of your hands. You had to remind yourself continually that you wanted to study this book, indeed that you had to; and you had repeatedly to invoke the image of the knowledge and the usefulness that you expected to gain from it in order to put up with the constant feeling of resistance, until you were convinced for other reasons that you might just as well leave it unread, that the gains would in fact be negligible and not worth the effort expended. Did the fault rest solely with you, with your lack of attention and your own inability to relate to the depth and profundity of that book? You don't appear to believe this. The mood you found yourself in when reading the works of other no less profound writers allowed you to form a more favourable opinion of yourself. You felt drawn to and captivated by them. You did not need to remember your resolve to study, or the advantages you hoped to gain. When your mind [Geist][4] was totally engrossed by what you were reading you had no need to look for any reason beyond reading it for its own sake, and the only thing that troubled you was tearing yourself from it when other duties called you away. Several times you found yourself perhaps in a similar situation to a certain French woman. When the court ball was officially begun, she was reading *La nouvelle Héloïse*.[5] She was informed that her carriage was ready but it was too early to travel to court. Two hours later there was still time enough when they reminded her. But two hours after that she found it was too late. She read all night long and this time sacrificed going to the ball altogether.

Thus it is with books, and thus it is with other works of art, as with nature. One thing leaves us cold and disinterested, or even repels us; another attracts, invites us to linger awhile in contemplation [Betrachtung][6] and lose ourselves in it.

This experience is all the more remarkable in that the reasons which one might at first sight choose in explanation are insufficient. The less serious and more superficial reader, who is only looking for enjoyment, and who can only learn anything if it is subtly disguised as such, may well generally prefer to be entertained by stories than to have to think and explore along with an author. But often the most detailed stories, packed with events each more exciting than the one before, fail to hold the attention of the reader; at the same time there are plenty of those who, without any regard for self-improvement, would rather reason with Voltaire or polemize with Lessing than be told about the adventures of the Swedish countess.[7] Therefore it certainly seems worthwhile – and it perhaps lies on our path – to investigate what it actually might be that on the one hand draws us so powerfully, whether to frivolities or to serious and important investigations, and on the other hand drives us uncontrollably in the opposite direction, however important or useful the subject matter in question might be.

This much is clear: that a work of the first sort may excite, stimulate and strengthen our appreciation of and capacity to appreciate its subject matter; that such a work is not simply the object of our intellectual [geistigen] engagement, for it gives us at the same time the ability to engage ourselves with it, so that we receive not just the gift but the hand with which we must grasp it. Such a work creates the spectacle and the audience at one and the same time and, like the life-force in the universe, imparts first movement and structure to dead matter and then in the same breath spiritual life to that structure.[8] Conversely, a work of the other sort restrains and impedes the very capacity [Sinn] which we need. Because of a constant feeling of resistance it finally exhausts and kills it, so that the mechanism operating the mind [Geist], which is constantly about to come to a standstill, must be set in motion once again by renewed pressure from the mainspring, from the absolute self-activity [Selbstthätigkeit][9] within, only to be thwarted again at the very next instant. In the first case our understanding [Verstand] thinks or our imagination [Einbildungskraft] composes spontaneously along with the artist, just as he wills, without our control. The appropriate concepts [Begriffe] or the forms intended shape and order themselves before our inner [geistigen] eye, without our believing we have had a hand in it.[10] But in the second case we must always watch ourselves under strict surveillance; we must constantly repeat the commandment of attentiveness and see that it is observed. The moment we turn our inner eye away our attention is swiftly diverted from its object. Fancy [Phantasie], left to its own devices, once more seeks out familiar ground, and likewise the spirit [Geist] relapses into dull brooding. In a word, works of the first sort seem to possess a vitalizing force [belebende Kraft] in relation to the inner sense, and especially in relation to that particular sense which is attuned to grasp it. Works of the other sort may be ordered, thorough and useful – they may be everything one might care to name – but that force they do not possess.

This vitalizing force in a work of art we call 'spirit' [Geist], and its absence 'spiritlessness' [Geistlosigkeit]. And so here we are with the subject of our inquiry before us.

How does a work created by man receive that vitalizing force and where does the ingenious [geistvolle] artist learn the secret of breathing it into a work of art? While looking at his work I discover with pleasant surprise gifts and talents in myself which I didn't know I possessed. In gauging the effect of his work did he assume these talents in me? Without doubt, for where else would his success come from? But who revealed to him my innermost being, to which I myself was a stranger? Perhaps if he transported me to celestial realms through elevating representations of religious scenes, or shattered me with the terrors of the Last Judgement, or drew tears from me with the sufferings of sweet forbearing innocence, then this could come about. But regardless of this it remains astonishing how he contrives for me to become absorbed in his writings – which I hold only as writings – and to entertain sensations which are only too real. With the same confidence his pen describes a country dance or his brush outlines a wild flower on the canvas, and my heart is always his certain captive. Where is the mysterious connection between such means and such an end, and through what art has he divined what cannot be discovered by any amount of meditation?

Second Letter

You take up the question raised at the end of my previous letter and answer it in the following way:

"Nowhere else but in the depths of his own breast can the ingenious [geist-volle] artist have discovered what lies in mine, though it is hidden from my own eyes and from everyone else's. He reckons on the agreement of others, and he does so rightly. We see that under his influence the mass, if it be at all cultivated, actually comes together as one soul; that all individual differences in disposition and feeling disappear; that the same fear or the same pity or the same intellectual [geistige] pleasure lifts and moves all hearts. In as much as he is an artist he must have in him that which is common to all developed souls, and instead of the individual disposition which differentiates and divides others from it, the common disposition [Universalsinn] of collective humanity, as it were, and this alone must dwell in him at the moment of inspiration [Begeisterung]. We are all different from one another in many ways. No one person is exactly the same as another, neither as far as concerns his spiritual nor his physical character.

Nevertheless we must all possess, to a greater or lesser extent, according to the degree of similarity or difference in education and experience, either on the surface of our mind [Geist] or in its more hidden depths, certain common characteristics. For we understand each other, we can communicate with each other, and all human intercourse from the beginning of time has been nothing but an uninterrupted struggle from generation to generation in which each individual tries to make every other with whom he comes into contact in the course of his life agree with him. What is not so easy for the ordinary man, and what he doesn't quite succeed in doing, the artist achieves by altering the ambition and giving up the idea of projecting his individuality on others. On the contrary he sacrifices it and takes instead those common characteristics which occur in each one of us, moulding them to form the individual character of his mind [Geist] and his work. Therefore what inspires him is called genius [Genius], and great genius, an essence from a higher sphere in which all lowly and earthly limitations determining the individual character of earthbound men can no longer be distinguished and merge together in a soft haze.

Since the means which he uses to awaken and engage this common sense [Gemeinsinn],[11] and to silence individuality for as long as he has us under his influence; – since these means and the necessary connection which exists between them and their effect cannot easily be discovered by reflection, nor by any reference to their purpose through concepts [Begriffe]:[12] so only through experience, through his own inner experience of self, can the artist become acquainted with them. At least, any attempts to discover them by other routes have failed. The artist has already felt what he makes us feel after him, and the same forms which he conjures up before our eyes – regardless as to how they appeared before his own – have already lulled him into that sweet intoxication, that delightful madness which takes hold of us all at his singing, before his vibrant canvas, or at the sound of his flute. Cool self-possession [Besonnenheit][13] returns to him again and with sober artistry he portrays what he saw in his ecstasy in order to draw the whole of mankind into his delusion, the dear memory of which still fills him with sweet emotion, and to spread the burden of guilt which the founding of his kind placed upon him amongst the whole species. Wherever there are developed human beings the evidence of his long-extinguished inspiration [Begeisterung] will be celebrated by re-enactment to the end of time."[14]

Thus you solve the task in hand, and I think you are right. But let us jointly examine your argument further, break it down into its finer parts, and trace their development from the roots, so that we can form a definite idea of this common disposition [Universalsinn] which you use as the basis of your explanation. And let us see clearly how the impression, which you say is made on that faculty [Sinn] in the artist's mind, is created, and grasp – as far as it can be grasped – why it is able to communicate itself so easily and so universally.[15]

You say that totally apart from all external experience and without any outside help the artist develops from the depths of his nature [Gemüth] what lies hidden from all in the human soul; that guided by his powers of divination he sets forth the characteristics common to the whole of humanity, which have not shown themselves as such in any previous experience. But the one thing in man which is independent and utterly incapable of being determined from outside we call "drive" [Trieb]. This and this alone is the single and highest principle governing self-activity [Selbstthätigkeit] in us. This alone makes us independent, observing and acting beings. However much external things may influence us, they do not go so far as to bring out in us something which was not already present in them, nor do they produce an effect contrary to their underlying nature. Self-activity in man, which determines his character and distinguishes him from the rest of nature, placing him outside her laws, must itself be based on something peculiar to him. This peculiarity is drive. A human being is above all human because of drive, and what kind of a person he is depends on the greater or lesser force [Kraft] and effectiveness of drive, of the inner living and striving.[16]

Only through drive is man an image-producing being [vorstellendes

Wesen]. Even if, as some philosophers would have it, we could let objects
provide him with the material of his representation [Vorstellung], letting
images [Bilder] flow to him from all sides via things, he would still need self-
activity to be able to grasp them and shape them into a representation, which
the lifeless creatures in space around us are without, although the images
floating through the whole universe must stream over them as they do over us.
We need self-activity to arrange these representations in a motivated way:
now to observe the outward form of a plant, so as to be able to recognize it
again and distinguish it from other similar types; now to look into the laws
which might have governed nature's formation of that plant; now to find out
how it might be used as food or clothing or as medicine. We need self-activity
in order unceasingly to intensify and extend our cognitive knowledge [Erk-
enntniss][17] of objects. Through it alone the star, which for the unschooled
countryman remains a tiny lamp by the light of which to gather up his farm
implements, becomes for the astronomer a large solid celestial body moving at
immeasurable distances according to immutable laws.

   To the extent that this kind of drive seeks the generation of knowledge we
can call it, in this respect and for the sake of clarity and brevity, the "knowledge-drive" [Erkenntnisstrieb], as if it were one particular *basic drive* [*Grund-
trieb*], which it is not. It and all the other specific drives and forces which we
may still call by this name are simply particular manifestations of the one
indivisible primary force [Grundkraft] in man, and we must be very careful to
refrain from interpreting such expressions in any other way, in this or in any
other philosophical work. The knowledge-drive accordingly is always satisfied
to a certain extent: every man has certain cognitions [Erkenntnisse], and
without them he would be something other than a man. In general therefore
this drive manifests itself in the effect it produces. From this we return to the
cause in the self-active subject, and only in this way do we arrive at an idea
[Idee] of the nature of this drive and a recognition [Erkenntniss] of its laws.

   Drive is not always satisfied, in that it does not simply seek knowledge of the
thing as it is, but looks for definition, variation and development of the thing as
it ought to be. Then it is called "practical" – and this in the narrowest sense, for
strictly speaking all drive is practical in that it urges us to self-activity, so that in
this sense everything in man is based on the practical drive, for there is nothing
in him except through self-activity. Alternatively, when it goes in search of a
certain particular representation purely for its own sake, and in no way for the
sake of a thing which might correspond to it, or just for cognitive knowledge of
this thing, then, since it does not yet have a name in its generality, we will
provisionally give it one and call it the "aesthetic", as a branch of it has been so
named before.[18] It is clear that an understanding [Kenntniss] of this drive and
of the knowledge-drive cannot be reached by the same route, i.e. by tracing the
cause from the effect. So the question arises as to how one does arrive at such an
understanding. But before we answer this question let us make a sharper
distinction between the drives themselves as put forward above.

The knowledge-drive aims at cognitive knowledge as such, and for the sake of cognition. It leaves us quite indifferent to the being [Wesen] of the thing, its outer or inner qualities. Under its guidance we want nothing more than to be aware of what these qualities are: we are aware, and we are satisfied. Here the representation has no other value and serves no other function beyond being fully in accordance with the fact [Sache]. It is the practical drive which seeks out the qualities of things, for the sake of qualities. We recognize this only too well when this drive is stimulated. But we are not satisfied with this. It must be different, and different in a determinate way. In the case of the knowledge-drive there is posited a thing which is completely self-determining, without any of our help, and the drive seeks to reproduce it in our mind, with these determinations and with no others, through free self-activity. In the case of the practical drive there is posited as fundamental a representation whose existence [Daseyn] and content are created through free self-activity in the soul, and the drive seeks to bring forward something that corresponds to it in the sensible world. In both cases the drive seeks neither the representation alone nor the thing alone, but a harmony between the two; only in the first case the representation ought to conform itself to the thing, and in the second case the thing to the representation.

It is quite a different matter with the drive which we have just named the aesthetic.[19] It is directed towards a representation, and a particular [bestimmte] representation, exclusively for the sake of its determination [Bestimmung] and its determination as a pure representation. As far as this drive is concerned the representation is an end in itself. It does not derive its value from harmonizing with the object – on which no store is set in this connection – but has value in itself. It is not the replication of reality but a free unrestrained form of the image which is sought. Without any interdetermination [Wechselbestimmung] between it and an object such a representation stands isolated as the ultimate goal of the drive. It is not related to any thing which it governs or is governed by. Just as a representation whose very substance is created through absolute self-activity is at the basis of the practical determination [Bestimmung], so a representation created in the same way is at the basis of the aesthetic, with the difference that the latter need not, like the former, be presented with something that corresponds to it in the sensible world. Just as the knowledge-drive has as its ultimate goal a representation, and is satisfied when this is formed, so it is with the aesthetic, now with the difference that a representation of the first type should harmonize with the object, whereas the aesthetic representation does not have to harmonize with anything at all. It is possible that a presentation [Darstellung] of the aesthetic image should be called for in the sensible world; but this does not occur by means of the aesthetic drive, whose task is completed with the creation of the image in the soul, but rather by means of the practical drive, which for some reason intervenes in the order of representations and sets up a possible outward and extraneous focus for the replicated image [Nachbildung] in the real world.

Likewise it can happen that a representation of an object which really exists harmonizes completely with the aesthetic drive, but in that case the ensuing satisfaction of this drive is in no way concerned with the empirical truth of the representation. The image created would be no less pleasing if it were empty, and it does not give any more pleasure because it happens at the same time to embody cognitive knowledge. It could not be otherwise – I remind you of this in passing, in order to make myself clearer, but not to draw any premature conclusions – it could not be otherwise if both these incompatible drives, one to leave things as they are and the other to work upon them everywhere and *ad infinitum*, are to unite and present to us a single indivisible man, according to our usual view of the matter. Or, looking at them in the manner described above, which strictly speaking is the only correct way:[20] if both drives are one and the same and only the conditions of their expression are to be distinguished. Drive could not aim at the representation of the thing without aiming at the representation for its own sake. Just as impossible would be a drive which would work on the thing itself and modify it on the basis of a representation which lay beyond all experience or any possible experience, if there were no drive or faculty to create representations independent of the real nature of things.

How do these two drives just mentioned manifest themselves, if the aesthetic drive never produces, and the practical drive by no means always produces actions [Handlungen] which would make it possible to observe them? Even so, the following means of tracking them down still remains. Since the drive, in the way it begins having an effect on man and then takes over, arouses and stimulates total self-activity and focusses it completely on something specific, whether it be an object ouside him or a representation within him; so necessarily the fortuitous harmony in a sentient being, which man must certainly be, between the given and this tendency of self-activity, must be revealed in man's overwhelming awareness of self, of his force [Kraft] and of his range [Ausbreitung], which we call a feeling of pleasure. Conversely, the chance disharmony between the given and this same tendency must be revealed through an equally overwhelming feeling of impotence and constraint, which we call a feeling of displeasure. So let us conceive of a force in a magnet, and of a drive behind this force, a drive to attract anything made of iron which comes within its sphere of influence. Let it really attract a piece of iron: its drive expresses itself and is satisfied, and if we confer upon the magnet the power of feeling then a feeling of satisfaction, i.e. a feeling of pleasure, would necessarily be aroused in it. If on the other hand we allow the weight of the iron to exceed the force of the magnet, then the drive still remains inside it, since it really would attract the iron if we subtracted the amount by which the magnet is outweighed; but it is not satisfied, and if the magnet is once again given the power of feeling then it must necessarily feel a resistance to and a restriction and limitation of its force. In a word, it must feel displeasure. This is the sole source of all pleasure and displeasure.[21]

Both drives, the practical as well as the aesthetic, express themselves in this way, but with a difference. As we have already said, the practical drive pursues an object outside man, one whose existence must be seen as independent of him in that no action ensues or could ensue. Certainly the as yet unshaped concept [Begriff] of this object is there in the soul. Something takes place in the mind [Gemüth] through which the drive is expressed and signified for consciousness: namely, the concept of that towards which it is directed. The nature of the drive is characterized by this. It can be felt and is felt, and in this instance is called a 'desire' [Begehren] – a desire, in so far as the conditions in which the object can become real are not regarded as being within our power. If they do come within our power, and we decide to make the effort and the sacrifices necessary to make them real, then our desire is raised to the level of volition [Wollen]. When faced with an existing object, in this case one can predict what will arouse pleasure or displeasure, for only the actual existence of the object arouses such a feeling. One can therefore differentiate between the nature of the practical drive and the object, and thus between the satisfaction of this drive and the lack of it. The human spirit [Geist] takes on as it were something that belongs to it, an expression of its own actions outside itself, and with no difficulty it sees in the objects its own form, as if in a mirror. It is quite different with the aesthetic drive. It is not directed at anything outside man, but towards something which is only to be found within him. No prior representation of its objects is possible because its object is itself only a representation. The nature of the drive is therefore not characterized by anything except by satisfaction or the lack of it. The one does not permit itself to be distinguished from the other, but both happen together. What is in us as the result of the aesthetic drive does not reveal itself through a desire, but only through an unexpectedly surprising but completely unmotivated and purposeless feeling of either well-being or discomfort, which bears no comprehensible relation to the other workings of our mind [Gemüth]. To continue the example: let us present to the magnet, which has a drive to attract a piece of iron outweighing the capacity of its force, the representation [Vorstellung] of this iron. Then it will *desire* to attract it. And if it can muster a force beyond its inherent capacity, to the extent of detracting as much from the iron as is in excess of its own capacity to attract; and if the urge to attract this iron is stronger than its antipathy (i.e. the refusal of the iron to have the weight reduced), then it will *experience volition* [*wollen*][22] to attract it. If we take away from the magnet this ability to posit [vorzustellen] both the iron outside itself and its ability to attract it, and simply leave it with drive, force, and self-sensation [Selbstgefühl], then it will experience a feeling of displeasure when the heaviness of the iron outweighs its own force, and a feeling of pleasure when, the weight having been taken away without its knowing, it is able to attract the iron. It cannot explain this feeling, which is not connected to anything it recognizes, and which is just like our feeling of aesthetic pleasure or displeasure – but does not stem from the same source. But imagine, as a fitting image for the aesthetic mood, the sweet songster of the night. Imagine, as you can well do along with the poet, that her soul is pure song; imagine her spirit as a striving to form the most perfect harmony, and its particular notes as the representative images [Vorstellungen] of this soul. Unaware of herself, the songster performs [treibt] up and down the octaves according to the inclination of her spirit; gradually it develops its whole capacity through the myriad of harmonies. Each new chord is on a new rung on the ladder of development and is in harmony with the basic drive of the songster, which she is unaware of; for we have given her no representations other than the notes themselves, so that she cannot make judgements about their connection with what is for her a chance harmony. In just the same way the direction of the aesthetic drive lies hidden from our eyes, and we similarly cannot compare the representations developing in us with that which obeys wholly other laws. All the same that harmony must arouse a pleasure in her which fills her whole being, the causes of which she could not for that very reason adduce. But she carries on her inner and secret life in the following tones: its development is not yet complete, this chord does not yet express her whole being, and that pleasure is turned to displeasure in a flash; then both dissolve into greater pleasure with the next note, but return again to drive the singer once more. Her life floats on the surging waves of aesthetic feeling, as does the life of art in every true genius.[23]

So it is easy for the practical drive to make itself known to consciousness in all sorts of ways through its various functions, and it seems quite possible to learn to know it thoroughly and exhaustively by starting out from one's own inner experience. But as far as the aims of the aesthetic drive are concerned, more impediments arise. There seems to be no way of penetrating far enough into the depths of our minds [Geistes] to reach it, other than by trying either to reach it through external experience regardless, waiting to see *whether* and *how* it will reveal itself in these conditions, or by leaving things to chance, blindly trusting one's imagination [Einbildungskraft] and waiting to see how its multifarious creations affect us. But in both cases one is still in danger of confusing a feeling of pleasure based on an obscure, undeveloped, perhaps completely empirical and individual practical consciousness with aesthetic pleasure proper. And so we are always left uncertain as to whether there is such a drive as that which we have described as the aesthetic, or whether all the things we take to be expressions of it are a subtle delusion. We could never guess with certainty, from previous actual experience, what would give pleasure; and the conclusions that what had given us pleasure must give everyone pleasure would remain without foundation.

Consider the position, that aesthetic representations can only develop first and foremost in and by means of experience which is directed towards cognitive knowledge: then you are confronted by a new difficulty. But looked at from another angle this becomes a relief, and the only thing that facilitates the transition from the sphere of knowledge to that of aesthetic feeling.

You see another difficulty: even knowledge is not in the first place sought for its own sake, but for a purpose beyond it. At the first level of development [Bildung], both of the individual and of the whole species, the practical drive in its baser expression outstrips all others, seeking the maintenance and external well-being of animal life. So likewise the knowledge-drive begins by serving this need, in order by so doing to develop the capacity for an independent subsistence. Because of the harshness of nature, or because of the advance of our fellow men against us in struggle, we have no time to linger in contemplation of the things around us. We seize busily on their useful qualities in order to get the best out of them, with constant misgivings about the disadvantages in practice which might follow from a false view of them. Hastily we hurry away from this hard-won cognitive knowledge to the exploitation of these things, and are very careful not to lose a moment in gaining the tools which we could use for the immediate attainment of our ends. Mankind must first attain a certain external well-being and security. The cry of want from within must first be silenced, and strife from without must be settled, before we can observe and linger over our contemplations, and abandon ourselves during this leisurely and liberal contemplation to aesthetic impressions, even if it must be coldbloodedly, without reference to the needs of the moment, and even with the danger of going astray. Thus the calm surface of the water captures the beautiful image of the sun; the outlines drawn in pure light dance and are thrown together and engulfed in the mighty face of the inconstant waves.

Hence the periods and regions of serfdom [Knechtschaft] are also those of tastelessness [Geschmacklosigkeit]; and if it is on the one hand inadvisable to allow men to be free before their aesthetic sense is developed, so on the other hand it is impossible to develop it before they are free. Thus the idea [Idee] of elevating men through aesthetic education [ästhetische Erziehung] to be worthy of freedom, and to freedom itself, will get us into a vicious circle if we do not find beforehand a means of arousing the courage of the individual amongst the throng to be neither the master nor the slave of anyone.[24] In such a time it is all that the oppressed one can do to keep himself alive under the boot of the oppressor, to get enough air and not let himself be completely trodden down. The oppressor himself can only maintain his equilibrium, and not lose his balance during the twistings and turnings of the victim. The burden and the pressure on him are increased because of his unnatural and irremediable position. Because of this the contortions of the victim only get more panic-stricken and daring, and the repression of the other more severe, so that through a very understandable interaction the evil increases in a dismal progression. Neither of the two has time – and they will have increasingly less time – to breathe, to look calmly around himself and let his senses open up to the delightful influence of beneficent nature. Both retain all their lives the taste [Geschmack] they embraced then, when nothing confined them but their swaddling-clothes: the taste for garish colours which violently stimulate the dulled eye, and for the gloss of precious metals. The needy craftsman hurries to appease this taste in the one person who is well-off, in order to reap the scant reward which he needs to live. Thus art declined during the Roman empire at the same rate as freedom, until under Constantine it became a slave to barbarian pomp.[25] Thus the emperor of China's elephants are clad in heavy gold ornaments, and the horses of the kings of Persia drink from cups of solid gold.

No more depressing, but more repugnant and more disturbing for art, is the sight of those under freer skies and milder men of power, who stand in the centre between the two extremes, and who are allowed by the world to be free, but who do not make use of this last remnant of freedom, which, it seems, a genius watching over mankind has thrown into the constitution as seed for harvesting by future generations. No, they press their attentions on the rulers, who are themselves tired of the eternal uniformity, against their will, and grieve that no one acknowledges their bowing and scraping, nor gives them a political importance which they do not in themselves have. Then, with mathematical precision, all forms of culture [Bildung] are estimated according to their future use: speculation which wanders harmlessly at will is asked what it has to offer before it crosses the threshold; novels and plays are searched for their fine morals; one has no chagrin in publicly admitting that one finds an Iphigenia or an epistle in the same vein unpoetic; and Homer himself would probably be called an insipid poetaster if he were not excused for the sake of his Greekness.[26]

But just that aforementioned condition that we must begin our life with experience, as we have said before, reveals to us the only possible transition to spiritual life. As soon as that pressing urgency is removed, no longer driving us to snatch up greedily any possible mental acquisition [Geisteserwerb] only to be able to expend it when the need dictates, then the drive for cognitive knowledge is aroused for the sake of knowledge itself. We begin by letting our inner [geistig] eye wander over objects and linger awhile; we look at them from several angles without considering a possible use for them, and take the risk of making a dubious assumption only to await the right explanation in peace. We are seized by the single noble avarice of collecting the wealth of the spirit [Geistesschätze] for the sake of having it and to delight in looking at its items, since we do not need them to live and they are not imprinted with the stamp of the mint which alone has currency. We dare to invest our riches in attempts which could fail, being more indifferent to the possible loss. We have taken the first step in separating ourselves from the animal in us. Liberalmindedness [Liberalität der Gesinnungen] comes into being – the first degree of humanity.[27]

During this peaceful and unmotivated contemplation of objects, when our mind [Geist] is secure and not keeping a watch on itself, our aesthetic sense develops with reality as its guide without our having anything to do with it. But after both have gone down the same path for a distance, it breaks loose at the parting of the ways and continues independent of and unaccompanied by reality. Thus your eye often rested on the land to the west of your country dwelling. If you could look at it completely disinterestedly, not trying to see how you might escape the night attacks of bands of thieves, then you would not just see the green grass and beyond that the different sorts of clover and beyond that the tall corn, and commit to memory what was there; but your contemplative eye would linger with pleasure on the fresh green of the grass, would look further at the numerous blossoms of the clover, and would glide softly over the rippling waves of the corn towards the heights beyond. There ought, you would say, to be a little village at the top under some trees, or perhaps a wood. But you would not desire to have a house in the village, nor to walk in the wood. It would have been just the same to you if, without your knowing it, someone had conjured up what you wished for by means of an optical illusion. How did this come about? Well, your aesthetic sense had already been aroused in the contemplation of the first objects, in that they satisfied it unexpectedly; but it was offended that this view should cease so abruptly, and that your eye should sink into empty space beyond the heights. According to its requirements the view should have resolved itself in a suitable manner, in order to complete and round off the beautiful whole that had been begun; and your imagination [Einbildungskraft], guided up to now by the aesthetic sense, was able to meet this need itself.[28]

You see in this example a short history of the development of our whole aesthetic faculty [Vermögen]. During peaceful contemplation, which no longer concerns itself with knowledge of what has been long recognized, but which extends as it were further out beyond the object, the aesthetic sense develops in the soul at rest, when intellectual curiosity [Wissbegierde] has been stilled and the knowledge-drive has been satisfied. One object has our approval quite without interest, i.e. we judge it to be in conformity with a certain rule (which we will not go into any further)[29] without attaching any greater value to it. Another object does not receive this approval, and would not unless we took great pains to make it other than it is. It now remains to be shown that we likewise possess a certain sense and a certain awareness [Kenntniss] which is no more than that, which will not lead to anything, and which cannot be used for anything. This faculty is called taste [Geschmack], and the same term chiefly applies to the skill in making correct and generally acceptable judgements in this respect; its opposite is tastelessness.

Out of this contemplation, which still continues to hold on to the thread of reality but wherein we are no longer concerned with the real nature of things, but rather with their oneness with our spirit, the imagination, born to be free, soon attains total freedom. Having arrived in the sphere of the aesthetic drive it remains there, even when the drive deviates from nature and portrays forms not as they are but as they ought to be according to the requirements of this drive. This free creative ability is called "spirit" [Geist]. Taste judges the given, but spirit creates. Taste is the complement and fulfilment of liberality, spirit that of taste itself. One can have taste without spirit, but not spirit without taste. Through spirit the sphere of taste, which is confined within the bounds of nature, is enlarged. The products of spirit create new objects and further develop taste, albeit without elevating it to the status of spirit itself. Everyone can cultivate taste, but it is doubtful whether everyone can raise himself to the level of spirit.

The infinite and unlimited objective of our drive is called the "idea" [Idee], and in as much as a part of it may be presented as a sensible image [Bild], then it is called the "ideal" [Ideale]. Spirit is therefore a faculty of the ideal.[30]

Spirit leaves the bounds of reality behind it, and in its own special sphere there are no bounds. The drive to which it is entrusted passes into the infinite; through it the spirit is led ever onwards from one vista to another, and when it has attained the goal it had in view new horizons open up to it. In the pure, clear aether of the land of its birth there are no vibrations other than those it creates with its own wings.

Third Letter[31]

It is only the capacity [Sinn] for the aesthetic which gives us our first firm viewpoint for introspection. Genius resides there and reveals its hidden depths to the rest of us through art, its companion. It is the same sense [Sinn] which gives living expression to the well-known and well-formed self within us.

Spirit seeks the development of the inner life in man; the development of drive, and indeed of a particular drive, which raises him as an intelligent being over the whole sensible world, and removes him from its influence. The sensible world alone is diverse, and only in so far as we are connected to it at a point entirely invisible to us, and are open to its influence, are we different as individuals. The spirit is one, and what is laid down by the essence of reason [Vernunft] is the same in all rational individuals. One person may prefer this dish, another another; one may prefer this, another that colour. But the influences of the creations of the spirit are generally valid for all men in all ages under all skies, even if they are not equally valued. For everyone there is a point on the ladder of spiritual development [Geistesbildung] at which a particular work would make the impression intended and would necessarily have to do so, even if they had not already reached this point, or were simply unable to reach it on this side of the grave because they started at the bottom of the ladder and because of the brevity of human existence. What the in-spired man [Begeisterte] finds in his breast lies in every human breast, and his capacity is the common capacity [Gemeinsinn] of the whole species.[32]

Partly to test out this sense on others, and partly to communicate to them what is so attractive to it, the genius [das Genie] dresses the forms which appear undisguised before his spiritual eye in more tangible elements, and presents them thus to his contemporaries.

First, on the *testing out* of this sense: not because he needs the approval of the crowd to believe in what is revealed to him through an irresistible feeling at the moment of inspiration – a feeling as irresistible as that of his own existence – but really to shore up his belief in advance against the time when loss of fervour and doubts might set in for himself. "My work is created from the richness of human nature, therefore it must and ought to please everyone who is a part of that, and it will be immortal, like human nature itself"; this is his conclusion. The spiritless writer, who has not the remotest idea of his high calling, turns this round and concludes: "My work will be read by the throng, it will line the pockets of the booksellers, and the reviewers will compete to praise it, therefore it is excellent." But nevertheless, the belief of the first kind of writer in himself will not make him scorn the approval of educated [gebildeter] people and see it as anything other than a bonus. Thus the believer is sure that a providential eye is presiding over him and that a better life awaits him beyond the grave; and in certain moods, the opposition of the whole world of rational beings would not move him an inch, since his belief does not come to him from outside, but he has discovered it in his own heart. Nevertheless he questions and investigates carefully, in the dark forebodings of anxious hours, whether others believe the same thing, and at such times he might well need just such a lightly valued support as the agreement of others. Yet the true genius never loses his composure because of the coldest reception or the loudest criticism of his greatest works. He is sure of his case and of the spirit which dwells within him without his having had anything to do with it; but out of respect for it he wants it to be recognized and respected by others. It is the same with everything that we accept just because of our feeling [Gefühl] and can only believe.[33] When everyone present unanimously assures us that an object which we believe we have glimpsed is not there, then, if we are at all aware of the illusions created by our senses and our imagination, we become confused and begin to look in ourselves for the reasons behind this phenomenon. We believe much more strongly in our inner feeling, but we like even this to be supported by the feelings of others.

Now to the *communication* of the mood [Stimmung] of the genius. As you have observed yourself, there is in all of us the drive to make the people round us as like ourselves as possible, and to duplicate ourselves in them as closely as we can. This is all the more so when we are justified in this aspiration because of our own higher development [Bildung]. Only the unjust egoist wishes to be the sole representative of his kind, and cannot endure anyone else like him; but the noble person would like everyone to be like him, and does everything within his power to bring this about. This is how it is with the inspired darling of nature. He would like to see his own beloved image reflected back to him from all other souls. Thus he imprints the mood of his spirit into a physical form. What goes on in the soul of the artist, the numerous twistings and turnings of his inner life and of his self-active force [selbstthätigen Kraft], cannot be described. No language has found the words for it, and if they were found then the pregnant fullness of its life would be lost in the description gradually drawn out to one simple thread. Life can be presented only in living action; and just as for all ordered activities of the human spirit, its free exercise must have an object to work on in which its inner nature is revealed through the way it operates. Thus the fundamental principle of *sound* exists in the harmonious pulsations and vibrations of the string, which would produce and determine one another, fulfil their inner potential, and even form the note to just the same extent in a vacuum. But only in the surrounding air do they have an external medium for creating their effect. They impress themselves on it and reproduce themselves again and again until they reach the ears of the delighted listener; and it is from this marriage alone that the sound which echoes in our soul is born. In the same way the inspired artist expresses the mood of his nature [Gemüthes] in a flexible physical form, and the motion, action and continuity of his forms is the expression of the inner vibrations of his soul. This motion [Bewegung] should arouse in us the same mood that was in him. He lent his soul to dead matter so that it could communicate itself to us.[34] Our spirit is the final goal of his art, and those forms are the intermediaries between him and us, as the air is the intermediary between our ear and the string.

This inner mood of the artist is the spirit [Geist] of the work he creates, and the contingent forms in which he expresses it are the embodiment or the letter [Buchstabe] of it.

It is here that the need for artistic technique comes in.

Whoever wishes to work upon objects according to a certain mood must understand how to do so, and to do so with facility, so that no resistance is apparent and so that, in his hands, dead matter seems to have taken on formative structure [Bildung] and organization of its own accord. As soon as matter resists and effort is needed to conquer it, then the aesthetic mood is broken, and nothing remains but the sight of the worker who is striving to achieve his purpose – a not unworthy sight, but one which we did not want here. People have often confused this facility of artistic technique with spirit itself. It is certainly the determining condition for the expression of spirit, and anyone who sets to work must already have acquired it; but it is not spirit. Through it alone nothing but an empty strumming is produced, a play of sound which is nothing more than just that, which does not rise up to ideas [Ideen], and at most expresses a wilfulness [Muthwillen] and a wasted energy which secretly one wishes could have been put to better use. It is true that the lightest and most careless brushstroke executed by the true genius will have a veneer of those ideas. But the mere technician will never with his highest skills produce anything but a mechanical work, which at the very most might induce one to marvel at its structure.

So, with the most recent masterpieces of the most favoured darling of nature in our own nation – with Tasso, Iphigenia, and with the lightest brushstrokes of the same artist since then[35] – with them, I say, it is not the simplicity of narrative, nor the language which flows softly and without bombast, which attracts the cultivated reader so strongly. It is not the letter, but the spirit.

With the same simplicity of plot, and the same facility and nobility of language, it is possible to produce a very insipid, bland and feeble work. It is the mood [Stimmung] which dominates in these works: this noblest flower of humanity, which was only once put forth by nature under a Grecian sky, and by one of her miracles was repeated in the north. Upon our souls there is impressed the living image of that long-terminated culture, which no longer counters the attacks of fate with strenuous twistings and turnings, and which would lose everything rather than the pure equanimity of its character and the easy grace [Grazie] of the motions of its mind [Gemüths]; that reliance in and upon itself, which no longer needs to strain to summon up its strength [Kraft] and brace itself against opposition, but which stands firm on its feet; that indifference of spirit which, despite their bearing down upon us, gives things no more appreciation than they deserve in being the objects of our contemplation, and which may win aesthetic pleasure from their agreeable forms, or a slight smile (as the Graces smile) from their distorted ones; the image of that perfection of humanity, which feels itself detached rather than torn from the sensible world, and which can do without it, without any feeling of displeasure, just as easily as it can enjoy it in its own way. With pleasure we find ourselves placed in a world in which alone such a mood is possible, and in a society all of whose members are upright and benevolent, and whose divisions are not caused by bad will but by the storms of adverse fate (for we can never be indifferent to injustices brought about by free beings: they will always arouse serious disapproval, and never the slight smile brought about by the blows of irrational nature). Under the influence of the artist we discover with satisfied self-love a poise in ourselves, which we do not usually have during the course of our lives. We feel ourselves raised higher and ennobled, and heartfelt love is the reward of the poet who coaxes us so sweetly in order to improve us.

Every person has a very precise sense of the sort of cultivation [Ausbildung] that he needs next, and may in a period of delusion [Täuschung] opt to find in himself that which a vague presentiment tells him is actually on the next level of culture [Cultur] that he has to attain. A considerable part of our public has not yet got to the stage where all that is missing is grace in its movements,[36] and facility and unconstraint in the expression of its force [Kraftäusserung]. Many lack force itself. For them, portrayals [Darstellungen] such as those of which we have been speaking are unpalatable. They confuse that restrained force, which actually comes from an abundance of force, and which they do not recognize, with the absence of force, which they know all too well. They prefer to see themselves tricked by images of the crude but vigorous [kraft-volle] customs of our ancestors – a genre that is as good as any other, if it is treated with spirit – or they take pleasure in the whimsical contortions of our mediocre chivalric romances, and in high-flown and presumptuous speeches.

Two different epochs of human culture [Cultur], with all their modulations, have been given to the poet about whom I am speaking to plot out. He took the last stage of his own age, only to set it down again at the first. But his genius, as it had to, flew over the slow process of time. He created his own public, as every true artist must; he worked for posterity, and if our species has risen higher it is not without his doing.[37]

Those two conditions, that of the first original inspiration and that of its presentation in corporeal form, are not always separate in the soul of the artist, though they must be carefully distinguished by the exact inquirer. There are artists who take hold of and grip their inspiration firmly, look at the materials around them, and choose the most suitable for its expression; who watch themselves carefully while they work; who first seize the spirit and then search for the lump of clay into which they breathe the living soul. There are others in whom the spirit and the corporeal form are born simultaneously, and from whose souls the whole new living thing tears itself away at the same time. The former create the most fully fashioned and finely meditated works, all of whose parts show the finest symmetry both in themselves and in relation to the whole; but the more sensitive eye may notice here and there the hand of the artist in the joining together of spirit and corporeal form. These two things are intimately joined in the works of the second kind of artist, just as they are in nature's workshop, and the complete life permeates even the most outward parts. And, just as in the works of nature, one discovers here and there small aberrations whose purpose cannot be defined, but which could not be removed without damaging the whole. Our nation has masters of both the above kinds.

Certain higher moods, as has been said, are not for common eyes, and cannot be communicated to them. And, with those others who are open to such communication, it is certainly not apparent how it happens that the work soars up to them. Observers who are not very critical are therefore tempted to ascribe the motive [bewegende] force, which only spirit has, to the form and structure of the physical object.[38] The proportions of this object and the rules according to which it is formed are to be estimated, learned and practised through art, since, as admitted above, the corporeal form of the most brilliant [geistreich] work is itself produced only through art. There are several causes which can move the most spiritless man to imitate the mechanical part of a work which has spiritual quality, and since even this has its merits, some onlookers do not lose anything by it. Such craftsmen are literalists [Buchstäbler]. The spiritless man who is incapable even of mechanical art is a bungler. Let Pygmalion place his statue-come-to-life before the eyes of jubilant people; he ought – for nothing prevents us from enlarging upon the legend – to have given her, as well as life, the secret advantage of being seen as living only by those full of spirit [von geistvollen Augen], remaining cold and dead for the common and the dull. Doesn't it take more to become famous? Think of it – while the whole populace pays homage to the artist, a man who also knows how to wield his chisel measures exactly the proportions of the statue with ruler and compasses, goes away, prepares his work, puts it next to that of the artist – and there are many who can find no difference between the two.[39]

The rules governing art which are to be found in the textbooks are concerned mostly with its mechanical side. They must be interpreted in the spirit, and not according to the letter. Thus they teach us how to invent the plot, and how to communicate and gradually develop it; and it is certainly necessary for the artist to understand this. Even if he understands nothing more than the observation of these rules, he still ends up with a good story, which excites curiosity, entertains, and satisfies. But we demanded more of him than this. The oneness of spiritual mood which dominates his work, and which is to be imparted to the mind [Gemüth] of the reader, is the soul of the work. If this mood is indicated, developed and maintained victoriously throughout, then the work is complete, whether or not the outward events have satisfied mere curiosity. The triumph of this mood over its numerous interruptions is the true evolution. Although the thoughtless reader who wanted to hear a fairy story may yet ask what happened next.[40]

They advise us to employ illusion [zu täuschen]. By means of the story, the literalist believes, he musters all his arts to get us to take his fairy tale for a real event, and if it fails then he assures us on his word of honour that he is telling a true story. So indeed he continues, until all the gullible [alle Gaffer] are lost in wonder. But he should not believe that he has delivered up a work of art. Our elevation to a wholly other mood, one which is strange to us and in which we forget our individuality, – that is the true illusion, and for this final purpose the literal truth of a story, which is all that the literalist values, is insufficient. People act in these stories more or less in the way we too would act in the same circumstances.

They hold forth about pure morals. And whoever can and wants to carry on this good work of making important moral doctrines forcefully available to us in stories, let him do it. He seeks to bring us to the point of choosing the better path by our own free decision: he deserves our thanks, and his efforts are not always lost on us. But he ought to recognize what he is, and not put himself in a category to which he does not belong. The inspired [begeisterte] artist does not address himself at all to our freedom. So little does he do so that, on the contrary, his magic begins only when we have given it up. Through his art he momentarily raises us, through no agency of our own, to a higher sphere. We do not become any better for it. But the unploughed fields of our minds [Gemüths] are nevertheless opened up, and if for other reasons we one day decide in freedom to take possession of them, we find half the resistance removed and half the work done.[41]

(The continuation did not appear)

Foreword to

The Vocation of Man
[Die Bestimmung des Menschen]

1800

Translated by Roderick M. Chisholm in Fichte (1956), pp. 3–4 (slightly modified).

German texts in *SW*, II, 167–8; and in Fichte (1964–), I, 6, pp. 189–90.

Introductory note

This work of 1800, only the foreword to which is included here, represents one of Fichte's frequent attempts to reach a wider audience than that open to the technical procedures of the critical philosophy; one might compare Coleridge's self-consciousness about the precise kinds of readers envisaged by his various works, although in Coleridge's career we can trace a move toward a highly specialized readership, rather than a constant engagement with both popular and technical versions of his thought.

By employing the form of the dialogue Fichte is doing his utmost to create an incentive for the act of self-reference requested in the foreword, and so central to Romantic aesthetics in general; the same can be said of his use of a dramatic speaker.

FOREWORD

This work has for its subject matter that part of the new philosophy which is of use outside the academy, set forth in that order in which it would naturally present itself to unsophisticated [kunstlos] reflection. The more profound arguments by which subtle objections and extravagances of overrefined understandings are to be met fall beyond the limits of our task; so, too, whatever is but the foundation of some other positive science, and whatever belongs to pedagogy in its widest sense, that is, to the deliberate and the arbitrary education of the human race. Such objections are not made by the natural understanding; positive science we leave to its scholars [Gelehrten]; and the education of the human race, in so far as that depends upon human effort, we leave to its appointed teachers and statesmen.

This book, therefore, is not intended for professional philosophers, for they will find nothing in it that has not been already set forth in other writings of the same author. It ought to be intelligible to all readers who are able to understand a book at all. To those who wish only to repeat, in somewhat varied order, certain phrases which they have already learned by rote, and

94

who mistake this business of the memory for real understanding, it will doubtless be found unintelligible.

This book is intended to attract and animate the reader, and to elevate him from the world of sense into a region beyond it. At least, the author is conscious that he has not entered upon his task without such inspiration [Begeisterung]. Often, indeed, the fire with which we commence an undertaking disappears during the toil of execution; and thus, at the conclusion of a work, we are in danger of doing ourselves injustice upon this point. In short, whether the author has succeeded or not in attaining his object can be determined only by the effect which the work produces on the readers to whom it is addressed, and in this the author has no voice.

I must, however, remind my reader that the "I" who speaks in this book is not the author himself; it is the author's wish that the reader himself will assume this character. And it is to be hoped that the reader – instead of resting content with a merely historical apprehension of what is here said – will actually hold converse with himself during the act of reading; that he will deliberate, draw conclusions, and form resolutions, like his imaginary representative; and thus, by his own labour and reflection, develop and build up purely out of himself that mode of thought the mere picture of which is presented to him in the book.

Selections from

On the Nature of the Scholar,
and his Manifestations in the Sphere of Freedom
[Über das Wesen des Gelehrten und seine
Erscheinungen im Gebiete der Freiheit]

Lectures given at Erlangen in the summer of 1805

What follows is a heavily revised text of (selections from) the translation by William Smith in Fichte (1889), I, 209–317. German text in *SW*, VI, 347–447.

Introductory note

These lectures constitute another of Fichte's public or exoteric statements of his philosophical priorities, and in many ways extend the themes of the 1794 lectures *On the Vocation of the Scholar*: see Fichte (1889), I, 149–205; *SW*, VI, 289–346. Here he had emphasized the social function and identity of learning, arguing strongly against Rousseau's notion of the corrupting tendency of a scholar class (*SW*, VI, 335f.) whilst maintaining the ideal of minimal government.

The following lectures might seem in the first place to have very little to do with aesthetics, but it becomes apparent at a certain point in the argument that the scholar and the artist are defined each in terms of the other, and that what Fichte is working toward is some sort of socially manifested aesthetic identity. One might compare Shelley's broad and inclusive idea of poetry in *A Defence of Poetry*: it can exist in laws, in institutions, and in architecture, as well as in the literary mode commonly so named (which yet remains its pre-eminent form) – in short, in anything that is essentially creative and capable of inspiring cultural regeneration. Fichte would have said much the same of *Geist*, or, in this case, of *Genie* (genius).

If *Geist* has dropped out of the privileged place it occupied in the argument of *On the Spirit and the Letter in Philosophy*, it yet defines exactly what the scholar class must possess in order to function properly.

Various parts of the exposition in the later *Addresses to the German Nation* (1807–8) should also be consulted in this context. There, for example, he speaks of poetry in particular as having a special role in putting into action the principles of the transcendental philosophy. A living language "has within itself the power of infinite poetry, ever refreshing and renewing its youth, for every stirring of living thought in it opens up a new vein of poetic enthusiasm [Begeisterung]. To such a language, therefore, poetry is the highest and best means of flooding the life of all with the spiritual culture that has been attained." See Fichte (1968), p. 68; *SW*, VII, 334. The whole argument is very much in the spirit of Shelley.

Lecture III

OF THE PROSPECTIVE SCHOLAR GENERALLY, AND IN PARTICULAR
OF ABILITY [TALENT] AND INDUSTRY [FLEISS]

It is the idea [Idee] itself which, by its own inherent force, creates for itself an independent and personal life in man, constantly maintains itself in this life, and by means of it arranges [vermittelst] the outward world in its own image. The natural man cannot by his own strength raise himself to the supernatural; he must be raised thereto by the force of the supernatural. This self-forming and self-supporting life of the idea in man manifests itself as love – strictly speaking as love of the idea for itself, but in the world of appearances [in der Erscheinung] as love of man for the idea.[1] This was set forth in our *first lecture*.

So it is with love in general, and it is no different in the particular case of love of knowledge [Erkenntniss] of the idea, which is the knowledge the scholar is called upon to acquire. The love of the idea wholly for itself and in particular for its essential clarity and luminosity [Klarheit] shows itself in those men whom it has inspired, and of whose being it has fully possessed itself, as knowledge of the idea. In the fully developed scholar this appears with a well-defined and perfect clarity; in the prospective scholar, as a striving toward such clarity as it can attain under the circumstances in which he is placed. Following the plan laid out in the opening lecture, we shall speak in the first place of the prospective [angehender] scholar.

In him the idea in the first place strives to apprehend itself in a definite form, and to establish for itself a fixed place amid the tide of manifold representations [Vorstellungen] which flows in ceaseless change through his soul. In this effort he is seized with a presentiment of a truth still unknown to him, of which he has as yet no clear concept. He feels that every newly felt apprehension still falls short of the full and perfect truth [das Rechte], without being able to say distinctly in what it is deficient, or *how* that truth which is to take its place can be attained. This striving of the idea within him becomes henceforward his essential life, and its highest and deepest drive [Trieb], superseding his hitherto sensuous [sinnlich] and egoistical drive, which was directed only at the maintenance of his personal existence and physical well-being. It subordinates this latter to itself, and thereby extinguishes it as his exclusive and fundamental drive. Actual personal need continues to demand its satisfaction as hitherto; but that satisfaction does not continue, as it has hitherto continued, even when its immediate needs have been met, to be the engrossing thought, the ever-present object of reflection, the motive to all conduct and action in the thinking being. As the sensuous nature has hitherto asserted its rights, so now does emancipated thought, armed with new force, in its own strength and without outward compulsion or ulterior design, return from the strange land into which it has been led captive to its own proper home, and set itself upon the path which leads towards that much wished-for unknown whose light streams upon it from afar. Towards that unknown it is unceasingly attracted, and in meditating upon it and striving after it, it employs its best spiritual forces.

This drive towards an obscure, imperfectly discerned spiritual state is commonly named genius [Genie], and on good grounds. It is a supernatural inclination in man, attracting him to a supernatural object, thus indicating his affinity with the spiritual world and his original home in that world. Whether we suppose that this drive which, absolutely considered, should lead to the pursuit of the divine idea in its primitive unity and indivisibility, does originally and at the first appearance of any particular individual in the world of sense so shape itself that he can lay hold of the idea only at some specific point of contact, and only from that point penetrate gradually to the whole; or whether we hold that this essential point of contact is determined for the individual during the first application of his force [Kraft] on the manifold materials which surround it, and always occurs in that material which chance presents at the precise moment that the force is sufficiently developed – whichever of these opinions we adopt,[2] still, as far as its outward appearance is concerned, the drive which shows itself in man and urges him onward will always exhibit itself as a drive towards some particular side of the one in-itself-indivisible idea. Or, as we may express it, after the principles laid down in our last lecture, without fear of being misunderstood: as a drive towards one particular idea in the sphere of all possible ideas. Or again, when this drive is given the name of genius, then genius will always appear as a specific genius – whether for philosophy, poetry, natural science, legislation or the like – and never as genius purely in general. According to the first of the above opinions this specific genius possesses its distinguishing character as an innate determination. According to the second it is originally a universal quality of genius [Genialität] determined to a particular genius [Genie] only by the accident of culture. The resolution of this conflict of opinion lies beyond the limits of our present task.

However it may be resolved, two things are evident. First, in general, the indispensability of previously existing spiritual culture, and of preliminary acquaintance with concepts and known things, so that any genius which is present may disclose itself. Second, in particular, the necessity of bringing concepts of many different kinds within the reach of every man, so that either the inborn specific genius may come into contact with its appropriate material, or the genius not born to such specificity may freely choose one from among the many. Future genius reveals itself even in this preliminary spiritual culture. Its drive is toward knowing [Wissen], from the first toward knowing only as knowing: it manifests itself solely as a desire to know [Wissbegierde].

But even when this drive has visibly manifested itself, either in the active investigation of some problem that attracts it or in happy anticipations of its solution, there are still required a persevering industry [Fleiss] and an uninterrupted searching. The question has often been raised whether natural ability [Talent] or industry be the more essential in scientific knowledge [Wissenschaft]. I answer: both must be united. The one is of little worth without the other. Natural ability or genius [Genie][3] is nothing more than the drive of the idea to assume a definite form; for the idea has no content or embodiment in itself, but only first shapes such a thing for itself out of the surrounding scientific materials of its time, and this industry alone can supply. On the other hand industry can do nothing more than provide the elements of this embodiment. It cannot unite them organically or breathe into them a living spirit. This can only be done by the idea, which reveals itself as natural ability. To become impressed on the surrounding world is the purpose for which the living idea dwelling in the true scholar seeks an embodiment for itself. It must become the highest principle of life and the innermost soul of this world – it must therefore take on the same forms that are borne by it, establish itself in them as its own proper dwelling place, and regulate with a free discretion [Willkür] the movements of all their individual parts according to the natural purposes of each, just as a healthy man can set his own limbs in motion. As for him in whom the indwelling genius proceeds but half way in its embodiment, and stops here – whether because the paths of learned culture are inaccessible to him, or because he does not follow them through idleness or presumptuous self-conceit – between him and his age, and therefore between him and every possible age, and the whole human race in every stage of its culture, an impassable gulf is established and all means of mutual influence cut off. Whatever may now dwell within him – or, more strictly speaking, whatever he may have acquired in the course of his developing culture – he is unable to explain clearly either to himself or others, or to make it the deliberate rule of his actions and thus realize it in the world. He lacks the two necessary elements of the true life of the idea – clarity and freedom. Clarity: his fundamental concept is not thoroughly transparent to his own mind, he cannot follow it securely through all its modifications, from its innermost source where it descends immediately from the divinity upon his soul, to all those points at which it has to manifest and embody itself in the actual world, and through the different forms which it must assume under different conditions.[4] Freedom, which springs from clarity and can never exist without it: for he does not recognize at first sight in each appearance that comes before him the form [Gestalt] which the concept must take in it, and the means by which one must control it; nor has he those means at his free disposal. He is commonly called a fanatic [Schwärmer], and rightly so.[5] He, on the contrary, in whom the idea perfectly reveals itself, looks out upon and thoroughly penetrates all reality by its light. Through the idea itself he understands all related objects – how they have become what they are, what is true [recht] in them, what is still wanting and how the want must be supplied; and he has besides the means of supplying that want completely in his free power. The embodiment of the idea is then for the first time completed in him, and he is a finished scholar. The point where the scholar passes into the free artist is the perfecting of the scholar. Hence it is obvious that even when genius has disclosed itself and visibly become a self-forming life of the idea, untiring industry is necessary to its perfect completion. To show that, at the point where the scholar reaches maturity, the cultural moment [Bildungs-Epoche] of the artist begins, and that this too requires industry, so that it shall be infinite, lies not within our present inquiry; we allude to it only in passing.

But what am I saying? That industry is required even after the appearance of genius, as if I would call it forth by my prescription, my advice, my demonstration of its necessity, and thus expected to rouse to exertion those in whom it is wanting? Rather let us say that where genius is really present then industry is found there spontaneously, and develops with a steady growth, and ceaselessly drives the progressive scholar onwards towards perfection. On the contrary where industry is not to be found then it is not genius nor the impulse [Antrieb] of the idea which has shown itself, but only some mean and unworthy motive in place of it.

The idea is not the ornament of the individual (strictly speaking there is no such thing as individuality in the idea) but seeks to flow forth in the whole human race, to animate it with new life and to mould it after its own image. This is the distinctive character of the idea, and whatever is without this character is not the idea. Wherever, therefore, it attains such life, it irresistibly strives after this universal efficacy not through the life of the individual but through its own essential nature. It thus drives everyone in whom it has an abode as though he were a passive instrument, even against the will and wish of his sensuous, personal nature. It drives him forward to this universal efficacy, to the skill which is demanded for its exercise, and to the industry which is necessary for the acquisition of that skill. Wholly of itself and quite without need of the personal premeditation of its instrument, it never ceases from spontaneous activity and self-development, until it has attained whatever living form its particular circumstances will allow it as a means of grasping its surroundings. Wherever a man, having availed himself of the existing and accessible means for the acquisition of learned culture (for the second case, where those means do not exist or are inaccessible, does not belong to our present subject), wherever, I say, such a man remains inactive, and satisfied with the persuasion that he possesses something resembling the idea or genius, then in him there is neither idea nor genius, but only a vain, ostentatious disposition which assumes a singular and fantastic costume in order to attract notice. Such a disposition shows itself at once in a self-congratulatory contemplation of its own parts and endowments, dwelling on these in complacent indolence commonly accompanied by contemptuous disparagement of the personal qualities and gifts of others. On the other hand, he who is constantly urged on by the idea has no time left to think about himself. Lost with all his senses in the object he has in view, he never weighs his own ability for grasping it against those of other men. Ability [Talent], where it is present, sees its object [Sache] only, and never sees itself, as the healthy eye fixes itself upon something beyond it but never looks round upon its own brightness. But if the idea does indeed not belong to one of the kind described above, then what is it that animates him and moves him to those eager and restless efforts which we behold? It is mere pride and self-conceit, and the desperate ambition, in spite of natural disqualification, to assume a character which does not belong to him; these inspire, impel and spur him on, and stand for him in place of genius. And what is it that he produces, and that appears to the common eye as if it were the idea? – though the common eye is itself neither clear nor pure, and is in particular incapable of appreciating the sole criteria of all true ideals: clarity, freedom, self-possession [Besonnenheit], artistic form – what is it, I say? Either something he has thought up himself, or something which has accidentally occurred to him; which he does not, indeed, understand, but which he nevertheless hopes may appear new, *frappant*, paradoxical, and therefore blaze forth far and wide.[6] With this he commits himself to the wheel of fortune, trusting that in the aftermath he himself or someone else may discover a meaning therein. Or else he has borrowed it from others, cunningly distorting, disarranging and unsettling it so that its original form cannot easily be recognized; and, by way of precaution, depreciating as utterly barren and unprofitable the source from whence it came, lest the unprejudiced observer might be led to inquire whether he has not possibly obtained from thence that which he calls his own.

In a word: self-contemplation, self-admiration, and self-flattery (though the last may remain unexpressed and even carefully shrouded from an eye other than his own); these, and the things that spring from them, indolence and a disdain for the things in the treasure of learned culture as it already exists, are sure signs of the absence of true ability [Talent]. Conversely, forgetfulness of self in the object [Sache] pursued, entire devotion to that object, and inability to entertain any thought of self in its presence, are the inseparable accompaniments of true ability. It follows that such ability is in every stage of its growth and especially during its early development marked by an amiable modesty and a retiring bashfulness. Ability knows least of all about itself. It is present, and works and rules with silent power, long before it comes to consciousness of its own nature. Whoever is constantly looking back upon himself to see how it stands with him, and of what powers he can boast, and who is the first discoverer of them – in him there is nothing truly significant.

Should there then be any blossoming ability here among you, far be it from me to wound its native modesty and diffidence by any general invitation to you to scrutinize yourselves to see whether or not you might be in possession of the idea. Much rather would I earnestly dissuade you from such self-investigation. And that this advice may not seem to you the suggestion of mere pedantic school-wisdom, and perhaps of extravagant caution, but may commend itself to your minds as arising from absolute necessity, I would add that you cannot answer this question for yourselves, nor can you obtain any sure answer from anyone else. Therefore truth is not elicited by any premeditated self-investigation, through which on the contrary the youth is taught a self-contemplation and conceited brooding over himself, through which at length everyone becomes an intellectual and moral ruin. There are many signs by which we may know that the ability which possibly lies concealed in a student has not yet declared itself. But there is only one decisive criterion by which we may determine whether such ability has or has not ever existed in him, and that criterion can be applied only after the result has become apparent. Whoever has really become a mature scholar and artist in the sense in which we have used these words – grasping the world through a clear, penetrating idea, and able to impress that idea upon the world at every point – then he has had ability [Talent], he has been seized by the idea, and it may now confidently be said that he has been seized by it. He who, notwithstanding the most industrious study, has arrived at maturity without having raised himself to the idea, has then been without ability and without communion with the idea; and he too may then be judged. But neither of these judgements can be passed upon him who is still upon the way.

This disposition of things, which is as wise as it is necessary, leaves but one course open to the youthful student who cannot know with certainty whether or not ability dwells within him: namely, that he continue to act as though there were latent within him that which must at last come to light; that he subject himself to all conditions and place himself in all circumstances in which, if present, it may come to light; and that, with untiring industry and the true devotion of his whole mind, he avail himself of all the means which learned culture offers to him. In the worst case, if at the termination of his studies he should discover that out of the mass of learning which he has accumulated no spark of the idea has shone upon him, there yet remains for him at least a consciousness, a consciousness more indispensable to man than even genius [Genie] itself, and without which the possessor of the greatest genius is far less worthy than he: the consciousness that if he has not risen higher then no blame can be attached to him, and that the point at which he has stopped short is the place assigned to him by God, whose will he will joyfully obey. No one need pride himself upon ability, for it is the free gift of the divinity. But of honest industry and true devotion to his nature any man may well be proud. Indeed, this thorough integrity of purpose is itself the divine idea in its most common form, and no really honest mind is without communion with the divinity.

Moreover, the knowledge which he has acquired by means of this sincere effort after something higher will render him always a suitable instrument in the hands of the man of higher culture, who has attained possession of the idea. To such a man he will unhesitatingly submit without grudge or jealousy, and without any unsatisfied struggle after an elevation for which he was not formed. He will follow his guidance with a true loyalty which shall have become to him a second nature, and thus he will obtain a sure consciousness of having fulfilled his vocation, the last and highest thing which in any sphere of life a man can attain.

Lecture VIII

OF RULERS [REGENTEN]

He in whom learned culture has actually accomplished its end, which is to put the cultured man in possession of the idea, shows by the manner in which he regards and practises the calling of the scholar that his occupation is honourable and holy to him before all other things. In its relation to the progressive improvement of the world, the idea may be expressed either in actual life and conduct or in pure concepts. In the first of these modes it is expressed by those who guide and order, in an original manner and as the ultimate free principle, the relations of men – both their relations among themselves (or their legal conditions) and to passive nature (the rule of reason over the irrational world); and who possess the right and calling, either by themselves or in concert with others, to think, judge and resolve independently concerning the actual arrangement of these relations. We have to speak today of the holy purpose and practice of this occupation. As we have already taken precautions against misunderstanding by a strict definition of our meaning, we shall for the sake of brevity term those who practise this calling *rulers*.

The business of the ruler has been described in our early lectures, and so definitely, that no further analysis is necessary for our present purpose. We have now only to show what capacities and talents must be possessed by the ruler, and by what estimate and application of his calling he proves that he holds it to be a holy one.

He who undertakes to guide his age and direct and order its constitution must be raised above it. He must not merely possess a historical knowledge of it, but must thoroughly understand and comprehend [begreifen] it. The ruler possesses in the first place a living concept [Begriff] of that relation of human life which he undertakes to superintend. He knows its essential nature, meaning and purpose. Further, he perfectly understands the changing and adventitious forms which it may assume in actuality without prejudice to its essential nature. He knows the particular form that it has assumed at the present time, and the new forms through which it must be led nearer and nearer to its unattainable ideal. No part of its present form is, in his view, necessary and unchangeable, but is only an incidental point in a progression by which it is constantly rising towards higher perfection. He knows the whole of which that condition is a part, and of which every improvement of it must still remain a part, and he never loses sight of this whole in contemplating the improvement of individual parts. This knowledge gives to his inventive spirit the means of accomplishing the improvements he may devise, and the same knowledge secures him from the mistake of disorganizing the whole by the supposed improvement of individual parts. His eye always combines the part with the whole, and the ideal of the whole with its manifestation in actuality.

He who cannot look upon human affairs with this unfettered vision is never a ruler, whatever station he may occupy, nor can he ever become one. His mode of thought itself, and his faith in the unchangeableness of the present, places him in a state of subordination and makes him an instrument of whoever created that arrangement of things in whose permanence he believes. This frequently happens, and thus all generations do not have actual rulers. Great spirits of previous times often rule over succeeding ages long after their death, by means of men who are nothing in themselves, but only continuations and prolongations of their lives. Very often, too, this is no misfortune. But those who desire to understand human life with deeper insight ought to know that these men are not true rulers, and that under them the age does not move forward, but rests – perhaps to gain strength for new creations.[7]

The ruler, as I have said, thoroughly comprehends that relation of human life which he undertakes to superintend. He knows its essential character, as it is and ought to be in particular, and looks upon it as the absolute divine will for man. It is not for him a means to the attainment of any end whatsoever, nor in particular to the production of human happiness; but he grasps it as in itself an end, as the absolute mode, order and form in which the human race should live.

Thus his occupation is ennobled and dignified in the first place in accordance with the nobility of his mode of thought. To direct all his faculties and aspirations and to devote his whole life to the purpose that mortal men may fall out as little as possible with each other in the short span of time during which they have to live together; that they may have something to eat and drink, and wherewithal to clothe themselves, until they make way for another generation which again shall eat and drink and clothe itself – this occupation would appear to a noble mind as a very unworthy destiny. The ruler, after our picture of him, is secure against this view of his calling. Through the concept of human relations by which he is animated, the race among which he practises his vocation is likewise ennobled. He who has constantly to keep in view the infirmities and weaknesses of men, who has daily to govern these things, and who has frequent opportunities of observing their general meanness and corruption, seeing nothing more than these, cannot be much disposed to honour or to love them. And indeed those powerful spirits who have filled the most prominent places among men but have not been penetrated by true religious feeling have at no time been known to bestow much honour or respect upon their species. In his estimate of mankind, the ruler as we have defined him looks beyond that which they are *actually* [*wirklich*] to that which they are in the *divine concept* – that is therefore to that which they may be, ought to be, and one day surely will be. He is thus filled with a reverence for a species called to so high a destiny. Love is not required of him. Indeed, if you think more deeply, it is even a kind of arrogance for a ruler to presume to love the whole human species, or even his own nation – to assure it of his love and, as it were, make it dependent upon it. A ruler of the sort we have described is free from this kind of love: his reverence for humanity as the image and protected child of the divinity more than substitutes for it.

He grasps [begreift] his occupation as the divine concept [Begriff] at work in the human species, and its practice as the divine concept at work in himself, the particular individual. He recognizes in himself one of the first and immediate servants of the divinity, one of the material organs through which it enters into communion with actuality. Not that this thought excites him to vain self-exaltation; for he who is penetrated by the idea has lost his personality in it, and has no longer any feeling of self remaining, except that of employing his personal existence truly and conscientiously in his high calling. He knows very well that he has not been given this intuition of the idea and this force [Kraft] as a self, as a particular individual, but that he has received them. He knows that he can add nothing to what has been given him except its honest and conscientious use; and he knows that the humblest of men can do this in the same degree as he can himself, and that such a one would have the same value in the sight of the divinity as he does in his station. He who knows how to value higher and more substantial distinctions will not be dazzled by the outward rank and elevation above other men, which have been given not to his person but to his dignity [Würde], and which are only the conditions of the possession of this dignity. In a word: he looks upon his calling not as a friendly service which he renders to the world but as his absolute personal duty and obligation, by the performance of which alone he obtains, maintains and justifies his personal existence, and without which he would pass away into nothing.

This view of his calling, as the divine call in him, supports and justifies him before himself in an important difficulty which must very often occur to him who conscientiously follows this occupation; and it makes his step firm, determined, and unwavering. In no circumstances indeed should the individual, considered strictly as an individual, be sacrificed to the whole, however unimportant the individual and however great the nature and the interest of the whole that is at stake. But the parts of the whole must often be placed in danger on its account. This danger then itself, and not the ruler, selects its victims from among individual men. How could a ruler, who apprehends no other destiny for the human species than happiness here below – how could he answer to his conscience for the danger and possible sacrifice of any individual victim, since that individual must have had as good a claim to happiness as any other? How could such a ruler, for example, answer to his conscience for determining upon a just war, one undertaken for the support of national independence, threatened either immediately or prospectively? – for the victims who would fall in such a war, and the many evils thereby inflicted upon humanity? The ruler who sees a divine calling in his occupation stands firm and immovable before all these doubts, overtaken by no unmanly weakness. Is the war just? Then it is the will of god that there should be war, and it is God's will with him that he resolve upon it. Let sacrifices be made as they must; it is again the divine will that chooses them. God has the most perfect right over all human life and well-being, for both have proceeded from him and will return to him, and in his creation nothing can be lost. So also in the business of legislation. There must be a general law, and it must be administered absolutely without exception. The universality of the law cannot be given up for the sake of one individual who thinks his case so peculiar that he is aggrieved by the strict enforcement of the law, even though his allegation may have some truth in it. Let him bring the small injustice done to himself as a sacrifice to the general support of justice among men. [8]

The divine idea, ruling in the ruler and through him moulding the relations of his age and nation, now becomes his whole and single life. This indeed is the case with the idea under any form in which it may enter man: he cannot have, nor permit, nor endure any life within him except this. He comprehends this life with clear consciousness as the immediate divine activity and energy within him, as the fulfilment of the divine will in and by his person. It is unnecessary to repeat the proofs which we have already adduced in general, that through this consciousness his thought is sanctified, transfigured, and bathed in God. Everyone needs religion, everyone may acquire it, and with it everyone may obtain blessedness; most of all, as we have seen above, does the ruler need it. Unless he clothe his occupation in the light of religion he can never pursue it with a good conscience. Without this, nothing remains for him but thoughtlessness and a mere mechanical carrying on of his vocation, without giving account to himself of its reasonableness or justice; or if not thoughtlessness, then want of principle, obduracy, insensibility, and hatred and contempt for the human race.

The idea, formed out of and for his own particular life, leads the life of the ruler in place of his own. It alone drives him; nothing else in its place. His personality has long since gone over to the idea – how then can any motive now arise from it? He lives in *glory* [*Ehre*], transfused in God to work his eternal work; how then can *fame*, the judgement of mortal and perishable men upon him, have any meaning for him? Devoted to the idea with his whole being, how can he ever seek to pamper or to spare himself? His own person and all personality has disappeared in the divine concept of the order of the whole. He thinks this order, and only through it does he think of individuals; hence neither friend nor foe, neither favourite nor adversary, finds a place before him. All alike, and he himself among them, are lost forever in the concept of the independence and equality of all.

Only the idea drives him, and where it does not do so then he has no life but remains quiescent and inactive. He will never act or rouse himself to exertion merely that something may come to pass, or that he may gain a reputation for activity; for he never desires that something might merely happen, but that the will of the idea might be accomplished. Until it speaks, he too is silent: he has no voice but for it. He does not respect the old because it is old, yet just as little does he desire novelty for its own sake. He looks for what is better and more perfect than the present, and until this rises before him in its clarity, and as long as charge would lead only to difference and not improvement, then he remains inactive, and concedes to the old the privilege it derives from prior establishment.

In this way does the ideal wholly possess and pervade him, without intermission or reserve, and there remains nothing either of his person or in the course of his life that does not burn as a perpetual offering before its altar. Thus he is the most immediate manifestation [Erscheinung] of God in the world.

That there is a God is made evident by a very little serious reflection upon the external world. We must end at last by resting all existence which demands an extrinsic foundation upon a being the fountain of whose life is within himself; by allying the fugitive phenomena, seen as flowing changes on the stream of time, with something lasting and unchangeable. And the divinity appears immediately visible, and perceivable even through all outer senses, entering the world in the conduct of divine men. In their behaviour the unchangeableness of the divine nature manifests itself in the firmness and intrepidity of human will, which no power can force from its prescribed path. In it, God's inner clarity expresses itself in the human grasp and enveloping of all earthly things in the one which endures forever. In it God's influence expresses itself, not simply in happiness, which is not what God's influence consists in, but in the ordering, ennobling and dignifying of the human species. A divine life is the most decisive proof that man can give of the presence [Daseyn] of god.[9]

It is the business of all mankind to see that the conviction of the divine presence without which the very roots of their own being pass away into nothing, shall never perish and disappear from among them. Above all this is the business of the rulers as the highest disposers of human affairs. It is not their part to bring forward the theoretical proof from the grounds of reason, or to regulate the mode in which this proof shall be adduced by the second class of scholars;[10] but the practical [factische] proof falls to them to demonstrate in their own lives, and that in the highest degree. Declare for their authority and overall stability and sureness, for their all-seeing clarity, for their ordering and ennobling spirit for us, and we would then see God face to face in their works, and need no other proof. God is, we would say, for they are, and he is in them.

Lecture IX

OF THE ORAL SCHOLAR-TEACHER

Besides those possessors of the idea whose occupation it is to introduce the idea immediately into life by guiding and ordering the affairs of men, there is yet another class, namely those who are strictly speaking and by pre-eminence called scholars; they express the idea directly in concepts, and their calling is to maintain among men the conviction that there is, in truth, a divine idea accessible to human thought, to raise this idea unceasingly to greater clarity and precision, and thus to transmit it from generation to generation fresh and radiant in ever-renewed youth.

The latter calling again divides itself into two very different occupations, according to the immediate purpose in view and the mode of its attainment. Either the minds of men are to be trained and cultivated to a capacity for receiving the idea, or the idea itself is to be produced in a definite form for those who are already prepared for its reception. The first occupation has particular men for its primary and immediate objects. In it the only use that is made of the idea is as a means of training and cultivating these men so that they may become capable of comprehending it through itself and by their own independent effort. In this occupation it follows that regard must be had solely to the men who are to be cultivated; to the level of their culture and their capacity for being cultivated. In this context an influence is valuable only in so far as it may be efficiently applied to those individuals for whom it is especially intended.[11] The second occupation has for its object the idea itself, and the developing and fashioning of it into a distinct concept. It has no reference whatsoever to any subjective disposition or capacity of men, and has no one especially in view as particularly called to or fitted for the reception of the idea in the form thus given to it. Its production [Werk] itself settles and determines by itself who shall grasp it, and it is addressed only to those who can grasp it. The first object will be best and most fittingly attained by the verbal discourses of the scholar-educator; the second through scholarly writings. . . .

Lecture X

OF THE AUTHOR [SCHRIFTSTELLER]

To complete and close our overall survey of the calling of the scholar, we have today to speak of the calling of the author.

I have hitherto contented myself with setting forth purely and clearly the idea of the specific objects of my inquiry, without turning aside to glance at the actual state of things in the present age. It is almost impossible to proceed in this way with the subject I am to discuss today. The concept of the author is as good as unknown in our age, and something most unworthy usurps its name. This is the particular disgrace of the time, and the true source of all its other evils in the realm of knowledge. The inglorious has become glorious and is encouraged, honoured and rewarded.

According to the almost universally received opinion it is a merit and an honour for a man to have printed something, merely because he has printed it and without any regard for what it is that is thus printed and what its consequences might be. And those who, as the phrase goes, review the works of others – who undertake to announce the fact that somebody has printed something and to describe it – also lay claim to the highest rank in the republic of learning. It is almost inexplicable that such an absurd opinion could have arisen and taken root, when we consider the subject in its true light.

This is how the matter stands: in the latter half of the last century reading took the place of some other amusements which had gone out of fashion. This new luxury from time to time demanded new fashionable goods, for it is of course quite impossible that one should read over again something one has already read, or those things our forefathers have read before us, just as it would be altogether unbecoming to appear frequently in fashionable society in the same costume, or to dress according to the notions of one's grandfather. The new want gave birth to a new trade, striving to nourish and enrich itself by supplying the wares now in demand: namely, bookselling. The success of those who first undertook this trade encouraged others to engage in it, until in our own days it has come to the point that this mode of obtaining a livelihood is greatly overextended, and the quantity of goods produced is much too large in proportion to the consumers. Like the dealer in any other commodity, the book-merchant orders his goods from the manufacturer solely with the view of bringing them to the market. At times also he buys uncommissioned goods which have been manufactured only on speculation. The author who writes for the sake of writing is this manufacturer. It is impossible to conceive of a reason why the book manufacturer should take precedence over any other manufacturer; he ought rather to feel that he is far inferior to the others, in that the luxury to which he panders is more pernicious than others. It may indeed be useful and profitable to him that he find a merchant for his wares, but how it should be an honour is not easy to discover. Of course, no value can be set on the judgement of the publisher, which is only a judgement on the saleableness or unsaleableness of the goods.[12]

Amid this bustle and pressure of the literary trade, a lucky thought struck someone: that is, to make one periodical book out of all the books which were printed, so that the reader of this book might be spared the trouble of reading any other. It was fortunate that this last purpose was not entirely successful, and that everybody did not take to reading this last book exclusively, since then no others would have been bought and consequently no others printed, so that this book itself, being constantly reliant upon other books for the possibility of its own existence, must likewise have remained unprinted.

He who undertook such a work, commonly called a 'learned library' or 'literary gazette' etc., had the advantage of seeing his work prosper by the charitable contributions of many anonymous individuals, and of thus earning honour and profit by the labour of others. To veil his own poverty of ideas he pretended to pass judgement on the authors whom he quoted – a shallow pretence to the thinker who looks below the surface. For either the book is a bad book, as most books are at present, and printed only that there might be one more book in the world (and in this case it ought never to have been written, and is a nullity, and so any judgement upon it is a nullity also); or the book is the sort of work that we shall describe below as a true literary [schrift-

stellerisch] work, and then is the result of a whole energetic life devoted to art
or science, so that it would call for another entire life as energetic as the first to
be employed in its judgement. Final judgement cannot be passed upon such a
work in a couple of sheets put out within three or six months after its appearance. How can there be any honour in contributing to such collections? On
the contrary, a good mind will rather be disposed to labour on a connected
work, originated and planned out by itself, than to allow the current of its
thoughts to be interrupted by every temporary phenomenon, lasting only
until something else interrupts the interruption itself. The disposition to watch
the thoughts of others continually, and to hang our own attempts at thinking,
God willing, upon them, is a certain sign of immaturity and of a weak and
dependent ability [Talent]. Or does the honour lie in the fact that those who
undertake such works should consider us capable of filling the office of judge,
actually making it over to us? In fact their judgement goes no deeper than
that of a common unlettered printer, and applies to the saleableness or unsaleableness of the goods, and to the outward reputation which may thereby
accrue to their critical academy [Recensions-Institute].[13]

I am aware that what I have now said might seem very paradoxical. All of
us who are connected in any way with exact knowledge [Wissenschaft], which
in this connection may be termed literature [Literatur], grow up in the belief
that the literary industry is a blessing, an advantage, and an honourable
distinction of our cultivated and philosophical age. Very few have the power
to see through this presupposition and recognize its emptiness. The only
apparent circumstance that can be adduced in defence of such perverted
industry is in my opinion this: that thereby an extensive public is kept alive,
roused to attention, and as it were held together, so that should anything of
real value and importance be brought before it, a public shall be found
already in existence, and will not have to be first called together. But I answer
that, in the first place, the means appear much too extensive for the end
contemplated. It seems too great a sacrifice that many generations should
spend their time upon nothing in order that some future generation might be
able to occupy itself with something. Moreover it is by no means true that a
public is merely kept alive by this misdirected industry; it is at the same time
perverted, vitiated and ruined for the appreciation of anything truly valuable.
Much that is excellent has made its appearance in our age – I shall mention
only the Kantian philosophy – but this very industriousness of the literary
market has destroyed, perverted and degraded it so that its spirit has fled; now
only a ghost of it stalks about, which no one can venerate.

The scholarly history [Gelehrten-Geschichte] of our own day shows the real
thinker how writing for writing's sake may be honoured and applauded. A few
only excepted, our authors have in their writings borne worse testimony
against themselves than anyone else could have given against them. No even
moderately well-disposed person would be inclined to consider the writers of
our day so shallow, perverse and spiritless as the majority show themselves in

their works. The only way to retain any respect for this age, or any desire to influence it, is to assume that those who proclaim their opinions aloud are inferior men, and that only among those who keep silence may be found some who are capable of teaching better things.

Thus, when I speak of the literary calling, it is not the literary trade of our age that I mean, but something quite other than that.

I have already set forth the concept of authorship, in distinguishing it from that of the oral teacher of prospective scholars. Both have to express and communicate the idea in language, the latter for particular individuals by whose capacity for receiving it he must be guided, and the former without regard to any individual and in the most perfect form that can be given to it in his age.

The author must represent the idea, and he must therefore be a partaker of it. All works of authorship are either works of art [Kunst] or of science [Wissenschaft]. Whatever may be the subject of a work of the first class, it is evident that since it does not directly express any special concept and thus teaches the reader nothing, it can only awaken the idea within him and furnish it with a fitting embodiment; otherwise it would be but an empty play of words and have no real content.[14] And whatever may be the subject of a scientific work, the author of it must not conceive of scientific knowledge in a merely historical fashion, only as it is received from others; he must have worked through it ideally and for himself in some one of its aspects, and produce in it a self-creative, new and hitherto unknown form. If he be but a link in the chain of historical tradition, and can do no more than hand down to others the doctrine as he himself has received it, and only in the form in which it already exists in the work whence he has obtained it, then let him leave others in peace to draw from the fountain from which he has drawn. What need is there of his officious mediation and meddling? To do over again that which has been done already is to do nothing, and no man who possesses common honesty and conscientiousness will allow himself to indulge in such idleness. Can his age then furnish him with no occupation suited to his powers, that he must thus employ himself in doing what he need not do? It is not necessary that he write an entirely new work in some branch of scientific knowledge, but only a better work than any hitherto existing. He who cannot do this should, emphatically, not write; it is a crime, a want of honesty to do so, which at the most can be excused only by his thoughtlessness and utter lack of any true concept of the business he has undertaken.

He must express the idea in language, in an intelligible manner and in a perfect form. The idea must therefore have become in him so clear, living and independent, that it of itself speaks out to him in words and, penetrating to the innermost spirit of his language, frames thence an embodiment for itself by its own inherent force. The idea itself must speak, not the author. His will, his individuality, his peculiar method and art, all must disappear from his page, so that only the method and art of his idea may live the highest life that it can attain in his language and in his time. As he is free from the obligation under which the oral teacher works – to accommodate himself to the capacities of others – so he does not have this excuse to plead before himself. He has no specific reader in view; he constructs his reader and lays down to him the law which he must obey. There may be printed productions addressed only to a certain age and certain circle – we shall see afterwards under what conditions such writings may be necessary – but these do not belong to the class of essentially literary [schriftstellerisch] works of which we now speak; they are printed discourses, which are printed because the circle to which they are addressed cannot be brought together.

In order that the idea may thus in his person become master of his language, it is necessary that the author shall first have acquired a mastery over that language. The idea does not seize upon the language directly, but only through him as its possessor. This indispensable mastery of the author over his language is acquired only by preparatory exercises, long continued and persevered in, which are studies for future works but have in themselves no essential value. The conscientious scholar writes them, indeed, but will never allow them to be printed. It requires, I say, long and persevering exercise; but happily these conditions mutually promote each other. As the idea becomes more vivid, language spontaneously appears, and as facility of expression is increased the idea flows forth in greater clarity.

These are the first and most necessary conditions of all true authorship. The idea itself – to express his idea in language in a particular way – is that which lives in him, and alone lives in him within whom the presentiment has arisen that he may one day send forth a literary work. It is this which drives him on in his preparations for that work, as well as in the future completion of his design.

By this idea he is inspired with a dignified and sacred conviction in the literary calling. The work of the oral scholar-teacher is in its immediate application only a work for its time, modified by the degree of culture possessed by those who are entrusted to his care. Only in so far as he can venture to suppose that he is cultivating future teachers worthy of their calling, who in their turn will train others for the same task, and so on without end, can he regard himself as working for eternity. But the work of the author is in itself a work for eternity. Even should future ages transcend the knowledge [Wissenschaft] expressed in his work, he has not therein recorded this knowledge alone, but also the fixed and settled character of his age in relation to it; and this will preserve its interest as long as the human race endures. Independent of all vicissitude and change, his characters [Buchstabe] speak in every age to all men who are able to make them live, and thus they continue their inspiring, elevating and ennobling work even to the end of time.[15]

The idea, in this its acknowledged sacredness, drives him on, and it alone drives him. He does not believe that he has attained anything until he has attained all, until his work stands before him in the purity and perfectness he has striven to attain. Devoid of love for his own person, and faithfully devoted to the idea by which he is constantly guided, he recognizes with certain vision and in its true character every trace of his former nature which remains in his expression of the idea, and strives unceasingly to free himself from it. As long as he is not conscious of this absolute freedom and purity, he has not attained his end, but still works on. In such an age as we have already described, where the quotation [Notiz] of knowledge has greatly increased and has even fallen into the hands of some who are better fitted for any occupation than for this one, it may be necessary for him to give some preliminary account of his labours. Other modes of communication, such as for example that of the oral scholar-teacher, may require such a preliminary account from him. But he will never put forth these required writings for anything else than what they are: preliminary announcements adapted to a certain age and certain circumstances. He will never regard them as finished works destined for immortality.

The idea alone drives him on, and nothing else. All personal concerns have disappeared from his sight. I do not speak of his own person, and of his having entirely forgotten himself in his purpose; this has already been sufficiently explained. But the personality of others has no more weight with him than his own, as against the truth and the idea. I do not mention his not encroaching upon the rights of other scholars or authors in their civic or personal relations. That is altogether below the dignity of one who has to do with real facts [Sache], and it is also below the dignity of these discourses to make mention of it.[16] But this I will say: that he will not allow himself to be restrained by forbearance towards any person whatsoever from demolishing error and establishing truth in its place. The worst insult that can be offered, even to a half-reasoning man, is to suppose that he can be offended by the exposure of an error he has entertained, or the proclamation of a truth which has escaped his notice. From this bold and open profession of truth as he recognizes it, without regard to any man, he will allow nothing to lead him away, not even the politely expressed contempt of the so-called fashionable world which can conceive of the literary calling only by analogy with its own social circles, and would impose the etiquette of the court upon the conduct of the scholar.

Here I close these lectures. If one of my thoughts has entered into any now present, and shall abide there as a guide to something better, then perhaps it may sometimes awaken the memory of these lectures and of me. Only in this way do I desire to live in your recollection.

Part 3

Schelling

Friedrich Wilhelm Joseph von Schelling

(1775–1854)

After a theological education during which he enjoyed the company and friendship of Hegel and Hölderlin (see Nauern, 1971), Schelling was appointed at the age of twenty-three to a professorship at Jena, where he became the colleague of Fichte and soon the friend of Schiller, Tieck, Goethe and others; he married A.W. Schlegel's divorced wife Caroline in 1803. After professorships at Würzburg, Munich and Erlangen, he moved to Berlin in 1841.

Like Fichte, Schelling is relatively unfamiliar to the English-speaking tradition; it is only recently that a translation of the major work of his early period, the *System of Transcendental Idealism*, has appeared (1978). His thought is difficult, partly because it is more than usually uncongenial to English-speaking philosophical preoccupations, tending as it does toward a synthesis of everything (self, nature, science and religion), and partly because scholars have had to concentrate on the task of plotting the different phases of Schelling's career, which has become something of a nightmare question for historians of philosophy. In the context of scientific theory Schelling is perhaps the major exponent of the *Naturphilosophie* (at least among the philosophers), purporting as it does to establish the grounds of an inner connection between all forms of life and expression on organic and dynamic principles. Although this may seem remote to us its intentions are not totally at odds with the ambitions of those among modern physicists engaged in the search for a unified field theory, and it has been argued that Schelling's writings might have had a formative effect on, for example, the discovery of electro-magnetism by Oersted: see Esposito (1977), pp. 137ff. In theology, Schelling's gradual elucidation of an element of evil was an important incorporation of a traditional problem into the spectrum of Idealism. In epistemology, his continuation and elaboration of Fichte's conviction of the simultaneous positing of self and other proved to be an important stage in the gradual bringing together of subjectivity and nature – a trend which indeed became much less gradual thanks to Schelling. In fact, it is with Schelling that German Romantic philosophy becomes most fully idealist, and it is also with Schelling that aesthetics are for the first and only time allowed to stand with philosophy as the ultimate and absolute expression of what is true and of value.

Further reading

Despite his obscurity and difficulty, it is also arguable that Schelling had a greater and more immediate influence on the English tradition than any of the other philosophers represented in this anthology, by virtue of Coleridge's famous borrowings (but see the general introduction for Coleridge's reservations about this). On his importance in this respect, see Wellek (1931), pp. 95–102; Orsini (1969), pp. 192–237; McFarland (1969), pp. 146ff.; Ashton (1980), pp. 53–5; and for his typological suitability to an elucidation of English Romanticism, see Hirsch (1960). Lewes (1857), pp. 591f. may be consulted for a (brief) mid-century view of Schelling's general contribution to philosophy; for a more up to date account, see Copleston (1965a), pp. 121–82. Two recent studies in English may also be recommended (although they restrict their focus, much can be learned from them): Esposito (1977) and Brown (1977). See also Seidel (1976) and Nauern (1971).

There are no extended accounts of Schelling's aesthetics in English. Wellek (1955), II, 74–82, manages to say a great deal in very little space; and Engell (1981), pp. 301–27, is very helpful within the limits of its chosen topic, the imagination. Fackenheim (1954) has transcribed the leading ideas of Schelling's untranslated lecture series of 1802–3 and 1804–5, on the *Philosophy of Art* (selections from which appear below), and there is a longer and more detailed paraphrase in Gibelin (1933).

For translations of Schelling's works into English – and there is much still to be done here if we are to have a representation of the range of his thought – see the bibliography: Schelling (1936), (1942), (1966), (1974), (1978), (1980). See also the bibliography by Schneeberger (1954).

Conclusion to
System of Transcendental Idealism
[*System des transcendentalen Idealismus*]

1800

Concluding sections

Translated by Albert Hofstadter (very slightly modified) in Hofstadter and Kuhns (1964), pp. 362–77.

German text in *Sämtliche Werke* (1856–61), III, 612ff.

Introductory note

By the time he published the *System of Transcendental Idealism* in 1800, Schelling had already initiated the exposition of his philosophy of nature, which removed the hypothetical element from the argument of Kant's 'Critique of Teleological Judgement' and put forward as a matter of fact that nature is a coherent and self-evolving system moving toward ends in a purposive way. In this work, broadly speaking, he explores the implications of this philosophy for self-consciousness, starting *from* self-consciousness in the true spirit of the transcendental method as maintained by Fichte. Before the final sections, here translated, Schelling has worked through all the primitive and developing stages of self-consciousness in its positing of the not-self, or objective world, and the consequent reflective intuition of self as free intelligence. The *System* is one of the masterpieces of German Idealism, both in itself and because of its important prefiguring of some of the central issues in Hegel's philosophy: it incorporates an argued recognition of other selves and the element of biographical and historical time, as well as a wider social dimension of ethics and politics – synthesizing into a single argument subjects which Fichte had tended to deal with separately, albeit synoptically.

What makes the *System* unique from our particular point of view is that it is the only major philosophical text to argue for aesthetics and the fine arts as the pinnacle and conclusive representation of its insights. As early as 1796, in his prospectus for a system of philosophy, Schelling had been emphatic about the role of aesthetics:

I am convinced that the highest act of reason, the one in which she encompasses all Ideas, is an aesthetic act . . . The philosopher must possess just as much aesthetic power as the poet . . . the poetic act alone will outlive all the arts and sciences.

Schelling (1966), pp. xii–xiii

Much of the thinking behind this assertion seems to have to do with the capacity of the art object to reach a wider public than abstract philosophy alone can do:

Unless we have made the Ideas aesthetic, i.e. mythological, they are of no interest to the people; and conversely, until mythology has been made rational, the philosopher can only be ashamed of it.

Schelling (1966), p. xiii

What is envisaged here, at the tender age of twenty-one, is remarkably coherent as a forecasting of Schelling's preoccupations over the years to come: a synthesis of art and philosophy, representative as they are of the same truths in different ways, and a relation of both to the available body of shareable representations held in common by a community: a "mythology".

In the *System*, as we see from what follows, art is argued to be superior to philosophy – though on other occasions they are ranked equally – for its effectiveness in representing objectively the union of mind and nature, spirit and matter; or rather, in making it clear that the mind that is in nature is identifiable with the nature that is in the mind.

Section VI

DEDUCTION OF A UNIVERSAL ORGAN OF PHILOSOPHY, OR MAIN PROPOSITIONS OF THE PHILOSOPHY OF ART ACCORDING TO PRINCIPLES OF TRANSCENDENTAL IDEALISM

1. Deduction of the art product in general

The postulated intuition [Anschauung][1] should comprehend what exists separated in the appearance of freedom and in the intuition of the product of nature, namely, *identity of conscious and unconscious in the ego* and *consciousness of this identity*. The product of this intuition will thus be contiguous on the one side with the product of nature and on the other side with the product of freedom, and it will have to unite within itself the characteristics of both. If we know the product of intuition, then we also know the intuition itself. We therefore need only deduce the product in order to deduce the intuition.

The product will have in common with the product of freedom the fact that it is produced with conscious intent, and with the product of nature that it is produced unconsciously.[2] In the first respect it will consequently be the inverse of the organic product of nature. If unconscious (blind) activity is reflected as conscious by the organic product then inversely by the product here discussed conscious activity will be reflected as unconscious (objective); or, if the organic product reflects for me unconscious activity as determined by conscious activity, then inversely, the product which is here deduced will reflect conscious activity as determined by unconscious activity. More briefly: nature begins unconscious and ends conscious; its production is not *purposive* [zweckmässig] but its product indeed is. The ego, in the activity here discussed, must begin with consciousness (subjectively) and end in the unconscious, or *objectively*; the ego is conscious as regards production, unconscious as regards the product.[3]

How shall *we*, however, explain transcendentally for ourselves an intuition of this nature, in which unconscious activity, as it were, works its way through conscious activity to perfect identity with it? We reflect first on the fact that the activity is supposed to be a conscious one. Now it is plainly impossible that something objective should be produced with consciousness, which nevertheless is here required. Only what arises unconsciously is objective; the genuinely objective element in that intuition therefore cannot be introduced by means of *consciousness*. On this point we may appeal immediately to the proofs that have already been adduced in regard to free action, namely, that the objective element in free action arises in it by force of something independent of freedom.[4] The difference is merely this: (a) that in free action the identity of both activities must be annulled [aufgehoben] precisely in order that the action should thereby appear as free: here, on the other hand, in *consciousness* itself, and without the negation of consciousness, both should appear as one. Also (b) the two activities in free action can *never* become absolutely identical. Hence, again, the object of free action is necessarily an *infinite* one, never fully realized; for were it fully realized, then the conscious and the objective activity would collapse into one, i.e., the appearance of *freedom* would vanish.[5] Now what was simply impossible through freedom is to be possible through the action here postulated, which, however, just on this account, must cease to be a free action and become one in which freedom and necessity are absolutely united. But the production was to have occurred with consciousness, which is impossible unless both the activities are separated. Here, therefore, is a clear contradiction. I shall set it forth once more. Conscious and unconscious activity are to be absolutely one in the product, just as they are also in the organic product; but they are to be one in a different way – both are to be one *for the ego itself*. But this is impossible unless the ego is conscious of the production. But if the ego is conscious of the production, then the two activities must be separate, since this is a necessary condition for consciousness of production. The two activities must therefore be one, for otherwise there is no identity; the two must be separate, for otherwise there is identity, but not for the ego. How is this contradiction to be resolved?

Both activities must be separated for the sake of the appearance, the objectivation [Objektivwerdens] of production, just as they must be separated in free action for the sake of the objectivation of intuition. But they cannot be separate *to infinity*, as in free action, because the objective phase would then never be a complete representation of the relevant identity.[6] The identity of the two was to have been broken up only for the sake of consciousness, but the production is to end in unconsciousness. Hence there must be a point where both fall together into one and conversely, where both fall together into one, the production must cease to appear free.

Once this point in the production is arrived at, the productive process must cease absolutely, and it must be impossible for the producer to continue to produce. For the condition of all producing is just the opposition of conscious and unconscious activity, whereas these are here supposed to meet absolutely; so that in intelligence all strife is ended, all contradiction resolved.

Intelligence will thus terminate in full recognition of the identity expressed in the product, as one whose principle lies in itself; i.e., it will terminate in a complete self-intuition. Now since it was the free tendency to self-intuition in this identity that originally brought about the self-estrangement of intelligence, the feeling that accompanies this intuition will be a feeling of infinite satisfaction. The whole productive drive [Trieb zu produciren] comes to rest with the completion of the product; all contradictions are resolved [aufgehoben], all riddles unravelled. Since the production proceeded from freedom, i.e., from an infinite opposition of the two activities, intelligence will not be able to ascribe to *freedom* the absolute unification of the two in which the production ends. For simultaneously with the completion of the product all appearance of freedom is removed; intelligence will feel itself surprised and *blessed* by that unification, i.e., it will regard it as though it were a freely bestowed favour of a higher nature that has by means of it made the impossible possible.

But this unknown, which here brings objective and conscious activity into unexpected harmony, is none other than that Absolute which contains the universal ground of the pre-established harmony between the conscious and the unconscious. If, then, this Absolute is reflected from the product, it will appear to intelligence as something above it and which itself, in opposition to freedom, adds the element of purposelessness to that which was begun with consciousness and purposeful intention.[7]

This unchangeable identity, which cannot arrive at consciousness and is only reflected from the product, is for the producer exactly what destiny is for the actor, i.e., an obscure unknown power that adds the element of perfection, completion, or objectivity to the fragmentary work of freedom. And, as the power that realizes *non-prefigured* ends by means of our free action without our knowledge, indeed itself against our will, is called destiny, so the incomprehensible principle which adds the objective to the conscious without the cooperation of freedom and in a certain way in opposition to freedom, in which what is united in the above-mentioned eternally flees from itself, is signified by the obscure concept of *genius* [*Genie*].[8]

The postulated product is none other than the product of genius, or, since genius is possible only in art, the *product of art*.

The deduction is finished and we now have nothing to do but show by a complete analysis that all the characteristic traits of the postulated production converge in the aesthetic process.

That all aesthetic production rests on an opposition of activities may properly be inferred from the declaration by all artists that they are involuntarily impelled to the creation of their works, that they merely satisfy an irresistible impulse of their nature through such production. For if every impulse originates in a contradiction in such a way that, given the contradiction, the free activity occurs involuntarily, then the artistic impulse must also proceed from such a feeling of an inner contradiction. But this contradiction, since it sets into motion the whole man with all his powers, is without doubt a contradiction that seizes upon the *ultimate in him*, the root of his entire existence. It is as though in the rare persons who are, above all others, artists in the highest sense of the word, the immutable identity, on which all existence rests, has put off the raiment with which it clothes itself in others and now, just as it is immediately affected by things, with equal immediacy reaffects everything. Consequently it can only be the contradiction between the conscious and the unconscious in free action that sets the artistic impulse into motion, just as, once more, it can only be given to art to satisfy our infinite striving as well as to resolve the ultimate and most extreme contradiction in us.

Just as aesthetic production starts from the feeling of an apparently irresolvable contradiction, so, according to the testimony of all artists and of all who participate in their inspiration, it comes to a close in the feeling of an *infinite* harmony. That this feeling, which accompanies the closure, is at the same time an *emotion*, a being *moved* [*Rührung*], already demonstrates that the artist ascribes the complete resolution of the contradiction which he discovers in his work not [alone] to himself but to a spontaneous gift of his nature; which, however inexorably it sets him into contradiction with himself, with equal grace removes the pain of this contradiction from him. For just as the artist is driven to production involuntarily and even against his inner resistance (hence the maxims among the ancients: *pati Deum*, etc.,[9] and hence in general the image of being inspired by a breath from without), so the objective element comes about in his production as though without his co-operation, i.e., itself in a purely objective way. Just as the fateful man does not accomplish what he intends or has in view, but rather what he must, by an incomprehensible destiny under whose influence he stands, so the artist, however specifically purposeful he may be, nevertheless, in regard to what is truly objective in his creation, seems to stand under the influence of a power that sets him apart from all other men and compels him to express or represent things he does not himself fully see through and whose meaning is infinite. Now since that absolute confluence of the two mutually fleeing activities is not at all further explicable, but is merely an *appearance*, which, though incomprehensible, cannot be denied, art is the sole and eternal revelation that exists and the miracle which, even if it had existed only once, must have persuaded us of the absolute reality of that highest principle.

Moreover, if art is brought to completion by two thoroughly different activities, then genius is neither the one nor the other but that which is above both. If we must seek in one of these two activities, namely conscious activity, for what is usually called *art*, but which is merely one part of art, namely, the part that is practised with consciousness, deliberation, and reflection, which can also be taught and learned, received from others, and attained by one's own practice, then, on the other hand, we must seek in the unconscious, which also enters into art, for that in art which cannot be learned, cannot be attained by practice or in any other way, but can only be inborn by the free gift of nature, and which is what we may call in one word the *poetry* [*Poesie*] in art.[10]

Obviously, then, it would be utterly futile to ask which of the two constituents is prior to the other; for in fact either without the other has no value and only the two in conjunction can bring forth the highest. For though that which cannot be achieved by practice but is native with us is generally considered the nobler of the two, the gods have so firmly tied the exercise of that original power to painstaking human effort, to industry and deliberation, that without art, poetry, even where it is innate, produces only products that appear lifeless, in which no human understanding can take delight, and which repel all judgement and even intuition by the completely blind force at work in them. On the contrary, it is rather to be expected that art might be able to accomplish something without poetry than poetry without art, partly because a person can hardly be by nature devoid of poetry, while many have no art, and partly because persistent study of the ideas of the great masters can to some degree compensate for an original lack of objective power.[11] Still, only a semblance of poetry can arise in this way, which is easily distinguishable by its superficiality, in contrast with the inexhaustible depth which the true artist, though he works with the greatest presence of mind [Besonnenheit],[12] puts into his work involuntarily and which neither he nor anyone else is able to penetrate completely. There are also many other characteristics by which such mere semblance of poetry is distinguishable, e.g., the great value it places on the merely mechanical features of art, the poverty of the form in which it moves itself, etc.

It is evident also that as neither poetry nor art can produce a perfected work singly each by itself, so the two existing in separation cannot produce such a work. Consequently, because the identity of the two can only be original, and is absolutely impossible and unattainable through freedom, the complete work of art is possible only through genius, which for this reason is for aesthetics what the ego is for philosophy, namely, that which is highest, absolutely real, which itself never becomes objective but is the cause of everything objective.[13]

2. Character of the art product

(A) The work of art reflects for us the identity of conscious and unconscious activity. But the opposition of the two is infinite, and it is overcome [aufgehoben] without any contribution of freedom. The basic character of the work of art is thus an *unconscious infinity* (synthesis of nature and freedom). The artist seems to have presented in his work, as if instinctively, apart from what he has put into it with obvious intent, an infinity which no finite understanding can fully unfold. To make this clear to ourselves merely by one example, Greek mythology – of which it is undeniable that it includes within itself an infinite meaning and symbols for all Ideas – arose among a people and in a manner both of which make it impossible to assume any thorough-going intentionality [Absichtlichkeit] in its discovery and in the harmony with which everything is unified into a single great whole. So it is with every true work of art: each is susceptible of infinite interpretation, as though there were an infinity of intentions within it, yet we cannot at all tell whether this infinity lay in the artist himself or whether it resides solely in the art-work. On the other hand, in a product that merely simulates the character of a work of art, intention and rule lie on the surface and appear so limited and bounded that the product is nothing other than a faithful impression of the conscious activity of the artist and is altogether merely an object for reflection, but not for intuition, which loves to immerse itself in what it intuits and can come to rest only in the infinite.[14]

(B) Every aesthetic production starts from the feeling of an infinite contradiction. Hence also the feeling that accompanies the completion of the art product must be the feeling of such a satisfaction, and this feeling must in turn go over into the work of art itself. The outward expression of the work of art is therefore the expression of repose and of quiet grandeur, even where the greatest tension of pain or of joy is to be expressed.[15]

(C) Every aesthetic production starts from an intrinsically infinite separation of both activities, which are separated in every free production. Since, however, both these activities are to be presented in the product as united, an infinite will be finitely presented by this product. But the infinite finitely presented is beauty. The basic character of every work of art, which comprehends within itself both of the foregoing characters, is therefore *beauty*, and without beauty there is no work of art. For although there are sublime works of art as well, and beauty and sublimity are in a certain respect opposite (in that a natural scene, for instance, can be beautiful without thereby being sublime, and conversely), still the opposition between beauty and sublimity is one that occurs only in regard to the object and not in regard to the subject of intuition. For the difference between a beautiful and a sublime work of art rests only on the fact that where beauty exists the infinite contradiction is resolved [aufgehoben] in the object itself, whereas where sublimity exists the contradiction is not unified in the object itself but is merely raised to a level at which it involuntarily overcomes itself [sich aufhebt] in the intuition, which then is as good as if it were *removed* [*aufgehoben*] from the object. It can also be shown easily that sublimity rests on the same contradiction as beauty. For whenever an object is called sublime, a magnitude is apprehended by unconscious activity which cannot be apprehended in conscious activity; the ego is thereby set into a conflict with itself which can end only in an aesthetic intuition that places both activities in an unanticipated harmony. However, the intuition, which lies here not in the artist but in the intuiting subject itself, is completely involuntary, because the sublime (quite unlike the merely marvellous, which likewise poses the imagination with a contradiction which, however, it is not worth the effort to resolve) sets all the powers of the mind in motion in order to resolve the contradiction that threatens one's entire intellectual existence.[16]

Now that the characteristics of the work of art have been derived, its *difference* from all other products has also been brought to light.

For the work of art distinguishes itself from the organic product of nature chiefly by the fact that (a) the organic being presents still unseparated what aesthetic production presents after separation but united; (b) organic production does not start out from consciousness, hence also not from an infinite

contradiction, which is a condition of aesthetic production. The organic product of nature will therefore also not necessarily be *beautiful* if beauty is exclusively the resolution of an infinite contradiction; and if it is beautiful, then its
beauty will seem simply accidental, because the condition of its existence
cannot be thought of as existing in nature. From this the altogether unique
interest in natural beauty – not in so far as it is beauty in general but in so far
as it is definitely *natural* beauty – can be explained. Our view regarding the
imitation of nature as the principle of art becomes clear from the foregoing.
For far from its being the case that a merely accidentally beautiful nature
should give the rule of art, what art produces in its perfection is the principle
and the norm for judging the beauty of nature.[17]

It is easy to determine what the distinction is between the aesthetic product
and the *ordinary art product*. In its principle, all aesthetic production is absolutely free, since the artist can indeed be impelled to produce by a contradiction, but only by one that lies in the highest region of his own nature, whereas
all other production is occasioned by a contradiction that lies outside the real
producer and hence all such production has its end outside itself. From its
independence of external ends there springs the sanctity and purity of art.
This goes so far that it excludes not only affinity with everything that is merely
sensuous enjoyment (to demand which of art is the peculiar characteristic of
barbarism), or with the useful (to demand which is possible only to an age
that places the highest efforts of the human spirit in economic discoveries), but
even affinity with everything that belongs to morality. Indeed, it leaves far
below it science itself, which in view of its disinterestedness borders most
closely upon art, merely because it is always directed to a goal beyond itself
and in the end must itself serve as a mere means for the highest, i.e. art.[18]

As for the relation of art to science in particular, they are both so opposed in
tendency that, were science ever to have accomplished its whole task as art
always has accomplished its, both would have to converge and become one –
which is the proof of completely opposite tendencies. For although science, in
its highest function, has one and the same problem as art, yet this problem,
because of the manner of its solution, is an infinite one for science. We can thus
say that art is the model [Vorbild] for science, and wherever art may be, there
science must first join it.[19] From this we can see why and to what extent there
is no genius in the sciences, not because it would be impossible for a scientific
problem to be solved in a "genial" way, but because the very problem whose
solution can be discovered by genius is also soluble mechanically. Of such a
sort, e.g., is the Newtonian system of gravitation, which could have been a
'genial' discovery – and in its first discoverer, Kepler, really was – but could
equally well have been a wholly scientific [scientifische] discovery, as it became through Newton. Only what art produces is possible *solely* and alone
through genius, because in every task that art has fulfilled an infinite contradiction has been resolved. What science produces *can* be produced by genius,
but it is not necessarily so produced. Genius, therefore, is and remains prob-

lematic in science, i.e., one can always definitely say where it is not, but never where it is. There are only a few characteristic traits from which we can deduce a genius in science. (That we have to deduce it already demonstrates a wholly unique state of affairs here.) E.g., genius is certainly not present where a whole, such as a system, arises part by part and as if by composition. Conversely, genius would have to be presupposed wherever it is clear that the idea of the whole has preceded the individual parts. For, since the idea of the whole cannot grow distinct except by unfolding itself in the individual parts, while, again, the individual parts are possible only through the idea of the whole, there appears to be a contradiction here which is possible only through an act of genius, i.e., through an unexpected confluence of unconscious and conscious activity. Another reason for imputing genius in science would be if someone were to say and assert things whose meaning he could not have wholly penetrated (whether in view of the time in which he lived or in comparison with his other utterances), where he thus expressed something apparently with consciousness which, nevertheless, he could only have expressed unconsciously. Yet that these grounds of imputation can be highly deceptive can easily be demonstrated in a number of ways.

Genius is differentiated from everything that is mere talent [Talent] or skill by the fact that it resolves a contradiction which is absolute and resolvable by nothing else.[20] In all production, even in the most ordinary every-day variety, an unconscious activity works together with conscious activity; but only a production whose condition was an infinite opposition of both activities is aesthetic and is possible *only* through genius.

3. Corollaries

Having derived the nature and character of the art product as fully as was required for the present investigation, nothing remains but to give an account of the relation in which the philosophy of art stands to the whole system of philosophy in general.

1. Philosophy as a whole starts from, and must start from, a principle which, as the absolute identity, is completely nonobjective. How then is this absolutely nonobjective principle to be evoked in consciousness and understood, which is necessary if it is the condition of understanding the whole of philosophy? No proof is needed of the impossibility of apprehending or presenting it by means of concepts [Begriffe]. Nothing remains, therefore, but that it be presented in an immediate intuition; yet this itself seems incomprehensible and, since its object is supposed to be something absolutely nonobjective, even self-contradictory. If, however, there were nevertheless such an intuition, which had as object that which was absolutely identical, in itself neither subjective nor objective, and if on behalf of this intuition, which can only be an intellectual intuition, one were to appeal to immediate experience, by what means could this intuition be established as objective, i.e., how could we establish beyond doubt that it does

not rest on a merely subjective illusion, unless there were an objectivity belonging to the intuition which was universal and acknowledged by all men? This universally acknowledged and thoroughly undeniable objectivity of intellectual intuition is art itself. For aesthetic intuition is precisely intellectual intuition become objective.[21] The work of art merely reflects to me what is otherwise reflected by nothing, that absolutely identical principle which has already divided itself in the ego. Thus what for the philosopher divides itself already in the first act of consciousness, and which is otherwise inaccessible to any intuition, shines back to us from its products by the miracle of art.

But not only the first principle of philosophy and the first intuition from which it proceeds, but also the whole mechanism which philosophy deduces and on which it itself rests, becomes objective for the first time through aesthetic production.

Philosophy starts out from an infinite dichotomy of opposed activities; but all aesthetic production rests on the same dichotomy, which latter is completely resolved [aufgehoben] by each artistic representation. What then is the marvellous faculty by which, according to the assertions of philosophers, an infinite opposition annuls itself [sich aufhebt] in productive intuition? We have until now been unable to make this mechanism fully comprehensible because it is only the faculty of art that can fully disclose it. This productive faculty under consideration is the same as that by which art also attains to the impossible, namely, to resolve [aufzuheben] an infinite contradiction in a finite product. It is the poetic faculty which, in the first potency, is original intuition, and conversely it is only productive intuition repeating itself in the highest potency that we call the poetic faculty.[22] It is one and the same thing that is active in both, the sole capacity by which we are able to think and comprehend even what is contradictory – the imagination [Einbildungskraft].[23] Hence also it is products of one and the same activity that appear to us beyond consciousness as real and on the hither side of consciousness as ideal or as a world of art. But precisely this fact, that under otherwise entirely identical conditions of origin, the genesis of one lies beyond consciousness and that of the other on this side of consciousness, constitutes the eternal and ineradicable difference between the two.

For while the real world proceeds wholly from the same original opposition as that from which the world of art must proceed (bearing in mind that the art world must also be thought of as a single great whole, and presents in all of its individual products only the one infinite), nevertheless the opposition beyond consciousness is infinite only to the extent that an infinite is presented by the objective world as a *whole* and never by the individual object, whereas for art the opposition is infinite in regard to *each individual object*, and every single product of art presents infinity. For if aesthetic production proceeds from freedom, and if the opposition of conscious and unconscious activity is absolute precisely for freedom, then there exists really only a single absolute work of art, which can to be sure exist in entirely different exemplars but which yet is only one, even though it should not yet exist in its most original form. To this view it cannot be objected that it would be inconsistent with the great freedom with which the predicate "work of art" is used. That which does not present an infinite immediately or at least in reflection is not a work of art. Shall we, e.g., also call poems works of art that by their nature present merely what is individual and subjective? Then we shall also have to apply the name to every epigram that records a merely momentary feeling or current impression.[24] Yet the great masters who worked in these literary types sought to achieve objectivity only through the *whole* of their writings, and used them only as means whereby to represent a whole infinite life and to reflect it by a many-faceted mirror.

2. If aesthetic intuition is only intellectual intuition become objective, then it is evident that art is the sole true and eternal organon as well as document of philosophy, which sets forth in ever fresh forms what philosophy cannot represent outwardly, namely, the unconscious in action and production and its original identity with the conscious. For this very reason art occupies the highest place for the philosopher, since it opens to him, as it were, the holy of holies where in eternal and primal union, as in a single flame, there burns what is sundered in nature and history and what must eternally flee from itself in life and action as in thought. The view of nature which the philosopher composes artificially [künstlich] is, for art [Kunst], original and natural. What we call nature is a poem that lies hidden in a mysterious and marvellous script. Yet if the riddle could reveal itself, we would recognize in it the Odyssey of the spirit which, in a strange delusion, seeking itself, flees itself; for the land of phantasy [Phantasie] toward which we aspire gleams through the world of sense only as through a half-transparent mist, only as a meaning does through words. When a great painting comes into being it is as though the invisible curtain that separates the real from the ideal world is raised [aufgehoben]; it is merely the opening through which the characters and places of the world of fantasy, which shimmers only imperfectly through the real world, fully come upon the stage. Nature is nothing more to the artist than it is to the philosopher; it is merely the ideal world appearing under unchanging limitations, or it is merely the imperfect reflection of a world that exists not outside but within him.

What is the derivation of this affinity of philosophy and art, despite their opposition? This question is already sufficiently answered by the foregoing.

We conclude therefore with the following observation. A system is completed when it has returned to its starting point. But this is precisely the case with our system. For it is just that original ground of all harmony of the subjective and the objective which could be presented in its original identity only by intellectual intuition, that was fully brought forth from the subjective and became altogether objective by means of the work of art, in such a way that we have conducted our object, the ego itself, gradually to the point at which we ourselves stood when we began to philosophize.

But now, if it is art alone that can succeed in making objective with universal validity what the philosopher can only represent subjectively, then it is to be expected (to draw this further inference) that as philosophy, and with it all the sciences that were brought to perfection by it, was born from and nurtured by poetry in the childhood of science, so now after their completion they will return as just so many individual streams to the universal ocean of poetry from which they started out. On the whole it is not difficult to say what will be the intermediate stage in the return of science to poetry, since one such intermediate stage existed in mythology before this seemingly irresolvable breach occurred. But how a new mythology (which cannot be the invention of an individual poet but only of a new generation that represents things as if it were a single poet) can itself arise, is a problem for whose solution we must look to the future destiny of the world and the further course of history alone.[25]

General observation on the whole system

If the reader who has followed our progress attentively up to this point once more contemplates the organization of the whole, he will doubtless make the following observations.

The entire system falls between two extremes, of which one is characterized by intellectual and the other by aesthetic intuition. What intellectual intuition is for the philosopher, aesthetic intuition is for his object. The former, since it is necessary merely for the particular orientation of mind [Geist] adopted in philosophizing, does not at all occur in ordinary consciousness. The latter, since it is nothing but intellectual intuition become objective or universally valid, *can* at least occur in every consciousness. But this also makes it possible to see that and why philosophy *as* philosophy can never be universally valid. Absolute objectivity is given to art alone. If art is deprived of objectivity, one may say, it ceases to be what it is and becomes philosophy; give objectivity to philosophy, it ceases to be philosophy and becomes art. Philosophy, to be sure, reaches the highest level, but it brings only, as it were, a fragment of man to this point. Art brings *the whole man*, as he is, to that point, namely to a knowledge of the highest of all, and on this rests the eternal difference and the miracle of art.

Furthermore, the whole continuity of transcendental philosophy rests merely on a continuous potentiation of self-intuition, from the first, simplest stage in self-consciousness to the highest stage, the aesthetic.

The following are the potencies that the object of philosophy traverses so as to produce the total structure of self-consciousness.

The act of self-consciousness in which at the beginning the absolutely identical principle divides itself is nothing but an act of *self-intuition in general*. Consequently, nothing definite can yet be posited by this act in the ego, since it is only through it that all definiteness in general is posited. In this first act the identity first becomes subject and object simultaneously, i.e., it becomes in general ego – not for itself but for philosophizing reflection.

(What the identity is abstracted from and, as it were, might be *before* this act, cannot at all be asked. For it is that which can reveal itself *only* through self-consciousness and can in no way separate itself from this act.)

The second self-intuition is that by which the ego intuits the definiteness posited in the objective aspect of its activity, which occurs in sensation. In this intuition the ego is *an object for itself*, whereas in the preceding one it was object and subject only for the philosopher.

In the third self-intuition the ego becomes an object for itself also as sensing, i.e., the previously subjective phase in the ego is transposed into an objective phase. Everything in the ego, consequently, is now objective, or the ego is *wholly* objective and *as* objective it is simultaneously subject and object.

From this moment of consciousness nothing will therefore be able to remain behind except what exists, in accordance with the consciousness that has already arisen, as the absolutely objective (the external world). In this intuition, which is already potentiated and for that very reason productive, there is contained in addition to the objective and subjective activities which are *both* objective here, still a third, a genuinely intuiting or *ideal* activity, the very same as later comes to view as *conscious* activity. But since it is merely the third of the other two, it cannot separate itself from them nor be set in opposition to them. Thus there is a conscious activity already comprised in this intuition, or the unconscious objective element is determined by a conscious activity, except that the latter is not differentiated as such.

The following intuition will be that by which the ego intuits itself as productive. However, since the ego is now *merely* objective, this intuition will also be *merely* objective, i.e., once again unconscious. There is indeed in this intuition an ideal activity which has as its objective the intuiting, virtually ideal activity comprised within the preceding intuition; the intuiting activity here is thus an ideal one to the second potency, i.e., a purposive activity which is, however, unconsciously purposive. What remains behind of this intuition in consciousness will thus indeed appear as purposive, but not as a purposively produced product. Such a result is *organization* [*Organisation*] throughout its entire range.[26]

By the way of these four stages the ego is completed as intelligence.[27] It is apparent that up to this point nature keeps pace with the ego, and hence that nature doubtless lacks only the final feature, whereby all the intuitions attain for it the same significance they have for the ego. But what this final feature may be will become evident from what follows.

If the ego were to continue to be *merely* objective, self-intuition could potentiate itself on and on to infinity; in this way the series of products in nature would merely be increased, but consciousness would never arise. Consciousness is possible only in so far as the merely objective element in the ego becomes objective *for the ego itself*. For the ego is absolutely identical with that *merely* objective phase. The ground, therefore, can only lie outside the ego, which is gradually narrowed, by progressive delimitation, to intelligence and even to individuality. *Outside* the individual, however, i.e., independent of it, there is only *intelligence itself*. But intelligence itself must (according to the deduced mechanism) limit itself, where it is, to individuality. The ground sought outside the individual can therefore lie only in *another individual*.

That which is absolutely objective can become an object *for the ego itself* only by means of the influence of another rational being. But the design of such an influence must already have lain in this latter being. Thus freedom is always already presupposed in nature (nature does not generate it), and where it is not already present as a first principle it can never arise. Here, therefore, it becomes evident that although nature is completely equal to intelligence up to this point and runs through the same potencies as intelligence, nevertheless freedom, *if* it exists (*that* it exists, however, cannot be proved theoretically), must be superior to nature (*natura prior*).

Hence a new sequence of actions, which are not possible by means of nature but leave it behind, begins at this point.

The absolutely objective element or the lawfulness of intuition becomes an object for the ego itself. But intuition becomes an object for the intuiting agent only by means of will [Wollen]. The objective element in will is intuition itself, or the pure lawfulness of nature; the subjective element is an ideal activity directed upon that lawfulness in itself; the act in which this happens is the *absolute act of will* [*absolute Willensakt*].

For the ego the absolute act of will itself becomes once more an object in that, for the ego, the objective element in will, directed toward something external, becomes object in the form of natural impulse, while the subjective element, directed toward lawfulness in itself, becomes object in the form of absolute will, i.e., categorical imperative.[28] But this, again, is not possible without an activity superior to both. This activity is *free choice* or *free will* [*Willkür*], or consciously free activity.

Now if this consciously free activity (which is opposed to the objective activity present in action, although it has to become one with it immediately) is intuited in its original identity with the objective activity (which is absolutely impossible by means of freedom) then there arises thereby the highest potency of self-intuition. Since this itself already lies above and beyond the *conditions* of consciousness and rather is itself consciousness self-creative from the beginning, it must appear to be simply accidental wherever it is; and this simply accidental feature in the highest potency of self-intuition is what is signified by the idea of *genius* [*Genie*].

These are the moments in the history of self-consciousness, invariable and fixed for all knowledge, which are expressed in experience by a continuous sequence of levels that can be exhibited and pursued from simple matter to organization (by which unconsciously productive nature returns into itself) and from that point through reason and free choice up to the highest union of freedom and necessity in art (by which nature, become consciously productive, closes and consummates itself in itself).

From
Philosophy of Art
[Philosophie der Kunst]

Lectures given in Jena in the winter of 1802–3, and repeated in 1804–5 in Würzburg

Translated by Elizabeth Rubenstein.

German text in *SW*, V, 718f.

Introductory note

Schelling's 1802–3 lectures are openly and consciously eclectic, drawing frequently upon the work of August Wilhelm and Friedrich Schlegel as well as upon other contemporaries and precursors. To try to recover all the borrowings and overlaps, and to assess the precise degree of Schelling's deviations from them, would be a considerable scholarly task, one which the present editor has not attempted. This is especially true of the account of Shakespeare, who had been widely translated into German (although the great Schlegel and Tieck translation was only 'under way' when Schelling was giving these lectures), and was already regarded as an adopted son by the German critics and theorists. Some account of the place of Shakespeare in German Romanticism can be gained by consulting Stahl (1947), Pascal (1937), and Ralli (1932), I, 108f.

Crabb Robinson (1929), p. 119, noted the remarks Schelling delivered at a dinner party in December 1802:

the Raptures with which he speaks of Shakespear are boundless – tho' he praises so mystically & so metaphysically that you wo⁰ not be able to comprehend one Word of his Eulogy And he does not scruple to say that not one of the Editors of Shakespear has the least presentimᵗ or suspicion of his real Worth: Shakespear is a sealed book to the whole english Nation.

This mood of excessive praise does not however completely accord with the arguments of the lectures, given below.

On modern dramatic poetry

I shall continue with an exposition of tragedy and comedy in the modern dramatists. So as not to be completely submerged in this vast sea, I shall seek to draw attention to the few major points on which modern drama *differs* from the ancient, and to remark on its *coincidence* with it, and on its own specific features. I shall base these relationships once again on the determinate view [Anschauung] of what we must recognize as the most important phenomena in modern tragedy and comedy. Therefore in considering the major points I shall refer especially to Shakespeare.

The first thing which we must begin by considering is that the *combination* [*Mischung*] *of opposites*, thus of the tragic and comic especially, is the fundamental principle of modern drama. The following reflection will serve to make us grasp the importance of this combination: the tragic and the comic could be presented in a state of completeness as an unsublimated [nicht aufgehobenen] indifference,[1] but then the poetry [Poesie] would have to be neither tragic nor comic. It would be quite a different genre: it would be epic poetry. In epic poetry the two elements which are stressfully at variance in the drama are not united but yet not truly separate. The combination of these two elements in such a way that they do not appear at all separate cannot therefore be the distinguishing feature of modern tragedy, which entails rather a combination in which both are clearly differentiated and in such a way that the poet shows himself to be simultaneously master of both, as is Shakespeare, who focusses dramatic energy toward both opposite poles. And the *most heartrending* Shakespeare is in Falstaff and in Macbeth.

Yet we can consider this combination of opposing elements as the striving of modern drama to return to the epic, without thereby becoming epic; just as on the other hand the same poetry in the epic strives toward the dramatic through the novel. This poetry thus overcomes the pure limits of the higher art forms from both sides.

For this *combination* it is necessary that the poet has not simply got pieces of tragedy and pieces of comedy at his command, but that he should be a master of nuances; like Shakespeare, who in the comic is tender, adventurous and witty all at the same time, as in *Hamlet*, and earthy (as in the Falstaff plays) without ever being vulgar; just as in the tragic he is devastating (as in *Lear*), punishing (as in *Macbeth*), and stirring, touching and calming, as in *Romeo and Juliet* and in other plays in the mixed mode.

Let us now look at the subject matter of modern tragedy. This also had to have a mythological dignity [Würde], at least in its most perfect manifestation. There were therefore only three possible sources out of which the subject matter could be derived. The separate myths which, like those of Greek tragedy, had not unified themselves into epic wholes, remained outside the broad circle of the universal epic: they were expressed in the modern world through the *novellas*. Legendary or poetic history [Historie] provided a second source. The third source is made up of religious myths and legends and the stories of the saints. Shakespeare took material from the first two of these, since the third did not provide subject matter suited to his age and to his nation. It was especially the Spanish, among them Calderón, who took material from here. Shakespeare, therefore, found his material ready made. In this sense he was not an *inventor*, but in the way he used, arranged and brought to life his materials he showed himself in *his* sphere to be like the ancient dramatists and to be the wisest of artists. It has been remarked and it is a fact that Shakespeare committed himself to the exact details of the given material, especially that of the novellas; that he included everything, down to the most minor circumstance, and left nothing out (this is a practice which could perhaps often throw light on the apparently groundless elements in some of his plots), changing what he was given as little as possible.[2]

Here too he is like the ancients – except Euripides, who as the more frivolous poet deliberately distorts the myths.

The next undertaking is [to decide] how far or not the essence of ancient tragedy is present in the modern. Is there a true idea of fate to be found in modern tragedy? Indeed, of that higher fate which in itself incorporates freedom?

As observed, Aristotle defines the supreme instance of tragedy as occurring when a just man commits a crime by mistake [Irrthum]. It must be added that this mistake is inflicted by necessity or by the gods, possibly even *against* freedom.[3] According to the concepts of the Christian religion this last example would seem to be impossible. Those powers which undermine the will and inflict not only harm but *evil* are themselves evil and infernal powers.

At the very least if a mistake caused by divine decree were to bring about calamity and crime, then in that same religion according to which this were a possibility there would also have to be the possibility of a corresponding forgiveness. This is certainly there in Catholicism which, by its nature a mixture of the sacred and the profane, ordains sin in order to demonstrate the power of the means of grace in the forgiveness of sin. Thus in Catholicism the possibility of the *true* tragic fate existed, though it differed from that of the ancients.[4]

Shakespeare was a Protestant, and this possibility was not open to him. If there is a fate in his work it can only be of a twofold nature. Harm is brought about by conjuring up evil and demonic powers, but according to Christian concepts these cannot be invincible, and resistance to them should *and* can be made. The inescapability of their effect, in so far as it is made apparent, is reflected in and reverts to the character [Charakter] or subject. So it is with Shakespeare. Character takes the place of the ancient tragic fate [Schicksal], but he places within it such a mighty destiny [Fatum] that it can be no longer regarded as free. Indeed, it stands forth as insuperable necessity.

A demonic trickery lures Macbeth into murder but there is no objective need for the deed. Banquo does not allow himself to be beguiled by the voice of the witches, but Macbeth does. Therefore it is character which decides.

The childish folly of an old man is presented in Lear in the manner of a confusing delphic oracle, and the sweet Desdemona has to submit to the dark stain which is coupled with jealousy.

Because he had to place the necessity for the crime in the *character*, Shakespeare has had for the same reason to deal with the case *not* accepted by Aristotle as tragic, that of the criminal who plunges from happiness into misfortune with a terrible indifference.[5] In the place of fate in itself he has *nemesis* in all its forms, where horror is overwhelmed by horrors, one wave of blood drives the next one on, and the curse of the cursed is constantly being fulfilled, as the Wars of the Roses exemplify in English history. He *has* to show himself as a barbarian since he undertakes to show the worst kind of barbarity, such as the brutal battles of families amongst themselves, where all art [Kunst] seems at an end and brute force takes its place, as it is said in *Lear*:

> It will come,
> Humanity must perforce prey on itself,
> Like monsters of the deep.[6]

But here there are signs to be found that he has sent the grace [Anmuth] of art amongst the *furies*, who do not appear in their own shapes. Such is Margaret's love lament over the head of her unlawful and guilty lover and her parting from him.[7]

Shakespeare ends the sequence with Richard III, whom he makes pursue and attain his goal with monstrous energy, until he is driven from the heights of his achievement into the tight corner of despair. In the turmoil of the battle in which he is defeated he calls out, irretrievably lost:

> A horse! a horse! my kingdom for a horse![8]

In *Macbeth*, revenge forces its way step by step towards a nobler criminal led astray by an immoderate ambition, in such a way that, deceived by demonic illusions, he believes it to be far away.

A more gentle, indeed the mildest nemesis is to be found in *Julius Caesar*. Brutus does not perish so much because of avenging powers as because of the very mildness of a fine and tender disposition which moves him to take the wrong measures after the deed. He had made of his deed a sacrifice to virtue, as he believed he had to, and thereby sacrifices himself to it.

The difference between this nemesis and true *fate* [*Schicksal*] is however very significant. It comes from the real world and is rooted in *reality*; it is the nemesis that governs history, and Shakespeare found it *there* like the rest of his material. What brings it about is *freedom* quarrelling with *freedom*; it is a *sequence of events* [*Succession*], and the revenge is not immediately one with the crime.

In the cycle of the Greek presentations a nemesis also dominates, but here necessity is limited and punished directly by necessity, and each situation taken on its own was a completed action.

From the very beginning all the tragic myths of the Greeks belonged more to art, and a steady communication and interpenetration of gods and men, as of fate, was natural to them, as well as the concept of an irresistible influence. Perhaps *chance* [*Zufall*] itself plays a part in one of the most unfathomable of Shakespeare's plays (*Hamlet*), but Shakespeare perceived it *with* its consequences: it is therefore intended by him and makes the greatest sense.

If after this we want to express in one word what Shakespeare is in relation to the sublime nature of ancient tragedy, then we will have to name him as the greatest inventor in *the realm of character* [*Charakteristischen*]. He cannot portray that sublime and as it were purified and transfigured beauty which proves itself against fate and becomes one with moral goodness – he cannot portray the beauty that he does portray in such a way that it appears in the *whole* and so that the totality of each work bears its image. He *knows* the highest beauty only as individual character. He has not been able to subordinate everything to it, because as a modern, who conceives of the eternal not within limits but in the unlimited, he is too diffuse in his universality. The ancients had a concentrated universality, a totality not in multiplicity but in unity.[9]

There is *nothing* in man that Shakespeare did not touch on, but he treats it individually whereas the Greeks treat it in its totality. The highest and the lowest elements in human nature lie dispersed in him: he knows *everything*, every passion, every state of mind, in youth and age, in the king and the shepherd boy. From the volumes of his works one would be able to recreate the lost earth. That ancient lyre on its own managed to draw the whole world out of *four* notes; the new instrument has a thousand strings.[10] It splits up the harmony of the universe in order to recreate it, and thus it is always less soothing for the soul. The austere, all-assuaging beauty can only exist in simplicity.

In accordance with the nature of the romantic principle modern comedy does not present the action as pure or isolated, or with the representational limits [plastischen Beschränkung] of ancient drama, but it presents all that goes with it at the same time. Only Shakespeare has given his tragedy the most concentrated wealth of detail and succinctness in every part as well as in the broad whole, but yet without any arbitrary excess and in such a way that it appears as the richness of nature itself, apprehended by artistic necessity. The intention of the *whole* remains clear, but then again plunges to inexhaustible depths where all points of view can be absorbed.

It goes without saying that with this kind of universality Shakespeare's world is not a limited one, and is not an ideal world, in as much as the ideal world itself is a limited and closed one. But on the other hand it is not the world that is directly opposed to the ideal, the formal [conventionelle] world by which the miserable taste of the French has replaced the ideal.

Shakespeare never portrays either an ideal or a formal world but always the *real* world. The ideal appears in him in the construction of his plays. Moreover he is able to place himself with ease into every nationality and period as if it were his own, i.e. he draws them as *wholes* untroubled by less important details.

What men undertake, how and where they are able to do it, all this Shakespeare knew. He is therefore at home everywhere; nothing is strange or astonishing to him. He observes a much higher spectacle than that of customs and times. The style of his plays is determined by the subject and they differ one from another (in no way according to chronology) according to the harshness, softness, regularity or freedom of the verses, and the brevity and abruptness or the length of the sentences.

Now, to make mention of what remains to be said about the outward structure of modern tragedy, and in order not to waste time describing the necessary changes which must result from the differences already mentioned (such as the abandoning of the three unities, the division of the whole into scenes, etc.): so, again, the *combination* of prose and verse in modern drama is the outward expression of its inwardly mixed epic and dramatic nature. Leaving aside the so-called domestic or inferior tragedies [Trauerspielen] where the characters quite justifiably express themselves in prose, its use *from time to time* was necessary just because of the exposition of dramatic richness in secondary characters. Shakespeare has shown himself a master in this combination of prose and verse and in observing what is right as far as the language is concerned; not only in individual instances but in the work as a whole. Thus in *Hamlet* the structure of the sentences is confused, abrupt, troubled like the hero. In the historical plays based on early and more recent English and on Roman history, there prevails a very discrepant tone in terms of cultivation and purity. In the Roman plays there is almost no verse. On the other hand in the English plays, especially those based on early history, there is a great deal that is exceedingly picturesque [pittoresk].

The accusations of perversity and even coarseness that people make against Shakespeare are mostly not valid, and are only considered to be so by a narrow and feeble taste. Yet by no one does his true greatness go more unrecognized than by his fellow countrymen, the *English* critics and admirers. They cling to single presentations of passion or of a character; to the psychology, to scenes, to words, without any feeling for the whole, or for art. When one takes a look at the English critics, as Tieck says very tellingly, it is as if, travelling in a beautiful landscape, one were to pass by an inn in front of which drunken peasants were squabbling.[11]

That Shakespeare wrote by some happy inspiration and in completely unconscious mastery of his art is a very common error and a myth put about by a completely misinformed age, one which began in England with Pope.[12] Of course the Germans often misunderstood him, not just because they perhaps knew him only from a crude translation, but because the belief in art had disappeared altogether.

The poems of Shakespeare's youth – the *Sonnets*, *Adonis*, and *Lucrece* – testify to an extremely love-worthy nature and to a very *heartfelt*, *subjective* feeling, not to any unconscious genius-inspired storm or stress [Genie-Sturm oder Drang].[13] After this Shakespeare lived wholly in the world, as far as his environment allowed, until he began to reveal his existence in a world without any bounds, and to set it down in a series of works of art which truly portray the total infinity of art and nature.

Shakespeare's genius [Genius] is so all-encompassing that his name, like Homer's, could be taken to be a collective name; and as has indeed already happened, his works could be ascribed to different authors. (Here the individual is collective in the same way that the work is with the ancients.)

We might still view Shakespeare's art with a kind of hopelessness if we were absolutely bound to regard him as the zenith of romantic art in the drama; for barbarism must first be allowed him in order that he be seen as great, indeed divine within it. In his unboundedness Shakespeare cannot be compared with any of the ancient tragedians, but we must however be allowed to hope for a Sophocles of the differentiated [differenzürten] world, and to hope for appeasement in an art which is as it were *sinful*. At least the possibility of the fulfilment of this expectation seems to have been hinted at by a hitherto less well known source.[14]

On Dante in Relation to Philosophy
[Über Dante in philosophischer Beziehung]

1803

Translated by Elizabeth Rubenstein.

German text in *SW*, V, 152–63. First published in *Kritisches Journal der Philosophie*, II (1803), 35–50.

Introductory note

Schelling's essay on Dante in many ways continues the themes outlined in the remarks on Shakespeare. Dante's importance as the prototype of the modern artist depends upon his creation of an individual mythology; thus he sets an example for other possible representations of the fragmented world.

   Much of what Schelling says here is taken over (and acknowledged) by A.W. Schlegel in his *Lectures on Fine Art and Literature* (see 1962–74, IV, 169–81), who also finds Dante prophetic of the whole of modern poetry. Schlegel had written on Dante earlier, and had himself translated the *Inferno* along with sections of the other two parts of the *Divine Comedy*. Schelling's essay is apparently in reaction to Friedrich Bouterwek's negative judgement in his *Geschichte der Poesie und Beredsamkeit* (1801): see Wellek (1955), II, 80.

Those who love the past more than the present will not find it strange to find themselves drawn away from its not always rewarding aspects and taken back to such a distant monument of philosophy combined with poetry as the works of Dante, which have long been overshadowed by the sacrosanctness of antiquity.

   As justification for the space which these thoughts here occupy, I demand for the time being no other admission than that the poem to which they refer presents one of the most remarkable problems concerning the philosophical and historical construction of art. What follows will show that this inquiry contains within it a far more general one, which concerns the circumstances of philosophy itself, and is of no less interest for philosophy than for poetry. Their reciprocal merging, to which the whole modern age is inclined, demands equally determinate conditions on both sides.[1]

> In the Holy of Holies,
> where religion and poetry ally,

stands Dante as the high priest and he who initiates the whole course of modern art. Representing not just one single poem but the whole genre of modern poetry, and even a genre in its own right, the *Divine Comedy* stands so completely apart that no theory abstracted from individual models is adequate to describe it. As a world of its own, it demands its own theory. The author gave it the epithet 'divine' because it deals with theology and divine things; he called it a 'comedy' according to the basic concepts of this and of the opposite genre: because of the terrifying beginning and happy outcome, and because the mixed nature of his poem, whose subject matter is part sublime and part humble, makes a mixed kind of recitation necessary.

But it is easy to see that it cannot be called 'dramatic' according to the generally accepted concepts, because it does not portray a limited action. In as much as Dante himself is viewed as the main protagonist, one who serves as the link between the immeasurable series of visions and portraits, and who behaves passively rather than actively, then the poem might seem to approach the novel. But this definition does so little justice to the poem that it could be called 'epic', after another more common view [Vorstellung], since there is no sequential continuity in the objects portrayed.[2] To view it as a didactic poem is equally impossible, since it is written with a much more imprecise form and intention than that of the didactic poem. It is therefore not a particular example of any of the above, nor is it merely a combination of various parts of each. It is a quite unique and as it were organic fusion of all the elements of these genres, which cannot be reproduced by any arbitrary skill [Kunst]. It is an absolutely individual thing, not comparable to anything outside itself.

Broadly speaking, the subject matter of the poem is the clear-cut, essential identity of the whole age in which the poet lived, the imbuing of its events with the ideas [Ideen] of religion, scientific knowledge [Wissenschaft] and poetry [Poesie], conceived of in the most superior mind of that century. But it is not our intention to look at the poem in its immediate relation to its own time, but rather to see it in its universal validity [Allgemeingültigkeit] and in its role of archetype for the whole of modern poetry.

The necessary law governing the as yet undetermined, far-away point where the great epic of modern times, which has revealed itself up to now only rhapsodically and in single manifestations, emerges as a complete totality, is this: that the individual moulds that part of the world revealed to him into a whole, and creates his own mythology [Mythologie] from the material of his age, from its history and its scientific learning. For just as the ancient world is in general a world of types, so the modern is one of individuals. There it is the general that is truly particular; the species acts as a single individual. Here on the other hand the point of departure is particularity, which is supposed to become general. For that reason everything among the ancients is enduring and everlasting. Number seems to have no force, since the concept of the general fuses with that of the individual. Among the moderns change and alteration are a constant law. Not a completed, closed circle but one to be endlessly expanded through individuality determines its modifications, and because universality is of the essence of poetry, the necessary requirement is this: that through the most supreme uniqueness the individual should become universally valid again. Through fully developed particularity he must become once more absolute. It is through the sheer individuality of his poem, comparable to nothing else, that Dante is the creator of modern art, which cannot be conceived of without this arbitrary necessity and necessary arbitrariness.

From the very beginnings of Greek poetry, in Homer onwards, we see a poetry clearly distinct from scientific learning and philosophy, and this process of separation continued right up to the total polarization of poets and philosophers, who sought in vain to effect a harmony through allegorical explanations of the Homeric poems. In more recent times scientific knowledge has moved ahead of poetry and mythology, which indeed cannot be mythology without being universal and drawing into itself all elements of the existing culture – science, religion, art itself – and combining not just the material of the present but also that of the past to form a perfect unity. Since art demands the completed, the self-contained, and the limited, while the spirit of the modern world pushes towards the unlimited and tears down every barrier with unshakable determination, the individual must enter into this conflict, but with absolute freedom. He must seek to achieve lasting shapes out of the confusion of the age, and into the arbitrarily produced forms of the images of his poetry [Dichtung] he must again impart universal validity.

This Dante has done. He had the material of present as of past history in front of him. He could not work it into a pure epic, partly because of its nature, partly because by so doing he would have excluded other aspects of the culture of his time. Contemporary astronomy, theology and philosophy also belonged to this whole. He could not present them in a didactic poem because he would thereby limit himself once more, and in order to be universal his poem had to be at the same time historical. There was need of a completely freely willed [willkürlich] invention, emanating from the individual and able to combine this material and shape it organically into a whole. To present the ideas of philosophy and theology in symbols [Symbole] was impossible because there was no symbolic mythology in existence.[3] No more could he make his poem completely allegorical, because it would then no longer be historical. Therefore it had to be a completely unique mixture of the allegorical and the historical. In the exemplary poetry [Poesie] of the ancients no alternative of this kind was possible.[4] Only the individual was able to seize it, only free invention pure and simple could pursue it.

Dante's poem is not allegorical in the sense that the figures simply stand for something else, without being independent of this meaning and thus something in themselves. On the other hand none of them is independent of the meaning in such a way that it becomes one with the idea itself, and more than allegorical of it. There is thus in Dante's poem a quite unique middle point between allegory and symbolic-objective forms. For example, there is no doubt – and the poet has explained it himself elsewhere – that Beatrice is an allegory, namely of theology. So also her companions, and many other figures. However they still register in their own right and enter as historical characters, without for that purpose being symbols.

In this respect Dante is archetypal, since he has expressed what the modern poet must do in order to set forth in its entirety and in a poetic whole the history and culture of his time and the particular mythological material that is before him. He must combine the allegorical and the historical with absolute freedom of choice [Willkür]. He must be allegorical, and is so against his will, because he cannot be symbolic; and historical, because he must be poetic. The invention that he produces is in this respect unique every time, a world unto itself, wholly dependent on the personality.

In a similar way the one German poem of universal proportions joins together the most extreme aspects of the struggles of the age by the wholly individual invention of a partial mythology: the figure of Faust. However, this may be regarded as a comedy far more in the Aristophanic sense than is Dante's poem, and as divine in a different and more poetic sense.[5]

The energy with which the individual shapes the particular combination of the available materials of his life and times determines the extent to which it receives mythological force. Because of the place in which he sets them, which is eternal, Dante's characters already take on a kind of eternity. But not only the real events taken from his own times, like the story of Ugolino amongst others, but also what he has wholly invented, like the fate of Ulysses and his companions, take on in the context of his poem a truly mythological conviction.

To present Dante's philosophy, physics and astronomy purely in and for themselves would only be of minor interest, since his true uniqueness lies solely in the manner of their merging with poetry. The Ptolemaic cosmology, which is to some extent the basis of poetic edifice, already has a mythological colouring in itself; but if his philosophy is generally described as Aristotelian, then what must be understood here is not the purely peripatetic version but rather the particular connection current at that time between it and Platonic ideas, one which reveals itself on repeated investigations of the poem.[6]

We do not wish to dwell on the force and integrity of individual points, nor on the simplicity and infinite naivety of the individual images in which he expresses his philosophical ideas, such as the well-known one of the soul, which emerges from the hands of God as a little girl, childlike in its laughter and crying, an innocent little soul that knows nothing beyond what is controlled by its joyous creator, turning gladly to what amuses it.[7] We are only concerned with the generally symbolic form of the whole, in whose absoluteness the universal validity and eternal nature of this poem is more than anywhere else apparent.

If the union of philosophy and poetry even at the most elementary level of synthesis is viewed as didactic poetry then it is necessary, because the poem should be without any ulterior motive, that the intention to instruct is again in itself overcome and turned into an absolute, so that it can seem to exist for its own sake. This is however only conceivable if knowledge [Wissen], as image of the universe and in complete harmony with it, is in and for itself poetic, as with the most original and beautiful poetry. Dante's poem is a much more elevated interpenetration of scientific learning and poetry, and all the more must its form, even in its freer self-sufficiency, be attuned to the general paradigm of the world view [Weltanschauung].

The division of the universe and the arrangement of the subject matter into three realms, the *Inferno*, *Purgatorio*, and *Paradiso* is, independent of the particular significance of these concepts in Christianity, also a general symbolic form, so that one does not see why each age depicted in the same way could not have its divine comedy. Just as for recent drama the five-act form is regarded as usual, because each event can be seen in its beginning, continuation, culmination, progress to completion and actual ending; so for the higher prophetic poetry which expresses a whole age that trichotomy of Dante's is conceivable as a general form, but one whose filling out would be endlessly varied as it is revitalized by the power of original invention. That form is eternal, not only as outward form but also as sensuous [sinnbildlich] expression of the inner paradigm of all scientific knowledge and poetry, and is capable of containing within it the three great domains of science and culture: nature, history, and art. Nature, as the birthplace of all things, is eternal night, and as that unity through which they have their being in themselves, it is the aphelion of the universe, the place of distance from God as the true centre.[8] Life and history, whose nature is a succession of step by step advances, is simply a refining process, a transition to an absolute state. This is present only in art, which anticipates eternity, and is the *Paradiso* of life, truly at the centre.

Looked at from all sides Dante's poem is not therefore a single work of a particular time and stage of culture, but is archetypal through its universal validity, which it unites with absolute individuality. Its universality excludes no aspects of life and culture, and its form finally is not a particular paradigm but above all the paradigm of the contemplation of the universe.

The particular internal structure of the poem can certainly not have universal validity, since it is formed according to the concepts of the time and the particular intentions of the poet. On the other hand, as can only be expected of such an artistic and totally deliberate work, the universal inner paradigm is symbolized externally by the shape, colour and tone of the three great sections of the poem.

Given the uncommon nature of his subject matter Dante needed a kind of authentication for the detailed form of his inventions, which only the scientific learning of his age could give him. This is for him, as it were, the mythology and the general foundation which supports the bold edifice of these inventions. But even in details he remains quite true to his intention of being allegorical without ceasing to be historical and poetic. Hell, purgatory and paradise are so to speak simply the physical and structural expression of the system of theology. The measurements, numbers and proportions which he observes within it were prescribed by scientific learning, and here he deliberately gave up freedom of invention in order to give his poem, which was unlimited as far as the material was concerned, necessity and limitation through form. The universal sacredness and significance of the numbers is another exterior form on which his poetry is based. Thus for him all the logical and syllogistic erudition of his time is mere form, which must be conceded to him if we are to arrive at that region in which his poetry exists.

Nevertheless in this attachment to religious and scientific representations Dante never seeks any kind of common poetic probability as the most universally valid thing that his age had to offer. Indeed, he overcomes all inclination to pander to the coarser faculties [Sinnen]. His first entry into hell takes place, as it had to, without any unpoetic attempt to motivate it or make it comprehensible; it is a state similar to a vision, without there being any intention of making this state account for it. His elevation through the eyes of Beatrice, through which the divine force so to speak transmitted itself to him, is expressed in a single line.[9] The wondrous nature of his own encounters he turns directly into a figure of the secrets of religion, and gives credence to them through the still higher mystery, such as when he makes his absorption into the moon, which he compares to a ray of light being in water but not cleaving it, into an image of God's incarnation.[10]

To explain the fullness of art and the depth of intention in the internal construction of the three parts of the world in detail would be a special science in itself. This was recognized by his nation a short time after the death of the poet, for they set up a special Dante Chair, which Boccaccio was the first to take up.

What is universally meaningful in the first section shines through each of the three parts of the poem, and not only in their particular inventions; the law which applies to them expresses this meaningfulness still more precisely in the inner and spiritual rhythm through which they are set against one another. Just as the *Inferno* is the most objectively terrible in its subject matter, so it is the strongest in expression and the strictest in diction, sombre and full of dread in its very choice of words. In one part of *Purgatorio* a deep stillness prevails, as the laments of the nether world grow silent, and on its hills, the forecourts of heaven, everything is glorious.[11] *Paradiso* is a true music of the spheres.

The diversity and variety of the punishments in the *Inferno* have been thought out with an almost unparalleled inventiveness. There is nothing other than a poetic connection between the crimes and the torments. Dante's spirit is not outraged by the horrific; indeed, he goes to the extreme limit of horror. But it can be shown in each individual case that he never ceases to be sublime and therefore truly beautiful. For what those who are not in a position to grasp the whole have singled out as base or inferior is not so in the sense that they mean but is a necessary element of the mixed nature of the poem, for which reason Dante himself calls it 'comedy'. The hatred of evil and the anger of a divine mind, as expressed in Dante's terrifying composition, are not the portion of ordinary souls. The generally held view is indeed very doubtful: that it was the exile from Florence, before which he had dedicated his poetry almost solely to love, that had first spurred on his mind (already inclined to the serious and the extraordinary) to the highest inventiveness, in which he breathed forth the whole of his life, the whole density of his heart and fatherland, together with his displeasure over them.[12] But the vengeance that he takes in the *Inferno* is taken in the name of the Last Judgement. He speaks with prophetic force as an authorized criminal judge; not from personal hatred, but as a pious soul outraged by the atrocities of the times, and with a love of the fatherland long since unknown. Thus he represents himself at one point in the *Paradiso*:

> If e'er the sacred poem, that hath made
> Both Heaven and earth copartners in its toil,
> And with lean abstinence, through many a year,
> Faded my brow, be destined to prevail
> Over the cruelty, which bars me forth
> Of the fair sheep-fold, where, a sleeping lamb
> The wolves set on and fain had worried me;
> With other voice, and fleece of other grain,
> I shall forthwith return; and, standing up
> At my baptismal font, shall claim the wreath
> Due to the poet's temples.[13]

He moderates the horrors of the torments of the damned by his own feeling, which at the final goal of so much misery almost so overcomes his vision that he desires to weep, and Virgil says to him: "Why are you afflicted?"[14]

It has already been remarked that most of the punishments in *Inferno* symbolize the crimes which are punished by them, but several are symbolic in a much more general context. One particular example of this type is the portrayal of a metamorphosis where two natures change into and through one another and, so to speak, exchange material identity.[15] None of the metamorphoses of antiquity can measure up to this in terms of invention, and if a naturalist or didactic poet were able to draw up with such force sensuous images of the eternal metamorphosis of nature, he might indeed call himself fortunate.

As already observed, the *Inferno* differs from the other parts not only in terms of the outward form of the presentation, but also because it is chiefly concerned with the realm of figures [Gestalten] and is thus the tangibly embodied [plastische] part of the poem. *Purgatorio* must be recognized as the picturesque. Not only are the penances which are here imposed on the sinners in part quite pictorially treated, even going so far as mirth; but the pilgrimage over the sacred mount of the place of penance in particular presents a rapid succession of fleeting views, scenes, and manifold effects of light.[16] At its final limits, after the poet has arrived at Lethe, the greatest splendour of painting and colour opens up in the descriptions of the ancient divine groves of that region, of the heavenly clarity of the waters that are clouded by their eternal shadows, of the virgin whom he encounters on the shore, and of the arrival of Beatrice in a cloud of flowers, under a white veil crowned with olives, wrapped in a green mantle, and clad in purple living flame.[17]

The poet has forced his way to the light through the centre of the earth. In the darkness of the underworld only shapes [Gestalt] could be distinguished. In *Purgatorio* the light is kindled by earthly matter, and becomes colour. In *Paradiso* only the pure music of light remains, the reflection ceases, and the poet raises himself gradually to the contemplation [Anschauung] of the transparent, pure substance of the Godhead itself.

The view of the cosmos at the time of the poet, and of the properties of the stars and the extent of their movement, is, invested with mythological dignity, the foundation upon which his inventions in this part of the poem rest. And if in this sphere of absoluteness he nevertheless allows gradations and differences to appear, then he overcomes [aufhebt] them with the splendid pronouncement which he has spoken forth by one of the sister souls he encounters on the moon: that every place in heaven is paradise.[18]

The structure of the poem requires that the highest principles of theology be discussed, precisely because of the elevation through paradise. The high respect for this science is exemplified by the love for Beatrice. It is necessary that in the same measure as contemplation [Anschauung] melts into the purely universal so poetry loses its forms and becomes music. In this respect the *Inferno* might appear as the most poetic part. But certainly nothing can be taken separately here, and the particular excellence of every part of the poem can only be understood and truly recognized in its harmony with the whole. If the relationship of the three parts is taken as a whole, then it has to be seen that the *Paradiso* is the purely musical and lyrical part by the very intention of the poet, who demonstrates this in external forms through the frequent use of the Latin words of church hymns.

The extraordinary greatness of this poem, which shines forth in the interpenetration of all elements of poetry and art, in this way fully reaches outward manifestation. This divine work is neither plastic, nor picturesque, nor musical, but all of these at the same time and in a mutual harmony. It is not dramatic, not epic, not lyric, but a completely individual and unparalleled combination of all of these.

At the same time I believe that I have shown that it is prophetic and exemplary [vorbildlich] for the whole of modern poetry. It contains all the attributes of modern poetry within it, and emerges from the frequently blended subject matter of the same as the first vintage to spread over earth to heaven, the first fruit of transfiguration. Those who want to get to know the poetry of more recent times at its source, rather than according to superficial concepts, may test themselves against this great and severe spirit [Geist], in order to know the means by which the totality of the modern age can be grasped, and that no easily created bond unites it. Those who are not called to do this may apply to themselves the words at the beginning of the first part:

All hope abandon, ye who enter here.[19]

Selections from
Concerning the Relation of the Plastic Arts to Nature
[Über das Verhältnis der bildenden Künste
zur Natur]

An oration on the name day of the King, 1807[1]

Translated by Michael Bullock (slightly amended) in Read (1968), pp. 323–58.

German text in *SW*, VII, 291–329.

Introductory note

This is the work from which Coleridge seems to have borrowed most directly for one of his 1818 lectures, reprinted as *On Poesy or Art* in (1954), II, 253–63; Shawcross' notes should be consulted on the precise relations of the two texts, as well as the general accounts of the Coleridge–Schelling relation mentioned above.

As perhaps befits its occasion, a public lecture on the name day of the King, this is Schelling's most rhapsodic statement of the potential of the fine arts for representing the essential truths put forward more patiently by philosophy. The conceptual heritage of *Kraft*, variously translated here as 'force', 'energy', or 'power', is expanded into what Schelling seems to see as a challenge to the empty formalism of post-Kantian aesthetics. In its place he offers an organically interdetermining equilibrium or harmony in tension between form and essence, replacing Kant's scrupulously limited relations of analogy between art and nature by a firm argument for their identity.

[Schelling sets the scene of his argument by referring to the unenlivened notion of nature held to by most of the ancients and their modern admirers. Nature is empirical material for imitation, not living soul. Even Winckelmann, who was "the first to think of looking at works of art in the light of the modes and laws of the eternal works of nature", failed to bridge the gap completely.]

. . . Everywhere nature first confronts us in more or less hard form and closed in. It is like that serious and silent beauty which does not attract attention by clamorous signs, does not catch the common eye. How can we, so to speak, spiritually melt this apparently hard form, so that the unadulterated energy of things fuses with the energy of our spirits, forming a single cast?[2] We must go beyond form, in order to regain it as comprehensible, living and truly felt. If you look at the most beautiful forms, what is there left once you have mentally eliminated the operative principle from them? Nothing but purely inessential qualities, such as extension and spatial relationship. Does the fact that one part of matter is beside and outside the other contribute anything to its inner essentiality, or does it rather contribute nothing whatever? Obviously the latter. It is not coexistence that makes form, but the kind of coexistence: this, however, can only be determined by a positive force, which rather runs counter to the existence of things outside one another and subordinates the manifoldness of the parts to the unity of a concept [Begriff], from the force operating in a crystal to that which, like a gentle magnetic current, gives to the material parts in human constructions [Bildungen] such an attitude and position in relation to one another as enables the concept, the essential unity and beauty, to become visible.[3]

But it is not enough for essence in form to be manifest to us as the active principle in general, as spirit and practical [werkthätige] science, for us to lay hold of it alive. All unity must be spiritual in kind and derivation, and what is the aim of all investigation of nature if not to find science [Wissenschaft] itself therein? For that which contained no intelligence [Verstand] could not serve as an object for the intelligence either; what was without knowledge could not itself be known. The science by which nature operates is not, of course, one which, like the human, is linked to itself by reflection; in it the concept does not differ from the deed, nor the design from its execution. Hence raw matter tends, so to speak, blindly toward regular shape, and unwittingly assumes purely stereometric forms, which certainly appertain to the realm of concepts and are something spiritual within the material. The most sublime art of number and mensuration is inherent in the stellar system, which performs it in its movements without any concept of it. More distinctly, although beyond their own apprehension, is living knowledge manifest in animals, which we consequently observe achieving numberless effects that are much more splendid than they themselves: the bird which, intoxicated by music, surpasses itself in soulful notes; the little artistically gifted creature which, without practice or instruction, accomplishes simple architectural works – all, however, conducted by a super-powerful spirit that gleams in single flashes of knowledge, but nowhere emerges as the full sun, as it does in man.

This practical science is, in nature and man, the link between concept and form [Form], between body and soul. Every thing is ministered over by an eternal concept, designed in the infinite intelligence; but through what does this concept enter into reality and physical existence? Solely through creative science, which is just as necessarily linked to the infinite intelligence [Verstand] as, in the artist, that part of his being which apprehends the idea [Idee] of non-sensuous beauty is linked to that which gives it sensuous representation. If that artist is to be called happy and pre-eminently deserving of praise upon whom the gods have bestowed this creative spirit, so will the work of art appear excellent in the degree to which it shows us this unfalsified natural force of creation and effectiveness contained, as it were, within a single outline.

It has long been perceived that not everything in art is the outcome of consciousness, that an unconscious force must be linked with conscious activity and that it is the perfect unanimity and mutual interpenetration of the two which produces the highest art.[4] Works which lack this seal of unconscious science are recognizable by the palpable absence of a life which is autonomous and independent of their creator, while on the contrary, where it is in operation, art simultaneously imparts to its work, with the greatest lucidity of the intelligence, that unfathomable reality by virtue of which it resembles a work of nature.

The dictum that art, to be art, must first withdraw from nature and only return to it in its final consummation, has frequently been offered as an elucidation of the artist's position in relation to nature. It seems to us that the true meaning of this can be no other than the following. In all natural beings the living concept is manifested in blind operation only: if it were the same in the artist he would differ in no way from nature. If, however, he were consciously to subordinate himself entirely to nature and reproduce the existent with servile fidelity he would produce masks, but no works of art. Thus, he must withdraw from the product or creature, but only in order to raise himself to the level of creative energy and apprehend it spiritually. This bears him aloft into the realm of pure concepts; he loses the creature, to regain it with thousand-fold interest, and so return, in this sense at least, to nature. The artist ought indeed to emulate this spirit of nature, which is at work in the core of things and which speaks forth in form and shape only as sense-images [Sinnbilder]; and only in so far as he has apprehended it in living imitation has he himself created something true. For works arising out of the combination of forms which are already beautiful in themselves would be devoid of all beauty, since that which now actually constitutes the beauty of the work or the whole can no longer be form. It is above form, it is essence, the universal, the vision and expression of the indwelling spirit of nature.

There is little room for doubt as to the view to be taken of this prevailing demand for the so-called idealization of nature in art. It seems to spring from a manner of reasoning according to which it is not truth, beauty and goodness, but the opposite of all these that is the real.[5] If the real were indeed the opposite of truth and beauty the artist would not have to exalt or idealize it, but to eliminate [aufheben] and destroy it in order to create something good and beautiful. But how could anything except truth be real, and what is beauty if it is not full and complete existence? Accordingly, what higher purpose could art have other than to depict that which exists in nature and in fact? Or how could it set itself the task of surpassing so-called real nature, since it would be bound always to lag behind the latter? For does it impart sensually real life to its works? This statue does not breathe, is not moved by a pulse-beat nor warmed by blood. But both that ostensible superiority and this apparent lagging behind prove to be the outcome of one and the same principle, once we make the purpose of art the portrayal of that which truly exists. Works of art appear to be endowed with life on the surface only: in nature life seems to penetrate deeper and to be entirely blended with substance. But does not the ceaseless metamorphosis of matter and the universal lot of ultimate dissolution apprise us of the inessentiality of this amalgamation and that it is no intimate fusion? Thus art, by endowing its works with a merely superficial animation, in fact represents as non-existent only that which does not exist. How does it come about that, to everyone whose sensibility [Sinn] is to some degree educated, imitations of the real which are pushed to the point of illusion appear in the highest degree unreal, making, indeed, the impression of spectres, whereas a work in which the concept is regnant strikes every such observer with the full force of truth and actually transports him for the first time into the genuinely real world? How does this come about, if not through the more or less obscure feeling which tells him that the concept is the only living element in things and all else vain and unsubstantial shadow? The same principle explains all cases brought forward in contradiction of it and quoted as examples of the surpassing of nature by art. If it halts the rapid course of human years, if it links the vigour of masculine prime with the gentle charm [Reiz] of early youth, or shows a mother to her grown-up sons and daughters in the full possession of robust beauty, what else is it doing but eliminating [aufhebt] that which is inessential – time? If, as the excellent man of discernment remarked, every natural growth has only one moment of true and consummate beauty, we may say that it also has only one moment of complete existence.[6] At this moment it is what it is for all eternity: beyond this its lot is merely a becoming and a passing away. Art, by depicting the creature at this moment, raises it up out of time and presents it in its pure being, in the eternity of its life.

Once everything positive and essential had been mentally eliminated from form [Form], it was bound to appear restrictive and, so to speak, hostile to essence [Wesen] and the same theory which had conjured up the false and feeble ideal inevitably operated in the direction of the formless in art at the same time. In any case, if form were necessarily restrictive to essence it would exist independently of it. But if it exists with and through essence, how could the latter feel restricted by that which it creates itself? Violence might certainly be done to essence by form which was imposed upon it, but never by that which flows out of itself.[7] It is bound rather to rest satisfied in the latter and feel its existence to be autonomous and self-enclosed. Definiteness of form in nature is never a negation but always an affirmation. Generally, of course, you think of a body's shape as a restriction which it undergoes; if, however, you were to turn your attention to creative force, it would strike you as the bounds which this latter sets itself and within which it appears as a truly meaningful force. For the ability to set one's own bounds is everywhere regarded as an excellence, indeed as one of the highest.

Similarly, most people look upon the single creature as a negative, namely as that which is not the whole or all: the single creature, however, does not subsist through its limitation, but through the force that inhabits it, by means of which it asserts itself as a whole on its own in relation to the whole.

Since much of the power of singleness, and therefore of individuality as well, is manifested as living character, a negative conception [Begriff] of the former necessarily results in an inadequate and erroneous view of the characteristic in art. Dead and of an unbearable hardness would be the art that aimed to portray the empty husk or limitation of the individual. To be sure, we do not ask for the individual; we ask to see more, namely its living concept. But if the artist recognizes the vision and essence of the idea [Idea] creating within him and stresses these, he fashions the individual into a world of its own, a genus, an eternal prototype; and whoever has grasped the essence need have no fear of hardness and severity either, for they are the precondition of life. Nature, which appears in its consummation as the greatest mildness, we see operating in every independent creature in the direction of definiteness, indeed first and foremost of hardness and self-enclosedness. Just as the whole of creation is a work of the greatest renunciation [Entäußerung], so must the artist begin by denying himself and descending into the single-creature, not shunning separateness nor the pain, indeed the torment, of form. From its first works onward nature is entirely characteristic; the energy of fire, the flash of light it imprisons in hard stone and the lovely soul of sound in harsh metal; even at the threshold of life and with organic configuration already planned, it relapses into petrifaction, overcome by the power of form. The life of the plant consists in silent receptiveness; but within what a precise and strict outline is this patient life enclosed? Only with the animal kingdom does the struggle between life and form seem really to commence: its first works it conceals in hard shells, and where these are laid aside the animate world reunites with the realm of crystallization through the art impulse [Kunsttrieb]. Finally, it steps forth bolder and freer, and active living characters appear which are the same throughout whole genera. Admittedly, art cannot begin at such a deep level as nature. If beauty is equally distributed everywhere, there are nonetheless various degrees of the manifestation and evolution of the essence and, hence, of beauty: but art demands a certain fullness of beauty, and would like to strike up, not the single sound or note, nor even the separate chord, but the whole choral melody of beauty at once. It therefore prefers to seize directly upon that which is highest and most evolved, the human figure. For since it is not given it to encompass the immeasurable whole, and since there appear in all other creatures only single refulgences, and in man alone the existence [Seyn] full, entire and bereft of nothing, it is not only permissible but actually incumbent upon it to see the whole of nature in man alone. But just because the latter gathers together everything at one point, it also repeats its whole manifoldness and traverses the same path, along which it has already passed in its broad compass, for the second time in a narrower one. Here then arises the demand upon the artist first to be faithful and truthful in the limited particulars, in order to emerge consummate and beautiful in the whole. Here it is a question of wrestling, not in flaccid and feeble, but in strong and courageous combat, with the creative spirit of nature which, in the human kingdom also, apportions character and stamp in unfathomable manifoldness.

The exercise of restraint in the recognition of that which renders the singularity of things positive must preserve him from emptiness, flabbiness and inner nothingness, before he dare aim at achieving the extreme of beauty in constructions of the greatest simplicity with infinite content, by means of the ever higher combination and ultimate fusion of manifold forms.

Only by the consummation of form can form be destroyed and this, of course, is the final goal of art in the characteristic.[8] But just as apparent agreement comes more easily to shallow souls than to others, but is inwardly valueless, so is it in art with swiftly achieved outer harmony devoid of the fullness of content; and if theory and teaching have to counteract the spiritless imitation of beautiful forms, they must also combat, above all, the inclination toward flabby, characterless art, whose bestowal of high-sounding titles upon itself merely serves to conceal its inability to fulfil art's basic conditions.

[After further remarks on Winckelmann's account of Greek art, on the fundamental necessity of the "characteristic", and on its specific manifestations in sculpture and painting, Schelling goes on to discuss the relation of beauty and passion.]

. . . Here we come upon that well-known theoretical precept which demands that the real outburst of passion [Leidenschaft] shall be as far as possible moderated, in order not to violate beauty of form. We, however, believe it necessary rather to invert this precept and express it by saying that passion ought to be moderated precisely by beauty itself. For it is very much to be feared that the moderation thus demanded will also be negatively understood, since the true requirement is rather to oppose passion by a positive force. For just as virtue does not consist in the absence of passions, but in the power of the spirit over them, so beauty is not safeguarded by their removal or reduction but by the power of beauty over them. The forces of passion must therefore really show; it must be evident that they could rebel utterly, but are held down by the power of character and break on the forms of firmly grounded beauty, as break the waves of a mighty river that rises just to the level of its banks, but cannot overflow them. Otherwise this enterprise of moderation would merely resemble that of the shallow moralists who, in order to cope with man, prefer to mutilate nature in him and have so thoroughly eliminated everything positive from his actions that the people gloat over the spectacle of great crimes, in order to enliven themselves with the sight at least of something positive.

In nature and art, essence first strives for the realization or representation of itself in singleness. Hence, the greatest severity of form is exhibited in the beginnings of both; for without bounds the boundless could not be manifested; if there were no harshness, mildness could not exist, and if unity is to be made palpable this can only be done through singularity, isolation and conflict. Initially, therefore, the creative spirit makes its appearance entirely lost in form, inaccessible, enclosed and even to a large degree austere. But the more it succeeds in uniting its whole fullness within one creature,[9] the more it gradually abates its severity, and where it fully accomplishes form, so that it rests therein and is the complete expression of itself, it grows lighthearted, so to speak, and begins to move in gentle lines. This is the condition of the most beautiful maturity and bloom, where the pure vessel stands consummate, the spirit of nature is liberated from its bonds and feels its kinship with the soul. Like a gentle dawn suffusing the whole figure, it announces the approaching soul; it is not yet there, but everything makes ready to receive it by the quiet play of gentle movements: the rigid outlines melt and grow soft; a lovely essence that is neither sensual nor spiritual, but inapprehensible, spreads over the figure and clings to all the outlines and to every motion of the limbs. This essence, inapprehensible as we stated, and yet perceptible to everyone, is what the Greeks termed *charis* and what we know as grace [Anmuth].[10]

[The argument continues with an account of representations of the human soul in relation to grace, which in its sensuous manifestation becomes "once more merely the husk and body of a higher life . . . the loftiest relation of art to nature is attained by its making the latter a means of rendering visible the soul within it".]

. . . Painting, however, seems quite differently circumstanced to sculpture [Skulptur]. For the former does not represent by means of corporeal things like the latter, but by light and colour, that is by noncorporeal and, to some extent, spiritual media; also, it does not present its images as being the objects themselves, but expressly wishes them to be looked upon as images. By its very nature, therefore, it lays less stress upon matter than sculpture, and for this reason it seems, in spite of raising substance above spirit, to be able with impunity to sink deeper below itself than could sculpture in the same case and, on the other hand, to lay with all the greater warrant a distinct overemphasis on the soul. Where it strives after the most exalted, it will in any case ennoble the passions by character or moderate them by grace, or show the power of the soul in them; on the other hand, however, precisely those loftier passions which depend upon the soul's kinship with a supreme being are fully adapted to its nature. Indeed, if sculpture effects a perfect counter-balance between the force by which a being exists outwardly and functions in nature and that by which it lives inwardly and as a soul, and excludes mere passion even from matter, so, on the other hand, may painting reduce the character of energy and activity in the latter to the advantage of the soul, transmuting it into that of submission and sufferance, through which it seems that man became more receptive to the promptings of the soul and of loftier influences in general.

This antithesis alone is sufficient to explain not only the inevitable paramountcy of sculpture [Plastik] in antiquity and of painting in modern times, in that the former had an entirely sculptural outlook as well, while the latter make the soul itself into the suffering organ of higher revelations; this also demonstrates that to strive after the sculptural [Plastischen] in form and portrayal does not suffice, and that it is necessary above all to think and feel sculpturally, i.e. in the antique manner, as well.[11] But if the debauching of sculpture into the painterly is a corruption of art, so the retrenchment of painting within the preconditions and forms of sculpture is to impose an arbitrary limitation upon it. For if the former, like weight, operates upon one point, so may painting, like light, fill creatively the whole universe.

[Schelling goes on to make observations on the history of painting. After the formative and primitive energies of Michelangelo, "elegance" (Grazie) is born in Leonardo. Then we have the sophistication of the spirit–matter relation by the technique of chiaroscuro in Correggio and then Raphael.]

. . . After the confines of nature have been overcome, and the monstrous, the fruit of the initial liberty, suppressed, and shape and form beautified by the presentiment of the soul: the heavens brighten, the softened earthly element is able to merge with the heavenly and the latter, in turn, with the gently human. Raphael takes possession of serene Olympus and leads us with him away from earth into the concourse of the gods, of the abiding, blessed beings. The flower of life at its most cultivated and the fragrance of imagination [Phantasie], together with the savour of the spirit, breathe in unison from his works. He is no longer a painter, he is a philosopher, a poet at the same time. Beside the power of his spirit stands wisdom, and as he portrays things, so they are ordered in eternal necessity. In him art has reached its goal, and because the pure equipoise of divine and human can hardly exist at more than one point, the seal of uniqueness is set upon his works.

[Guido Reni, in whose work "every element of sculptural harshness and severity has been eliminated", and whose paintings seem "to operate almost with pure light", is presented as a high point in the casting off of matter from spirit and the attainment of "soul". Schelling then describes how this sequence in the history of art applies to the contemporary artist.]

. . . The demand that art, like every other living thing, must set out from its first beginnings and to renew its vitality must always return to them afresh, may appear a harsh doctrine in an age that has been so often told how it can appropriate the most refined beauty ready-made from existing works of art, and thus reach its ultimate goal at one step. Do we not already possess the excellent and the consummate, and why should we go back to the primitive and unrefined? If the great authors of the newer art had thought like this, we should never have come to see their miracles. They too had before them the creations of the ancients, pieces of sculpture in the round and sublime works of low relief, which they could have translated directly into paintings.[12] But this expropriation of a beauty not won by itself and therefore also unintelligible, did not satisfy an art-impulse which went entirely to the original and out of which the beautiful was to be regenerated in liberty and primordial vigour. Hence, it did not hesitate to appear plain, artless and dull by the side of those sublime ancients, and to enclose art in an insignificant-looking bud until the time of grace was come. Why else do we still regard these works of the old masters, from Giotto to the teacher of Raphael, with a kind of reverence and even a certain predilection, than because the fidelity of their endeavour and the great seriousness of their calm, voluntary restrictedness compel our respect and admiration? The present generation bears the same relation to them as they do to the ancients. No living tradition, no bond of organically continuous cultural growth links their age to ours: to become their equals we must recreate art along their path, but with our own energy. Even that Indian summer of art at the end of the sixteenth and beginning of the seventeenth century was able to conjure up a few fresh blooms on the old stem, but no fertile seeds, and still less itself to plant a new stem of art. But to put away the consummate works of art and seek out its still plain and simple beginnings, in order to imitate them, as some have wished to do, would be merely a fresh and perhaps still greater misapprehension; they themselves would not be a return to the original, the very plainness would be affectation and become a hypocritical pretence.

[Art is dependent for its essential "inspiration" upon a public context, "as the more delicate plants are upon air and weather". Such a fertile environment, says Schelling, "is more safely and lastingly preserved for us by the clement overlordship of a paternal regent than by a democratic government". Without some relation to a creative public opinion the artist is condemned to isolation and eccentricity, to mere subservience to fashion.]

. . . A different inspiration [Begeisterung] falls to the lot of different epochs. Can we not expect one for this age, since the new world now in the process of formation, as it is already present partly outwardly and partly inwardly and in the mind, can no longer be measured by the yardsticks of previous opinion and everything loudly demands a larger scale and announces a complete revival? Must not that sense which has once again opened up nature and history also give back to art its great themes? To try to draw sparks from burnt-out ashes and kindle from them a universal blaze is a vain endeavour. But no more than a change in ideas [Ideen] themselves is required to lift up art out of its lassitude; no more than fresh knowledge and new belief capable of inspiring it to the work whereby it might manifest, in a rejuvenated life, a splendour resembling that which is past. To be sure, an art the same in all respects as that of past centuries will never come again; for nature never repeats itself. A Raphael of that particular kind will never again exist, but there will be another who has attained to the highest level of art in the same original manner. Only let that basic precondition be not lacking and the reawakened art, like its predecessor, will show its destined goal in its first works: if it sets forth differently from a fresh primal energy, grace will already be present, even though veiled, in its fashioning of the defined characteristic, and in both the soul will be already preordained. Works which arise after this manner are necessary and eternal, even in their initial imperfection.

We may as well confess that in this hope for the rebirth of an absolutely original art, it is pre-eminently the fatherland we have in view. Even at the time when art was reawakened in Italy, the vigorous growth of the art of our great Albrecht Dürer sprang forth first from out of our own soil; how typically German, and yet how akin to that whose sweet fruits the gentler sun of Italy brought to perfect maturity. This nation, from which proceeded the revolution [Revolution] of thought in the new Europe, to whose intellectual power [Geisteskraft] the greatest inventions bear witness, which has given laws to the heavens and whose investigations have penetrated most deeply into the earth, in whom nature has implanted more deeply than in any other a steadfast feeling for the right and an inclination toward the recognition of first causes, this nation must reach its conclusion in an original art. . . .

Part 4

Schopenhauer

Arthur Schopenhauer

(1788–1860)

At first sight Schopenhauer seems to articulate an entirely different kind of philosophy from that of his Idealist predecessors and contemporaries. Where Fichte and Schelling had spoken of the truth of the absolute and its relation to the divine idea, Schopenhauer puts forward the blind impulses of the will. He is deterministic where they aspired to an activity of ideal freedom, aggressively elitist where they tried to be democratic, and stoically pessimistic where they might seem improbably optimistic. In fact, that part of his exposition which comes closest to what we have traced so far as the 'tradition' is to be found in his case for the redeeming status of the aesthetic.

Unlike those he so bitterly attacked, Schopenhauer spent very little of his life within the universities. When he did start lecturing at Berlin in 1820, without holding a Chair, he pointedly arranged his courses to coincide with Hegel's, thus committing himself to a nearly non-existent audience. When these lectures failed he retired from the academic life and spent his time writing, remaining in almost complete obscurity until towards the very end of his life. Lewes (1857) does not even mention his name.

Schopenhauer placed himself directly in the tradition of Plato and Kant, declaring that most of what had been written since Kant was a waste of time. He had little time for Schelling, and Fichte was for him "a mere sophist and not a real philosopher"; Hegel was his favourite target, as the producer of "monstrous articulations of words that cancel and contradict one another", and that "gradually destroy so completely his ability to think, that henceforth hollow, empty flourishes and phrases are regarded by him as thoughts" (1974a, I, 141, 23; compare II, 501ff. and 1969, I, 429).

The first volume of his great work, *The World as Will and Representation*, was written in Dresden between 1814 and 1818, and published in 1819, although its significance did not begin to be appreciated until many years later. The second edition of 1844 appeared with a second volume of fifty chapters expanding on the content of the original, and a third edition, further revised, was published in 1859. Even in 1851 his obscurity was such that the two volumes of *Parerga and Paralipomena* were published in an imprint of 750. The author received ten free copies but no payment! (1974a, I, xi–xii).

As has been said, Schopenhauer saw himself as the only significant successor to Kant, though as we have seen the movement away from concentration on the unchanging operations of mind towards the positing of some dynamic and practical version of what Schopenhauer calls the "will" is evident also in Fichte's treatment of the "drives" [Trieben] and Schelling's of "force" [Kraft]. Moreover, I have explained in the general introduction that one receives a very one-sided view of Kant if one reads him only in the great *Critiques*. The writings on history and society, and above all the arguments of the *Anthropology*, reveal a mood of biologistic pessimism much closer to the spirit of Schopenhauer than to that of any other among Kant's successors; consider, for example, Kant's remarks on the inevitability of egotism, on the fundamental force of the sex drive and the urge for self-preservation, on the ubiquity of pain, and on the function of aggression and competition as nature's means of keeping the species in good health (1974, pp. 10, 100, 141ff.). These are the residual insights of Enlightenment materialism which are not allowed to impinge upon the founding of transcendental idealism, though they can occasionally be glimpsed behind it. And they were more or less ignored by Kant's followers, until Schopenhauer.

Apart from those on whom he exercised a direct influence – Hardy, Gissing, Thomas Mann, Wagner, Nietzsche, Freud, Wittgenstein and others – one looks to the tradition of Malthus and Darwin for analogues of the ideas we find explored in Schopenhauer. Striving and desiring are now the very essence of the human condition: we live in constant motion "without any possibility of that rest for which we are always longing. We resemble a man running down hill who would inevitably fall if he tried to stop" (1974a, II, 284). Schopenhauer means the simile to count. We are in contradiction with ourselves, wanting to rest even knowing that we cannot (it is Nietzsche who will try to insist on the joyousness or freedom of such a predicament), and the downhill road leads to dusty death. All forms of practical or scientific knowledge are expressions of the will, the inscrutable primary drive which is the true "thing in itself" and which forces us necessarily to obey its demands, whatever consoling fictions we may invent as responsible for our behaviour. Stridently contemptuous of theology, as he felt Kant to have been in spite of the efforts of his misty-minded followers (1974a, I, 188), Schopenhauer employs the "will" as the ground of a rigid determinism. The whole form and body of man is its outward manifestation (II, 176), and the differences between individuals which it creates are not to be mediated by the machinations of civil society (II, 229f.), which only imperfectly masks by legislation the nature of the egotistic drive (211f.). Where Schelling had put forward an idealist vitalism wherein all matter was infused with and impelled by the idea, Schopenhauer insists on a more materialized primary force:

the parts of the body must correspond completely to the chief demands and desires by which the will manifests itself . . . Teeth, gullet, and intestinal canal are objectified hunger; the genitals are objectified sexual impulse; grasping hands and nimble feet correspond to the more indirect strivings of the will which they represent.

Schopenhauer (1969), I, 108

There are only two alternatives open to the individual – and only to the individual, for they can never be coordinated successfully into social forms – if he would escape total and continual subservience to the demands of the will: asceticism and art. Asceticism is in one sense the higher of the two, since it can endure through time as a subjective condition, and through it we may approach what can be salvaged of conventional ethics. Aesthetic creation or response is a more temporary source of relief, though its products do survive for others to experience. Art results from the individual's having an oversupply of will, a surplus beyond what is necessary to meet the demands of practical needs and desires. Thus it can produce a pure form of knowing, will-inspired indeed but not related to contingent necessities and therefore open to intersubjective consensus (as in Kant). The object is recognized as Platonic Idea, "as persistent form of the whole species of things", and the self as "pure, will-less subject of knowledge" (1969, I, 195).

Further reading

Schopenhauer's reading was extraordinarily broad, and unlike some of his predecessors with their emphasis on the *a priori*, he illustrates his case with abundant examples from the whole range of world literatures and religions. I have selected passages from the first volume of *The World as Will and Representation* (1819). The corresponding passages in volume two should also be consulted, as well as the essay 'On the Metaphysics of the Beautiful and Aesthetics' (1974a, II, 415–52). Useful preliminary accounts of Schopenhauer's aesthetics can be found in Copleston (1965b), pp. 43–8; Knox (1936); and Wellek (1955), II, 308–18. The recent bibliography by Arthur Hübscher (1981) is very helpfully arranged, and lists a wide range of works on Schopenhauer's aesthetics, as well as studies of his relation to and influence upon later literary writers, among them Beckett, Browning, Gissing, Hardy, Lawrence and Melville. Sorg (1975) may also be consulted. Most of Schopenhauer's major writings are available in good English translations, thanks to the efforts of E.F.J. Payne. His philosophy in general is remarkable for its wholeness and coherence over the years of its exposition. For a recent overview, see Hamlyn (1980).

Selections from
The World as Will and Representation
[Die Welt als Wille und Vorstellung]

Volume I, 1819

The translation is a very slightly modified reprint of that by E.F.J. Payne (1969).

German text in *Arthur Schopenhauers sämtliche Werke*, ed. Deussen, vol. I.

§36

History follows the thread of events; it is pragmatic in so far as it deduces them according to the law of motivation [Motivation], a law that determines the appearing will where that will is illuminated by knowledge [Erkenntniß]. At the lower grades of its objectivity, where it still acts without knowledge, natural science as etiology considers the laws of the changes of its phenomena, and as morphology considers what is permanent in them. This almost endless theme is facilitated by the aid of concepts [Begriffe] that comprehend the general, in order to deduce from it the particular. Finally, mathematics considers the mere forms, that is, time and space, in which the Ideas [Ideen] appear drawn apart into plurality for the knowledge of the subject as individual. All these, the common name of which is science, therefore follow the principle of sufficient reason in its different forms, and their theme remains the phenomenon, its laws, connexion, and the relations resulting from these.[1] But now, what kind of knowledge is it that considers what continues to exist outside and independently of all relations, but which alone is really essential to the world, the true content of its phenomena, that which is subject to no change, and is therefore known with equal truth for all time, in a word, the *Ideas [Ideen]* that are the immediate and adequate objectivity of the thing-in-itself, of the will? It is *art*, the work of genius [Genius]. It repeats the eternal Ideas apprehended through pure contemplation [Kontemplation],[2] the essential and abiding element in all the phenomena of the world. According to the material in which it repeats, it is sculpture, painting, poetry, or music. Its only source is knowledge of the Ideas; its sole aim is communication of this knowledge. Whilst science, following the restless and unstable stream of the fourfold forms of reasons or grounds and consequents, is with every end it attains again and again directed farther, and can never find an ultimate goal or complete satisfaction, any more than by running we can reach the point where the clouds touch the horizon; art, on the contrary, is everywhere at its goal. For it plucks the object of its contemplation from the stream of the world's course, and holds it isolated before it. This particular thing, which in that stream was an infinitesimal part, becomes for art a representative of the whole, an equivalent of the infinitely many in space and time. It therefore pauses at this particular thing; it stops the wheel of time; for it the relations vanish; its object is only the essential, the Idea. We can therefore define it accurately as *the way of considering things independently of the principle of sufficient reason*, in contrast to the way of considering them which proceeds in exact accordance with this principle, and is the way of science and experience. This latter method of consideration can be compared to an endless line running horizontally, and the former to a vertical line cutting the horizontal at any point. The method of consideration that follows the principle of sufficient reason is the rational method, and it alone is valid and useful in practical life and in science. The method of consideration that looks away from the content of this principle is the method of genius [geniale Betrachtungsart], which is valid and useful in art alone. The first is Aristotle's method; the second is, on the whole, Plato's. The first is like the mighty storm, rushing along without beginning or aim, bending, agitating, and carrying everything away with it; the second is like the silent sunbeam, cutting through the path of the storm, and quite unmoved by it. The first is like the innumerable violently agitated drops of the waterfall, constantly changing and never for a moment at rest; the second is like the rainbow silently resting on this raging torrent. Only through the pure contemplation described above, which becomes absorbed entirely in the object, are the Ideas comprehended; and the nature of *genius* consists precisely in the pre-eminent ability for such contemplation. Now as this demands a complete forgetting of our own person and of its relations and connexions, the *gift of genius [Genialität]* is nothing but the most complete *objectivity*, i.e., the objective tendency of the mind [Geist], as opposed to the subjective directed to our own person, i.e., to the will. Accordingly, genius is the capacity to remain in a state of pure perception, to lose oneself in perception [Anschauung],[3] to remove from the service of the will the knowledge which originally existed only for this service. In other words, genius is the ability to leave entirely out of sight our own interest, our willing, and our aims, and consequently to discard entirely our own personality for a time, in order to remain *pure knowing subject*, the clear eye of the world; and this not merely for moments, but with the necessary continuity and self-presence [Besonnenheit] to enable us to repeat by deliberate art what has been apprehended, and "what in wavering apparition gleams fix in its place with thoughts that stand for ever!"[4] For genius [Genius] to appear in an individual, it is as if a measure of the power of knowledge must have fallen to his lot far exceeding that required for the service of an individual will; and this superfluity of knowledge having become free, now becomes the subject purified of will, the clear mirror of the inner nature of the world. This explains the animation, amounting to disquietude, in men of genius, since the present can seldom satisfy them, because it does not fill their consciousness. This gives them that restless zealous nature, that constant search for new objects worthy of contemplation [Betrachtung], and also that longing, hardly ever satisfied, for men of like nature and stature to whom they may open their hearts. The common mortal, on the other hand, entirely filled and satisfied by the common present, is absorbed in it, and, finding everywhere his like, has that special ease and comfort in daily life which are denied to the man of genius. Imagination [Phantasie] has been rightly recognized as an essential element of genius; indeed, it has sometimes been regarded as identical with genius, but this is not correct. The objects of genius as such are the eternal Ideas, the persistent, essential forms of the world and of all its phenomena; but knowledge of the Idea is necessarily knowledge through perception, and is not abstract. Thus the knowledge of the genius would be restricted to the Ideas of objects actually present to his own person, and would be dependent on the concatenation of circumstances that brought them to him, did not imagination extend his horizon far beyond the reality of his personal experience, and enable him to construct all the rest out of the little that has come into his own actual apperception [Apperception],[5] and thus to let almost all the possible scenes of life pass by within himself. Moreover, the actual objects are almost always only very imperfect copies of the Idea that manifests itself in them. Therefore the man of genius requires imagination, in order to see in things not what nature has actually formed, but what she endeavoured to form, yet did not bring about, because of the conflict of her forms with one another which was referred to in the previous book.[6] We shall return to this later, when considering sculpture. Thus imagination extends the mental horizon of the genius beyond the objects that actually present themselves to his person, as regards both quality and quantity. For this reason, unusual strength of imagination is a companion, indeed a condition, of genius. But the converse is not the case, for strength of imagination is not evidence of genius; on the contrary, even men with little or no touch of genius may have much imagination. For we can consider an actual object in two opposite ways, purely objectively, the way of genius grasping the Idea of the object, or in the common way, merely in its relations to other objects according to the principle of sufficient reason, and in its relations to our own will. In a similar manner, we can also perceive an imaginary object in these two ways. Considered in the first way, it is a means to knowledge of the Idea, the communication of which is the work of art. In the second case, the imaginary object is used to build castles in the air, congenial to selfishness and to one's own whim, which for the moment delude and delight; thus only the relations of the phantasms so connected are really ever known. The man who indulges in this game is a dreamer [Phantast]; he will easily mingle with reality the pictures that delight his solitude, and will thus become unfit for real life. Perhaps he will write down the delusions of his imagination, and these will give us the ordinary novels of all kinds which entertain those like him and the public at large, since the readers fancy themselves in the position of the hero, and then find the description very "nice".[7]

As we have said, the common, ordinary man, that manufactured article of nature which she daily produces in thousands, is not capable, at any rate continuously, of a consideration of things wholly disinterested in every sense, such as is contemplativeness [Beschaulichkeit] proper. He can direct his attention to things only in so far as they have some relation to his will, although that relation may be only very indirect. As in this reference that always demands only knowledge of the relations, the abstract concept of the thing is sufficient and often even more appropriate, the ordinary man does not linger long over the mere perception [Anschauung], does not fix his eye on an object for long, but, in everything that presents itself to him, quickly looks merely for the concept under which it is to be brought, just as the lazy man looks for a chair, which then no longer interests him. Therefore he is very soon finished with everything, with works of art, with beautiful natural objects, and with that contemplation of life in all its scenes which is really of significance everywhere. He does not linger; he seeks only his way in life, or at most all that might at any time become his way. Thus he makes topographical notes in the widest sense, but on the consideration [Betrachtung] of life itself as such he wastes no time. On the other hand, the man of genius [der Geniale], whose power of knowledge is, through its excess, withdrawn for a part of his time from the service of his will, dwells on the consideration of life itself, strives to grasp the Idea of each thing, not its relations to other things. In doing this, he frequently neglects a consideration of his own path in life, and therefore often pursues this with insufficient skill. Whereas to the ordinary man his faculty of knowledge is a lamp that lights his path, to the man of genius it is the sun that reveals the world. This great difference in their way of looking at life soon becomes visible even in the outward appearance of them both. The glance of the man in whom genius [Genius] lives and works readily distinguishes him; it is both vivid and firm and bears the character of contemplativeness [Beschaulichkeit], of contemplation [Kontemplation]. We can see this in the portraits of the few men of genius which nature has produced here and there among countless millions. On the other hand, the real opposite of contemplation, namely spying or prying, can be readily seen in the glance of others, if indeed it is not dull and vacant, as is often the case. Consequently a face's "expression of genius" consists in the fact that a decided predominance of knowing over willing is visible in it, and hence that there is manifested in it a knowledge without any relation to a will, in other words, a *pure knowing*.[8] On the other hand, in the case of faces that follow the rule, the expression of the will predominates, and we see that knowledge comes into activity only on the impulse of the will, and so is directed only to motives [Motive].

As the knowledge of the genius, or knowledge of the Idea, is that which does not follow the principle of sufficient reason, so, on the other hand, the knowledge that does follow this principle gives us prudence and rationality in life, and brings about the sciences. Thus individuals of genius will be affected with the defects entailed in the neglect of the latter kind of knowledge. Here, however, a limitation must be observed, that what I shall state in this regard concerns them only in so far as, and while, they are actually engaged with the kind of knowledge peculiar to the genius. Now this is by no means the case at every moment of their lives, for the great though spontaneous exertion required for the will-free comprehension of the Ideas necessarily relaxes again, and there are long intervals during which men of genius stand in very much the same position as ordinary persons, both as regards merits and defects.[9] On this account, the action of genius has always been regarded as an inspiration [Inspiration], as indeed the name itself indicates, as the action of a superhuman being different from the individual himself, which takes possession of him only periodically. The disinclination of men of genius to direct their attention to the content of the principle of sufficient reason will show itself first in regard to the ground of being, as a disinclination for mathematics. The consideration of mathematics proceeds on the most universal forms of the phenomenon, space and time, which are themselves only modes or aspects of the principle of sufficient reason; and it is therefore the very opposite of that consideration that seeks only the content of the phenomenon, namely the Idea expressing itself in the phenomenon apart from all relations. Moreover, the logical procedure of mathematics will be repugnant to genius, for it obscures real insight and does not satisfy it; it presents a mere concatenation of conclusions according to the principle of the ground of knowing. Of all the mental powers, it makes the greatest claim on memory, so that one may have before oneself all the earlier propositions to which reference is made. Experience has also confirmed that men of great artistic genius have no aptitude for mathematics; no man was ever very distinguished in both at the same time. Alfieri relates that he was never able to understand even the fourth proposition of Euclid. Goethe was reproached enough with his want of mathematical knowledge by the ignorant opponents of his colour theory.[10] Here, where it was naturally not a question of calculation and measurement according to hypothetical data, but one of direct knowledge by understanding cause and effect, this reproach was so utterly absurd and out of place, that they revealed their total lack of judgement just as much by such a reproach as by the rest of their Midas-utterances. The fact that even today, nearly half a century after the appearance of Goethe's colour theory, the Newtonian fallacies still remain in undisturbed possession of the professorial chair even in Germany, and that people continue to talk quite seriously about the seven homogeneous rays of light and their differing refrangibility, will one day be numbered among the great intellectual peculiarities of mankind in general, and of the Germans in particular. From the same above-mentioned cause may be explained the equally well-known fact that, conversely, distinguished mathematicians have little susceptibility to works of fine art. This is expressed with particular naivety in the well-known anecdote of that French mathematician who, after reading Racine's *Iphigenia*, shrugged his shoulders and asked: "Qu'est-ce que cela prouve?"[11] Further, as keen comprehension of relations according to the laws of causality and motivation really constitutes prudence or sagacity, whereas the knowledge of genius is not directed to relations, a prudent man will not be a genius in so far as and while he is prudent, and a genius will not be prudent in so far as and while he is a genius. Finally, perceptual knowledge generally, in the province of which the Idea entirely lies, is directly opposed to rational or abstract knowledge, which is guided by the principle of the ground of knowing.[12] It is also well known that we seldom find great genius united with pre-eminent rationality; on the contrary, men of genius are often subject to violent emotions and irrational passions. But the cause of this is not weakness of the faculty of reason, but partly unusual energy of that whole phenomenon of will, the individual genius. This phenomenon manifests itself through vehemence of all his acts of will. The cause is also partly a preponderance of knowledge from perception through the senses and the understanding over abstract knowledge, in other words, a decided tendency to the perceptual [Anschauliche]. In such men the extremely energetic impression of the perceptual outshines the colourless concepts so that conduct is no longer guided by the latter, but by the former, and on this very account becomes irrational. Accordingly, the impression of the present moment on them is very strong, and carries them away into thoughtless actions, into emotion and passion. Moreover, since their knowledge has generally been withdrawn in part from the service of the will, they will not in conversation think so much of the person with whom they are speaking as of the thing they are speaking about, which is vividly present in their minds. Therefore they will judge or narrate too objectively for their own interests; they will not conceal what it would be more prudent to keep concealed, and so on. Finally, they are inclined to soliloquize, and in general may exhibit several weaknesses that actually are closely akin to madness. It is often remarked that genius and madness have a side where they touch and even pass over into each other, and even poetic inspiration [Begeisterung] has been called a kind of madness; *amabilis insania*, as Horace calls it (*Odes*, iii, 4); and in the introduction to *Oberon* Wieland speaks of "amiable madness". Even Aristotle, as quoted by Seneca (*De Tranquillitate Animi*, xv, 16 [xvii, 10]), is supposed to have said: "nullum magnum ingenium sine mixtura dementiae fuit."[13] Plato expresses it in the above-mentioned myth of the dark cave (*Republic*, Bk 7) by saying that those who outside the cave have seen the true sunlight and the things that actually are (the Ideas), cannot afterwards see within the cave any more, because their eyes have grown unaccustomed to the darkness; they no longer recognize the shadow-forms correctly. They are therefore ridiculed for their mistakes by those others who have never left that cave and those shadow-forms. Also in the *Phaedrus* (245a), he distinctly says that without a certain madness there can be no genuine poet, in fact (249d) that everyone appears mad who recognizes the eternal Ideas in fleeting things. Cicero also states: *Negat enim sine furore Democritus quemquam poetam magnum esse posse; quod idem dicit Plato* (*De Divinatione*, i, 37).[14] And finally, Pope says:

> Great wits to madness sure are near allied.
> And thin partitions do their bounds divide.[15]

Particularly instructive in this respect is Goethe's *Torquato Tasso*, in which he brings before our eyes not only suffering, the essential martyrdom of genius as such, but also its constant transition into madness. Finally, the fact of direct contact between genius and madness is established partly by the biographies of great men of genius, such as Rousseau, Byron, and Alfieri, and by anecdotes from the lives of others. On the other hand, I must mention having found, in frequent visits to lunatic asylums, individual subjects endowed with unmistakably great gifts. Their genius appeared distinctly through their madness which had completely gained the upper hand. Now this cannot be ascribed to chance, for on the one hand the number of mad persons is relatively very small, while on the other a man of genius is a phenomenon rare beyond all ordinary estimation, and appearing in nature only as the greatest exception. We may be convinced of this from the mere fact that we can compare the number of the really great men of genius produced by the whole of civilized Europe in ancient and modern times, with the two hundred and fifty millions who are always living in Europe and renew themselves every thirty years. Among men of genius, however, can be reckoned only those who have furnished works that have retained through all time an enduring value for mankind. Indeed, I will not refrain from mentioning that I have known some men of decided, though not remarkable, mental superiority who at the same time betrayed a slight touch of insanity. Accordingly, it might appear that every advance of the intellect beyond the usual amount, as an abnormality, already disposes to madness. Meanwhile, however, I will give as briefly as possible my opinion about the purely intellectual ground of the kinship between genius and madness, for this discussion will certainly contribute to the explanation of the real nature of genius, in other words, of that quality of the mind which is alone capable of producing genuine works of art. But this necessitates a brief discussion of madness itself.[16]

A clear and complete insight into the nature of madness, a correct and distinct conception of what really distinguishes the sane from the insane, has, so far as I know, never yet been found. Neither the faculty of reason nor understanding can be denied to the mad, for they talk and understand, and often draw very accurate conclusions. They also as a rule, perceive quite correctly what is present, and see the connexion between cause and effect. Visions [Visionen], like the fancies of an overwrought brain, are no ordinary symptom of madness; delirium falsifies perception [Anschauung], madness the thoughts. For the most part, mad people do not generally err in the knowledge of what is immediately *present*; but their mad talk relates always to what is *absent* and *past*, and only through these to its connexion with what is present. Therefore, it seems to me that their malady specially concerns the *memory*. It is not, indeed, a case of memory failing them entirely, for many of them know a great deal by heart, and sometimes recognize persons whom they have not seen for a long time. Rather is it a case of the thread of memory being broken, its continuous connexion being abolished, and of the impossibility of a uniformly coherent recollection of the past. Individual scenes of the past stand out correctly, just like the individual present; but there are gaps in their recollection that they fill up with fictions [Fiktionen]. These are either always the same, and so become fixed ideas [Ideen];[17] it is then a fixed mania or melancholy; or they are different each time, momentary fancies; it is then called folly, *fatuitas*. This is the reason why it is so difficult to question a mad person about his previous life-history when he enters an asylum. In his memory the true is for ever mixed up with the false. Although the immediate present is correctly known, it is falsified through a fictitious connexion with an imaginary past. Mad people therefore consider themselves and others as identical with persons who live merely in their fictitious past. Many acquaintances they do not recognize at all, and, in spite of a correct representation or mental picture [Vorstellung] of the individual actually present, they have only false relations of this to what is absent. If the madness reaches a high degree, the result is a complete absence of memory; the mad person is then wholly incapable of any reference to what is absent or past, but is determined solely by the whim of the moment in combination with fictions that in his head fill up the past. In such a case, we are then not safe for one moment from ill-treatment or murder, unless we constantly and visibly remind the insane person of superior force. The mad person's knowledge has in common with the animal's the fact that both are restricted to the present; but what distinguishes them is that the animal has really no representation at all of the past as such, although the past acts on it through the medium of custom. Thus, for instance, the dog recognizes his former master even after years, that is to say, it receives the accustomed impression at the sight of him; but the dog has no recollection of the time that has since elapsed. On the other hand, the madman always carries about in his faculty of reason a past in the abstract, but it is a false past that exists for him alone, and that either all the time or merely for the moment. The influence of this false past then prevents the use of the correctly known present which the animal makes. The fact that violent mental suffering or unexpected and terrible events are frequently the cause of madness, I explain as follows. Every such suffering is as an actual event always confined to the present; hence it is only transitory, and to that extent is never excessively heavy. It becomes insufferably great only in so far as it is a lasting pain, but as such it is again only a thought, and therefore resides in the *memory*. Now if such a sorrow, such painful knowledge or reflection, is so harrowing that it becomes positively unbearable, and the individual would succumb to it, then nature, alarmed in this way, seizes on *madness* as the last means of saving life. The mind [Geist], tormented so greatly, destroys, as it were, the thread of its memory, fills up the gaps with fictions, and thus seeks refuge in madness from the mental suffering that exceeds its strength, just as a limb affected by mortification is cut off and replaced with a wooden one. As examples, we may consider the raving Ajax, King Lear, and Ophelia;[18] for the creations of the genuine genius, to which alone we can here refer, as being generally known, are equal in truth to real persons; moreover, frequent actual experience in this respect shows the same thing. A faint analogy of this kind of transition from pain to madness is to be found in the way in which we all frequently try, as it were mechanically, to banish a tormenting memory that suddenly occurs to us by some loud exclamation or movement, to turn ourselves from it, to distract ourselves by force.

Now, from what we have stated, we see that the madman correctly knows the individual present as well as many particulars of the past, but that he fails to recognize the connexion, the relations, and therefore goes astray and talks nonsense. Just this is his point of contact with the genius; for he too leaves out of sight knowledge of the connexion of things, as he neglects that knowledge of relations which is knowledge according to the principle of sufficient reason, in order to see in things only their Ideas, and to try to grasp their real inner nature which expresses itself to perception, in regard to which *one* thing represents its whole species, and hence, as Goethe says, one case is valid for a thousand. The individual object of his contemplation, or the present which he apprehends with excessive vividness, appears in so strong a light that the remaining links of the chain, so to speak, to which they belong, withdraw into obscurity, and this gives us phenomena that have long been recognized as akin to those of madness. That which exists in the actual individual thing, only imperfectly and weakened by modifications [Modifikationen], is enhanced to perfection, to the Idea of it, by the method of contemplation used by the genius. Therefore he everywhere sees extremes, and on this account his own actions tend to extremes. He does not know how to strike the mean; he lacks cool-headedness, and the result is as we have said. He knows the Ideas perfectly, but not the individuals. Therefore it has been observed that a poet may know *man* profoundly and thoroughly, but *men* very badly; he is easily duped, and is a plaything in the hands of the cunning and crafty.[19]

§37

Now according to our explanation, genius consists in the ability to know, independently of the principle of sufficient reason, not individual things which have their existence only in relation, but the Ideas of such things, and in the ability to be, in face of these, the correlative of the Idea, and hence no longer individual, but pure subject of knowing. Yet this ability must be inherent in all men in a lesser and different degree, as otherwise they would be just as incapable of enjoying works of art as of producing them.[20] Generally they would have no susceptibility at all to the beautiful and to the sublime; indeed, these words could have no meaning for them. We must therefore assume as existing in all men that power of recognizing in things their Ideas, of divesting themselves for a moment of their personality, unless indeed there are some who are not capable of any aesthetic pleasure at all. The man of genius excels them only in the far higher degree and more continuous duration of this kind of knowledge. These enable him to retain that self-presence [Besonnenheit] necessary for him to repeat what is thus known in a voluntary and intentional work, such repetition being the work of art. Through this he communicates to others the Idea he has grasped. Therefore this Idea remains unchanged and the same, and hence aesthetic pleasure is essentially one and the same, whether it be called forth by a work of art, or directly by the perception [Anschauung] of nature and of life. The work of art is merely a means of facilitating that knowledge in which this pleasure consists. That the Idea comes to us more easily from the work of art than directly from nature and from reality, arises solely from the fact that the artist, who knew only the Idea and not reality, clearly repeated in his work only the Idea, separated it out from reality, and omitted all disturbing contingencies. The artist lets us peer into the world through his eyes. That he has these eyes, that he knows the essential in things which lies outside all relations, is the gift of genius and is inborn; but that he is able to lend us this gift, to let us see with his eyes, is acquired, and is the technical side of art. Therefore, after the account I have given in the foregoing remarks of the inner essence of the aesthetic way of knowing in its most general outline, the following more detailed philosophical consideration of the beautiful and the sublime will explain both simultaneously, in nature and in art, without separating them further. We shall first consider what takes place in a man when he is affected by the beautiful and the sublime. Whether he draws this emotion directly from nature, from life, or partakes of it only through the mediation of art, makes no essential difference, but only an outward one.

§38

In the aesthetic method of contemplation we found *two inseparable constituent parts*: namely, knowledge of the object not as individual thing, but as Platonic *Idea*, in other words, as persistent form of this whole species of things; and the self-consciousness of the knower, not as individual, but as *pure, will-less subject of knowledge*. The condition under which the two constituent parts appear always united was the abandonment of the method of knowledge that is bound to the principle of sufficient reason, a knowledge that, on the contrary, is the only appropriate kind for serving the will and also for science. Moreover, we shall see that the *pleasure* produced by contemplation of the beautiful arises from those two constituent parts, sometimes more from the one than from the other, according to what the object of aesthetic contemplation may be.

All *willing* [*Wollen*] springs from lack, from deficiency, and thus from suffering. Fulfilment brings this to an end; yet for one wish that is fulfilled there remain at least ten that are denied. Further, desiring [das Begehren] lasts a long time, demands and requests go on to infinity; fulfilment is short and meted out sparingly. But even the final satisfaction itself is only apparent; the wish fulfilled at once makes way for a new one; the former is a known delusion, the latter a delusion not as yet known. No attained object of willing can give a satisfaction that lasts and no longer declines; but it is always like the alms thrown to a beggar, which reprieves him today so that his misery may be prolonged till tomorrow. Therefore, so long as our consciousness is filled by our will, so long as we are given up to the throng of desires with its constant hopes and fears, so long as we are the subject of willing, we never obtain lasting happiness or peace. Essentially, it is all the same whether we pursue or flee, fear harm or aspire to enjoyment; care for the constantly demanding will, no matter in what form, continually fills and moves consciousness; but without peace and calm, true well-being is absolutely impossible. Thus the subject of willing is constantly lying on the revolving wheel of Ixion, is always drawing water in the sieve of the Danaides, and is the eternally thirsting Tantalus.

When, however, an external cause or inward disposition suddenly raises us out of the endless stream of willing, and snatches knowledge from the thraldom of the will, the attention is now no longer directed to the motives of willing, but comprehends things free from their relation to the will. Thus it considers things without interest, without subjectivity, purely objectively; it is entirely given up to them in so far as they are merely representations [Vorstellungen], and not motives. Then all at once the peace, always sought but always escaping us on that first path of willing, comes to us of its own accord, and all is well with us. It is the painless state, prized by Epicurus as the highest good and as the state of the gods; for that moment we are delivered from the miserable pressure of the will. We celebrate the Sabbath of the penal servitude of willing; the wheel of Ixion stands still.

But this is just the state that I described above as necessary for knowledge of the Idea, as pure contemplation, absorption in perception, being lost in the object, forgetting all individuality, abolishing [Aufhebung] the kind of knowledge which follows the principle of sufficient reason, and comprehends only relations. It is the state where, simultaneously and inseparably, the perceived individual thing is raised to the Idea of its species, and the knowing individual to the pure subject of will-less knowing, and now the two, as such, no longer stand in the stream of time and of all other relations. It is then all the same whether we see the setting sun from a prison or from a palace.[21]

Inward disposition, predominance of knowing over willing, can bring about this state in any environment. This is shown by those admirable Dutchmen who directed such purely objective perception to the most insignificant objects, and set up a lasting monument of their objectivity and spiritual peace in paintings of *still life*. The aesthetic beholder does not contemplate this without emotion, for it graphically describes to him the calm, tranquil, will-free frame of mind of the artist which was necessary for contemplating such insignificant things so objectively, considering them so attentively, and repeating this perception with such thought. Since the picture invites the beholder to participate in this state, his emotion is often enhanced by the contrast between it and his own restless state of mind, disturbed by vehement willing, in which he happens to be. In the same spirit landscape painters, especially Ruysdael, have often painted extremely insignificant landscape objects, and have thus produced the same effect even more delightfully.

So much is achieved simply and solely by the inner force of an artistic disposition; but that purely objective frame of mind is facilitated and favoured from without by accommodating objects, by the abundance of natural beauty that invites perception [Anschauen], and even presses itself on us. Whenever it presents itself to our gaze all at once, it almost always succeeds in snatching us, although only for a few moments, from subjectivity, from the thraldom of the will, and transferring us into the state of pure knowledge. This is why the man tormented by passions, want, or care, is so suddenly revived, cheered, and comforted by a single, free glance into nature. The storm of passions, the pressure of desire and fear, and all the miseries of willing are then at once calmed and appeased in a marvellous way. For at the moment when, torn from the will, we have given ourselves up to pure, will-less knowing, we have stepped into another world, so to speak, where everything that moves our will, and thus violently agitates us, no longer exists. This liberation of knowledge lifts us as wholly and completely above all this as do sleep and dreams. Happiness and unhappiness have vanished; we are no longer the individual; that is forgotten; we are only pure subject of knowledge. We are only that *one* eye of the world which looks out from all knowing creatures, but which in man alone can be wholly free from serving the will. In this way, all difference of individuality disappears so completely that it is all the same whether the perceiving eye belongs to a mighty monarch or to a stricken beggar; for beyond that boundary neither happiness nor misery is taken with us. There always lies so near to us a realm in which we have escaped entirely from all our affliction; but who has the strength to remain in it for long? As soon as any relation to our will, to our person, even of those objects of pure contemplation, again enters consciousness, the magic is at an end. We fall back into knowledge governed by the principle of sufficient reason; we now no longer know the Idea, but the individual thing, the link of a chain to which we also belong, and we are again abandoned to all our woe. Most men are almost always at this standpoint, because they entirely lack objectivity, i.e., genius. Therefore they do not like to be alone with nature; they need company, or at any rate a book, for their knowledge remains subject to the will. Therefore in objects they seek only some relation to their will, and with everything that has not such a relation there sounds within them, as it were like a ground-bass, the constant, inconsolable lament, "It is of no use to me." Thus in solitude even the most beautiful surroundings have for them a desolate, dark, strange, and hostile appearance.

Finally, it is also the blessedness of will-less perception [Anschauen] which spreads so wonderful a spell over the past and the distant, and by a self-deception presents them to us in so flattering a light. For by our conjuring up in our minds days long past spent in a distant place, it is only the objects recalled by our imagination, not the subject of will, that carried around its incurable sorrows with it just as much then as it does now. But these are forgotten, because since then they have frequently made way for others. Now in what is remembered, objective perception is just as effective as it would be in what is present, if we allowed it to have influence over us, if, free from will, we surrendered ourselves to it. Hence it happens that, especially when we are more than usually disturbed by some want, the sudden recollection of past and distant scenes flits across our minds like a lost paradise. The imagination recalls merely what was objective, not what was individually subjective, and we imagine that that something objective stood before us then just as pure and undisturbed by any relation to the will as its image now stands in the imagination; but the relation of objects to our will caused us just as much affliction then as it does now. We can withdraw from all suffering just as well through present as through distant objects, whenever we raise ourselves to a purely objective contemplation of them, and are thus able to produce the illusion that only those objects are present, not we ourselves. Then, as pure subject of knowing, delivered from the miserable self, we become entirely one with those objects, and foreign as our want is to them, it is at such moments just as foreign to us. Then the world as representation [Vorstellung] alone remains; the world as will [Wille] has disappeared.

In all these remarks, I have sought to make clear the nature and extent of the share which the subjective condition has in aesthetic pleasure, namely the deliverance of knowledge from the service of the will, the forgetting of oneself as individual, and the enhancement of consciousness to the pure, will-less, timeless subject of knowing that is independent of all relations. With this subjective side of aesthetic contemplation [Beschauung] there always appears at the same time as necessary correlative its objective side, the intuitive apprehension of the Platonic Idea. But before we turn to a closer consideration of this and to the achievements of art in reference to it, it is better to stop for a while at the subjective side of aesthetic pleasure, in order to complete our consideration of this by discussing the impression of the *sublime*, which depends solely on it, and arises through a modification of it. After this, our investigation of aesthetic pleasure will be completed by a consideration of its objective side.[22]

But first of all, the following remarks appertain to what has so far been said. Light is most pleasant and delightful; it has become the symbol of all that is good and salutary. In all religions it indicates eternal salvation, while darkness symbolizes damnation. Ormuzd dwells in the purest light, Ahriman in eternal night.[23] Dante's Paradise looks somewhat like Vauxhall in London, since all the blessed spirits appear there as points of light that arrange themselves in regular figures. The absence of light immediately makes us sad, and its return makes us feel happy. Colours directly excite a keen delight, which reaches its highest degree when they are translucent. All this is due to the fact that light is the correlative and condition of the most perfect kind of knowledge through perception, of the only knowledge that in no way directly affects the will. For sight, unlike the affections of the other senses, is in itself, directly, and by its sensuous effect, quite incapable of pleasantness or unpleasantness of *sensation* in the organ; in other words, it has no direct connexion with the will. Only perception [Anschauung] arising in the understanding can have such a connexion, which then lies in the relation of the object to the will. In the case of hearing, this is different; tones can excite pain immediately, and can also be directly agreeable sensuously without reference to harmony or melody. Touch, as being one with the feeling of the whole body, is still more subject to this direct influence on the will; and yet there is a touch devoid of pain and pleasure. Odours, however, are always pleasant or unpleasant, and tastes even more so. Thus the last two senses are most closely related to the will, and hence are always the most ignoble, and have been called by Kant the subjective senses.[24] Therefore the pleasure from light is in fact the pleasure from the objective possibility of the purest and most perfect kind of knowledge from perception. As such it can be deduced from the fact that pure knowing, freed and delivered from all willing, is extremely gratifying, and, as such, has a large share in aesthetic enjoyment. Again, the incredible beauty that we associated with the reflection of objects in water can be deduced from this view of light. That lightest, quickest, and finest species of the effect of bodies on one another, that to which we owe also by far the most perfect and pure of our perceptions [Wahrnehmungen], namely the impression by means of reflected light-rays, is here brought before our eyes quite distinctly, clearly, and completely, in cause and effect, and indeed on a large scale. Hence our aesthetic delight from it, which in the main is entirely rooted in the subjective ground of aesthetic pleasure, and is delight from pure knowledge and its ways.[25]

§39

All these considerations are intended to stress the subjective part of aesthetic pleasure, namely, that pleasure in so far as it is delight in the mere perceptual knowledge as such, in contrast to the will. Now directly connected with all this is the following explanation of the frame of mind which has been called the feeling of the *sublime*.

It has already been observed that transition into the state of pure perception occurs most easily when the objects accommodate themselves to it, in other words, when by their manifold and at the same time definite and distinct form they easily become representatives of their Ideas, in which beauty, in the objective sense, consists. Above all, natural beauty has this quality, and even the most stolid and apathetic person obtains therefrom at least a fleeting aesthetic pleasure. Indeed, it is remarkable how the plant world in particular invites one to aesthetic contemplation, and, as it were, obtrudes itself thereon. It might be said that such accommodation was connected with the fact that these organic beings themselves, unlike animal bodies, are not immediate objects of knowledge. They therefore need the extrinsic, intelligent individual in order to come from the world of blind willing into the world of the representation. Thus they yearn for this entrance, so to speak, in order to attain at any rate indirectly what directly is denied to them. For the rest, I leave entirely undecided this bold and venturesome idea that perhaps borders on the fanatic [Schwärmerei], for only a very intimate and devoted contemplation of nature can excite or justify it.[26] Now so long as it is this accommodation of nature, the significance and distinctness of its forms, from which the Ideas individualized in them readily speak to us; so long as it is this which moves us from knowledge of mere relations serving the will into aesthetic contemplation, and thus raises us to the will-free subject of knowing, so long is it merely the *beautiful* that affects us, and the feeling of beauty that is excited. But these very objects, whose significant forms invite us to a pure contemplation of them, may have a hostile relation to the human will in general, as manifested in its objectivity, the human body. They may be opposed to it; they may threaten it by their might that eliminates all resistance, or their immeasurable greatness may reduce it to nought. Nevertheless, the beholder may not direct his attention to this relation to his will which is so pressing and hostile, but, although he perceives and acknowledges it, he may consciously turn away from it, forcibly tear himself from his will and its relations, and, giving himself up entirely to knowledge, may quietly contemplate, as pure, will-less subject of knowing, those very objects so terrible to the will. He may comprehend only their Idea that is foreign to all relation, gladly linger over its contemplation, and consequently be elevated precisely in this way above himself, his person, his willing, and all willing. In that case, he is then filled with the feeling of the *sublime*; he is in the state of exaltation, and therefore the object that causes such a state is called *sublime*. Thus what distinguishes the feeling of the sublime from that of the beautiful is that, with the beautiful, pure knowledge has gained the upper hand without a struggle, since the beauty of the object, in other words that quality of it which facilitates knowledge of its Idea, has removed from consciousness, without resistance and hence imperceptibly, the will and knowledge of relations that slavishly serve this will. What is then left is pure subject of knowing, and not even a recollection of the will remains. On the other hand, with the sublime, that state of pure knowing is obtained first of all by a conscious and violent tearing away from the relations of the same object to the will which are recognized as unfavourable, by a free exaltation, accompanied by consciousness, beyond the will and the knowledge related to it. This exaltation must not only be won with consciousness, but also be maintained, and it is therefore accompanied by a constant recollection of the will, yet not of a single individual willing, such as fear or desire, but of human willing in general, in so far as it is expressed universally through its objectivity, the human body. If a single, real act of will were to enter consciousness through actual personal affliction and danger from the object, the individual will, thus actually affected, would at once gain the upper hand. The peace of contemplation would become impossible, the impression of the sublime would be lost, because it had yielded to anxiety, in which the effort of the individual to save himself supplanted every other thought. A few examples will contribute a great deal to making clear this theory of the aesthetically sublime, and removing any doubt about it. At the same time they will show the difference in the degrees of this feeling of the sublime. For in the main it is identical with the feeling of the beautiful, with pure will-less knowing, and with the knowledge, which necessarily appears therewith, of the Ideas out of all relation that is determined by the principle of sufficient reason. The feeling of the sublime is distinguished from that of the beautiful only by the addition, namely the exaltation beyond the known hostile relation of the contemplated object to the will in general. Thus there result several degrees of the sublime, in fact transitions from the beautiful to the sublime, according as this addition is strong, clamorous, urgent, and near, or only feeble, remote, and merely suggested. I regard it as more appropriate to the discussion to adduce first of all in examples these transitions, and generally the weaker degrees of the impression of the sublime, although those whose aesthetic susceptibility in general is not very great, and whose imagination is not vivid, will understand only the examples, given later, of the higher and more distinct degrees of that impression. They should therefore confine themselves to these, and should ignore the examples of the very weak degree of the above-mentioned impression, which are to be spoken of first.

Just as man is simultaneously impetuous and dark impulse of willing (indicated by the pole of the genitals as its focal point), and eternal, free, serene subject of pure knowing (indicated by the pole of the brain),[27] so, in keeping with this antithesis, the sun is simultaneously the source of *light*, the condition for the most perfect kind of knowledge, and therefore of the most delightful of things; and the source of *heat*, the first condition of all life, in other words, of every phenomenon of the will at its higher grades. Therefore what heat is for the will, light is for knowledge. For this reason, light is the largest diamond in the crown of beauty, and has the most decided influence on the knowledge of every beautiful object. Its presence generally is an indispensable condition; its favourable arrangement enhances even the beauty of the most beautiful. But above all else, the beautiful in architecture is enhanced by the favour of light, and through it even the most insignificant thing becomes a beautiful object. Now if in the depth of winter, when the whole of nature is frozen and stiff, we see the rays of the setting sun reflected by masses of stone, where they illuminate without warming, and are thus favourable only to the purest kind of knowledge, not to the will, then contemplation of the beautiful effect of light on these masses moves us into the state of pure knowing, as all beauty does. Yet here, through the faint recollection of the lack of warmth from those rays, in other words, of the absence of the principle of life, a certain transcending of the interest of the will is required. There is a slight challenge to abide in pure knowledge, to turn away from all willing, and precisely in this way we have a transition from the feeling of the beautiful to that of the sublime. It is the faintest trace of the sublime in the beautiful, and beauty itself appears here only in a slight degree. The following is an example almost as weak.

Let us transport ourselves to a very lonely region of boundless horizons, under a perfectly cloudless sky, trees and plants in the perfectly motionless air, no animals, no human beings, no moving masses of water, the profoundest silence. Such surroundings are as it were a summons to seriousness, to contemplation, with complete emancipation from all willing and its cravings; but it is just this that gives to such a scene of mere solitude and profound peace a touch of the sublime. For, since it affords no objects, either favourable or unfavourable, to the will that is always in need of strife and attainment, there is left only the state of pure contemplation, and whoever is incapable of this is abandoned with shameful ignominy to the emptiness of unoccupied will, to the torture and misery of boredom. To this extent it affords us a measure of our own intellectual worth, and for this generally the degree of our ability to endure solitude, or our love of it, is a good criterion. The surroundings just described, therefore, give us an instance of the sublime in a low degree, for in them with the state of pure knowing in its peace and all-sufficiency there is mingled, as a contrast, a recollection of the dependence and wretchedness of the will in need of constant activity. This is the species of the sublime for which the sight of the boundless prairies of the interior of North America is renowned.

Now let us imagine such a region denuded of plants and showing only bare rocks; the will is at once filled with alarm through the total absence of that which is organic and necessary for our subsistence. The desert takes on a fearful character; our mood becomes more tragic. The exaltation to pure knowledge comes about with a more decided emancipation from the interest of the will, and by our persisting in the state of pure knowledge, the feeling of the sublime distinctly appears.

The following environment can cause this in an even higher degree. Nature in turbulent and tempestuous motion; semi-darkness through threatening black thunder-clouds; immense, bare, overhanging cliffs shutting out the view by their interlacing; rushing, foaming masses of water; complete desert; the wail of the wind sweeping through the ravines. Our dependence, our struggle with hostile nature, our will that is broken in this, now appear clearly before our eyes. Yet as long as personal affliction does not gain the upper hand, but we remain in aesthetic contemplation, the pure subject of knowing gazes through this struggle of nature, through this picture of the broken will, and comprehends calmly, unshaken and unconcerned, the Ideas in those very objects that are threatening and terrible to the will. In this contrast is to be found the feeling of the sublime.[28]

But the impression becomes even stronger, when we have before our eyes the struggle of the agitated forces of nature on a large scale, when in these surroundings the roaring of a falling stream deprives us of the possibility of hearing our own voices. Or when we are abroad in the storm of tempestuous seas; mountainous waves rise and fall, are dashed violently against steep cliffs, and shoot their spray high into the air. The storm howls, the sea roars, the lightning flashes from black clouds, and thunder-claps drown the noise of storm and sea. Then in the unmoved beholder of this scene the twofold nature of his consciousness reaches the highest distinctness. Simultaneously, he feels himself as individual, as the feeble phenomenon of will, which the slightest touch of these forces can annihilate, helpless against powerful nature, dependent, abandoned to chance, a vanishing nothing in face of stupendous forces; and he also feels himself as the eternal, serene subject of knowing, who as the condition of every object is the supporter of this whole world, the fearful struggle of nature being only his mental picture or representation; he himself is free from, and foreign to, all willing and all needs, in the quiet comprehension of the Ideas. This is the full impression of the sublime. Here it is caused by the sight of a power beyond all comparison superior to the individual, and threatening him with annihilation.

The impression of the sublime can arise in quite a different way by our imagining a mere magnitude in space and time, whose immensity reduces the individual to nought. By retaining Kant's terms and his correct division, we can call the first kind the dynamically sublime, and the second the mathematically sublime, although we differ from him entirely in the explanation of the inner nature of that impression, and can concede no share in this either to moral reflections or to hypostases from scholastic philosophy.[29]

If we lose ourselves in contemplation of the infinite greatness of the universe in space and time, meditate on the past millennia and on those to come; or if the heavens at night actually bring innumerable worlds before our eyes, and so impress on our consciousness the immensity of the universe, we feel ourselves reduced to nothing; we feel ourselves as individuals, as living bodies, as transient phenomena of will, like drops in the ocean, dwindling and dissolving into nothing. But against such a ghost of our own nothingness, against such a lying impossibility, there arises the immediate consciousness that all these worlds exist only in our representation, only as modifications of the eternal subject of pure knowing. This we find ourselves to be as soon as we forget individuality; it is the necessary, conditional supporter of all worlds and

of all periods of time. The vastness of the world, which previously disturbed
our peace of mind, now rests within us; our dependence on it is now annulled
[aufgehoben] by its dependence on us. All this, however, does not come into
reflection at once, but shows itself as a consciousness, merely felt, that in some
sense or other (made clear only by philosophy) we are one with the world, and
are therefore not oppressed but exalted [gehoben] by its immensity. It is the
felt consciousness of what the Upanishads of the Vedas express repeatedly in
so many different ways, but most admirably in the saying already quoted: *Hae
omnes creaturae in totum ego sum, et praeter me aliud (ens) non est* (*Oupnek'hat*, Vol. I,
p. 122).[30] It is an exaltation beyond our own individuality, a feeling of the
sublime.

We receive this impression of the mathematically sublime in quite a direct
way through a space which is small indeed as compared with the universe, but
which, by becoming directly and wholly perceptible [wahrnehmbar] to us,
affects us with its whole magnitude in all three dimensions, and is sufficient to
render the size of our own body almost infinitely small. This can never be
done by a space that is empty for perception [Wahrnehmung], and therefore
never by an open space, but only by one that is directly perceivable in all its
dimensions through delimitation, and so by a very high and large dome, like
that of St Peter's in Rome or of St Paul's in London. The feeling of the sublime
arises here through our being aware of the vanishing nothingness of our own
body in the presence of a greatness which itself, on the other hand, resides only
in our representation, and of which we, as knowing subject, are the supporter.
Therefore, here as everywhere, it arises through the contrast between the
insignificance and dependence of ourselves as individuals, as phenomena of
will, and the consciousness of ourselves as pure subject of knowing. Even the
vault of the starry heavens, if contemplated without reflection, has only the
same effect as that vault of stone, and acts not with its true, but only with its
apparent, greatness.[31] Many objects of our perception [Anschauung] excite
the impression of the sublime; by virtue both of their spatial magnitude and of
their great antiquity, and therefore of their duration in time, we feel ourselves
reduced to nought in their presence, and yet revel in the pleasure of beholding
them. Of this kind are very high mountains, the Egyptian pyramids, and
colossal ruins of great antiquity.

Our explanation of the sublime can indeed be extended to cover the ethical,
namely what is described as the sublime character. Such a character springs
from the fact that the will is not excited here by objects certainly well
calculated to excite it, but that knowledge retains the upper hand. Such a
character will accordingly consider men in a purely objective way, and not
according to the relations they might have to his will. For example, he will
observe their faults, and even their hatred and injustice to himself, without
being thereby stirred to hatred on his own part. He will contemplate their
happiness without feeling envy, recognize their good qualities without
desiring closer association with them, perceive the beauty of women without

hankering after them. His personal happiness or unhappiness will not violently affect him; he will be rather as Hamlet describes Horatio:

> for thou hast been
> As one, in suffering all, that suffers nothing;
> A man, that fortune's buffets and rewards
> Hast ta'en with equal thanks, *etc.*
>
> (Act III, sc. 2)[32]

For, in the course of his own life and in its misfortunes, he will look less at his own individual lot than at the lot of mankind as a whole, and accordingly will conduct himself in this respect rather as a knower than as a sufferer.

§42

I return to our discussion of the aesthetic impression. Knowledge of the beautiful always supposes, simultaneously and inseparably, a purely knowing subject and a known Idea as object. But yet the source of aesthetic enjoyment will lie sometimes rather in the apprehension of the known Idea, sometimes rather in the bliss and peace of mind of pure knowledge free from all willing, and thus from all individuality and the pain that results therefrom. And in fact, this predominance of the one or the other constituent element of aesthetic enjoyment will depend on whether the intuitively grasped Idea is a higher or a lower grade of the will's objectivity. Thus with aesthetic contemplation (in real life or through the medium of art) of natural beauty in the inorganic and vegetable kingdoms and of the works of architecture, the enjoyment of pure, will-less knowing will predominate, because the Ideas here apprehended are only low grades of the will's objectivity, and therefore are not phenomena of deep significance and suggestive content. On the other hand, if animals and human beings are the object of aesthetic contemplation or presentation, the enjoyment will consist rather in the objective apprehension of these Ideas that are the most distinct revelations of the will. For these exhibit the greatest variety of forms, a wealth and deep significance of phenomena; they reveal to us most completely the essence of the will, whether in its violence, its terribleness, its satisfaction, or its being broken (this last in tragic situations), finally even in its change or self-overcoming [Selbstaufhebung], which is the particular theme of Christian painting. Historical painting and the drama generally have as object the Idea of the will enlightened by full knowledge. We will now go over the arts one by one, and in this way the theory of the beautiful that we put forward will gain in completeness and distinctness.

[§§43–5 develop a hierarchy among the fine arts, with architecture at the bottom, as the lowest grade of the will's objectivity; followed by landscape painting, animal painting, and sculpture, then representation of the human form. The argument reaches poetry in §51, below, and culminates in music in §52, not included here. Music is the point at which the Idea is entirely left behind and the pure will finds its true expression.]

§46

It is obvious that, in the famous group, Laocoön is not crying out, and the universal and ever-recurring surprise at this must be attributable to the fact that we should all cry out in his place. Nature also demands this; for in the case of the most acute physical pain and the sudden appearance of the greatest bodily fear, all reflection that might induce silent endurance is entirely expelled from consciousness, and nature relieves itself by crying out, thus expressing pain and fear at the same time, summoning the deliverer and terrifying the assailant. Therefore Winckelmann regretted the absence of the expression of crying out; but as he tried to justify the artist, he really made Laocoön into a Stoic who considered it beneath his dignity to cry out *secundum naturam*,[33] but added to his pain the useless constraint of stifling its expression. Winckelmann therefore sees in him "the tried spirit of a great man writhing in agony, and trying to suppress the expression of feeling and to lock it up in himself. He does not break out in a loud shriek, as in Virgil, but only anxious sighs escape him", and so on (*Werke*, Vol. VII, p. 98; the same in more detail in Vol. VI, pp. 104 *seq.*).[34] This opinion of Winckelmann was criticized by Lessing in his *Laocoön*, and improved by him in the way mentioned above. In place of the psychological reason, he gave the purely aesthetic one that beauty, the principle of ancient art, does not admit the expression of crying out. Another argument he gives is that a wholly fleeting state, incapable of any duration, should not be depicted in a motionless work of art. This has against it a hundred examples of excellent figures that are fixed in wholly fleeting movements, dancing, wrestling, catching, and so on. Indeed, Goethe, in the essay on the Laocoön which opens the *Propyläen* (p. 8), considers the choice of such a wholly fleeting moment to be absolutely necessary.[35] In our day, Hirt (*Horae*, 1797, tenth St.), reducing everything to the highest truth of the expression, decided the matter by saying that Laocoön does not cry out because he is no longer able to, as he is on the point of dying from suffocation.[36] Finally, Fernow (*Römische Studien*, Vol. I, pp. 426 *seq.*) weighed and discussed all these three opinions; he did not, however, add a new one of his own, but reconciled and amalgamated all three.[37]

I cannot help being surprised that such thoughtful and acute men laboriously bring in far-fetched and inadequate reasons, and resort to psychological and even physiological arguments, in order to explain a matter the reason of which is quite near at hand, and to the unprejudiced is immediately obvious. I am particularly surprised that Lessing, who came so near the correct explanation, completely missed the point.

Before all psychological and physiological investigation as to whether Laocoön in his position would cry out or not (and I affirm that he certainly would), it has to be decided as regards the group that crying out ought not to be expressed in it, for the simple reason that the presentation of this lies entirely outside the province of sculpture. A shrieking Laocoön could not be produced in marble, but only one with the mouth wide open fruitlessly endeavouring to shriek, a Laocoön whose voice was stuck in his throat, *vox faucibus haesit.*[38] The essence of shrieking, and consequently its effect on the onlooker, lies entirely in the sound, not in the gaping mouth. This latter phenomenon that necessarily accompanies the shriek must be motivated and justified first through the sound produced by it; it is then permissible and indeed necessary, as characteristic of the action, although it is detrimental to beauty. But in plastic art, to which the presentation of shrieking is quite foreign and impossible, it would be really foolish to exhibit the violent medium of shrieking, namely the gaping mouth, which disturbs all the features and the rest of the expression, since we should then have before us the means, which moreover demands many sacrifices, whilst its end, the shrieking itself together with its effect on our feelings, would fail to appear. Moreover there would be produced each time the ridiculous spectacle of a permanent exertion without effect. This could actually be compared to the wag who, for a joke, stopped up with wax the horn of the sleeping night watchman, and then woke him up with the cry of fire, and amused himself watching the man's fruitless efforts to blow. On the other hand, where the expression of shrieking lies within the province of expressive art, it is quite admissible, because it serves truth, in other words, the complete presentation of the Idea. So in poetry, which claims for perceptual presentation the imagination of the reader. Therefore in Virgil Laocoön cries out like an ox that has broken loose after being struck by an axe. Homer (*Iliad*, XX, 48–53) represents Mars and Minerva as shrieking horribly without detracting from their divine dignity or beauty.[39] In just the same way with acting; on the stage Laocoön would certainly have to cry out. Sophocles also represents Philoctetes as shrieking, and on the ancient stage he would certainly have done so. In quite a similar case, I remember having seen in London the famous actor Kemble in a piece called *Pizarro*, translated from the German.[40] He played the part of the American, a half-savage, but of very noble character. Yet when he was wounded, he cried out loudly and violently, and this was of great and admirable effect, since it was highly characteristic and contributed a great deal to the truth. On the other hand, a painted or voiceless shrieker in stone would be much more ridiculous than the painted music that is censured in Goethe's *Propyläen.*[41] For shrieking is much more detrimental to the rest of the expression and to beauty than music is; for at most this concerns only hands and arms, and is to be looked upon as an action characterizing the person. Indeed, to this extent it can be quite rightly painted, so long as it does not require any violent movement of the body or distortion of the mouth; thus for example, St Cecilia at the organ, Raphael's violinist in the Sciarra Gallery in Rome, and many others. Now since, on account of the limitations of the art, the pain of Laocoön could not be expressed by shrieking, the artist had to set in motion every other expression of pain. This he achieved to perfection, as is ably described by Winckelmann (*Werke*, Vol. VI, pp. 104 *seq.*), whose admirable account therefore retains its full value and truth as soon as we abstract from the stoical sentiment underlying it.[42]

§47

Because beauty with grace [Grazie] is the principal subject of sculpture, it likes the nude, and tolerates clothing only in so far as this does not conceal the form. It makes use of drapery, not as a covering, but as an indirect presentation of the form. This method of presentation greatly engrosses the understanding, since the understanding reaches the perception [Anschauung] of the cause, namely the form of the body, only through the one directly given effect, that is to say, the arrangement of the drapery. Therefore in sculpture drapery is to some extent what foreshortening is in painting. Both are suggestions, yet not symbolical, but such that, if they succeed, they force the understanding immediately to perceive what is suggested, just as if it were actually given.

Here I may be permitted in passing to insert a comparison relating to the rhetorical arts. Just as the beautiful bodily form can be seen to the best advantage with the lightest clothing, or even no clothing at all, and thus a very handsome man, if at the same time he had taste and could follow it, would prefer to walk about almost naked, clothed only after the manner of the ancients; so will every fine mind rich in ideas express itself always in the most natural, candid, and simple way, concerned if it be possible to communicate its thoughts to others, and thus to relieve the loneliness that one is bound to feel in a world such as this. Conversely, poverty of mind, confusion and perversity of thought will clothe themselves in the most far-fetched expressions and obscure forms of speech, in order to cloak in difficult and pompous phrases small, trifling, insipid, or commonplace ideas. It is like the man who lacks the majesty of beauty, and wishes to make up for this deficiency by clothing; he attempts to cover up the insignificance or ugliness of his person under barbaric finery, tinsel, feathers, ruffles, cuffs, and mantles. Thus many an author, if compelled to translate his pompous and obscure book into its little clear content, would be as embarrassed as that man would be if he were to go about naked.[43]

§49

The truth which lies at the foundation of all the remarks we have so far made on art is that the object of art, the depiction of which is the aim of the artist, and the knowledge of which must consequently precede his work as its germ and source, is an *Idea*, in Plato's sense, and absolutely nothing else; not the particular thing, the object of common apprehension, and not the concept [Begriff], the object of rational thought and of science. Although Idea and concept have something in common, in that both as unities represent a plurality of actual things, the great difference between the two will have become sufficiently clear and evident from what was said in the first book about the concept, and what has been said in the present book about the Idea.[44] I certainly do not mean to assert that Plato grasped this difference clearly; indeed many of his examples of Ideas and his discussions of them are applicable only to concepts. However, we leave this aside, and go our way, glad whenever we come across traces of a great and noble mind, yet pursuing not his footsteps, but our own aim. The *concept* is abstract, discursive, wholly undetermined within its sphere, determined only by its limits, attainable and intelligible only to him who has the faculty of reason, communicable by words without further assistance, entirely exhausted by its definition. The *Idea*, on the other hand, definable perhaps as the adequate representative of the concept, is absolutely perceptual [anschaulich], and, although representing an infinite number of individual things, is yet thoroughly definite. It is never known by the individual as such, but only by him who has raised himself above all willing and all individuality to the pure subject of knowing. Thus it is attainable only by the man of genius, and by him who, mostly with the assistance of works of genius, has raised his power of pure knowledge, and is now in the frame of mind of the genius. Therefore it is communicable not absolutely, but only conditionally, since the Idea, apprehended and repeated in the work of art, appeals to everyone only according to the measure of his own intellectual worth. For this reason the most excellent works of any art, the noblest productions of genius, must eternally remain sealed books to the dull majority of men, and are inaccessible to them. They are separated from them by a wide gulf, just as the society of princes is inaccessible to the common people. It is true that even the dullest of them accept on authority works which are acknowledged to be great, in order not to betray their own weakness. But they always remain in silence, ready to express their condemnation the moment they are allowed to hope that they can do so without running the risk of exposure. Then their long-restrained hatred of all that is great and beautiful and of the authors thereof readily relieves itself; for such things never appealed to them, and so humiliated them. For in order to acknowledge, and freely and willingly to admit, the worth of another, a man must generally have some worth of his own. On this is based the necessity for modesty in spite of all merit, as also for the disproportionately loud praise of this virtue, which alone of all its sisters is always included in the eulogy of anyone who ventures to praise a man distinguished in some way, in order to conciliate and appease the wrath of worthlessness. For what is modesty but hypocritical humility, by means of which, in a world swelling with vile envy, a man seeks to beg pardon for his excellences and merits from those who have none? For whoever attributes no merits to himself because he really has none, is not modest, but merely honest.

The *Idea* is the unity that has fallen into plurality by virtue of the temporal and spatial form of our intuitive apprehension [intuitive Apprehension]. The *concept*, on the other hand, is the unity once more produced out of plurality by means of abstraction through our faculty of reason; the latter can be described as *unitas post rem*, and the former as *unitas ante rem*.[45] Finally, we can express the distinction between concept and Idea figuratively, by saying that the *concept* is like a dead receptacle in which whatever has been put actually lies side by side, but from which no more can be taken out (by analytical judgements) than has been put in (by synthetical reflection).[46] The *Idea*, on the other hand, develops in him who has grasped it representations that are new as regards the concept of the same name; it is like a living organism, developing itself and endowed with generative force, which brings forth that which was not previously put into it.

Now it follows from all that has been said that the concept, useful as it is in life, serviceable, necessary, and productive as it is in science, is eternally barren and unproductive in art. The apprehended Idea, on the contrary, is the true and only source of every genuine work of art. In its powerful originality it is drawn only from life itself, from nature, from the world, and only by the genuine genius. Genuine works bearing immortal life arise only from such immediate responsiveness [Empfängniß]. Just because the Idea is and remains perceptual, the artist is not conscious *in abstracto* of the intention and aim of his work. Not a concept but an Idea is present in his mind; hence he cannot give an account of his actions. He works, as people say, from mere feeling and unconsciously, indeed instinctively. On the other hand, imitators, mannerists, *imitatores, servum pecus*,[47] in art start from the concept. They note what pleases and affects in genuine works, make this clear to themselves, fix it in the concept, and hence in the abstract, and then imitate it, openly or in disguise, with skill and intention. Like parasitic plants, they suck their nourishment from the works of others; and like polyps, take on the colour of their nourishment. Indeed, we could even carry the comparison farther, and assert that they are like machines which mince very fine and mix up what is put into them, but can never digest it, so that the constituent elements of others can always be found again, and picked out and separated from the mixture. Only the genius, on the other hand, is like the organic body that assimilates, transforms, and produces. For he is, indeed, educated and cultured by his predecessors and their works; but only by life and the world itself is he made directly productive through the impression of what is perceived; therefore the highest culture never interferes with his originality. All imitators, all mannerists apprehend in the concept the essential nature of the exemplary achievements of others; but concepts can never impart inner life to a work. The generation, in other words the dull multitude of any time, itself knows only concepts and sticks to them; it therefore accepts mannered works with ready and loud applause. After a few years, however, these works become unpalatable, because the spirit of the times [Zeitgeist], in other words the prevailing concepts, in which alone those works could take root, has changed. Only the genuine works that are drawn directly from nature and life remain eternally young and strong, like nature and life itself. For they belong to no age, but to mankind; and for this reason they are received with indifference by their own age to which they disdained to conform; and because they indirectly and negatively exposed the errors of the age, they were recognized tardily and reluctantly. On the other hand, they do not grow old, but even down to the latest times always make an ever new and fresh appeal to us. They are then no longer exposed to neglect and misunderstanding; for they now stand crowned and sanctioned by the approbation of the few minds capable of judging. These appear singly and sparingly in the course of centuries,[48] and cast their votes, the slowly increasing number of which establishes the authority, the only judgement-seat that is meant when an appeal is made to posterity. It is these successively appearing individuals alone; for the mass and multitude of posterity will always be and remain just as perverse and dull as the mass and multitude of contemporaries always were and always are. Let us read the complaints of the great minds of every century about their contemporaries; they always sound as if they were of today, since the human race is always the same. In every age and in every art affectation [Manier] takes the place of the spirit, which always is only the property of individuals. Affectation, however, is the old, cast-off garment of the phenomenon of the spirit which last existed and was recognized. In view of all this, the approbation of posterity is earned as a rule only at the expense of the approbation of one's contemporaries, and *vice versa*.[49]

§51

If with the foregoing observations on art in general we turn from the plastic and pictorial arts of poetry [Poesie], we shall have no doubt that its aim is also to reveal the Ideas, the grades of the will's objectification, and to communicate them to the hearer with that distinctness and vividness in which they were apprehended by the poetical mind. Ideas are essentially perceptual; therefore, if in poetry only abstract concepts are directly communicated by words, yet it is obviously the intention to let the hearer perceive the Ideas of life in the representatives of these concepts; and this can take place only by the assistance of his own imagination [Phantasie]. But in order to set this imagination in motion in accordance with the end in view, the abstract concepts that are the direct material of poetry, as of the driest prose, must be so arranged that their spheres intersect one another, so that none can continue in its abstract universality, but instead of it a perceptual representative appears before the imagination, and this is then modified further and further by the words of the poet according to his intention. Just as the chemist obtains solid precipitates by combining perfectly clear and transparent fluids, so does the poet know how to precipitate, as it were, the concrete, the individual, the perceptual representation, out of the abstract, transparent universality of the concepts by the way in which he combines them. For the Idea can be known only through perception, but knowledge of the Idea is the aim of all art. The skill of a master in poetry as in chemistry enables one always to obtain the precise precipitate that was intended. The many epithets in poetry serve this purpose, and through them the universality of every concept is restricted more and more till perceptibility is reached. . . .

Even in that method of treatment necessary to the historian, the inner essence, the significance of phenomena, the kernel of all those shells, can never be entirely lost, and can still be found and recognized by the person who looks for it. Yet that which is significant in itself, not in the relation, namely the real unfolding of the Idea, is found to be far more accurate and clear in poetry [Dichtung] than in history; therefore, paradoxical as it may sound, far more real, genuine, inner truth is to be attributed to poetry than to history. For the historian should accurately follow the individual event according to life as this event is developed in time in the manifold tortuous and complicated chains of reasons or grounds and consequents. But he cannot possibly possess all the data for this; he cannot have seen all and ascertained everything. At every moment he is forsaken by the original of his picture, or a false picture is substituted for it; and this happens so frequently, that I think I can assume that in all history the false outweighs the true. On the other hand, the poet has apprehended the Idea of mankind from some definite side to be described; thus it is the nature of his own self that is objectified in it for him. His knowledge, as was said above in connexion with sculpture, is half *a priori*; his ideal is before his mind, firm, clear, brightly illuminated, and it cannot forsake him. He therefore shows us in the mirror of his mind [Geist] the Idea purely and distinctly, and his description down to the last detail is as true as life itself.[50] The great ancient historians are therefore poets in the particulars where data forsake them, e.g., in the speeches of their heroes; indeed, the whole way in which they handle their material approaches the epic. But this gives their presentations unity, and enables them to retain inner truth, even where outer truth was not accessible to them, or was in fact falsified. . . .

The expression of the Idea of humanity, which devolves on the poet, can now be carried out in such a way that the depicted is also at the same time the depicter. This occurs in lyric poetry, in the song proper, where the poet vividly perceives and describes only his own state; hence through the object, a certain subjectivity is essential to poetry of this kind. Or again, the depicter is entirely different from what is to be depicted, as is the case with all other kinds of poetry. Here the depicter more or less conceals himself behind what is depicted, and finally altogether disappears. In the ballad [Romanze] the depicter still expresses to some extent his own state through the tone and proportion of the whole; therefore, though much more objective than the song, it still has something subjective in it. This fades away more in the idyll, still more in the romance [Roman], almost entirely in the epic proper, and finally to the last vestige in the drama, which is the most objective, and in more than one respect the most complete, and also the most difficult, form of poetry. The lyric form is therefore the easiest, and if in other respects art belongs only to the true genius who is so rare, even the man who is on the whole not very eminent can produce a beautiful song, when in fact, through strong excitement from outside, some inspiration enhances his mental powers. For this needs only a vivid perception of his own state at the moment of excitement. This is proved by many single songs written by individuals who have otherwise remained unknown, in particular by the German national songs, of which we have an excellent collection in the *Wunderhorn,* and also by innumerable love-songs and other popular songs in all languages.[51] For to seize the mood of the moment, and embody it in the song, is the whole achievement of poetry of this kind. Yet in the lyrics of genuine poets is reflected the inner nature of the whole of mankind; and all that millions of past, present, and future human beings have found and will find in the same constantly recurring situations, finds in them its corresponding expression. Since these situations, by constant recurrence, exist as permanently as humanity itself, and always call up the same sensations, the lyrical productions of genuine poets remain true, effective, and fresh for thousands of years. If, at the same time, the poet is the universal man, then all that has ever moved a human heart, and all that human nature produces from itself in any situation, all that dwells and broods in any human breast – all these are his theme and material, and with these all the rest of nature as well. Therefore the poet can just as well sing of voluptuousness as of mysticism, be Anacreon or Angelus Silesius, write tragedies or comedies, express the sublime or the common sentiment, according to his mood and disposition.[52] Accordingly, no one can prescribe to the poet that he should be noble and sublime, moral, pious, Christian, or anything else, still less reproach him for being this and not that. He is the mirror of mankind, and brings to its consciousness what it feels and does.

Now if we consider more closely the nature of the lyric proper, and take as examples exquisite and at the same time pure models, not those in any way approximating to another kind of poetry, such as the ballad, the elegy, the hymn, the epigram, and so on, we shall find that the characteristic nature of the song in the narrowest sense is as follows. It is the subject of the will, in other words, the singer's own willing, that fills his consciousness, often as a released and satisfied willing (joy), but even more often as an impeded willing (sorrow), always as emotion, passion, an agitated state of mind. Besides this, however, and simultaneously with it, the singer, through the sight of surrounding nature, becomes conscious of himself as the subject of pure, will-less knowing, whose unshakable, blissful peace now appears in contrast to the stress of willing that is always restricted and needy. The feeling of this contrast, this alternate play, is really what is expressed in the whole of the song, and what in general constitutes the lyrical state. In this state pure knowing comes to us, so to speak, in order to deliver us from willing and its stress. We follow, yet only for a few moments; willing, desire, the recollection of our own personal aims, always tears us anew from peaceful contemplation; but yet again and again the next beautiful environment, in which pure, will-less knowledge presents itself to us, entices us away from willing. Therefore in the song and in the lyrical mood, willing (the personal interest of the aims) and pure perception of the environment that presents itself are wonderfully blended with each other. Relations between the two are sought and imagined; the subjective disposition, the affection of the will, imparts its hue to the perceived environment, and this environment again imparts in the reflex its colour to that disposition. The genuine song is the expression or copy of the whole of this mingled and divided state of mind. . . .

In the course of life, these two subjects, or in popular language head and heart, grow more and more apart; men are always separating more and more their subjective feeling from their objective knowledge. In the child the two are still fully blended; it hardly knows how to distinguish itself from its surroundings; it is merged into them. In the youth all perception [Wahrnehmung] in the first place affects feeling and mood, and even mingles with these, as is very beautifully expressed by Byron:

> I live not in myself, but I become
> Portion of that around me; and to me
> High mountains are a feeling.
>
> (*Childe Harold's Pilgrimage*, III, 72)[53]

This is why the youth clings so much to the perceptual and outward side of things; this is why he is fit only for lyrical poetry, and only the mature man for dramatic poetry. We can think of the old man as at most an epic poet, like Ossian or Homer, for narration is characteristic of the old. . . .

Tragedy [Trauerspiel] is to be regarded, and is recognized, as the summit of poetic art, both as regards the greatness of the effect and the difficulty of the achievement. For the whole of our discussion, it is very significant and worth noting that the purpose of this highest poetical achievement is the description of the terrible side of life. The unspeakable pain, the wretchedness and misery of mankind, the triumph of wickedness, the scornful mastery of chance, and the irretrievable fall of the just and the innocent are all here presented to us; and here is to be found a significant hint as to the nature of the world and of existence. It is the antagonism of the will with itself which is here most completely unfolded at the highest grade of its objectivity, and which comes into fearful prominence. It becomes visible in the suffering of mankind which is produced partly by chance and error; and these stand forth as the rulers of the world, personified as fate through their insidiousness which appears almost like purpose and intention. In part it proceeds from mankind itself through the self-mortifying efforts of will on the part of individuals, through the wickedness and perversity of most. It is one and the same will, living and appearing in them all, whose phenomena fight with one another and tear one another to pieces. In one individual it appears powerfully, in another more feebly. Here and there it reaches thoughtfulness and is softened more or less by the light of knowledge, until at last in the individual case this knowledge is purified and enhanced by suffering itself. It then reaches the point where the phenomenon, the veil of Maya, no longer deceives it. It sees through the form of the phenomenon, the *principium individuationis*; the egoism resting on this expires with it. The *motives* [*Motive*] that were previously so powerful now lose their force, and instead of them, the complete knowledge of the real nature of the world, acting as a *quieter* [*Quietive*] of the will, produces resignation, the giving up not merely of life, but of the whole will-to-live itself. Thus we see in tragedy the noblest men, after a long conflict and suffering, finally renounce for ever all the pleasures of life and the aims till then pursued so keenly, or cheerfully and willingly give up life itself. . . .

Part 5
Hegel

Georg Wilhelm Friedrich Hegel

(1770–1831)

Along with Kant, Hegel is the most important figure represented in this volume, not only because of the thoroughness with which he addresses the major issues of his time, but also because of the range of his influence on later thinkers. In this second context his influence has been perhaps even greater than that of Kant, whose writings outside the great *Critiques*, for example those on psychology, history, and natural science, are little known except to specialists. This is, as we have seen, the result of a conscious decision on Kant's part about the limits of exact philosophy; with Hegel, the discipline once again expands to include everything that Kant had excluded from the transcendental method. Closer knowledge of his contemporaries, especially Fichte and Schelling, would certainly persuade the English-speaking reader that Hegel was less 'original' than he often seems to be, but this in no sense detracts from his importance. The expansion of Fichte's basic epistemology of self and other into a model for the understanding of a whole range of forms of culture and behaviour; the idealist theory of history; the influence (or not) on the young Marx and the consequent interest in Hegel of theorists of both left and right – these and other priorities have ensured Hegel's continuing importance to debates in philosophy, psychology, and the political and social sciences.

Intended for theology, along with his friends and co-seminarians Schelling and Hölderlin, Hegel went through the usual apprenticeship as a private tutor before settling at Jena in 1801. There are famous stories of his fleeing the city with the manuscript of the *Phenomenology of Spirit* under his arm, following the seizure of the city by the French (1807). Between 1808 and 1816 he was the headmaster of a *Gymnasium* or 'grammar school' in Nürnberg, and this period produced his second major work, the *Science of Logic* (1812–16). After a brief period at Heidelberg (1816–18) he became a professor at Berlin, a post which he held until his death in 1831, and through which he dominated the world of German philosophy (much to Schopenhauer's disgust!). The other major published works are the *Philosophy of Right* (1821) and the *Encyclopaedia of the Philosophical Sciences* (1830). Thanks to his influence on the British Hegelians of the later nineteenth century and his continued interdisciplinary importance, most of his work can be read in English, including the lecture courses in the history of philosophy, on the philosophy of religion, and on aesthetics.

Most of the priorities in Hegel's thought will be signalled in the notes as they relate to the specific concerns of the selections reprinted below. His system is nothing if not holistic, and most things lead to most other things. Perhaps the most important thing to emphasize at once is the pervasiveness of Hegel's interest in and deduction of an evolutionary history. Human history is the record of the gradual emergence of *Geist* to self-consciousness and self-definition. This word, which we have met before (most significantly in Fichte), has been variously rendered as 'mind' or 'spirit' by Hegel's translators, and it is indeed mind-spirit, the essentially formative and self-forming element in the self. The end of history will be the consummation of philosophy, art and religion having been both left behind and gathered within along the way – the emergence of absolute *Geist*, self-knowledge of God through man, a realm of pure thinking unmarked by sensuous representation.

The notion of a progressive and refining principle operating through history was not original to Hegel; similar ideas can be found in Schelling (though with less emphasis upon the progressive), in Fichte's *Characteristics of the Present Age*, and also in Herder, where they were the focus of some pointed scepticism from Kant (see 1963, pp. 27f.). But it is Hegel who works out the idea most fully. He places all sorts of restrictions on the incidence of *Geist* in history, as indeed he must do if he is to explain the obvious presence of forms of incoherence in a system whose scope is nevertheless total. Whilst history is argued to be subject to a rational process, the *Geist* which is the medium of that rationality is not present at all times in all places. When it is present and operative, it is seldom understood as such, and does not provide conscious instructions or a prospectus for those engaged in living through particular moments of history. This is the 'tragical' element in Hegel's thought, whereby knowledge of what has been most important always comes after the event. Here he stands with the Greeks, and we should remember this when making assessments of his vocabulary of 'world historical' figures, and so forth. In all these ways, Hegel's analysis bears close comparison with that of Shelley in *A Defence of Poetry*. Here too the dynamic principle in history, which Shelley calls "poetry" in the widest sense, operates through the unconscious and is prone to disappear or lie dormant for long periods of time, so that poets are the *unacknowledged* legislators of the world.

As history is partial and even immediately unpredictable in the short term (though a pattern appears to retrospection in the long term), so it is not a sphere from which we may deduce any simple feeling of well-being: "It is possible to consider history from the point of view of happiness, but history is not the soil in which happiness grows. The periods of happiness in it are the blank pages of history" (1980, pp. 78–9). Anxiety is the correlative of the partial or selective appearance of *Geist*, and even when it does appear its transformations are strenuous ones: "Development, therefore, is not just a harmless and peaceful process of growth like that of organic life, but a hard and obstinate struggle with itself" (p. 127). Thus alienation is central to the theory. *Geist* indeed appears by positing itself as other in a moment of rupture (ideally to be overcome), whether in the course of culture and history at large or in the individual life experience which Hegel (at times awkwardly) makes parallel to it. This whole process is "mediated by consciousness and will" (p. 126), so that there is always the possibility of failure, of arrestation, of fixation – one which may be total for an individual or culture at a given moment, though of course not so for the whole course of history. Again, the comparison with the dynamics of Greek tragedy comes to mind: the curse of the God must play itself out, but none of the protagonists can know this, or know when. Consequently they behave freely, and bring about the crucial even in a cloud of unknowing. Thus also for Hegel we are creatures of our times, and can operate only within their limits, or just beyond them if we happen (through no conscious decision of our own) to be world-historical. The famous examples of literary criticism in the *Phenomenology* (not reprinted here), the account of Sophocles' *Antigone* and the various remarks on Diderot's *Rameau's Nephew*, must be read in this light.

Geist makes progress by a movement that is simultaneously cancellation and incorporation or sublimation, a process Hegel calls *Aufhebung*. Progress is by negation, but negation involves both a destruction and carrying over: Hegel himself celebrates the double reading of the word in the *Science of Logic* (1969, pp. 106–8). In this way the traces of past transitions are available for recollection, or *Erinnerung* – a far more active process than mere remembrance, and one involving re-enacting, as Schelling also makes clear:

It is certain that whoever could write the history of his own life from its very ground, would have thereby grasped in a brief conspectus the history of the universe . . . all history . . . can only be relived . . . Whoever wishes knowledge of history must make the long journey, dwell upon each moment, submit himself to the gradualness of the development.   Schelling (1967), pp. 93–4

And so to art and aesthetics. The main point to grasp is that, after the exalted estimation of art in the (different) theories of Schelling and Schopenhauer, art is once again relegated by Hegel, though not (according to the logic I have just explained) in any sense deprived of essential content. Art is an early stage in the development of *Geist* toward self-recognition, a process further refined in religion, which is for Hegel the proper realm of *Vorstellung* or representational thought, and then consummated in philosophy. The high point of art is to be found in the civilization of the Greeks, for at that point in history art was closest to the total world-view of its society, and most fully incorporated its religious representations. Before and after the Greeks, art is either approaching or declining from this moment of exemplary coherence. But because the Greeks were pagans, *Geist* did not require the inward self-consciousness and the dissolution of outward form that are demanded by its Christian manifestations, later stages in its coming into being. The perfection of Greek art is therefore founded upon an element of incompletion, and we must always bear this in mind when reading Hegel. Greek civilization could embody itself most successfully in art, because art is unconscious creation, and because its gods regularly and readily took on human form; the Greeks had not yet perceived the 'higher' demands of self-consciousness and alienation – as Nietzsche also realized in trying to re-establish the viability of a pre-Christian ethics.

This schema does not however do justice to the richness of Hegel's view of art. Although art reaches its high point with the Greeks, it yet always exists in other and less completed forms at all moments of history, and as such is always available as an index to its time. This notion of the historical significance of art, its capacity to publicize and embody the essential elements of the particular culture in which it exists, has clearly been of the greatest importance to aesthetic theory and to literary criticism. Far more than Kant, who is interested strictly in the nature of the subjective judgement of taste and not at all in the psychology of the artist or in the history of art, and who therefore deliberately eschews examples, Hegel (like Schelling before him) ignores nothing in the history of art that seems to bear upon his case.

Further reading

This has made the task of selection more difficult than usual. Fortunately, Hegel's major pronouncements on art and aesthetics, those made in his course of lectures on the subject, have been recently and admirably translated by T.M. Knox (Hegel, 1975), with a superbly detailed index. Wellek (1955), II, 318–34, as so often, offers a fine introductory summary of the range of Hegel's literary criticism; see also Knox (1936), Kaminsky (1962), and Karelis (1979). Copleston (1965a) has a good general introduction to Hegel's thought, and among the various longer studies Taylor (1975) may be especially recommended; this book provides not only an account of Hegel's philosophy *per se*, but a very clear and comprehensive outline of its historical context, and I have found it particularly useful in writing the notes to this section of the anthology. Schelling (1978), pp. 199–214, should also be consulted for its philosophy of history. There is a bibliography by Steinhauer (1980).

Translations of Hegel into English began to appear only in the 1850s: see Muirhead (1927). Lewes (1857) had to cope with him in German: "Those who are utter strangers to German speculation will wonder, perhaps, how it is possible for such verbal quibbles to be accepted as philosophy" (p. 613). This reponse can be heard today, and is unlikely to disappear.

Selections from
On Classical Studies

Gymnasial-Reden, I: Am 29 September 1809

The translation is by Richard Kroner (slightly modified) in *G.W.F. Hegel: Early Theological Writings* (1971), pp. 321–30.

German text in *G.W.F. Hegel's Werke*, Vollständige Ausgabe, vol. XVI (1834), pp. 133–47.

Introductory note

The following excerpts are from a speech Hegel gave as rector of the *Gymnasium* (grammar school) at Nürnberg. As one might expect in a public oration, the style is rhapsodical and poetical, closer to that of the *Phenomenology* than to that of the next major published work, the *Science of Logic*. The spirit of Kant's essay *What is Enlightenment?* is once again evident in Hegel's argument for the cultivation of self-possession and "self-dependent value". But Hegel goes far beyond the brief remarks Kant makes (*CJ* §17) about the usefulness of the classical languages as models of taste. Here, it is the alien status of the classics that allows them to dramatize an educationally and spiritually advantageous version of the fortunate fall: our being cut off from them incites curiosity and desire (this being itself a basic element in Hegel's epistemology), and through their recovery we can achieve a fruitful return to our reconstituted and self-conscious selves. Schelling (1966), pp. 39–41, and Schopenhauer (1969), II, 66–7, may be compared here. The centrality of the Greek ideal to German Romantic thought had already been established by Winckelmann, Goethe, and Schiller, among others: see Hatfield (1964). In this speech, to an audience of grammar school students, Hegel's interest is primarily in the dynamics of language learning. The sections on language in the *Phenomenology of Spirit* (paragraphs 508ff., 652–3) should also be consulted.

. . . However, if we agree that excellence should be our starting point, then the foundation of higher study must be and remain Greek literature in the first place, Roman in the second. The perfection and glory of those masterpieces must be the spiritual bath, the secular baptism that first and indelibly attunes and tinctures the soul in respect of taste and knowledge [Geschmack und Wissenschaft]. For this initiation a general, perfunctory acquaintance with the ancients is not sufficient; we must take up our lodging with them, so that we can breathe their air, absorb their representations [Vorstellungen], their customs, one might even say their errors and prejudices, and become at home in this world – the most beautiful that ever has been. While the first paradise was that of *human nature*, this is the second, the higher paradise of the *human spirit* [*Menschengeistes*], which emerges like a bride from her chamber endowed with a yet more beautiful naturalness, with freedom, depth and serenity. The first wild glory of its dawn in the east is restrained by the grandeur of form and tames into beauty. The human spirit no longer here manifests its profundity in confusion, gloom or arrogance, but in perfect clarity [Klarheit]. Its serenity is not like the play of children; it is rather a veil spread over the melancholy which is familiar with the cruelty of fate but is not thereby driven to lose its freedom and moderation.[1] I do not believe I claim too much when I say that he who has never known the works of the ancients has lived without knowing what beauty is.

If we make ourselves at home in such an element then all the powers [Kräfte] of the soul are stimulated, developed and exercised; and, further, this element is a *unique material* through which we enrich ourselves and improve the very substance of our being.

It has been said that *activity of spirit* [*Geistesthätigkeit*] can be trained on *any material*, but best of all by external, useful and visible objects which are supposed to be most appropriate to the age of youth or childhood, since they pertain to the compass and manner of the representative faculty [Vorstellens] which this age has come to in and for itself.

One may doubt whether or not form and matter – training in itself and the objective circle of things on which we are trained – can be separated as if they had nothing to do with each other; but, even so, training as such is not the only thing that matters. As the plant not only trains its reproductive energies by enjoying light and air, but also absorbs its nourishment by this process, so likewise that material which the understanding and our faculty of soul use in developing and training themselves must at the same time be their nourishment. This subject matter is not the sort of material which is called 'useful', i.e. the sensuous materiality which is the object of immediate representation to the child; on the contrary it is only the content of spirit which has value and interest in and for itself that strengthens the soul. This content alone provides the independence and firmness, the substantial inwardness that is the mother of self-control and self-possession [Besonnenheit],[2] of presence and vigilance of spirit. It generates in the soul thus prepared and educated a kernel of self-dependent value, of absolute ends, which alone is the precondition of all usefulness in life and which it is important to plant in all citizens in all walks of life. Have we not seen in our own times that even states become unsteady, expose themselves to dangers and collapse, despite plenty of valuable resources, just because they have neglected and disdained to preserve such an inner citadel in the soul of their citizens; because they were interested in profit alone and directed their citizens to treat things spiritual as mere means?

The works of the ancients contain the most noble nourishment in the most noble form: golden apples in silver bowls. They are incomparably richer than all the works of any other nation or age. The greatness of their sentiments, their statuesque [plastische] virtue free from moral ambiguity, their patriotism, the grand manner of their deeds and characters, the multiplicity of their destinies, of their morals [Sitten] and constitutions – to recall these is enough to vindicate the assertion that in the compass of no other civilization was there ever united so much that was splendid, admirable, original, many-sided and instructive.

This richness, however, is intimately connected with the *language*, and only through and in language can we obtain it in all its special significance. The content can be given to us approximately by translations, but not the form, not the ethereal soul. Translations are like artificial roses which may resemble natural ones in shape, colour, and perhaps even scent, but which cannot attain their loveliness, delicacy, and softness of life. Whatever elegance and refinement the copy has belongs to the copy alone, and in it the contrast between the content and the form that has not grown out of that content makes itself felt unmistakably. Language is the musical element, the element of inwardness that fades away in the translation; it is the fine fragrance which makes possible the reader's sympathy of soul, and without which any ancient work tastes like Rhine wine that has lost its flavour.

This fact lays upon us what may seem like the harsh necessity of studying the ancient languages thoroughly and making them familiar to us as a prelude to enjoying their works to the greatest possible extent and in all their aspects and excellences. To complain about the trouble we have to undergo in learning the languages, and to regret or to fear that we have thus to neglect the learning of other things and the training of other abilities, is to find fault with fate because it has not given us this cycle of classical works in our own language. Only if we did thus have them would we possess a substitute for antiquity and be spared the laborious journey thither.

After having spoken about the *content* of education [Bildung], I wish to add some words about the *form* which its nature entails.

The progress of culture [Bildung] must not be regarded as the quiet continuation of a chain in which the new links are attached to the older ones with complete passivity; though with new material, yet without these new links working upon their predecessors. On the contrary, culture must have an earlier content and object upon which it works, and which it changes and forms anew. It is necessary that we appropriate the world of antiquity not only to possess it but even more to digest and transform it.[3]

But the substance of nature and spirit must have confronted us and taken the shape of something alien to us before it can become our *object*. Unhappy he whose immediate world of feelings has been alienated from him – for this means nothing less than the snapping of those bonds of faith, love and trust which unite heart and head with life in a holy friendship. For the alienation [Entfremdung] which is the condition of theoretical culture does not call for this social-moral [sittlich] pain, or the sufferings of the heart, but only the easier pain and stress of the representational imagination [Vorstellung] which is occupied with something not given in immediate experience, something foreign, something pertaining to recollection [Erinnerung], to memory and the thinking mind.[4]

But this demand for separation is so necessary that it expresses itself in us as a general and well-known impulse [Trieb]. What is strange and far away attracts our interest and lures us to activity and effort; it seems to be the more desirable the more remote it is and the less we have in common with it. The youth thinks himself lucky to leave his native land and live like Robinson Crusoe on a distant island.[5] It is a necessary illusion to seek first for profundity in the shape of distance; in fact, the depth and force [Kraft] to which we attain can only be measured by the distance between the point to which we were fleeing and the centre point in which we were at first engrossed and to which we shall finally again return.

This centrifugal force [Trieb] of the soul is above all the reason for the necessary separation by which it seeks to move away from its natural essence and condition, and why a remote and foreign world must be put before the youthful spirit [Geist]. The barrier best suited to perform this task of self-division for the sake of education [Bildung] is the world and language of the ancients. This world separates us from ourselves, but grants us at the same time the starting point and leading string for a return to ourselves; for a reconciliation with it and a rediscovery of ourselves, but now a selfhood seen in the truly universal essence of spirit.

If we apply to school education the general principle of this necessary process, which entails grasping the representative imagination [Vorstellung] of the ancients as well as their language as such, then it becomes evident that the mechanical side of this learning is not just a necessary evil. For it is the mechanical that is foreign to the spirit, and that awakens its desire to digest the indigestible food forced upon it, to bring to understanding what was hitherto lifeless and to assimilate it to its own condition.

Besides, with the mechanical elements in the learning of a language there is closely connected the *grammatical study* whose value cannot be too highly assessed, for it constitutes the beginning of a logical education [Bildung]. I mention this aspect last because it seems to be almost sunk in oblivion. Grammar has for its content the categories [Kategorien], special products and definitions of the understanding; therefore in learning it the understanding itself becomes *learned*. These most intellectual [geistigsten] essentials with which grammar first makes us acquainted are something very easy for youth to grasp; in fact, nothing in the world of spirit [nichts Geistiges] is easier. While youth does not yet possess the power of comprehending the many-sidedness of spiritual richness, those abstractions remain quite simple. They are so to speak the single letters [Buchstaben] or rather the vowels of the spiritual realm, with which we begin in order to spell it out and then learn to read it.[6]

Furthermore, grammar expounds the categories of the understanding in a way adapted to youth because it teaches them by distinguishing them through external marks mostly provided by the language itself. Knowledge thus achieved is somewhat better than that of colours like red or blue which everyone can distinguish without being able to define them according to Newton's hypothesis or some other theory. For it is of the utmost importance to have paid attention to these distinctions. Since the definitions of the under-standing [Verstandesbestimmungen] are *present in us* because we are an intel-lectual [verständige] entity, and we therefore understand them immediately: so the first step in education [Bildung] consists in our *owning* them, i.e. in our having made them the objects of our consciousness and being able to distin-guish them through their characteristic marks.

In that grammatical terminology teaches us to move in the realm of abstrac-tions, its study can be looked upon as elementary philosophy. This is why it is looked upon not just as a means but also as an end, in the Latin as much as in the German language classes. The general frivolity and superficiality which only the tremendous gravity and impact of the revolutions in our days was able to overcome had perverted the relation between means and ends in the field of linguistic studies as much as in all other fields, so that the material knowledge of a language was more highly esteemed than its rational [verständige] aspect.

Grammatical learning of an *ancient* language affords the advantage of necessarily implying a continuous and sustained activity of reason [Vernunft-thätigkeit]. In speaking our mother tongue, unreflective habit leads us to speak grammatically, but with an ancient language it is otherwise and we have to keep in view the significance which the understanding has given to the parts of speech, and call to our aid the rules of their combination. Thus a perpetual operation of subsuming the particular under the general and of specifying the general has to take place, and it is in precisely this that the activity of reason consists. Strict grammatical study is accordingly one of the most universal and noble forms of education.

Study of the ancients in their own language and grammatical instruction, taken together, constitute the *fundamental principle characteristic of our institution*. Though rich enough in itself, this *important benefit* does not comprise the whole range of knowledge to which our preparatory institute is an introduction. The classical authors to be read are so selected that the content of their writings is itself instructive, but apart from this the school offers lessons about other subjects which have a value in and for themselves or are particularly useful or beautiful. I need only mention these subjects here; their compass, treatment, order and gradation, and their relation to other subjects can be learned from the schedule that will be published and distributed. These subjects are, in general: religion, German language (including our classics), arithmetic, fol-lowed by algebra, geometry, geography, history, physiography (comprising cosmography, natural history, and physics), elements of philosophy, French, Hebrew (for future theologians), drawing and calligraphy. How little these subjects are neglected can be seen from a simple calculation. If we omit the last four subjects then the time given to the lessons in those first mentioned is exactly *as long as* that given to the ancient languages; but if we add those four subjects then the classical studies comprise not one half but only two-fifths of the whole curriculum.

[Five final paragraphs omitted.]

Selections from
Aesthetics: Lectures on Fine Art
[Vorlesungen über die Aesthetik]

Lectures given in Berlin between 1823 and 1829

The following translation is by T.M. Knox (slightly modified) in Hegel (1975); sections reprinted here are found on pp. 30–55, 602–11, 959–70.

German text in *Sämtliche Werke*, Jubiläumsausgabe in 20 vols. (1949–59), vols. XII, XIII, XIV.

Introductory note

These lectures were first published after Hegel's death by H.G. Hotho (1835; 2nd revised edn 1842), who worked partly from Hegel's own manuscript notes and partly from transcripts made by others of the courses given in 1823, 1826, and 1828–9. Hotho dates the earliest manuscripts at 1818, though he does not use them in his edition: see *SW*, XII, 3, 7.

Despite the less than ideal integrity of the text, these extensive lectures (1237 pages in Knox's translation) are a very coherent exposition of Hegel's ideas about art, and an indispensable source of arguments and examples for anyone concerned with Romantic aesthetics, in particular and in general. Intended from the first for public consumption, they tend to be easier to follow than the terse final paragraphs of the *Encyclopaedia* (see below) – they even contain jokes! – and more orderly than the famous passages of 'literary criticism' found in the earlier *Phenomenology*.

My selections are necessarily partial and can in no sense represent the whole range of Hegel's arguments. In the excerpts here reprinted, the reader will find some of the most explicit and available of all Romantic speculations on the relation of art to desire and appetite (Hegel's attention to this issue may be taken to signal how prophetic was the direction Schopenhauer had sensed in philosophy at large); on the moral faculty and on didacticism; and on the immediate predicament of art and the art instinct in Hegel's own time.

From the Introduction

(d) Now granted that the work of art is made by man as the creation of his spirit [Geist], a final question arises, in order to derive a deeper result from the foregoing [discussion], namely, what is man's *need* to produce works of art? On the one hand, this production may be regarded as a mere play of chance and fancies which might just as well be left alone as pursued; for it might be held that there are other and even better means of achieving what art aims at and that man has still higher and more important interests than art has the ability to satisfy. On the other hand, however, art seems to proceed from a higher impulse [Trieb] and to satisfy higher needs – at times the highest and absolute needs since it is bound up with the most universal views of life [Weltanschau-ungen] and the religious interests of whole epochs and peoples. This question about the non-contingent but absolute need for art, we cannot yet answer completely, because it is more concrete than an answer could turn out to be at this stage. Therefore we must content ourselves in the meantime with making only the following points.

The universal and absolute need from which art (on its formal side) springs has its origin in the fact that man is a *thinking* consciousness, i.e. that man draws out of himself and puts *before himself* [*für sich*] what he is and whatever else is. Things in nature are only *immediate* and *single*, while man as spirit *duplicates* himself, in that (i) he *is* as things in nature are, but (ii) he is just as much *for* himself; he intuits himself, represents himself, thinks, and only on the strength of this active placing himself before himself [Fürsichseyn] is he spirit. This consciousness of himself man acquires in a twofold way: *first, theoretically*, in so far as inwardly he must bring himself into his own consciousness, along with whatever moves, stirs, and presses in the human breast; and in general he must see himself, represent himself to himself, fix before himself what thinking finds as his essence, and recognize himself alone alike in what is summoned out of himself and in what is accepted from without. *Secondly*, man brings himself before himself by *practical* activity, since he has the impulse, in whatever is directly given to him, in what is present to him externally, to produce himself and therein equally to recognize himself. This aim he achieves by altering external things whereon he impresses the seal of his inner being and in which he now finds again his own characteristics [Bestimmungen].[1] Man does this in order, as a free subject, to strip the external world of its inflexible foreignness and to enjoy in the shape of things only an external realization of himself. Even a child's first impulse involves this practical alteration of external things; a boy throws stones into the river and now marvels at the circles drawn in the water as an effect in which he gains an intuition of something that is his own doing. This need runs through the most diversiform phenomena up to that mode of self-production in external things which is present in the work of art. And it is not only with external things that man proceeds in this way, but no less with himself, with his own natural figure which he does not leave as he finds it but deliberately alters. This is the cause of all dressing up and adorn-ment, even if it be barbaric, tasteless, completely disfiguring, or even pernici-ous like crushing the feet of Chinese ladies, or slitting the ears and lips. For it is only among civilized people that alteration of figure, behaviour, and every sort of mode of external expression proceeds from spiritual development [Bil-dung].[2]

The universal need for art, that is to say, is man's rational need to lift the inner and outer world into his spiritual consciousness as an object in which he recognizes again his own self. The need for this spiritual freedom he satisfies, on the one hand, within, by making what is within him explicit to himself, but correspondingly by giving outward reality to this his explicit self [Fürsichseyn], and thus in this duplication of himself by bringing what is in him into intuition [Anschauung] and knowledge [Erkenntnis], for himself and others. This is the free rationality of man in which all acting and knowing, as well as art too, have their basis and necessary origin. The specific need of art, however, in distinction from other action, political and moral, from religious representation and scientific knowledge, we shall see later.

(ii) [The Work of Art, as being for Apprehension by Man's Senses, is drawn from the Sensuous Sphere]

So far we have considered in the work of art the aspect in which it is made by man. We have now to pass on to its second characteristic [Bestimmung], namely that it is produced for apprehension by man's *senses* [*Sinn*] and therefore is more or less derived from the sensuous sphere.

(a) This reflection has given rise to the consideration that fine art is meant to arouse feeling [Empfindung], in particular the feeling that suits us, pleasant feeling. In this regard, the investigation of fine art has been made into an investigation of the feelings, and the question has been raised, 'what feelings should be aroused by art, fear, for example, and pity? But how can these be agreeable, how can the treatment of misfortune afford satisfaction?' Reflection on these lines dates especially from Moses Mendelssohn's times and many such discussions can be found in his writings.[3] Yet such investigation did not get far, because feeling is the indefinite dull region of the spirit; what is felt remains enveloped in the form of the most abstract individual subjectivity, and therefore differences between feelings are also completely abstract, not differences in the thing itself. For example, fear, anxiety, alarm, terror are of course further modifications of one and the same sort of feeling, but in part they are only quantitative intensifications, in part just forms not affecting their content, but indifferent to it. In the case of fear, for example, something is present in which the subject has an interest, but at the same time he sees the approach of the negative which threatens to destroy what he is interested in, and now he finds unmediated in himself the interest and the negative, both as contradictory affections of his subjectivity. But such fear cannot by itself condition any content; on the contrary, it is capable of receiving into itself the most varied and opposite contents. Feeling as such is an entirely empty form of subjective affectivity [Affektion]. Of course this form may be manifold in itself, as hope, grief, joy, pleasure; and, again, in this variety it may encompass different contents, as there is a feeling for justice, moral feeling [Gefühl], sublime religious feeling, and so on. But the fact that such content is present in different forms of feeling is not enough to bring to light its essential and specific nature. Feeling remains a purely subjective emotional state of mind in which the concrete thing vanishes, contracted into a circle of the greatest abstraction. Consequently the investigation of the feelings [Empfindungen] which art evokes, or is supposed to evoke, does not get beyond vagueness; it is a study which precisely abstracts from the content proper and its concrete essence and concept. For reflection on feeling is satisfied with observing subjective emotional reaction in its particular character, instead of immersing itself in the thing at issue, i.e. in the work of art, plumbing its depths, and in addition relinquishing mere subjectivity and its states. But in the case of feeling it is precisely this empty subjectivity which is not only retained but is the chief thing, and this is why men are so fond of having feelings. But this too is why a study of this kind becomes wearisome on account of its indefiniteness and emptiness, and disagreeable by its concentration on tiny subjective peculiarities.

(b) But since the work of art is not, as may be supposed, meant merely in general to arouse feelings (for in that case it would have this aim in common, without any specific difference, with oratory, historical writing, religious edification, etc.), but to do so only in so far as it is beautiful, reflection on the beautiful hit upon the idea of looking for a *special feeling of the beautiful*, and finding a specific *sense for the same*. In this quest it soon appeared that such a sense is no blind instinct, made firmly definite by nature, capable from the start in and by itself of distinguishing beauty. Hence *education* [*Bildung*] was demanded for this sense, and the educated sense of beauty was called *taste* which, although an educated appreciation and discovery of beauty, was supposed to remain still in the guise of immediate feeling. We have already touched on how abstract theories undertook to educate such a sense of taste and how it itself remained external and one-sided.[4] Criticism at the time of these views was on the one hand deficient in *universal* principles; on the other hand, as the *particular* criticism of *individual works* of art, it aimed less at grounding a more *definite judgement* – the implements for making one being not yet available – than at advancing rather the education of taste in general. Thus this education likewise got no further than what was rather vague, and it laboured only, by reflection, so to equip feeling, as a sense of beauty, that now it could find beauty wherever and however it existed. Yet the depths of the thing remained a sealed book to taste, since these depths require not only sensing and abstract reflections, but the entirety of reason and the solidity of the spirit, while taste was directed only to the external surface on which feelings play and where one-sided principles may pass as valid. Consequently, however, so-called 'good taste' takes fright at all the deeper effects [of art] and is silent when the thing at issue comes in question and externalities and incidentals vanish. For when great passions and the movements of a profound soul are revealed, there is no longer any question of the finer distinctions of taste and its pedantic preoccupation with individual details. It feels genius [Genius] striding over such ground, and, retreating before its might, finds the place too hot for itself and knows not what to do with itself.

(c) For this reason the study of works of art has given up keeping in view merely the education of taste and proposing only to exhibit taste. The *connois-seur* [*Kenner*] has taken the place of the man of taste or the judge of artistic taste. The positive side of connoisseurship, in so far as it concerns a thorough acquaintance with the whole sweep of the individual character of a work of art, we have already described as necessary for the study of art.[5] For, on account of its nature, at once material and individual, the work of art issues essentially from particular conditions of the most varied sort, amongst them especially the time and place of its origin, then the specific individuality of the artist, and above all the technical development of his art. Attention to all these aspects is indispensable for a distinct and thorough intuition of, and acquaint-ance with, a work of art, and indeed for the enjoyment of it; with them connoisseurship is principally preoccupied, and what it achieves in its way is to be accepted with gratitude. Now while such scholarship is justly counted as something essential, it still may not be taken as the single and supreme ele-ment in the relation which the spirit adopts to a work of art and to art in general. For connoisseurship, and this is its defective side, may stick at ac-quaintance with purely external aspects, the technical, historical, etc., and perhaps have little notion of the true nature of the work of art, or even know nothing of it at all; indeed it can even disesteem the value of deeper studies in comparison with purely positive, technical, and historical information. Yet connoisseurship, if it be of a genuine kind, does itself strive at least for specific grounds and information, and for an intelligent judgement with which after all is bound up a more precise discrimination of the different, even if partly external, aspects of a work of art and the evaluation of these.

(d) After these remarks on the modes of study occasioned by that aspect of the work of art which, as itself a sensuous object, gave it an essential relation to men as sensuous beings, we propose now to treat this aspect in its more essential bearing on art itself, namely (α) in regard to the work of art as an object, and (β) in regard to the subjectivity of the artist, his genius, talent [Genie, Talent], etc., yet without our entering upon what in this connection can proceed only from the knowledge of art in its universal concept. For here we are not yet really on scientific ground and territory; we are still only in the province of external reflections.

(α) Of course the work of art presents itself to sensuous apprehension. It is there for sensuous feeling, external or internal, for sensuous intuition and representation, just as nature is, whether the external nature that surrounds us, or our own sensitive nature within. After all, a speech, for example, can exist for sensuous representation and feeling. But nevertheless the work of art, as a sensuous object, is not merely for *sensuous* apprehension; its standing is of such a kind that, though sensuous, it is essentially at the same time for *spiritual* apprehension; the spirit is meant to be affected by it and to find some satisfac-tion in it.

This vocation and purpose [Bestimmung] of the work of art explains at once how it can in no way be a natural product or have in its natural aspect a natural vitality, whether a natural product is supposed to have a higher or a lower value than a *mere* work of art, as a work of art is often called in a depreciatory sense.

For the sensuous element in a work of art should be there only in so far as it exists for the human spirit, regardless of its existing independently as a sensuous object.

If we examine more closely in what way the sensuous is *there* for man, we find that what is sensuous can be related in various ways to the spirit.

(αα) The poorest mode of apprehension, the least adequate to spirit, is purely sensuous apprehension. It consists, in the first place, of merely looking on, hearing, feeling, etc., just as in hours of spiritual fatigue (indeed for many people at any time) it may be an amusement to wander about without thinking, just to listen here and look round there, and so on. Spirit does not stop at the mere apprehension of the external world by sight and hearing; it makes it into an object for its inner being which then is itself driven, once again in the form of sensuousness, to realize itself in things, and relates itself to them as *desire* [*Begierde*]. In this appetitive relation to the external world, man, as a sensuous individual, confronts things as they are individuals; likewise he does not turn his mind to them as thinker with universal categories of determination [Bestimmungen]: instead, in accord with individual impulses and interests, he relates himself to the objects, individuals themselves, and maintains himself in them by using and consuming them, and by sacrificing them works his own self-satisfaction. In this negative relation, desire requires for itself not merely the superficial appearance of external things, but the things themselves in their concrete physical existence. With mere pictures of the wood that it might use, or of the animals it might want to eat, desire is not served. Neither can desire let the object persist in its freedom, for its impulse drives it just to cancel [aufzuheben] this independence and freedom of external things, and to show that they are only there to be destroyed and consumed. But at the same time the person too, caught up in the individual, restricted, and nugatory interests of his desire, is neither free in himself, since he is not determined by the essential universality and rationality of his will, nor free in respect of the external world, for desire remains essentially determined by external things and related to them.

Now this relation of desire is not the one in which man stands to the work of art. He leaves it free as an object [Gegenstand] to exist on its own account; he relates himself to it without desire, as to an object [Objekt] which is for the contemplative [theoretische] side of spirit alone.[6] Consequently the work of art, though it has sensuous existence, does not require in this respect a sensuously concrete being and a natural life; indeed it ought not to remain on this level, seeing that it is meant to satisfy purely spiritual interests and exclude all desire from itself. Hence it is true that practical desire rates organic and inorganic individual things in nature, which can serve its purpose, higher than works of art which show themselves useless to serve it and are enjoyable only by other forms of the spirit.

(*ββ*) A second way in which what is externally present can be *for* the spirit is, in contrast to individual sense-perception and practical desire, the purely theoretical relation to *intelligence*. The theoretical study of things is not interested in consuming them in their individuality and satisfying itself and maintaining itself sensuously by means of them, but in coming to know them in their *universality*, finding their inner essence and law, and conceiving them in accordance with their concept [und sie ihrem Begriff nach zu begreifen]. Therefore theoretical interest lets individual things alone and retreats from them as sensuous individualities, since this sensuous individualism is not what intelligence tries to study. For the rational intelligence does not belong to the individual person as such in the way that desires do, but belongs to him as at the same time inherently universal. In as much as man relates himself to things in accordance with his universality, it is his universal reason which strives to find itself in nature and thereby to re-establish that inner essence of things which sensuous existence, though that essence is its basis, cannot immediately display. This theoretical interest [Interesse], the satisfaction of which is the work of *science* [*Wissenschaft*], art does not share, however, in this scientific form, nor does it make common cause with the impulses of purely practical desires. Of course science can start from the sensuous in its individuality and possess an idea [Vorstellung] of how this individual thing comes to be there in its individual colour, shape, size, etc. Yet in that case this isolated sensuous thing has as such no further bearing on the spirit, in as much as intelligence goes straight for the universal, the law, the thought and concept of the object; on this account not only does it turn its back on the object in its immediate individuality, but transforms it within; out of something sensuously concrete it makes an abstraction, something thought, and so something essentially other than what that same object was in its sensuous appearance. This the artistic interest, in distinction from science, does not do. Just as the work of art proclaims itself *qua* external object in its sensuous individuality and immediate determinateness in respect of colour, shape, sound, or *qua* a single intuition, etc., so the reflection on the work of art accepts it like this too, without going so far beyond the immediate object confronting it as to endeavour to grasp, as science does, the concept of this object as a universal concept.

From the practical interest of desire, the interest in art is distinguished by the fact that it lets its object persist freely and on its own account, while desire converts it to its own use by destroying it. On the other hand, the reflection on the work of art differs in an opposite way from theoretical consideration [Betrachtung] by scientific intelligence, since it cherishes an interest in the object in its individual existence and does not struggle to change it into its universal thought and concept.

(*γγ*) Now it follows from this that the sensuous must indeed be present in the work of art, but should appear only as the surface and as a pure *appearance* [*Schein*] of the sensuous. For in the sensuous aspect of a work of art the spirit seeks neither the concrete material stuff, the empirical inner completeness and development of the organism which desire demands, nor the universal and purely ideal thought. What it wants is sensuous presence which indeed should remain sensuous, but liberated from the scaffolding of its purely material nature. Thereby the sensuous aspect of a work of art, in comparison with the immediate existence of things in nature, is elevated to a pure *appearance*, and the work of art stands in the *middle* between immediate sensuousness and ideal thought. It is *not yet* pure thought, but, despite its sensuousness, is *no longer* a purely material existent either, like stones, plants, and organic life; on the contrary, the sensuous in the work of art is itself something ideal, but which, not being ideal as thought is ideal, is still at the same time there externally as a thing. If spirit leaves the objects free yet without descending into their essential inner being (for if it did so they would altogether cease to exist for it externally as individuals), then this pure appearance of the sensuous presents itself to spirit from without as the shape, the appearance, or the sonority of things. Consequently the sensuous aspect of art is related only to the two *theoretical* senses of *sight* and *hearing*, while smell, taste, and touch remain excluded from the enjoyment of art.[7] For smell, taste, and touch have to do with matter as such and its immediately sensible qualities – smell with material volatility in air, taste with the material liquefaction of objects, touch with warmth, cold, smoothness, etc. For this reason these senses cannot have to do with artistic objects, which are meant to maintain themselves in their real independence and allow of no *purely* sensuous relationship. What is agreeable for these senses is not the beauty of art. Thus art on its sensuous side deliberately produces only a shadow-world of shapes, sounds, and sights; and it is quite out of the question to maintain that, in calling works of art into existence, it is from mere impotence and because of his limitations that man produces no more than a surface of the sensuous, mere *schemata*.[8] These sensuous shapes and sounds appear in art not merely for the sake of themselves and their immediate shape, but with the aim, in this shape, of affording satisfaction to higher spiritual interests, since they have the power to call forth from all the depths of consciousness a sound and an echo in the spirit. In this way the sensuous aspect of art is *spiritualized*, since the *spirit* appears in art as made sensuous.

(β) But precisely for this reason an art-product is only there in so far as it has taken its passage through the spirit and has arisen from spiritual productive activity. This leads on to the other question which we have to answer, namely in what way the necessary sensuous side of art is operative in the artist as his objective productive activity. This sort and manner of production contains in itself, as subjective activity, just the same characteristics [Bestimmungen] which we found objectively present in the work of art; it must be a spiritual activity which yet contains at the same time the element of sensuousness and immediacy. Still it is neither on the one hand purely mechanical work, a purely unconscious skill in sensuous manipulation or a formal activity according to fixed rules to be learnt by heart, nor on the other hand is it a scientific production which passes over from the sensuous to abstract representations and thoughts or is active entirely in the element of pure thinking. In artistic production the spiritual and the sensuous aspects must be as one. For example, someone might propose to proceed in poetic composition by first apprehending the proposed theme as a prosaic thought and then putting it into poetical images, rhyme, and so forth, so that now the image would simply be hung on to the abstract reflections as an ornament and decoration. But such a procedure could produce only bad poetry, because in it there would be operative as *separate* activities what in artistic production has validity only as an undivided unity. This genuine mode of production constitutes the activity of artistic *imagination* [*Phantasie*].

This activity is the rational element which exists as spirit only in so far as it actively drives itself forth into consciousness, yet what it bears within itself it places before itself only in sensuous form. Thus this activity has a spiritual content which yet it configurates sensuously because only in this sensuous guise can it gain knowledge of the content. This can be compared with the characteristic mentality of a man experienced in life, or even of a man of quick wit and ingenuity, who, although he knows perfectly well what matters in life, what in substance holds men together, what moves them, what power dominates them, nevertheless has neither himself grasped this knowledge in general rules nor expounded it to others in general reflections. What fills his mind he always just makes clear to himself and others in particular cases, real or invented, in adequate examples, and so forth; for in his mode of representation anything and everything is shaped into concrete pictures, determined in time and space, to which there may not be wanting names and all sorts of other external circumstances. Yet such a kind of imagination [Einbildungskraft] rests rather on the recollection of situations lived through, of experiences enjoyed, instead of being creative itself. Recollection preserves and renews the individuality and the external fashion of the occurrence of such experiences, with all their accompanying circumstances, but does not allow the universal to emerge on its own account. But the productive imagination [Phantasie] of an artist is the imagination of a great spirit and heart, the apprehension and creation of representations and shapes, and indeed the exhibition of the profoundest and most universal human interests in pictorial and completely definite sensuous presentation.

Now from this it follows at once that, on one side, imagination [Phantasie] rests of course on natural gifts and talent in general, because its productive activity involves an aspect of sensuousness. We do indeed speak of 'scientific' talent too, but the sciences presuppose only the universal capacity for thinking, which, instead of proceeding in a natural way, like imagination, precisely abstracts from all natural activity; and so we are righter to say that there is no specifically scientific talent in the sense of a merely natural gift. Conversely, imagination has at the same time a sort of instinct-like productiveness, in that the essential figurativeness [Bildlichkeit] and sensuousness of the work of art must be present subjectively in the artist as a natural gift and natural impulse, and, as an unconscious operation, must also belong to the natural side of man.[9] Of course natural capacity is not the whole of talent and genius, since the production of art is also of a spiritual, self-conscious kind, yet its spirituality must somehow have in itself an element of natural picturing and shaping. Consequently almost anyone can get up to a certain point in an art, but to get beyond this point, where art proper only now begins, an inborn, higher talent for art is necessary.

As a natural gift, this talent declares itself after all in most cases in early youth, and it shows itself in the driving restlessness to shape a specific sensuous material at once in a lively and active way and to seize this mode of expression and communication as the only one, or as the most important and appropriate one. And so also an early technical facility, which up to a certain point is effortless, is a sign of inborn talent. For a sculptor everything turns into shapes, and from early years he lays hold of clay in order to model it. In short, whatever representations such talented men have, whatever rouses and moves them inwardly, turns at once into figure, drawing, melody, or poem.[10]

(γ) Thirdly, and lastly, the *subject matter* [*Inhalt*] of art is in a certain respect also drawn from the sensuous, from nature; or, in any case, even if the subject s of a spiritual kind, it can still be grasped only by displaying spiritual things, ike human relationships, in the shape of phenomena possessed of external ality.

(iii) [The Aim of Art]

Now the question arises of what interest or *end* man sets before himself when he produces such subject matter in the form of works of art. This was the third point which we adduced with regard to the work of art,[11] and its closer discussion will lead us on at last to the true concept of art itself.

If in this matter we cast a glance at what is commonly thought, one of the most prevalent ideas [Vorstellungen] which may occur to us is

(a) the principle of the *imitation of nature*. According to this view, imitation, as facility in copying natural forms just as they are, in a way that corresponds to them completely, is supposed to constitute the essential end and aim of art, and the success of this portrayal in correspondence with nature is supposed to afford complete satisfaction.

(α) This definition [Bestimmung] contains, *prima facie*, only the purely formal aim that whatever exists already in the external world, and the manner in which it exists there, is now to be made over again as a copy, as well as a man can do with the means at his disposal. But this repetition can be seen at once to be

(αα) a *superfluous* labour, since what pictures, theatrical productions, etc., portray imitatively – animals, natural scenes, human affairs – we already possess in our gardens or in our own houses or in matters within our narrower or wider circle of acquaintance. And, looked at more closely, this superfluous labour may even be regarded as a presumptuous game

(ββ) which falls far short of nature. For art is restricted in its means of portrayal [Darstellungsmitteln], and can only produce one-sided deceptions, for example a pure appearance of reality for *one* sense only, and, in fact, if it abides by the formal aim of *mere imitation*, it provides not the reality of life but only a pretence of life. After all, the Turks, as Mahommedans, do not, as is well known, tolerate any pictures or copies of men, etc. James Bruce in his journey to Abyssinia showed paintings of a fish to a Turk; at first the Turk was astonished, but quickly enough he found an answer: "If this fish shall rise up against you on the last day and say: 'You have indeed given me a body but no living soul', how will you then justify yourself against this accusation?"[12] The prophet too, as is recorded in the Sunna, said to the two women, Ommi Habiba and Ommi Selma, who had told him about pictures in Ethiopian churches: "These pictures will accuse their authors on the day of judgement."[13]

Even so, there are doubtless examples of completely deceptive copying. The grapes painted by Zeuxis have from antiquity onward been styled a triumph of art and also of the principle of the imitation of nature, because living doves are supposed to have pecked at them. To this ancient example we could add the modern one of Büttner's monkey which ate away a painting of a cockchafer in Rösel's *Insektbelustigungen* [*Amusements of Insects*] and was pardoned by his master because it had proved the excellence of the pictures in this book, although it had thus destroyed the beautiful copy of this expensive work.[14] But in such examples and others it must at least occur to us at once that, instead of praising works of art because they have deceived *even* doves and monkeys, we should just precisely censure those who think of exalting a work of art by predicating so miserable an effect as this as its highest and supreme quality. In sum, however, it must be said that, by mere imitation, art cannot stand in competition with nature, and, if it tries, it looks like a worm trying to crawl after an elephant.

(γγ) If we stay within the context of the continual, though comparative, failure of the copy compared with the original in nature, then there remains over as an aim nothing but taking pleasure in the trick of producing something like nature. And of course a man may enjoy himself in now producing over again by his own work, skill, and assiduity what otherwise is there already. But this enjoyment and admiration become in themselves the more frigid and cold, the more the copy is like the natural original, or they may even be perverted into tedium and repugnance. There are portraits which, as has been wittily said, are "disgustingly like", and Kant, in relation to this pleasure in imitation as such, cites another example, namely that we soon get tired of a man who can imitate to perfection the warbling of the nightingale (and there are such men); as soon as it is discovered that it is a man who is producing the notes, we are at once weary of the song.[15] We then recognize in it nothing but a trick, neither the free production of nature, nor a work of art, since from the free productive power of man we expect something quite different from such music which interests us only when, as is the case with the nightingale's warbling, it gushes forth purposeless from the bird's own life, like the voice of human feeling. In general this delight in imitative skill can always be but restricted, and it befits man better to take delight in what he produces out of himself. In this sense the discovery of any insignificant technical product has higher value, and man can be prouder of having invented the hammer, the nail, etc., than of manufacturing tricks of imitation. For this enthusiasm for copying merely as copying is to be respected as little as the trick of the man who had learnt to throw lentils through a small opening without missing. He displayed this dexterity before Alexander, but Alexander gave him a bushel of lentils as a reward for this useless and worthless art.[16]

(β) Now further, since the principle of imitation is purely formal, *objective beauty* itself disappears when this principle is made the end of art. For if it is, then there is no longer a question of the character of *what* is supposed to be imitated, but only of the *correctness* of the imitation. The object and content of the beautiful is regarded as a matter of complete indifference. Even if, apart from this, we speak of a difference between beauty and ugliness in relation to animals, men, localities, actions, or characters, yet according to that principle this remains a difference which does not properly belong to art, to which we have left nothing but imitation pure and simple. So that the above-mentioned lack of a criterion for the endless forms of nature leaves us, so far as the choice of objects and their beauty and ugliness are concerned, with mere *subjective taste* as the last word, and such taste will not be bound by rules, and is not open to dispute. And indeed if, in choosing objects for representation, we start from what *people* find beautiful or ugly and therefore worthy of artistic representation, i.e. from their taste, then all spheres of natural objects stand open to us, and none of them is likely to lack an admirer. For among us, e.g., it may not be every husband who finds his wife beautiful, but he did before they were married, to the exclusion of all others too; and the fact that the subjective taste for this beauty has no fixed rule may be considered a good thing for both parties. If finally we look beyond single individuals and their capricious taste to the taste of *nations*, this too is of the greatest variety and contrariety. How often do we hear it said that a European beauty would not please a Chinese, or a Hottentot either, since the Chinese has inherently a totally different conception of beauty from the negro's, and his again from a European's, and so on. Indeed, if we examine the works of art of these non-European peoples, their images of the gods, for example, which have sprung from their imagination [Phantasie] as sublime and worthy of veneration, they may present themselves to us as the most hideous idols; and while their music may sound in our ears as the most detestable noise, they on their side will regard our sculptures, pictures, and music, as meaningless or ugly.

(γ) But even if we abstract from an objective principle for art, and if beauty is to be based on subjective and individual taste, we soon nevertheless find on the side of art itself that the imitation of nature, which indeed appeared to be a universal principle and one confirmed by high authority, is not to be adopted, at least in this general and wholly abstract form. For if we look at the different arts, it will be granted at once that, even if *painting* and *sculpture* portray objects that appear to be like natural ones or ones whose type is essentially drawn from nature, on the other hand works of *architecture*, which is also one of the *fine* arts, can as little be called imitations of nature as works of *poetry* can, in so far as the latter are not confined, e.g., to mere description. In any case, if we still wanted to uphold this principle in relation to these latter arts, we would at least find ourselves compelled to take a long circuitous route, because we would have to attach various conditions to the proposition and reduce the so-called 'truth' of imitation to probability at least. But with probability we would again encounter a great difficulty, namely in settling what is probable and what is not, and, apart from this, we would not wish or be able to exclude from poetry all purely arbitrary and completely fanciful [phantastischen] inventions.

The aim of art must therefore lie in something still other than the purely mechanical imitation of what is there, which in every case can bring to birth only technical *tricks*, not *works*, of art. It is true that it is an essential element in a work of art to have a natural shape as its basis because what it portrays it displays in the form of an external and therefore also natural phenomenon. In painting, e.g., it is an important study to get to know and copy with precision the colours in their relation to one another, the effects of light, reflections, etc., as well as the forms and shapes of objects down to the last detail. It is in this respect, after all, that chiefly in recent times the principle of the imitation of nature, and of naturalism generally, has raised its head again in order to bring back to the vigour and distinctness of nature an art which had relapsed into feebleness and nebulosity; or, on the other hand, to assert the regular, immediate, and explicitly fixed sequences of nature against the manufactured and purely arbitrary conventionalism, really just as inartistic as unnatural, into which art had strayed. But whatever is right enough from one point of view in this endeavour, still the naturalism demanded is as such not the substantial and primary basis of art, and, even if external appearance in its naturalness constitutes one essential characteristic [Bestimmung] of art, still neither is the given natural world the *rule* nor is the mere imitation of external phenomena, as external, the *aim* of art.

(b) Therefore the further question arises: what, then, is the *content* of art, and why is this content to be portrayed? In this matter our consciousness confronts us with the common opinion that the task and aim of art is to bring home to our sense, our feeling, and our inspiration everything which has a place in the human spirit. That familiar saying "nihil humani a me alienum puto" art is supposed to make real in us.[17]

Its aim therefore is supposed to consist in awakening and vivifying our slumbering feelings, inclinations, and passions *of every kind*, in *filling* the heart, in forcing the human being, educated or not, to go through the whole gamut of feelings which the human heart in its inmost and secret recesses can bear, experience, and produce, through what can move and stir the human breast in its depths and manifold possibilities and aspects, and to deliver to feeling and contemplation for its enjoyment whatever the spirit possesses of the essential and lofty in its thinking and in the Idea [Idee] – the splendour of the noble, eternal, and true: moreover to make misfortune and misery, evil and guilt intelligible, to make men intimately acquainted with all that is horrible and shocking, as well as with all that is pleasurable and felicitous; and, finally, to let fancy [Phantasie] loose in the idle plays of imagination [Einbildungskraft] and plunge it into the seductive magic of sensuously bewitching visions and feelings. According to this view, art is on the one hand to embrace this universal wealth of subject matter in order to complete the natural experience of our external existence, and on the other hand to arouse those passions in general so that the experiences of life do not leave us unmoved and so that we might now acquire a receptivity for all phenomena. But such a stimulus is not given in this sphere by actual experience itself, but only through the appearance of it, since art deceptively substitutes its productions for reality. The possibility of this deception through the pure appearance-status [Schein] of art rests on the fact that, for man, all reality must come through the medium of intuition and representation, and only through this medium does it penetrate the heart and the will. Now here it is a matter of indifference whether a man's attention is claimed by immediate external reality or whether this happens in another way, namely through images, signs, and representations containing in themselves and portraying the material of reality. We can envisage things which are not real as if they were real. Therefore it remains all the same for our feelings whether it is external reality, or only the appearance of it, whereby a situation, a relation, or, in general, a circumstance of life, is brought home to us, in order to make us respond appropriately to the essence of such a matter, whether by grief or rejoicing, whether by being touched or agitated, or whether by making us go through the gamut of the feelings and passions of wrath, hatred, pity, anxiety, fear, love, reverence and admiration, honour and fame.

This arousing of all feelings [Empfindungen] in us, this drawing of the heart through all the circumstances of life, this actualizing of all these inner movements by means of a purely deceptive externally presented object is above all what is regarded, on the view we have been considering, as the proper and supreme power of art.

But now since, on this view, art is supposed to have the vocation of imposing on the heart and the representational imagination [Vorstellung] good and bad alike, strengthening man to the noblest ideals and yet enervating him to the most sensuous and selfish feelings of pleasure, art is given a purely formal task; and without any explicitly fixed aim would thus provide only the empty form for every possible kind of content and worth.

(c) In fact art does indeed have this formal side, namely its ability to adorn and bring before perception and feeling every possible material, just as the thinking of ratiocination can work on every possible object and mode of action and equip them with reasons and justifications. But confronted by such a multiple variety of content, we are at once forced to notice that the different feelings and representations, which art is supposed to arouse or confirm, counteract one another, contradict and reciprocally cancel [aufheben] one another. Indeed, in this respect, the more art inspires to contradictory [emotions] the more it increases the contradictory character of feelings and passions and makes us stagger about like Bacchantes or even goes on, like ratiocination [Raisonnement], to sophistry and scepticism.[18] This variety of material itself compels us, therefore, not to stop at so formal a definition [of the aim of art], since rationality penetrates this jumbled diversity and demands to see, and know to be attained, even out of elements so contradictory, a higher and inherently more universal end. It is claimed indeed similarly that the final end of the state and the social life of men is that *all* human capacities and *all* individual powers be developed and given expression in every way and in every direction. But against so formal a view the question arises soon enough: into what *unity* are these manifold formations to be brought together, what *single aim* must they have as their fundamental concept and final end? As with the concept of the state, so too with the concept of art there arises the need (a) for a *common* end for its particular aspects, but (b) also for a higher *substantial* end. As such a substantial end, the first thing that occurs to reflection is the view that art has the capacity and the vocation to mitigate the ferocity of desires.

(α) In respect of this first idea, we have only to discover in what feature peculiar to art there lies the capacity to cancel crudity and to bridle and educate impulses, inclinations, and passions. Crudeness in general is grounded in a direct selfishness of the impulses which make straightaway, precisely, and exclusively for the satisfaction of their appetite [Begierlichkeit]. But desire is all the cruder and imperious the more, as single and restricted, it engrosses the *whole man*, so that he loses the power to tear himself free, as a universal being, from this determinateness and become aware of himself as universal. And if the man says in such a case, as may be supposed, "The passion is stronger than *I*", then for consciousness the abstract "I" *is* separated from the particular passion, but only in a purely formal way, since all that is pronounced with this cleavage is that, in face of the power of the passion, the "I" as a universal is of no account whatever. Thus the ferocity of passion consists in the unity of the "I" as universal with the restricted object of its desire, so that the man has no longer any will beyond this single passion. Now such crudeness and untamed force of passion is *prima facie* mitigated by art, in that it gives a man an image [vorstellig macht] of what he feels and achieves in such a situation. And even if art restricts itself to setting up pictures of passions for intuition, even if indeed it were to flatter them, still there is here already a power of mitigation, since thereby a man is at least made aware of what otherwise he only immediately is. For then the man contemplates his impulses and inclinations, and while previously they carried him reflectionless away, he now sees them outside himself and already begins to be free from them because they confront him as something objective.

For this reason it may often be the case with an artist that, overtaken by grief, he mitigates and weakens for himself the intensity of his own feeling by setting it forth. Tears, even, provide some comfort; at first entirely sunk and concentrated in grief, a man may then in this direct way utter this purely inward feeling. But still more of an alleviation is the expression of one's inner state in words, pictures, sounds, and shapes. For this reason it was a good old custom at deaths and funerals to appoint wailing women in order that grief might be brought to intuition in its expression. For by expressions of condolence the burden of a man's misfortune is brought before his mind; if it is much spoken about he has to reflect on it, and this alleviates his grief. And so to cry one's eyes out and to speak out has ever been regarded as a means of freeing oneself from the oppressive burden of care or at least of relieving the heart. The mitigation of the power of passions therefore has its universal ground in the fact that man is released from his immediate imprisonment in a feeling and becomes conscious of it as something external to him, to which he must now relate himself in an ideal way. Art by means of its presentations [Darstellungen], while remaining within the sensuous sphere, liberates man at the same time from the power of sensuousness. Of course we may often hear favourite phraseology about man's duty to remain in immediate unity with nature; but such unity, in its abstraction, is purely and simply crudeness and ferocity, and by dissolving this unity for man, art lifts him with gentle hands out of and above imprisonment in nature. For man's preoccupation with artistic objects remains purely contemplative [theoretisch], and thereby it educates, even if at first only an attention to artistic portrayals in general, later on an attention to their meaning and to a comparison with other subjects, and it opens the mind to a general consideration of them and the points of view therein involved.

(β) Now on this there follows quite logically the second characteristic [Bestimmung] that has been attributed to art as its essential aim, namely the *purification* of the passions, instruction, and *moral* improvement. For the theory [Bestimmung] that art was to curb crudeness and educate the passions, remained quite formal and general, so that it has become again a matter of what *specific* sort of education [Bildung] this is and what is its essential aim.

(αα) It is true that the doctrine of the purification of passion still suffers the same deficiency as the previous doctrine of the mitigation of desires, yet it does at least emphasize more closely the fact that artistic presentations need a criterion for assessing their worth or unworthiness. This criterion is precisely an effectiveness in separating pure from impure in the passions. Such effectiveness therefore requires a content which can exercise this purifying force, and, in so far as producing such an effect is supposed to constitute the substantial aim of art, the purifying content will have to be brought into consciousness in accordance with its *universality* and *essentiality*.

(ββ) From this latter point of view, the aim of art has been pronounced to be that it should *instruct*. On this view, on the one hand, the special character of art consists in the movement of feelings and in the satisfaction lying in this movement, lying even in fear, in pity, in grievous emotion and agitation, i.e. in the satisfying enlistment of feelings and passions, and to that extent in a gusto, a pleasure, and delight in artistic subjects, in their presentation and effect. But, on the other hand, this aim of art is supposed to have its higher criterion only in its instructiveness, in *fabula docet*,[19] and so in the useful influence which the work of art may exert on the individual. In this respect the Horatian aphorism *Et prodesse volunt et delectare poetae*[20] contains, concentrated in a few words, what later has been elaborated in an infinite degree, diluted, and made into a view of art reduced to the uttermost extreme of shallowness. Now in connection with such instruction we must ask at once whether it is supposed to be contained in the work of art directly or indirectly, explicitly or implicitly. If, in general, what is at issue is a universal and non-contingent aim, then this end and aim, in view of the essentially spiritual nature of art, can itself only be a spiritual one, and moreover one which is not contingent but existing in and for itself. This aim in relation to teaching could only consist in bringing into consciousness, by means of the work of art, an absolutely essential [an und für sich wesentlichen] spiritual content. From this point of view we must assert that the more highly art is ranked the more it has to adopt such a content into itself and find only in the essence of that content the criterion of whether what is expressed is appropriate or not. Art has in fact become the first *instructress* of peoples.

If, however, the aim of instruction is treated as an aim in such a way that the universal nature of the content represented is supposed to emerge and be explained directly and explicitly as an abstract proposition, prosaic reflection, or general doctrine, and not to be contained implicitly and only indirectly in the concrete form of a work of art, then by this separation the sensuous pictorial form, which is precisely what alone makes a work of art a work of *art*, becomes a useless appendage, a veil and a pure appearance [Schein], expressly pronounced to be a *mere veil* and a mere pure appearance. But thereby the nature of the work of art itself is distorted. For the work of art should put before our eyes [vor die Anschauung] a content, not in its universality as such, but one whose universality has been absolutely individualized and sensuously particularized. If the work of art does not proceed from this principle but emphasizes the universality with the aim of [providing] abstract instruction, then the pictorial and sensuous element is only an external and superfluous adornment, and the work of art is broken up internally; form and content no longer appear as coalesced. In that event the sensuously individual and the spiritually universal have become external to one another.

Now, further, if the aim of art is restricted to this usefulness for *instruction*, the other side, pleasure, entertainment, and delight, is pronounced explicitly to be *inessential*, and ought to have its substance only in the utility of the doctrine on which it is attendant. But what is implied here at the same time is that art does not carry its vocation [Bestimmung], end, and aim in itself, but that its essence lies in something else to which it serves as a *means*. In that event art is only one amongst several means which are proved useful for and applied to the end of instruction. But this brings us to the boundary at which art is supposed to cease to be an end in itself, because it is reduced either to a mere entertaining game or a mere means of instruction.

(γγ) This boundary is most sharply marked if in turn a question is raised about a supreme aim and end for the sake of which passions are to be purified and men instructed. As this aim, *moral* [*moralische*] betterment has often been adduced in recent times, and the end of art has been placed in the function of preparing inclinations and impulses for moral perfection and of leading them to this final end. This idea [Vorstellung] unites instruction with purification, in as much as art, by affording an insight into genuinely moral goodness and so by instruction, at the same time incites to purification and only so is to accomplish the betterment of mankind as its utility and its highest aim.

Now as regards art in relation to this moral betterment, the same must be said, in the first place, about the aim of art as instruction. It is readily granted that art may not take immorality and the intention of promoting it as its principle. But it is one thing to make immorality the express aim of the presentation, and another not to take morality as that aim. From every genuine work of art a good moral may be drawn, yet of course all depends on interpretation and on *who* draws the moral. We can hear the most immoral presentations defended on the ground that one must be acquainted with evil and sins in order to be able to act morally; conversely, it has been said that the portrayal of Mary Magdalene, the beautiful sinner who afterwards repented, has seduced many into sin, because art makes repentance look so beautiful, and sinning must come before repentance.[21] But the doctrine of moral betterment, carried through logically, is not content with holding that a moral may be pointed from a work of art; on the contrary, it would want the moral instruction to shine forth clearly as the substantial aim of the work of art, and indeed would expressly permit the presentation of none but moral subjects, moral characters, actions, and events. For art can choose its subjects, and is thus distinct from history or the sciences, which have their material given to them.

In order, in this aspect of the matter, to be able to form a thorough estimate of the view that the aim of art is moral, we must first ask what specific standpoint of morality this view professes. If we keep more clearly in view the standpoint of the 'moral' as we have to take it in the best sense of the word today, it is soon obvious that its concept does not immediately coincide with what apart from it we generally call virtue, conventional life [Sittlichkeit],[22] respectability, etc. From this point of view a conventionally virtuous man is not *ipso facto moral*, because to be moral needs *reflection* [*Reflexion*], the specific consciousness of what accords with duty, and action on this preceding consciousness. Duty itself is the law of the will, a law which man nevertheless freely lays down out of himself, and then he ought to determine himself to this duty for the sake of duty and its fulfilment, by doing good solely from the conviction he has won that it is the good. But this law, the duty chosen for duty's sake as a guide out of free conviction and inner conscience, and then carried out, is by itself the abstract universal of the will and this has its direct opposite in nature, in sensuous impulses, selfish interests, passions, and everything grouped together under the name of feeling and emotion. In this opposition it is perceived that one side *cancels* the other, and since both are present in the subject as opposites, he has a choice, since his decision is made from within, between following either the one or the other. But such a decision is a *moral* one, from the standpoint we are considering, and so is the action carried out in accordance with it, but only if it is done, on the one hand, from a free conviction of duty, and, on the other hand, by the conquest not only of the particular will, natural impulses, inclinations, passions, etc., but also of noble feelings and higher impulses. For the modern moralistic view starts from the fixed opposition between the will in its spiritual universality and the will in its sensuous natural particularity; and it consists not in the complete mediation [Vermittelung] of these opposed sides, but in their reciprocal battle against one another, which involves the demand that impulses in their conflict with duty must give way to it.[23]

Now this opposition does not arise for consciousness in the restricted sphere of moral action alone; it emerges in a thorough-going cleavage and opposition between what is in and for itself and what is external reality and existence. Taken quite abstractly, it is the opposition of universal and particular, when each is fixed over against the other on its own account in the same way; more concretely, it appears in nature as the opposition of the abstract law to the abundance of individual phenomena, each explicitly with its own character; in the spirit it appears as the contrast between the sensuous and the spiritual in man, as the battle of spirit against flesh, of duty for duty's sake, of the cold command against particular interest, warmth of heart, sensuous inclinations and impulses, against the individual disposition in general; as the harsh opposition between inner freedom and the necessity of external nature, further as the contradiction between the dead inherently empty concept, and the full concreteness of life, between theory or subjective thinking, and objective existence and experience.

These are oppositions which have not been invented at all by the subtlety of reflection or the pedantry of philosophy; in numerous forms they have always preoccupied and troubled human consciousness, even if it is modern culture [Bildung] that has first worked them out most sharply and driven them up to the peak of harshest contradiction. Spiritual culture, the modern intellect

[Verstand], produces this opposition in man which makes him an amphibious animal, because he now has to live in two worlds which contradict one another. The result is that now consciousness wanders about in this contradiction, and, driven from one side to the other, cannot find satisfaction for itself in either the one or the other. For on the one side we see man imprisoned in the common world of reality and earthly temporality, borne down by need and poverty, hard pressed by nature, enmeshed in matter, sensuous ends and their enjoyment, mastered and carried away by natural impulses and passions. On the other side, he lifts himself to eternal ideas [Ideen], to a realm of thought and freedom, gives to himself, as *will* [*Wille*], universal laws and prescriptions [Bestimmungen], strips the world of its enlivened and flowering reality and dissolves it into abstractions, since the spirit now upholds its right and dignity only by mishandling nature and denying its right, and so retaliates on nature the distress and violence which it has suffered from nature itself. But for modern culture and its intellect this discordance in life and consciousness involves the demand that such a contradiction be resolved. Yet the intellect [Verstand] cannot cut itself free from the rigidity of these oppositions; therefore the solution remains for consciousness a mere *ought* [*Sollen*], and the present and reality move only in the unrest of a hither and thither which seeks a reconciliation without finding one. Thus the question then arises whether such a universal and thorough-going opposition, which cannot get beyond a mere ought and a postulated solution, is in general the absolute [an und für sich] truth and supreme end. If general culture has run into such a contradiction, it becomes the task of philosophy to supersede the oppositions, i.e. to show that neither the one alternative in its abstraction, nor the other in the like one-sidedness, possesses truth, but that they are both self-dissolving; that truth lies only in the reconciliation and mediation of both, and that this mediation is no mere demand, but what is absolutely accomplished and is ever self-accomplishing. This insight coincides immediately with the ingenuous faith and will [Wollen] which does have precisely this dissolved opposition steadily present to its view [vor der Vorstellung], and in action makes it its end and achieves it. Philosophy affords a reflective insight into the essence of the opposition only in so far as it shows how truth is just the dissolving of opposition and, at that, not in the sense, as may be supposed, that the opposition and its two sides *do not exist at all*, but that they exist reconciled.

Now since the ultimate end, moral betterment, has pointed to a higher standpoint, we will have to vindicate this higher standpoint for art too. Thereby the false position, already noticed, is at once abandoned: the position, namely, that art has to serve as a means to moral purposes, and the moral end of the world in general, by instructing and improving, and thus has its substantial aim, not in itself, but in something else. If on this account we now continue to speak of a final end and aim, we must in the first place get rid of the perverse idea [Vorstellung] which, in the question about an end, clings to the accessory meaning of the question, namely that it is one about utility.

The perversity here lies in this, that in that case the work of art is supposed to have a bearing on something else which is set before our minds as the essential thing or as what ought to be, so that then the work of art would have validity only as a useful tool for realizing this end which is independently valid on its own account outside the sphere of art. Against this we must maintain that art's vocation is to unveil the *truth* in the form of sensuous artistic configuration, to set forth the reconciled opposition just mentioned, and so to have its end and aim in itself, in this very setting forth and unveiling. For other ends, like instruction, purification, bettering, financial gain, struggling for fame and honour, have nothing to do with the work of art as such, and do not determine its nature.

(c) *The End of the Romantic Form of Art*[24]

Art, as it has been under our consideration hitherto, had as its basis the unity of meaning and shape and so the unity of the artist's subjective activity with his topic and work. Looked at more closely, it was the specific kind of this unification at each stage which provided, for the content and its corresponding portrayal, the substantial norm penetrating all artistic productions.

In this matter we found at the beginning of art, in the East, that the spirit was not yet itself explicitly free; it still sought for its Absolute [Absolute] in nature and therefore interpreted nature as in itself divine. Later on, the vision [Anschauung] of classical art represented the Greek gods as naive and inspired, yet even so essentially as individuals burdened with the natural human form as with an affirmative feature. Romantic art for the first time deepened the spirit in its own inwardness, in contrast to which the flesh, external reality, and the world in general were at first posited as negative [Nichtiges], even though the spirit and the Absolute had to appear in this element alone; yet at last this element could be given validity for itself again in a more and more positive way.

(α) These ways of viewing the world constitute religion, the substantial spirit of peoples and ages, and are woven into not art alone, but all the other spheres of the living present at all periods. Now just as every man is a child of his time in every activity, whether political, religious, or scientific, and just as he has the task of bringing out the essential content and the therefore necessary form of that time, so it is the vocation of art to find for the spirit of a people the artistic expression corresponding to it. Now so long as the artist is bound up with the specific character of such a world-view and religion, in immediate identity with it and with firm faith in it, so long is he genuinely in *earnest* with this material and its representation; i.e. this material remains for him the infinite and true element in his own consciousness – a material with which he lives in an original unity as part of his inmost self, while the form in which he exhibits it is for him as artist the final, necessary, and supreme manner of bringing before our intuition the Absolute and the soul of objects in general.[25] By the substance of his material, a substance immanent in himself, he is tied down to the specific mode of its exposition. For in that case the material, and therefore the form belonging to it, the artist carries immediately in himself as the proper essence of his existence which he does not imagine for himself but which he *is*; and therefore he only has the task of making this truly essential element objective to himself, to represent and develop it in a living way out of his own resources. Only in that event is the artist completely inspired by his material and its presentation; and his inventions are no product of caprice, they originate in him, out of him, out of this substantial ground, this stock, the content of which is not at rest until through the artist it acquires an individual shape adequate to its inner concept. If, on the other hand, we nowadays propose to make the subject of a statue or a painting a Greek god, or, Protestants as we are today, the Virgin Mary, we are not seriously in earnest with such material.[26] It is the innermost faith which we lack here, even if the artist in days when faith was still unimpaired did not exactly need to be what is generally called a pious man, for after all in every age artists have not as a rule been the most pious of men! The requirement is only this, that for the artist the content [of his work] shall constitute the substance, the inmost truth, of his consciousness and make his chosen mode of presentation necessary. For the artist in his production is at the same time a creature of nature, his skill is a *natural* talent; his work is not the pure activity of comprehension [Begreifen] which confronts its material entirely and unites itself with it in free thoughts, in pure thinking; on the contrary, the artist, not yet released from his natural side, is united directly with the subject matter, believes in it, and is identical with it in accordance with his very own self.[27] The result is then that the artist is entirely absorbed in the object; the work of art proceeds entirely out of the undivided inwardness and force of genius [Genie]; the production is firm and unwavering, and in it the full intensity [of creation] is preserved. This is the fundamental condition of art's being present in its integrity.

(β) On the other hand, in the position we have been forced to assign to art in the course of its development, the whole situation has altogether altered. This, however, we must not regard as a mere accidental misfortune suffered by art from without owing to the distress of the times, the sense for the prosaic, lack of interest, etc.; on the contrary, it is the effect and the progress of art itself which, by bringing before our intuition as an object its own indwelling material, at every step along this road makes its own contribution to freeing art from the content represented. What through art or thinking we have before our physical or spiritual eye as an object has lost all absolute interest for us if it has been put before us so completely that the content is exhausted, that everything is revealed, and nothing obscure or inward is left over any more. For interest is to be found only in the case of lively activity [of mind]. The spirit only occupies itself with objects so long as there is something secret, not revealed, in them. This is the case so long as the material is identical with the

substance of our own being. But if the essential world-views [Weltanschauun-
gen] implicit in the concept of art, and the range of the content belonging to
these, are in every respect revealed by art, then art has got rid of this content
which on every occasion was determinate for a particular people, a particular
age, and the true need to resume it again is awakened only with the need to
turn *against* the content that was alone valid hitherto; thus in Greece Aristo-
phanes rose up against his present world, and Lucian against the whole of the
Greek past, and in Italy and Spain, when the Middle Ages were closing,
Ariosto and Cervantes began to turn against chivalry.[28]

Now contrasted with the time in which the artist owing to his nationality
and his period stands with the substance of his being within a specific world-
view and its content and forms of portrayal, we find an altogether opposed
view which in its complete development is of importance only in most recent
times. In our day, in the case of almost all peoples, criticism [die Kritik],[29] the
cultivation of reflection, and, in our German case, freedom of thought have
mastered the artists too, and have made them, so to say, a *tabula rasa* in respect
of the material and the form of their productions, after the necessary particular stages of the romantic art-form have been traversed. Bondage to a particular subject matter and a mode of portrayal suitable for this material alone are
for artists today something past, and art therefore has become a free instrument which the artist can wield in proportion to his subjective skill in relation
to any material of whatever kind. The artist thus stands above specific conse-
crated forms and configurations and moves freely on his own account, independent of the subject matter and mode of conception in which the holy and
eternal was previously made visible to human apprehension. No content, no
form, is any longer immediately identical with the inwardness, the *nature*, the
unconscious substantial essence of the artist; every material may be indifferent
to him as long as it does not contradict the formal law of being simply
beautiful and capable of artistic treatment. Today there is no material which
stands in and for itself above this relativity [Relativität], and even if one
matter be raised above it, still there is at least no absolute need for its representation by *art*. Therefore the artist's attitude to his topic is on the whole much
the same as the dramatist's who brings on the scene and delineates different
characters who are strangers to him. The artist does still put his genius into
them, he weaves his web out of his own resources, but only out of what is
purely universal or quite accidental there, whereas its more detailed
individualization is not his. For this purpose he needs his supply of images,
modes of configuration, earlier forms of art which, taken in themselves, are
indifferent to him and only become important if they seem to him to be those
most suitable for precisely this or that material. Moreover, in most arts,
especially the visual arts, the topic comes to the artist from the outside; he
works to a commission, and in the case of sacred or profane stories, or scenes,
portraits, ecclesiastical buildings, etc., he has only to see what he can make of
his commission. For, however much he puts his heart into the given topic, that

topic yet always remains to him a material which is not in itself directly the substance of his own consciousness. It is therefore no help to him to adopt again, as that substance, so to say, past world-views, i.e. to propose to root himself firmly in one of these ways of looking at things, e.g. to turn Roman Catholic as in recent times many have done for art's sake in order to give stability to their mind and to give the character of something absolute [An-und-für-sich-seyenden] to the specifically limited character of their artistic product in itself.[30] The artist need not be forced first to settle his accounts with his mind or to worry about the salvation of his own soul. From the very beginning, before he embarks on production, his great and free soul must know and possess its own ground, must be sure of itself and confident in itself. The great artist today needs in particular the free development of the spirit; in that development all superstition [Aberglauben],[31] and all faith which remains restricted to determinate forms of vision and presentation, is degraded into mere aspects and features. These the free spirit has mastered because he sees in them no absolutely sacrosanct conditions for his exposition and mode of configuration, but ascribes value to them only on the strength of the higher content which in the course of his re-creation he puts into them as adequate to them.

In this way every form and every material is now at the service and command of the artist whose talent and genius is explicitly freed from the earlier limitation to one specific art-form.

(γ) But if in conclusion we ask about the content and the forms which can be considered as *specific* to this stage of our inquiry in virtue of its universal standpoint, the answer is as follows.

The universal forms of art had a bearing above all on the absolute truth which art attains and they had the origin of their particular differences in the specific interpretation of what counted for consciousness as the Absolute and carried in itself the principle for its mode of configuration. In this matter we have seen in symbolic art natural meanings appearing as the *content*, natural things and human personifications as the *form* of the representation; in classical art spiritual individuality, but as a corporeal, not inwardized present over which there stood the abstract necessity of fate; in romantic art spirituality with the subjectivity immanent therein, for the inwardness of which the external shape remained accidental. In this final art-form too, as in the earlier ones, the divine is the absolute [an und für sich] subject matter of art. But the divine had to objectify itself, determine itself, and therefore proceed out of itself into the secular content of subjective personality. At first the infinity of personality lay in honour, love, and fidelity, and then later in particular individuality, in the specific character which coalesced with the particular content of human existence. Finally this cohesion with such a specific limitation of subject matter was cancelled by humour [Humor] which could make every determinacy waver and dissolve and therefore made it possible for art to transcend itself. Yet in this self-transcendence art is nevertheless a withdrawal of man into himself, a descent into his own breast, whereby art strips away from itself all fixed restriction to a specific range of content and treatment, and makes *Humanus* its new holy of holies: i.e. the depths and heights of the human heart as such, universal humanity in its joys and sorrows, its strivings, deeds, and fates. Herewith the artist acquires his subject matter in himself and is the human spirit actually self-determining and considering, meditating, and expressing the infinity of its feelings and situations: nothing that can be living in the human breast is alien to that spirit any more.[32] This is a subject-matter which does not remain determined artistically in itself and on its own account; on the contrary, the specific character of the topic and its outward formation is left to capricious invention, yet no interest is excluded – for art does not need any longer to represent only what is absolutely at home at one of its specific stages, but everything in which man as such is capable of being at home.

In face of this breadth and variety of material we must above all make the demand that the actual presence of the spirit today shall be displayed at the same time throughout the mode of treating this material. The modern artist, it is true, may associate himself with the classical age and with still more ancient times; to be a follower of Homer, even if the last one, is fine, and productions reflecting the mediaeval veering to romantic art will have their merits too; but the universal validity, depth, and special idiom of some material is one thing, its mode of treatment another. No Homer, Sophocles, etc., no Dante, Ariosto, or Shakespeare can appear in our day; what was so magnificently sung, what so freely expressed, has been expressed; these are materials, ways of looking at them and treating them which have been sung once and for all. Only the present is fresh, the rest is paler and paler.

The French must be reproached on historical grounds, and criticized on the score of beauty, for presenting Greek and Roman heroes, Chinese, and Peruvians, as French princes and princesses and for ascribing to them the motives and views of the time of Louis XIV and XV; yet, if only these motives and views had been deeper and finer in themselves, drawing them into present-day works of art would not be exactly bad. On the contrary, all materials, whatever they be and from whatever period and nation they come, acquire their artistic truth only when imbued with living and contemporary interest. It is in this interest that artistic truth fills man's breast, provides his own mirror-image, and brings truth home to our feelings and representational imagination [Vorstellung]. It is the appearance and activity of imperishable humanity in its many-sided significance and endless all-round development which in this reservoir of human situations and feelings can now constitute the absolute content of our art.

If after thus determining in a general way the subject matter peculiar to this stage, we now look back at what we have considered in conclusion as the forms of the dissolution of romantic art, we have stressed principally how art falls to pieces, on the one hand, into the imitation of external objectivity in all its contingent shapes; on the other hand, however, into the liberation of subjectivity, in accordance with its inner contingency, in humour. Now, finally, still within the material indicated above, we may draw attention to a coalescence of these extremes of romantic art. In other words, just as in the advance from symbolic to classical art we considered the transitional forms of image, simile, epigram, etc.,[33] so here in romantic art we have to make mention of a similar transitional form. In those earlier modes of treatment the chief thing was that inner meaning and external shape fell apart from one another, a cleavage partly superseded by the subjective activity of the artist and converted, particularly in epigram, so far as possible into an identification. Now romantic art was from the beginning the deeper disunion of the inwardness which was finding its satisfaction in itself and which, since objectivity does not completely correspond with the spirit's inward being, remained broken or indifferent to the objective world. In the course of romantic art this opposition developed up to the point at which we had to arrive at an exclusive interest, either in contingent externality or in equally contingent subjectivity. But if this satisfaction in externality or in the subjective portrayal is intensified, according to the principle of romantic art, into the heart's deeper immersion in the object, and if, on the other hand, what matters to humour is the object and its configuration within its subjective reflex, then we acquire thereby a growing intimacy with the object, a sort of *objective* humour. Yet such an intimacy can only be partial and can perhaps be expressed only within the compass of a song or only as part of a greater whole. For if it were extended and carried through within objectivity, it would necessarily become action and event and an objective presentation of these. But what we may regard as necessary here is rather a sensitive abandonment of the heart in the object, which is indeed unfolded but remains a *subjective* spirited movement of imagination [Phantasie] and the heart – a fugitive notion, but one which is not purely accidental and capricious but an inner movement of the spirit devoted entirely to its object and retaining it as its content and interest.

In this connection we may contrast such final blossomings of art with the old Greek epigram in which this form appeared in its first and simplest shape, the form meant here displays itself only when to talk of the object is not just to name it, not an inscription or epigraph which merely says in general terms what the object is, but only when there are added a deep feeling, a felicitous witticism [Witz], an ingenious reflection, and an intelligent movement of imagination [Phantasie] which vivify and expand the smallest detail through the way that poetry treats it.[34] But such poems to or about something, a tree, a mill-lade, the spring, etc., about things animate or inanimate, may be of quite endless variety and arise in any nation, yet they remain of a subordinate kind and, in general, readily become lame. For especially when reflection and speech have been developed, anyone may be struck in connection with most objects and circumstances by something or other which he now has skill enough to express, just as anyone is good at writing a letter. With such a general sing-song, often repeated even if with new nuances, we soon become bored. Therefore at this stage what is especially at stake is that the heart, with its depth of feeling, and the spirit and a rich consciousness shall be entirely absorbed in the circumstances, situation, etc., tarry there, and so make out of the object something new, beautiful, and intrinsically valuable.

A brilliant example of this, even for the present and for the subjective spiritual depth of today, is afforded especially by the Persians and Arabs in the eastern splendour of their images, in the free bliss of their imagination [Phantasie] which deals with its object entirely contemplatively [theoretisch]. The Spaniards and Italians too have done excellent work of this kind. Klopstock does say of Petrarch: "Petrarch sang songs of his Laura, beautiful to their admirer, but to the lover – nothing."[35] Yet Klopstock's love-poems are full only of moral reflections, pitiable longing [Sehnsucht], and strained passion for the happiness of immortality – whereas in Petrarch we admire the freedom of the inherently ennobled feeling which, however much it expresses desire for the beloved, is still satisfied in itself. For the desire, the craving, cannot be missing in the sphere of these subjects, provided it be confined to wine and love, the tavern and the glass, just as, after all, the Persian pictures are of extreme voluptuousness. But in its subjective interest imagination [Phantasie] here removes the object altogether from the scope of practical craving; it has an interest only in this imaginative occupation, which is satisfied in the freest way with its hundreds of changing turns of phrase and conceits, and plays in the most ingenious manner with joy and sorrow alike. Amongst modern poets those chiefly possessed of this equally ingenious freedom of imagination, but also of its subjectively more heartfelt depth, are Rückert, and Goethe in his *West-östliche Divan*.[36] Goethe's poems in the *Divan* are particularly and essentially different from his earlier ones. In *Willkomm und Abschied* [*Welcome and Farewell*], e.g., the language and the depiction are beautiful indeed, and the feeling is heartfelt, but otherwise the situation is quite ordinary, the conclusion trivial, and imagination and its freedom has added nothing further. Totally different is the poem called *Wiederfinden* [*Meeting Again*] in the *Divan*. Here love is transferred wholly into the imagination, its movement, happiness, and bliss. In general, in similar productions of this kind we have before us no subjective longing, no being in love, no desire, but a pure delight in the topics, an inexhaustible self-yielding of imagination, a harmless play, a freedom in toying alike with rhyme and ingenious metres – and, with all this, a depth of feeling and a cheerfulness of the inwardly self-moving heart which through the serenity of the outward shape lift the soul high above all painful entanglement in the restrictions of the real world.

With this we may close our consideration of the *particular* forms into which the ideal of art has been spread in the course of its development. I have made these forms the subject of a rather extensive investigation in order to exhibit the content out of which too their mode of portrayal has been derived. For it is the content which, in art as in all human work, is decisive. In accordance with its concept, art has nothing else for its function but to set forth in an adequate sensuous present what is itself inherently rich in content, and the philosophy of art must make it its chief task to comprehend [begreifen] in thought what this fullness of content and its beautiful mode of appearance are.

Chapter III
Poetry

INTRODUCTION

1. The temple of classical *architecture* needed a god to live in it; *sculpture* places him before us in plastic beauty and gives to the material it uses for this purpose forms which by their very nature are not external to the spirit but are the shape immanent in the selected content itself. But the body, sensuousness, and ideal universality of the sculptural figure has contrasted with it both the subjective inner life and the particular character of the individual; and the content alike of the religious and the mundane life must gain actuality in the subjective and particular by means of a new art. This subjective and particular characteristic mode of expression *painting* introduces within the principle of the visual arts themselves, because it reduces the real externality of the shape to a more ideal appearance in colour and makes the expression of the inner soul the centre of the representation. Yet the general sphere in which these arts move, the first symbolic in type, the second ideally plastic, the third romantic, is the sensuous *external shape* [*Außengestalt*] of the spirit and things in nature.[37]

But the spiritual content, by essentially belonging to the inner life of consciousness, has at the same time an existence external to that life in the pure element of external appearance and in the vision to which the external shape is offered. Art must withdraw from this foreign element in order to enshrine its conceptions in a sphere of an explicitly inner and ideal kind in respect alike of the material used and the manner of expression. This was the forward step which we saw *music* taking, in that it made the inner life as such, and subjective feeling, something for apprehension by the inner life, not in visible shapes, but in the figurations in inwardly reverberating sound. But in this way it went to the other extreme, to an undeveloped subjective concentration, the content of which found once again only a purely symbolic expression in notes. For the note, taken by itself, is without content and has its determinate character only in virtue of numerical relations, so that although the qualitative character of the spiritual content does correspond in general to these quantitative relations which open out into essential differences, oppositions, and modulation, still it cannot be completely characterized qualitatively by a note. Therefore, if this qualitative side is not to be missing altogether, music must, on account of its one-sidedness, call on the help of the more exact meaning of words and, in order to become more firmly conjoined with the detail and characteristic expression of the subject-matter, it demands a text which alone gives a fuller content to the subjective life's outpouring in the notes. By means of this expression of representations and feelings the abstract inwardness of music emerges into a clearer and firmer unfolding of them. Yet on the one hand what it develops in this unfolding is not representations and their artistically adequate form but only their accompanying inner sentiment; on the other hand, music simply snaps its link with words in order to move at will and unhampered within its own sphere of sounds. Consequently, on its side too, the sphere of representations, which transcend the rather abstract inner life of feeling as such and give to their world the shape of concrete actuality, cuts itself free from music and gives itself an artistically adequate existence in the art of poetry.[38]

Poetry, the art of speech, is the third term, the *totality*, which unites in itself, within the province of the spiritual inner life and on a higher level, the two extremes, i.e. the *visual* arts and *music*. For, on the one hand, poetry, like music, contains that principle of the self-apprehension of the inner life as inner, which architecture, sculpture, and painting lack; while, on the other hand, in the very field of inner ideas [Vorstellens], intuitions, and feelings it broadens out into an objective world which does not altogether lose the determinate character of sculpture and painting. Finally, poetry is more capable than any other art of completely unfolding the totality of an event, a successive series and the changes of the heart's movements, passions, representations, and the complete course of an action.

2. But furthermore poetry is the third of the *romantic* arts, painting and music being the other two.

(a) Poetry (i) has as its general principle *spirituality* and therefore it no longer turns to heavy matter as such in order, like architecture, to form it symbolically into an analogous environment for the inner life, or, like sculpture, to shape into real matter the natural form, as a spatial external object, belonging to the spirit; on the contrary, it expresses directly for its own apprehension the spirit with all its imaginative and artistic conceptions [Konceptionen der Phantasie und Kunst] but without setting these out visibly and bodily for contemplation from the outside. (ii) Poetry, to a still ampler extent than painting and music, can comprise in the form of the inner life not only the inner consciousness but also the special and particular details of what exists externally, and at the same time it can portray them separately in the whole expanse of their individual traits and arbitrary peculiarities.

(b) Nevertheless poetry as a totality is on the other hand to be essentially distinguished from the specific arts whose characters it combines in itself.

(α) *Painting*, in this connection, has an overall advantage when it is a matter of bringing a subject before our eyes in its external appearance. For, with manifold means at its command, poetry can indeed likewise illustrate, just as the principle of setting something out for intuition is implicit in imagination [Phantasie] generally, but since the element in which poetry principally moves, i.e. representational imagination [die Vorstellung], is of a spiritual kind and therefore enjoys the universality of thought, poetry is incapable of reaching the definiteness of sense-perception. On the other hand, the different traits, which poetry introduces in order to make perceptible to us the concrete content of the subject in hand, do not fall together, as they do in painting, into one and the same whole which completely confronts us with all its details simultaneously; on the contrary, they occur separately because the manifold content of a representation can be expressed only as a succession. But this is a defect only from the sensuous point of view, one which the spirit can always rectify. Even where speech is concerned to evoke some concrete intuition, it does not appeal to the sensuous perception of a present external object but always to the inner life, to *spiritual* intuition, and consequently even if the individual traits only follow one another they are transferred into the element of the inwardly harmonious spirit which can extinguish a succession, pull together a varied series into *one* image and keep this image firmly in mind [in der Vorstellung] and enjoy it. Besides, this deficiency of sensuous reality and external definiteness in poetry as contrasted with painting is at once turned into an incalculable wealth. For since poetry is exempt from painting's restriction to a specific space and still more to one specific feature of a situation or an action, it is given the possibility of presenting a subject in its whole inward depth and in the breadth of its temporal development. Truth is absolutely concrete in virtue of comprising in itself a unity of essential determinations. But these develop in their appearance not only as juxtaposed in space, but in a temporal succession as a history, the course of which painting can only present graphically in an inappropriate way. Even every blade of grass, every tree has in this sense its history, alteration, process, and a complete totality of different situations. This is still more the case in the sphere of the spirit; as actual spirit in its appearance, it can only be portrayed exhaustively if it is brought before our minds [vor die Vorstellung] as such a course of history.

(β) As we saw, poetry has sounds as an external material in common with *music*. The wholly external material (ordinarily, though not philosophically, called 'objective') slips away finally, in the progressive series of the particular arts, into the subjective element of sound which cannot be seen, with the result that the inner life is made aware of itself solely by its own activity. But music's essential aim is to shape these sounds as *sounds*. For although in the course and progress of the melody and its fundamental harmonic relations the soul presents to feeling the inner meaning of the subject matter or its own inner self, nevertheless what gives music its own proper character is not the inner life as such but the soul, most intimately interweaved with its *sounding*, and the formation of this *musical* expression. This is so much the case that music becomes music and an independent art the more that what preponderates in it is the complete absorption of the inner life into the realm of sounds, not of the spirit as such. But, for this reason, it is capable only to a relative extent of harbouring the variety of spiritual representations and intuitions and the broad expanse of a richly filled conscious life, and in its expression it does not get beyond the more abstract and general character of what it takes as its subject or beyond vaguer deep feelings of the heart. Now in proportion as the spirit transforms this abstract generality into a concrete ensemble of ideas, aims, actions, and events and adds to this process their inspection *seriatim*, it deserts the inner sphere of imagination [Phantasie]. Consequently, simply on account of this transformation, any attempt to express this new-won wealth of the spirit wholly and exclusively through sounds and their harmony must be abandoned. Just as the material of sculpture is too poor to make possible the portrayal of the richer phenomena which it is painting's business to call to life, so now harmonious sounds and expression in melody cannot give full reality to the poet's imaginative creations. For these possess the precise and known definiteness of representations and an external phenomenal form minted for inner intuition. Therefore the spirit withdraws its content from sounds as such and is manifested by words which do not entirely forsake the element of sound but sink to being a merely external sign of what is being communicated. The musical note being thus replete with spiritual ideas becomes the sound of a word, and the word, instead of then being an end in itself, becomes a self-unindependent means of spiritual expression. This gives us, in accordance with what we established earlier, the essential difference between music and poetry. The subject matter of the art of speech is the entire world of ideas developed with a wealth of imagination, i.e. the spirit abiding by itself in its own spiritual element and, when it moves out to the creation of something external, using that only as a sign, itself different from the subject matter. With music, art abandons the immersion of the spirit in a tangible, visible, and directly present *shape*; in poetry it gives up the opposite element of *sound* and hearing, at least in so far as this sound is no longer formed into an adequate external object and the sole expression of the subject matter. Therefore the inner life does express itself [in music] but will not find its actual existence in the sensibility [Sinnlichkeit] (even if more ideal) of the notes, because it seeks this existence solely in itself, in order to express the content of the spirit as it is contained in the heart of imagination as imagination [Phantasie].

(c) If, *thirdly* and lastly, we look for the special character of poetry in its distinction from music, and from painting and the other visual arts, we find it simply in the above-mentioned subordination of the sensuous mode of presenting and elaborating all poetic subject matter. Since sound, as in music, or colour, as in painting, is no longer able to harbour and present that entire subject matter, the musical treatment of it by way of the beat, harmony, and melody necessarily disappears where and what is left is, in general, only the tempo of words and syllables, rhythm, and euphony, etc. And even these remain not as the proper element for conveying the subject matter but as a rather accidental externality which assumes an artistic form only because art cannot allow any external aspect to have free play purely by chance, arbitrarily, or capriciously.

(α) Granted the withdrawal of the spiritual content from sensuous material, the question arises at once: what, in default of sound, will now be the proper form of externality and objectivity in the case of poetry? We can answer quite simply: It is the *inner representational imagination* [*Vorstellen*] and *intuition* itself. It is *spiritual* forms which take the place of the sensuous ones and provide the material to be given shape, just as marble, bronze, colour, and musical notes were the material earlier on. For here we must not be led astray by the statement that representations and intuitions are in truth the *content* of poetry. This of course is true enough, as will be shown in detail later; but it is equally essential to maintain that representations, intuitions, feelings, etc., are the specific forms in which every content is apprehended and presented by poetry, so that, since the sensuous side of the communication always has only a subordinate part to play, these forms provide the proper material which the poet has to treat artistically. The thing in hand, the content, is to be objectified in poetry for the spirit's apprehension, yet this objectivity exchanges its previously external reality for an internal one, and it acquires an existence only within consciousness itself as something spiritually represented and intuited. Thus the spirit becomes objective to itself on its own ground and it has speech only as a medium, partly as a means of communication and partly as an external reality out of which, as out of a mere sign, it has withdrawn into itself from the very start. Consequently in the case of poetry proper it is a matter of indifference whether we read it or hear it read; it can even be translated into other languages without essential detriment to its value, and turned from poetry into prose, and in these cases it is related to quite different sounds from those of the original.[39]

(β) Further, this *second* question arises: granted that the inner representational imagination constitutes the material and form of poetry, *for what* is this material to be used? It is to be used for the absolute [an und für sich] truth contained in spiritual interests in general, yet not merely for their substance in its universality of symbolical meaning [in architecture] or its classical differentiation [in sculpture] but also for everything detailed and particular within this substance, and so for almost everything which interests and occupies the spirit in any way. Consequently the art of speech, in respect of its content and its mode of expounding it, has an enormous field, a wider field than that open to the other arts. Any topic, all spiritual and natural things, events, histories, deeds, actions, subjective and objective situations, all these can be drawn into poetry and fashioned by it.

(γ) But this most variegated material is not made poetic simply by being harboured in representation, for after all a commonplace mind can shape exactly the same subject matter into representations and have separate intuitions of it without achieving anything poetic. In this connection we previously called ideas the *material* and element which is only given a poetically adequate form when art has shaped it afresh, just as colour and sound are not already, as mere colour and sound, painting and music. We can put this difference in general terms by saying that it is not representation *as such* but the artistic imagination [Phantasie] which makes some material poetic; when, that is to say, imagination so lays hold of it that instead of confronting us as an architectural, sculptural, plastic, and painted shape or of sounding like musical notes, it can communicate with us in speech, in words and their beautiful spoken assembly.

The basic demand necessitated here is limited to this: (i) that the subject matter shall not be conceived either in terms of scientific or speculative *thinking* or in the form of wordless *feeling* or with the clarity and *precision* with which we perceive external objects, and (ii) that it shall not pass into representation with the accidents, fragmentations, and relativities of *finite* actuality. In this regard the poetic imagination has, for one thing, to keep to the mean between the abstract universality of thought and the sensuously concrete corporeal objects that we have come to recognize in the productions of the visual arts; for another thing, it has on the whole to satisfy the demands we made in the first part of these lectures in respect of any artistic creation, i.e. in its content it must be an end in itself and, with a purely contemplative [theoretische] interest, fashion everything that it conceives into an inherently independent and closed world. For only in this event does the content, as art requires, become by means of the manner of its presentation an organic whole which gives in its parts the appearance of close connection and coherence and, in contrast to the world of mutual dependence, stands there for its own sake and free on its own account.

3. The final point for discussion in connection with the difference between poetry and the other arts likewise concerns the changed relation which the poetic imagination introduces between its productions and the external material of their presentation.

The arts considered hitherto were completely in earnest with the sensuous element in which they moved, because they gave to a subject matter only a form which throughout could be adopted by and stamped on towering heavy masses, bronze, marble, wood, colours, and notes. Now in a certain sense it is true that poetry has a similar duty to fulfil. For in composing it must keep steadily in mind that its results are to be made known to the spirit only by communication in language. But this changes the whole relation to the material.

(a) The sensuous aspect acquires importance in the visual arts and in music. It follows that, owing to the specific *determinacy* of the material they use, it is only a *restricted* range of presentations that completely corresponds to particular real things existent in stone, colour, or sound, and the result is that the subject matter and the artistic mode of treatment in the arts considered hitherto is fenced in within certain limits. This was the reason why we brought each of the specific arts into close connection with only *one* of the *particular* artforms which this and no other art seemed best able to express adequately – architecture with the symbolic art-form, sculpture with the classical, painting and music with the romantic. It is true that the particular arts, below and above their proper sphere, encroached on the other art-forms too, and for this reason we could speak of classical and romantic architecture, and symbolic and Christian sculpture, and we also had to mention classical painting and music. But these deviations did not reach the real summit of art but either were the preparatory attempts of inferior beginning or else displayed the start of a transition to an art which, in this transition, seized on a content, and a way of treating the material, of a type that only a further art was permitted to develop completely.

In the expression of its content on the whole, architecture is poorest, sculpture is richer, while the scope of painting and music can be extended most widely of all. For with the increasing ideality and more varied particularization of the external material, the variety of the subject matter and of the forms it assumes is increased. Now poetry cuts itself free from this importance of the material, in the general sense that the specific character of its mode of sensuous expression affords no reason any longer for restriction to a specific subject matter and a confined sphere of treatment and presentation. It is therefore not linked exclusively to any specific form of art; on the contrary, it is the *universal* art which can shape in any way and express any content capable at all of entering the imagination [Phantasie], because its proper material is the imagination itself, that universal foundation of all the particular art-forms and the individual arts.

This is the point that we reached at the close of our treatment of the particular art-forms. Their culmination we looked for in art's making itself independent of the mode of representation peculiar to *one* of the art-forms and in its standing above the whole of these particular forms. Among the specific arts, the possibility of such a development in every direction lies from the very beginning in the essence of poetry alone, and it is therefore actualized in the course of poetic production partly through the actual exploitation of every particular form, partly through liberation from imprisonment in any exclusive type and character of treatment and content, whether symbolic, classical, or romantic.

(b) From this point of view too the position we have assigned to poetry in our philosophical development of the arts can be justified. Since poetry is occupied with the universal element in art as such to a greater extent than is the case in any of the other ways of producing works of art, it might seem that a philosophical explanation had to begin with it and only thereafter proceed to particularize the ways in which the other arts are differentiated by their sensuous material. But, as we have seen already in connection with particular art-forms, the process of development, regarded philosophically, consists on the one hand in a deepening of art's spiritual content, and on the other in showing that at first art only *seeks* its adequate content, then *finds* it, and finally *transcends* it. This conception [Begriff] of beauty and art must now also be made good in the *arts* themselves. We began therefore with architecture, which only strove after the complete representation of spiritual material in a sensuous element, so that art achieved a genuine fusion of form and content only in sculpture; with painting and music, on account of the inwardness and subjectivity of their content, art began to dissolve again the accomplished unification of conception and execution in the field of sense. This latter character poetry displays most strikingly because in its artistic materalization it is essentially to be interpreted as a withdrawal from the real world of sense-perception, and as a subordination of that world; yet not as a production that does not dare to embark yet on materialization and movement in the external world. But in order to expound this liberation philosophically it is first necessary to explain what it is from which art undertakes to free itself, and, similarly, how it is that poetry can harbour the entire content of art and all the forms of art. This too we have to regard as a struggle for a totality, a struggle that can be demonstrated philosophically only as the cancellation [Aufheben] of a restriction to the particular, which in turn implies a previous consideration of the one-sided stages, the unique value possessed by each being negated in the totality.

Only as a result of considering the series of the arts in this way does poetry appear as that particular art in which art itself begins at the same time to dissolve and acquire in the eyes of philosophy its point of transition to religious pictorial thinking [religiösen Vorstellung] as such, as well as to the prose of scientific thought. The realm of the beautiful, as we saw earlier, is bordered on one side by the prose of finitude and commonplace thinking, out of which art struggles on its way to truth, and on the other side the higher spheres of religion and philosophy [Wissenschaft] where there is a transition to that apprehension of the Absolute which is still further removed from the sensuous sphere.

(c) Therefore, however completely poetry produces the totality of beauty once and for all in a most spiritual way, nevertheless spirituality constitutes at the same time precisely the deficiency of this final sphere of art. In the system of the arts we can regard poetry as the polar opposite of architecture. Architecture cannot so subordinate the sensuous material to the spiritual content as to be able to form that material into an adequate shape of the spirit; poetry, on the other hand, goes so far in its negative treatment of its sensuous material that it reduces the opposite of heavy spatial matter, namely sound, to a meaningless sign instead of making it, as architecture makes its material, into a meaningful symbol. But in this way poetry destroys the fusion of spiritual inwardness with external existence to an extent that begins to be incompatible with the original conception of art, with the result that poetry runs the risk of losing itself in a transition from the region of sense into that of the spirit. The beautiful mean between these extremes of architecture and poetry is occupied by sculpture, painting, and music, because each of these arts works the spiritual content entirely into a natural medium and makes it intelligible alike to sense and spirit. For although painting and music, as romantic arts, do adopt a material which is already more ideal, yet on the other hand for the immediacy of tangible objects, which begins to evaporate in this enhanced ideality of the medium, they substitute the wealth of detail and the more varied configuration which colour and sound are capable of providing in a richer way than can be called for from the material of sculpture.

Poetry for its part likewise looks for a substitute: it brings the objective world before our eyes in a breadth and variety which even painting cannot achieve, at least on a single canvas, and yet this always remains only a real existence in the inner consciousness; and even if poetry in its need for an artistic embodiment makes straight for a strengthened sensuous impression, still it can produce this only by means foreign to itself and borrowed from painting and music; or else, in order to maintain itself as genuine poetry, it must always put these sister arts in the background, purely as its servants, and emphasize instead, as the really chief thing concerned, the spiritual idea, the imagination [Phantasie] which speaks to inner imagination [Phantasie].

So much in general about the conceptual relation of poetry to the other arts. The more detailed consideration of the art of poetry must be arranged as follows:

We have seen that in poetry both content and material are provided by our inner representational imagination. Yet this, outside art, is already the commonest form of consciousness and therefore we must in the first place undertake the task of distinguishing poetic from prosaic representation. But poetry should not abide by this inner poetical representation alone but must give its creations an expression in *language*. Here once again a double duty is to be undertaken. (i) Poetry must so organize its inner images that they can be completely adapted to communication in language; (ii) it must not leave this linguistic medium in the state in which it is used every day, but must treat it poetically in order to distinguish it from expressions in prose by the choice, placing, and sound of words.

But despite its expression in language, poetry is free in the main from the restrictions and conditions laid on the other arts by the particular character of their medium, and consequently it has the widest possibility of completely developing all the different genres that a work of art can permit of, independently of the one-sidedness of any particular art. For this reason the most perfect articulation of the different genres of poetry comes into view.

Accordingly our further course is

> *First*, to discuss poetry in general and the poetic work of art;
> *Secondly*, poetic expression;
> *Thirdly*, the division of this art into epic, lyric, and dramatic poetry.

From

The Philosophy of Spirit
[Die Philosophie des Geistes]

1830

A modified reprint of the translation by William Wallace, *Hegel's Philosophy of Mind* (1971), pp. 293–7.

German text in *SW*, X, 447–52.

Introductory note

These terse paragraphs are from the third part of the *Encyclopaedia of the Philosophical Sciences* of 1830, the book which Hegel regarded as the final statement and synthesis of his whole system of philosophy. As such, they are the 'essentialized' version of his views on the place of art, and stand in relation to his lectures much as does Schelling's conclusion to the *System of Transcendental Idealism* to his own expansive lecture course on the *Philosophy of Art*. In each case, the densely meditated abstract arguments are the skeletons of the lectures, and in each case the minimal nature of the exposition makes them very hard to read.

With the first version of the *Encyclopaedia*, in 1817, Hegel had tried to coordinate his major contributions to logic, epistemology and the natural sciences into a single coherent system. These sections on art represent the final version of this attempt; they constitute the first part of the last chapter, on "Absolute Spirit", and they are followed by equally terse accounts of revealed religion and of achieved philosophy.

It is noticeable that Hegel has much more to say here about the true art of the beautiful, i.e. classical art, than about the symbolic or romantic forms. This may be seen in terms of his conviction, expressed also elsewhere, that the Greeks went as far as can be gone in making art the medium of religion whilst remaining within what are for Hegel the necessary limits of art *vis-à-vis* a truly revealed religion (to be provided only by Christianity) on its way to the emergence of absolute spirit. Greek art is thus the most exemplary art for this part of the argument of the *Encyclopaedia*; it represents an intrinsic artistic perfection, whereas romantic art is bound to manifest itself as less perfect, pointing as it does to its own supersession as art. What is good news for absolute spirit is bad news for art. See Taylor (1975), pp. 201–6, for an account of similar arguments in the *Phenomenology*.

The following sections are by no means easy to understand, and the reader who seeks to find in them an available 'summary' might be referred to the preface to the *Phenomenology*, in which Hegel calls into question the whole possibility of a preface and insists, as did so many of his contemporaries, on the labour of reading in detail. Here, a reading of at least the selections from the *Aesthetics* (above) is probably a prerequisite for useful comprehension; see also the discussion in Taylor (1975), pp. 465–79.

A. Art

§556

The form of this knowledge [of the actuality of the spirit] is *immediate* (the moment of the finite existence of art). On the one hand it breaks up into a work of common externalized existence, into the subject which produces it, and which contemplates [anschauende] and admires it. On the other hand it is the concrete *intuition* and mental picture [*Anschauung* und Vorstellung] of the in-itself-absolute spirit as the *ideal*. In this ideal, or concrete shape born of the subjective spirit, the natural immediacy which is only a *sign* of the Idea [Idee] is so transfigured by the imagining [einbildenden] spirit in the expression of the Idea, that the shape or form shows it and it alone – the shape or form of *beauty*.

§557

The sensuous externality attaching to the beautiful, the *form* of *immediacy* as such, at the same time *qualifies* what it *embodies*, and the god has with his spirituality at the same time the stamp [Bestimmung] of a natural medium or existence upon him. He contains the so-called *unity* of nature and spirit, i.e. the *immediate*, the form of the intuition, but hence not the spiritual unity, in which the natural would be set forth only as ideal, as superseded [Aufgehobenes], and the spiritual content posited only in relation to itself. It is not the absolute spirit which enters this consciousness. On the subjective side the community has, of course, a customary ethical [sittlich] life, aware as it is of the spirituality of its essence; and its self-consciousness and actuality are herein elevated to substantial freedom. But encumbered with immediacy, the subject's freedom is only a customary mode [Sitte], without the infinite reflection into itself and the subjective inwardness of *conscience*. These considerations govern in their further development the devotion and the cult [Cultus] of the religion of fine art.[1]

§558

For the objects of intuition [Anschauungen] which it has to produce, art requires not only an external given material (by which is understood also subjective images and representations), but for the expression of spiritual content it must use the given forms of nature according to a significance which art anticipates and has within it. Of all such forms the human is the highest and the true, because only in it can the spirit have its corporeality and thereby its visible expression.

This disposes of the principle of the *imitation of nature* in art, a point on which it is impossible to come to an understanding while an antithesis remains thus abstract, i.e. as long as the natural is understood only in its externality, and not as the characteristic, meaningful natural form that signifies spirit.

§559

The absolute spirit cannot be made explicit in such singleness of forms. The spirit of fine art is therefore a limited popular spirit [Volksgeist], whose implicit [an sich seyende] universality breaks up into an indeterminate polytheism when steps are taken to specify its fullness in detail. With the essential limitedness of its content, beauty in general goes no further than a penetration of the intuition or the image by the agency of the spiritual; no further than something formal. So that the content of thought, or its representation, like the material it uses for its creation [Einbildung], can be of the most different and inessential kind, and the work still be something beautiful and a work of art.

§560

The one-sidedness of *immediacy* on the part of the ideal involves the opposite one-sidedness (§556), that it is something *made* by the artist. The subject is the *formal agent* [*Formelle*] of activity, and the *work of art* is then only an expression of the god when there is no sign of subjective *particularity* in it, and the power of the indwelling spirit is conceived and born into the world without admixture and unspotted by its contingent existence. But since freedom only exists as far as there is thought, then the activity filled with this indwelling power – the artist's *inspiration* [*Begeisterung*] – is to him like a foreign rule, like an *unfree* pathos. The *producing* has for its part the form of *natural* immediacy, and belongs to the *genius* [*Genie*] of the *particular subject*, and is at the same time a labour employing technical understanding and mechanical externalities. The work of art is to that extent also a work of free choice [Willkür], and the artist is the master of the god.[2]

§561

In a work thus inspired the *reconciliation* [*Versöhnung*] appears so firmly in its initial stage that it is immediately accomplished in the subjective self-consciousness, which is thus self-confident and cheerful, without profundity and without the sense of its opposition to the self-existing [an-und-für-sich-seyende] essence. On the other side of the perfection which is reached in such reconciliation, i.e. in the *beauty* of *classical* art, lies the art of *sublimity* – the *symbolic*, in which the figuration suitable to the idea [Idee] is not yet found, and thought is presented in a negative relation to the figure to which it goes forth and with which it wrestles, all the time trying to work itself into [einzubilden] it.[3] The meaning or content thus shows that it has not yet reached the infinite form, that it is not yet known nor does it know itself as free spirit. The content is only as the abstract god of pure thought, or a striving after him, that throws itself restless and unreconciled into all shapes, finding its goal in none of them.

§562

In another way the idea and its sensuous embodiment [Gestaltung] are incompatible; and that is where the infinite form, subjectivity, is not as in the former extreme a mere superficial personality, but is its inmost depth; and the god is known not as merely seeking his form or satisfying himself in an external form, but as finding himself only in himself, and thus giving himself his adequate figure in the spiritual world alone. This – *romantic* – art gives up the task of showing him as such in external shape and by means of beauty. It presents him as condescending only to appearance [Erscheinung], and the divine as the element of inwardness in an externality from which it always disengages itself. Thus the external here appears as contingent in relation to its true meaning.[4]

The philosophy of religion has to discover the logical necessity in the sequence of determinations leading to what is known as the absolute being. Next it must discover the particular determinations to which the kind of cult [Cultus] corresponds; and then see how the secular self-consciousness, the consciousness of that which is the highest motivation [Bestimmung] in man – in short how the nature of a nation's moral life [Sittlichkeit], the principle of its law, of its actual freedom and of its constitution, as well as of its art and science, corresponds to the principle that constitutes the substance of a religion. That all these elements of a nation's actuality constitute one systematic totality, and that one spirit [Geist] creates and informs them, is an insight from which follows the further one: that the history of religions coincides with the world-history.[5]

As regards the close connection of art with the various religions it may be further remarked that *beautiful* art can only belong to those religions in which the *spiritual* principle, though *concrete* and intrinsically free, is not yet absolute. In religions in which the idea has not yet been revealed and known in its free character, the need for art is still felt, in order to bring the representations of the *essence* [Vorstellung des *Wesens*] to consciousness in intuition and imagination [Anschauung und Phantasie]; for art is the sole organ in which the abstract and in itself indistinct content (a mixture of natural and spiritual elements) can try to bring itself to consciousness. But still this art is defective; its form is so because its subject matter and theme is so, and this defect reciprocally comes from the form being immanent in it. Its manifestations evidence a certain tastelessness and spiritlessness, for its inner identity is itself still afflicted with spiritlessness, and hence has not the power to transmute the external freely into significance and shape. *Beautiful* art, on the contrary, has as its condition the self-consciousness of the free spirit, and along with it the consciousness that compared with it the natural and sensuous has no standing of its own. It makes the natural wholly an expression of itself; spirit is the inner form that gives utterance to itself alone.

From this there follows the further and higher observation [Betrachtung] that the advent of art in a religion still in the bonds of sensuous externality shows that such a religion is on the decline. At the same time as it seems to give religion the supreme illumination, expression and brilliancy, it has lifted it out [hinausgehoben] of its limitation. In the sublime divinity to which the work of art succeeds in giving expression, the genius of the artist and the spectator find themselves at home with the particular sense and feeling, and satisfied and liberated; the perception [Anschauen] and consciousness of the free spirit is vouchsafed and attained. Beautiful art has thus from its side performed the same service as philosophy: it has purified the spirit from its thraldom. That religion in which the need for fine art is for that reason first generated has for its principle an other-world which is sensuous and unmeaning. The images *adored* by its devotees are hideous idols regarded as wonder-working talismans, which point to the spiritless objectivity of that other-world; bones perform a similar or even better service than such images. But even beautiful art is only a step on the way to liberation, never itself the true liberation. The genuine objectivity, which is only in the element of *thought* – the element in which alone the pure spirit is for the spirit, and where the freeing is simultaneous with reverence – is still absent in the sensuous beauty of the work of art, and yet more so in that external and unbeautiful sensuousness.[6]

§563

Beautiful art, like the religion peculiar to it, has its future in the true religion. The limited content of the idea passes in and for itself into the universality identical with infinite form – the intuition [Anschauung], the immediate knowledge bound to the sensuous, passes into a self-mediating knowledge, into an existence which is itself knowledge, into *revelation*. Thus the content of the idea has as its principle the determination of the free intelligence, and the absolute *spirit* is *for the spirit*.

Notes
Bibliography
Index

Notes

INTRODUCTION

1 Baumgarten (1973), p. 107. As well as Baumgarten, other figures such as Meier and Mendelssohn were important to the tradition from which Kant emerges; and the most popular recent candidate for the role of exemplary Romantic philosopher, following a trend initiated by Goethe himself, has been Karl Philipp Moritz (see Todorov (1982)). Accounts of German aesthetics prior to Kant may be found in E. Cassirer (1951), pp. 275–360 (Cassirer makes clear that it is an international context, in which Shaftesbury and Boileau were for example, important); Copleston (1964a), pp. 121–72; Wellek (1955), I, 144–200; Nivelle (1955); and Gay (1969), pp. 208–318. See also Vol. I of this series.

2 A sense of the social and historical contexts of German Romantic thought can be gained from Bruford (1935 and 1962), Menhennet (1973), and Kohlschmidt (1975), among others. See also Marshall Brown (1979).

3 There is a superb account of this whole subject in Blackall (1959). For a summary of the particular German dependence upon France and its culture and language, see Gay (1969), pp. 241–8.

4 Schleiermacher was also the author of a series of lectures on aesthetics, first delivered in 1819. Although they influenced Croce they have remained little known, and they do not exist in an English translation. The text is in Schleiermacher (1834–64), Pt III, vol. 7, and there is a very brief account of their content in Wellek (1955), II, 303–8. For an overview of Schleiermacher's career, see Copleston (1965a), pp. 183–93.

5 I do not mean to invoke the precise modern sense of this phrase in scientific discourse, though it is very much in the spirit of what Goethe and other Romantics would have desired, i.e. an explanation of apparently diverse phenomena by reference to a single process or force.

Most accounts of Goethe's life and thought include some assessment of his relation to contemporary philosophy. On the connection between the *CJ* and Goethe's scientific ideas, see E. Cassirer (1945). For a recent argument for the effect of the 'Critique of Aesthetic Judgement' on the revisions of *Wilhelm Meister*, see von Molnár (1981–2). For further details of the relations between the German Romantic writers and the philosophers, the literary histories of the period should be consulted, e.g. Korff (1923–57), Hettner (1961), as well as such recent standard editions of the major Romantics as are available or in process.

6 For the antecedents and analogues of this position appearing in the British tradition, see Meredith (1911), pp. 238–9. See also the important discussion of *sensus communis* or 'common sense' in Kant, *CJ*, §§40–3.

7 See Guyer (1979), pp. 224–37, for some very perceptive arguments about the de-

pendence of this position upon the founding doctrines of the *Critique of Pure Reason*, *vis-à-vis* the formal basis of all intuitions ordered in cognitive relations.

KANT

An Answer to the Question:
What is Enlightenment?

[Beck's notes are indicated by the initial B.]

1 More literally, "dare to be wise" (Horace, *Epistles*, I, 2, 40). B. notes that this was the motto adopted in 1736 by the Society of the Friends of Truth, an important circle in the German *Aufklärung*. For further information, see the introduction to *AE* by Wilkinson and Willoughby, pp. lxxiv–lxxv. Schiller borrows Kant's phrase and some of his thought in letter VIII. In the *Anthropology* of 1797, Kant has this to say of the Germans (1974, p. 180):

> The German's negative side is his tendency to imitate others and his diffidence about his ability to be original (which is diametrically opposed to the Englishman's defiance). Still worse, he has a certain mania for method which leads him to renounce the principle that, e.g., fellow citizens should approach equality, in favour of classifying them punctiliously according to degrees of precedence and hierarchy.

2 I have substantially altered the translation here, which seems to depend upon a misreading.

3 After the experience of the Terror in post-revolutionary France, many thinkers of the 1790s echoed this belief in the patient publication of truth unassisted by any revolutionary activity, Schiller and Godwin among them. That this is Kant's view even before the outbreak of the French Revolution should remind us that the argument was already available. In fact, Kant himself never completely lost faith in the evidence offered by the French experience for an intrinsic "moral disposition within the human race", and he could say this even in 1798 (cited by E. Cassirer (1981), p. 407; *Ak*. VII, 85).

4 Although Kant's technical distinction between *Verstand* and *Vernunft* had already been formulated by 1784, they appear to have their 'precritical' senses in this essay, as roughly synonymous. However, I have translated them as "understanding" and "reason" in order that the synonymity may *appear* as such.

5 The princely exception is Frederick the Great, King of Prussia from 1740 to 1786, whose own career went through a period of anti-authoritarianism followed by a cultivation of the military virtues. Whilst the size of Prussia doubled during his reign, he remains famous for his interest in philosophy and the arts and sciences – he played host to many of the *philosophes* – and is usually cited as the ideal of enlightened despotism.

6 In this distinction between "public" and "private" Kant seems to have in mind that between the published and the spoken word. We may infer from this that the written word is viewed as calling forth the most seriously meditated powers of its author and, reciprocally, the most authentic and rational faculties of its readers. It is thus a more proper medium for free speculation than say, oratory, which may become improperly persuasive. Cf. Fichte, *On the Nature of the Scholar*, and note 9, below.

7 "The emperor is not above the grammarians." Perhaps an allusion to a response to Voltaire said to have been made by Frederick the Great: "Caesar est supra gram-

maticam." But the sentiment was not original with Frederick, and has been attributed to the Emperor Sigismund at the Council of Constance (1414): "Ego sum rex Romanus et supra grammaticam" [B].

8 Cf. The preface to the first *Critique*: "Our age is, in especial degree, the age of criticism, and to criticism everything must submit" (Kant, 1933, p. 9) [B].

9 In fact, during the reign of his successor Frederick William II (1786–97) freedom of thought and publication was to be threatened again, and Kant himself would be forbidden to publish any further religious publications after *Religion Within the Limits of Reason Alone* (1793–4).

10 "Today I read in the *Büschingsche Wöchentliche Nachrichten* for 13 September an announcement of the *Berlinische Monatsschrift* for this month, which cites the answer to the same question by Mr Mendelssohn. But this issue has not yet come to me; if it had, I would have held back the present essay, which is now put forth only in order to see how much agreement in thought can be brought about by chance." [Kant's own note.] Mendelssohn's answer was that enlightenment lay in intellectual cultivation, which he distinguished from the practical. Kant, quite in line with his latter essay on theory and practice, refuses to make this distinction fundamental [B].

The Critique of Judgement

1 Kant's "faculty of desire" is to be understood in a precise sense as that through which we generate the wish that our representation [Vorstellung] should correspond to an object in the empirical world. We have, i.e., a mental image of something that we want to convert into actual experience. Such desire is of course not always satisfied (see the long footnote to *CJ*, I, 16, not included here), and in fact in its capacity for projection in advance of and even in despite of actual experience, it is a valuable signal of the independence of the mind and its capacity to generate the laws of freedom and practical reason. Kant distinguishes in this context between the lower and higher faculties of desire, the latter identical with reason in its capacity to determine the will without reference to empirical inclinations.

2 Kant uses two words which we have to translate as 'object', namely *Object* and *Gegenstand*. Meredith distinguishes between them by capitalizing the first letter of the former: "an object, regarded as merely presented to the mind, is *Gegenstand*; whereas an object, regarded as already something for the mind – a thought-object – is *Object*" (Meredith (1911), p. 229). (See also the long entry under *Objekt* in Eisler (1961).) I have preserved this distinction – though not his capitalization of the translation of *das Subject* – so that in what follows *Gegenstand* appears as 'object' and *Object* as 'Object'.

3 The "concept" [*der Begriff*] is one of the two or three most important terms in the vocabulary of the critical philosophy. For Kant, experience is composed by a synthesis of mental (*a priori*) and objective (contingent) elements. The concept is that "through which an object in general is thought (the category)", and in all acts of perception it is joined with the empirical "intuition" [*Anschauung*] through which it is given (Kant (1933), p. 162; B 146). Intuitions, which are sensible, would fail to 'produce' intelligible experience without the concepts of the understanding, and *vice versa*. For the "interest" of pure practical laws, see Kant (1956), p. 124; *Ak*. V, 120.

4 Kant's usual term for "universal" is *allgemein*, but here he incorporates the English words straight into German. The most likely source would seem to be Hume, for whom "general" is a familiar adjective, used both in opposition and loose apposition to "universal". Compare Kant with Hume in 'Of the Standard of Taste': "But

though all the general rules of art are founded only on experience and on the observation of the common sentiments of human nature, we must not imagine, that on every occasion, the feelings of men will be conformable to these rules" (Hume (1912), I, 270).

5 "Properly speaking, an *idea* [*Idee*] signifies a concept of reason, and an *ideal* [*Ideale*] the representation of an individual existence as adequate to an idea" (*CJ*, I, 76; and below, §17). Compare the distinction between aesthetic and rational ideas, neither of which are convertible to cognitions, made in the first remark appended to §57 (*CJ*, I, 209–10). Ideas are always to be distinguished from representations, which are mental pictures or images, although *Vorstellung* is often translated as "idea" in a non-specialized context. Kant's *Idee* is not Platonic: it is a guide to experience but has no metaphysical power.

6 Kant's term *Einbildungskraft*, or "imagination", signifies a faculty absolutely basic to all perception, and not an elevated or specifically artistic capacity, for which he tends to use *Genie* or *Phantasie*. But it is not a passive operation; it works to synthesize intuitions, though doing so in a normative way, at least in healthy and sane minds. See Kant (1933), pp. 141f., (A 115f.), and compare *CJ*, I, 30–2, 84–9. Imagination may be productive, rather than reproductive, when it is the "originator of arbitrary forms of possible intuitions" (*CJ*, I, 86), as it is in the judgement of taste. But this still does not make it 'creative' in any *exceptional* sense of the term. As ever, Kant is interested in the normal aesthetic response rather than the psychology of genius.

For arguments about a confusion in Kant's use of the term *Einbildungskraft*, see Engell (1981), pp. 128–39, and his mentor in this respect, Kemp-Smith (1923), pp. 227–34, 264–70. See also §§23, 49 of *CJ*.

7 A difficult but important point: Kant is extending the case made at the beginning of §9 about the dependence of aesthetic pleasure upon the assumed communicability of the state of mind to which it relates. If it were itself prior, then we would be back in the realm of empirical verification.

8 I.e. in the *Critique of Pure Reason*, wherein "schematism" is the term for the activity or process by which concepts and intuitions are mediated through representations. See Kant (1933), pp. 180f.; A 137f., B 176f.

9 Kant is not suggesting a tradition of exemplary works of art handed down through the generations as evidence of the universality of taste, but rather the fact that in any culture or moment of history there are going to be some things looked upon as exemplary, even if not the same things at all times. It is the universality of the *response*, or faculty of *mind*, that concerns him here.

10 "Models of taste with respect to the arts of speech must be composed in a dead and learned language; the first, to prevent their having to suffer the changes that inevitably overtake living ones, making dignified expressions become degraded, common ones antiquated, and ones newly coined after a short currency obsolete; the second to ensure its having a grammar that is not subject to the caprices of fashion, but has fixed rules of its own." [Kant's own note.] Compare Hegel's much more developed argument for the use of the classics in *On Classical Studies*, below, pp. 201–5.

11 I am not sure that Kant makes a strong or clear distinction between *Sittlichkeit* and *Moralität*, as Hegel does (see below, p. 281, n. 22), but he does tend to use the latter when emphatically self-prescribed behaviour is indicated. Kant's remarks on the physiological manifestations of the moral and aesthetic identity in the human form contain the seeds of the argument pursued by Schiller in his 1793 treatise *On Grace*

and Dignity [Über Anmuth und Würde]. Meredith (1911), p. 256 cites an interesting passage from Hugh Blair's *Lectures on Rhetoric and Belles Lettres* in this context; they were translated into German between 1785 and 1789.

12 "As telling against this explanation, the instance may be adduced, that there are things in which we see a form suggesting adaptation to an end, without any end being cognized in them – as, for example, the stone implements frequently obtained from sepulchral tumuli and supplied with a hole, as if for [inserting] a handle; and although these by their shape manifestly indicate a finality, the end of which is unknown, they are not on that account described as beautiful. But the very fact of their being regarded as art-products involves an immediate recognition that their shape is attributed to some purpose or other and to a definite end. For this reason there is no immediate delight whatever in their contemplation. A flower, on the other hand, such as a tulip, is regarded as beautiful, because we meet with a certain finality in its perception which, in our estimate of it, is not referred to any end whatever." [Kant's own note.] "Artifact" would be a better translation of *Kunstwerk* here, given that Kant clearly means an object produced for a purpose and not a work of fine art. Modern interests in various kinds of functional or primitive art would not *necessarily* be incompatible with Kant's argument that the perception of purpose precludes the feeling of delight; delight could, e.g., precede such a perception and remain distinct from it. But we would have to reassemble the details of this case to bring it round to this position!

13 William Marsden's *The History of Sumatra* (1783) had been translated as *Natürliche und bürgerliche Beschreibung der Insel Sumatra in Ostindien* (Leipzig, 1785).

14 Two (rare) examples in Kant's exposition, and it is significant that neither has anything to do with works of fine art. We may infer the contaminating presence of *interest* in the distinction between the bird's song and the human imitation, which has trained itself purposively to perfect an illusion. Compare *Anthropology* §13; and *CJ*, I, 162.

15 In *CJ* §13 Kant has already argued that the *pure* judgement of taste is independent of charm, which he regards as a quality additive or ornamental to form. But §14 suggests that there can be an empirical judgement of taste involving the merely agreeable – charm and emotion.

16 It is hard to follow Kant here in his assertion that the sublime is "less important and rich in consequences" than the beautiful, unless we limit the terms of the comparison, emphasizing the qualification *for nature*. For, given that the sublime is not concerned with *form*, it must function more readily than does the beautiful in referring us back to our own inner tendency to *introduce* sublimity into nature. As such it seems even more closely analogous to the operations of the moral faculty. Compare §27 below, and see also my comments in the general introduction.

For accounts of the importance of the sublime in eighteenth-century aesthetics, see Hipple (1957), Monk (1935), and Weiskel (1976).

17 Even the mathematically sublime, i.e., is related to the ideas of reason rather than to the concepts of the understanding, in that what is at work is an expanding act of perceiving relations, and never the specific computation of ratios – the onset of which, always possible, would be the passage out of the experience of the sublime. In this way the mathematically sublime does not allow the assumption of finality, and remains in accord with the argument that sublimity applies not to things in nature but to the mental processes operative upon them.

18 This habit of or tendency toward reifying our active powers, attributing them falsely to the material things through which we recognize them, is a very important

Romantic concern, shared explicitly by Wordsworth and Coleridge among others. As far as I know Kant is the first to use the term *Subreption* in a philosophical sense, taking it from the vocabulary of ecclesiastical law, where it denotes the concealment of facts.

19 The sublime and the beautiful taken together thus demonstrate the connection between the imagination and the faculties identified as transcendental by the first two *Critiques*: understanding and reason. As well as showing the symmetry of *CJ* with its two predecessors, this formulation again implies the closer relation of the sublime to moral experience, as compared to that of the beautiful. There is a stoical character to Kant's ethics, involving us as it does in an experience of subjective isolation before an unknowable or non-existent finality for which we are yet compelled to legislate. This is very much the spirit of his analysis of the sublime.

20 I.e. in the mathematically sublime. The dynamically sublime, now being discussed, concerns the imbalance of power, rather than magnitude, between nature and ourselves.

21 Once again, we see the emphasis on the need to avoid the rule of outer forms over inner spirit. Given the way in which institutions tend to employ such outer forms to represent their power, we can trace a strong analogy between Kant's argument (more fully developed for theology in *Religion Within the Limits of Reason Alone*) and those of Godwin against factions and parties, and that of Wordsworth against poetic diction. The common inheritance is that of the Enlightenment attack on various forms of superstition. See Simpson (1982a, 1982b). And compare Fichte in 1792:

Should we not be more intent in education on developing the feeling for the sublime? This is a way that nature herself opens to us to pass over from sensibility to morality; and in our age it is usually checked very early in us by frivolities and trinkets – and also, among other things, by theodicies and doctrines of happiness.

Fichte (1978), p. 51

22 Kant's use of the English *enthusiasm* signals his awareness of its place in the British tradition from at least Shaftesbury onwards. I have discussed the polemic against *Schwärmerei* in the general introduction.

23 Compare Burke (1759), Pt I, §11. This argument of Kant's accords with the frequently gloomy view (from the position of particular individuality) he expresses about history and civil society in the non-critical writings. Issues surrounding retirement, and the migration from the city to the country, provide some of the most important political–aesthetic themes in eighteenth-century English literature, as any perusal of Pope, Thomson, Cowper, Smollett, Crabbe, Goldsmith, etc. will demonstrate.

   Translations of the various parts of *Robinson Crusoe*, and even theatrical adaptations thereof, were enormously popular in Germany: see Price (1934), pp. 78–80. Kant mentions the Crusoe fantasy also in his *Conjectural Beginnings of Human History* (1786), as part of an attack on the myth of primitive innocence (see Kant (1963), pp. 67–8). Burke's treatise on the sublime and beautiful had been translated into German in 1773 (Riga), and again in 1784 (Erfurt). Meredith (1911) footnotes some of the parallels.

24 Against this exemplary statement of the Enlightenment case against superstition, we may quote Matthew Arnold's assimilation of Goethe in *Literature and Dogma*:

... 'Aberglaube', *extra-belief*, belief beyond what is certain and verifiable. Our word 'superstition' had by its derivation this same meaning, but it has come to be used in a merely bad sense, and to mean a childish & craven religiosity. With the German word it is not so; therefore Goethe can say with propriety and truth '*Aberglaube* is the poetry of life' ...

Arnold (1960–78), VI, 212

25 "We readily see that enlightenment, while easy, no doubt, *in thesi, in hypothesi* is difficult and slow of realization. For not to be passive with one's reason, but always to be self-legislative is doubtless quite an easy matter for a man who only desires to be adapted to his essential end, and does not seek to know what is beyond his understanding. But as the tendency in the latter direction is hardly avoidable, and others are always coming and promising with full assurance that they are able to satisfy one's curiosity, it must be very difficult to preserve or restore in the mind (and particularly in the public mind) that merely negative attitude (which constitutes enlightenment proper)." [Kant's own note.]

26 Note that in its relation to the other two *Critiques* judgement is here related most centrally to the question of consensus.

27 Yet another formulation of the relation between the beautiful and the moral. Note that it is the beauty of *nature*, and not that of art, which arouses an interest akin to the moral. Kant has already made the point that as soon as an interest is aroused then the judgement of taste ceases to be pure, but there he had in mind empirical interest (see §§13–14).

The "beautiful soul", which Kant defines as marking the preference for nature over art and for pure properties over social distinctions (*CJ*, 1, 159), was to become a *leitmotiv* in German Romanticism. Most famously, Schiller makes it the centrepiece of his essay *On Grace and Dignity* (1793). Here, what is for Kant a somewhat offhanded expression is developed into a fully argued concept, providing an alternative to what Schiller regarded as the excessive severity and abstractness of Kantian ethics. In Schiller's "beautiful soul" the moral instinct is so surely developed that the promptings of the will can be passively followed in the confidence that they will spontaneously embody moral action. Morality is thus taken out of the sphere of anxious self-consciousness. More common in women than in men, this reconciliation of freedom and determination is visibly embodied in *grace*. See Schiller (1943–), XX, 287–9.

The "beautiful soul" appears again in the title to Part II, book VI of Goethe's *Wilhelm Meister* (though one would not infer this from Carlyle's translation), and in Hegel, *Phenomenology of Spirit*, §632f. Although it is likely that Schiller's exact argument was not itself a determining influence on the British consciousness, at least in the early years of the nineteenth century, we can nevertheless observe variously weighted investigations of the relation between morality and spontaneity, ones which bear very close comparison with Schiller's case. For example, in the preface to *Lyrical Ballads* Wordsworth insists that the spontaneous overflow of powerful feelings that is poetry can only be proper if the poet has also thought long and deeply; it is the *habitual* discipline of the poet's thoughts and feelings that gives his statements the quality of apparent intuitions. Toward the end of chapter 13 of Austen's *Sense and Sensibility*, Marianne Dashwood tries to get away with a more fragile correlation of ethics with intuition. And by the time of the anti-self-consciousness crusade of Carlyle and Mill, the rational ingredient of Schiller's model (itself of course much less rational than Kant's) has been largely left aside.

28 An extreme statement of the opposite position would be by e.g. Brecht: that the artist take every opportunity to dramatize his presence in order to *prevent* his audience from reposing in the illusion of the natural. But if Kant and Brecht stand at opposite ends of this spectrum, it must be said that the movement away from Kant begins very quickly. Though few if any of the romantics would have subscribed wholeheartedly to the idea of art as a form of bad faith requiring our being regularly reminded of its status as mere appearance (indeed they are generally concerned

with the positive aspects of this fact), yet in Hegel we can see an emphasis on the importance of the very self-consciousness, and its appearance in labour, that Kant here ideally excludes. We should register also the strong formal incidence of themes of self-presence in Romantic poetry, often accompanied by anxieties about isolation or misunderstanding, even as we recognize other aspirations as its declared goals.

29 Compare Shelley: (1977), pp. 486, 504:

> A Poet is a nightingale, who sits in darkness and sings to cheer its own solitude with sweet sounds; his auditors are as men entranced by the melody of an unseen musician, who feel that they are moved and softened, yet know not whence or why . . . this power arises from within . . . and the conscious portions of our natures are unprophetic either of its approach or its departure.

30 Meredith's (1911) notes on this whole discussion of genius are especially full, and should be consulted for suggestions about Kant's relation to the British tradition. I have however altered his translation of *Geist* as "soul". This important section is obviously what Fichte has before him when he writes *On the Spirit and the Letter in Philosophy* (see below). What follows is Kant's most important definition of the aesthetic imagination.

31 Kant here means simply to subsume the particular under the general, and to explain that artistic genius is essentially connected to a faculty normal to the human mind (imagination). The term "talent" has no connotations of inferiority here.

32 Kant here – "und mit der Sprache, als bloßem Buchstaben, Geist verbindert" – specifically prefigures the title and subject of Fichte's essay (see below), and generally expounds that aspect of the imagination so popular among the Romantics: its capacity for renovation and discovery, for going beyond inherited associations and for producing new configurations.

33 Because the aesthetic idea now passes into an empirically available form – as poem, painting, statue – it must embody a concept, even though in its original apprehension no concept was adequate to it. We can distinguish between the concepts of the understanding necessary for the *existence* of a work of art and the indeterminate concepts to which it gives rise once it is in existence, and which were presumably in the artist's mind at the time of composition. See H.W. Cassirer (1938), pp. 278–85.

34 The desire to preserve the communicability of art and the continuity between the artist's faculties and those of ordinary human beings is central to Kant's purpose here; it is through the common possession of the understanding that shared experience of this sort is possible.

35 Compare Schiller on *Schein*, in *AE*, pp. 191–203; and see n. 7 to Hegel's *Aesthetics*, below. The declaration of poetry as the first among the fine arts, a view shared by Schelling and (ambiguously) by Hegel, has been felt to consort awkwardly with the emphasis on the visual arts in earlier parts of the *CJ*. The point is, I think, that the visual arts were more conducive to those parts of the argument stressing the absence of *interest* in the aesthetic response, painting and statuary being more prone to appetitive associations than the reading of words (for Kant, that is).

36 Once again, Kant's example makes clear that he has in mind the lower meaning of *Kunst* as "artifact".

37 For the very synthesis of art and nature that Kant here keeps apart, compare Coleridge (1972), p. 30:

> a Symbol . . . always partakes of the Reality which it renders intelligible; and while it enunciates the whole, abides itself as a living part in that Unity, of which it is the representative.

38 "We may, on the other hand, make use of an analogy to the above mentioned immediate physical ends to throw light on a certain union, which, however, is to be found more often in idea than in fact. Thus in the case of a complete transformation, recently undertaken, of a great people into a state, the word *organization* has frequently, and with much propriety, been used for the constitution of the legal authorities and even of the entire body politic. For in a whole of this kind certainly no member should be a mere means, but should also be an end, and, seeing that he contributes to the possibility of the entire body, should have his position and function in turn defined by the idea of the whole." [Kant's own note.]

39 Behind this emphasis is of course Kant's desire to pre-empt any hint of an argument for the existence of God from the evidence of a design in the created world. It is worth stressing yet again that in most of this exposition Kant has in mind our capacity to produce artifacts rather than fine art; he is interested in our production of things with a *purpose*, which we will be most tempted to relate to the productions of nature. (The beautiful, it will be remembered, is by definition never purposive.) This is important in view of the tendency of Kant's followers to apply these arguments to fine art, where they never belonged for their founder.

40 Meredith (1928), p. 170, notes as follows:

The reference to 'objective reality' in this passage . . . is certainly somewhat misleading . . . Kant presumably only means that organisms first give teleology a point of attachment in nature. The passage is one of several that are responsible for misinterpretations of Kant's teleology.

41 Any adequate footnote to this section of *CJ* would have to be of book-length proportions, and "splendid misery" would indeed be a suitable title. Within the general model of a fall both fortunate and unfortunate, many eighteenth-century thinkers were exploring the problems of the divisions in civil society (of labour, interest, wealth) and within the individual mind. Suffice it to say here that Kant is closer to the spirit of Hobbes and Mandeville, and to what will become the spirit of Malthus and the social Darwinists, than he is to the liberal sociologists of the nineteenth century. Kant (1963) should also be consulted for its arguments for the disjunctive relation of individual and species and the emergence of culture from strife. Evidence, if any were needed, that the arguments of the 'Critique of Teleological Judgement' are to be applied strictly to their declared contexts!

FICHTE

On the Spirit and the Letter in Philosophy

1 "The following three letters, which will be continued in a future issue, were written four years ago. I should like to remind you of this in order to explain the silence over recent events and comments which the title of this essay will call to mind." [Author's note of 1798.] Although the issue of the *Philosophische Journal* in which this work appeared is dated 1798, it did not in fact appear until 1800, and it was written in 1795, not 1794, as the Schiller–Fichte correspondence makes clear. One of the results of Fichte's quarrel with Schiller seems to have been a greater distance from his other Romantic contemporaries. The "recent events and comments" must refer principally to the atheism controversy which resulted in Fichte's leaving Jena, but he was also constantly involved in defending his system against interpretation as

excessive subjectivism. Léon (1922), I, 359 notes that he was in this context made a figure of fun in various contributions to the *Musenalmanach* in 1796.

2 In a note to letter 13 of *AE* Schiller had lamented the tendency he saw in Kant's followers toward the absolute separation of the rational-ideal from the empirical elements of experience, noting that "such a way of thinking is, it is true, wholly alien to the *spirit* of the Kantian system, but it may very well be found in the *letter* of it" (*AE*, p. 87). Schiller had also gone into this subject at greater length in *On Grace and Dignity* – see Schiller (1943–), XX, 283f. – and Kant's own definition of the aesthetic idea had included its capacity to synthesize the "spirit" with the "letter" (*CJ*, §49).

3 Compare Schiller, *AE*, p. 101:

> I am drawing ever nearer the goal towards which I have been leading you by a not exactly encouraging path. If you will consent to follow me a few steps further along it, horizons all the wider will unfold and a pleasing prospect perhaps requite you for the labour of the journey.

The doubts expressed about convincing the "neighbour" are in line with Fichte's general sense of the importance of vested interests in governing conviction and preventing us from being open to alternatives: see *SK*, pp. 12f. Schiller himself makes a similar point when he explains the quarrel as a result of their mutually different natures: see Fichte (1967), I, 487.

4 One of the noteworthy features of this work is its constant and conscious playing upon the various meanings of *Geist* and its adjectival compounds.

5 Rousseau's novel *Julie, ou la nouvelle Héloïse* (1761) was enormously popular in Europe; this anecdote is reported by Rousseau himself at the beginning of Bk XI of the *Confessions*.

6 Schiller defines *Betrachtung* as "the first liberal relation which man establishes with the universe around him" (*AE*, p. 183).

7 The reference is to C.F. Gellert's *Das Leben der schwedischen Gräfinn von G*** (1747–8, 2nd part 1763).

8 Compare Wordsworth in 1815:

> . . . every author, as far as he is great and at the same time *original*, has had the task of *creating* the taste by which he is to be enjoyed: so has it been, so will it continue to be. This remark was long since made to me by the philosophical Friend for the separation of whose poems from my own I have previously expressed my regret.
>
> Wordsworth (1974) III, 80

The friend was Coleridge.

9 "Self-activity" is one of the fundamental concepts of the *Wissenschaftslehre*, e.g.:

> The object is merely posited, insofar as there is resistance to an activity of the self; no such activity, no object. It is related as determinant to determinate. Only *in so far* as this activity is resisted, can an object be posited; and so far as it is not resisted, there is no object.   *SK*, p. 229

As a transcendental thinker Fichte here speaks of what must be *thought* to be the case. He is not speaking of the material world in itself, but saying that we can "never speak of the existence of an object without a subject" (p. 252).

10 Compare Coleridge (1954), II, 6, on "that willing suspension of disbelief for the moment, which constitutes poetic faith".

11 See the useful gloss on *Gemeinsinn* in Schiller, *AE*, pp. 314–16, and Kant's important discussion in *CJ*, §§20–2, 40.

12 This is the received doctrine from the *CJ*: aesthetic judgements cannot be applied to experience through concepts, but give rise to the same certainty (in the subject experiencing them) that they would have if they could.

13 *Besonnenheit*, which might also be translated as "composure" or "presence of mind", had been defined by Herder as the coordinating power holding together all the human faculties. See Blackall (1959), pp. 467, 471–2; Taylor (1975), pp. 19–20.

14 The burden of guilt, *Schuld* (perhaps "debt" or "responsibility"), is a puzzling reference, at least to me: *die Einrichtung* might be translated as "disposition" rather than "founding", in which case Fichte may mean simply to refer to the illusion that the artist has just experienced, and which he coolly sits down to reproduce for us. Or he may intend a more evocative reading, referring either to the idea that the emergence of the arts in civil society had been contingent upon a fall from some kind of natural state (this would not be a Fichtean viewpoint, but it is the friend speaking here); or to some among the various identifications in the classical tradition of artistic or prophetic power with guilt or danger (Orpheus, Teiresias, Prometheus etc.). Apollo, the patron of the arts, could also be the bringer of strife and madness, and the relation of madness to artistic genius was something of a commonplace from Plato (*Phaedrus* 245a) onwards; see Schopenhauer, below.

Schiller's manuscript version of the text includes the following remark ending this paragraph:

So stands Hüon firmly on his feet while everything around him swirls in a wild dance under the influence of the magic horn, which will echo into the most distant ages and carry away in the same rapture the spirits yet to be born, binding them through the flying moments in the same dance.

The reference is to C.M. Wieland's famous poem *Oberon* (1780). See Fichte (1964–), I, 6, p. 339.

15 Compare the account in the lecture version of the way in which *Geist* requires external form, and thus depends upon a corresponding spiritual capacity [Sinn] in the reader or beholder for its reactivation and comprehension: see Fichte (1964–), II, 3, pp. 319f. See also Schiller's essay of 1791, *Über Bürgers Gedichte*.

16 Fichte's use of the various drives [*Trieben*] in explaining experience definitely signals a move towards integrating the rational and the somatic, and an application of the critical philosophy to instinctual experience in a fashion not totally dissimilar from Schiller's (see *AE*, pp. 331–2). The same term [*Trieb*] makes a famous reappearance in Freud.

For Herder, poetry had been the art and emanation of *Kraft*: see Blackall (1959), pp. 471–2, and Clark (1942). Here Fichte seems to make *Kraft* merely a qualifier of drive, a measure of its degree; but this is modified somewhat by the next paragraph, which makes all drives merely different manifestations of the one primary *Grundkraft*. Compare Schiller, *AE*, p. 49: "drives are the only motive forces in the sensible world".

17 The translation is ungainly, but does preserve the specific meaning intended by Fichte; Meredith similarly always renders Kant's *Erkenntniß* as "cognition". Sometimes I have used the shorter form "knowledge", though Fichte almost always intends reference to empirical or contingent knowledge; a less exclusive reading is called for when he argues that this drive can be incorporated with an aesthetic potential (see below).

18 By Kant, presumably, who had been emphatic about the absence of interest in the aesthetic judgement and the irrelevance of any correspondence between its representation and the world of objects; perhaps also, implicitly, by Schiller.

19 I have departed from the text in introducing a new paragraph here, in hopes of making the exposition clearer. Schiller found a basic confusion in Fichte's account of the various drives, complaining of the absence of a "sensible" drive, one toward existence or matter [*Stoff*], as well as of the obscurity of the practical drive and consequently of the aesthetic. Fichte replied by defending the absence of a *Stofftrieb* in terms of the doctrine of the *Wissenschaftslehre*: all matter is posited by limitation of self-activity, not of itself, and the representation of matter *to the mind* belongs within the knowledge drive. See Fichte (1967), I, 468, 472. The basic problem concerns Fichte's practical drive, which seems at first to have little to do with the Kantian definition of the "practical" faculty as that of moral speculation. Here it seems to function as the precursor of future and possible cognitions, causing us to anticipate potential facts of experience through representations of what they might or ought to be. This need not exclude a moral potential: Fichte suggests below that there is a "baser" version of the drive "seeking the maintenance and external well-being of animal life", thus perhaps also implying a higher version. And the account of the practical drive in *SK* (pp. 232ff., 244) is more explicit about the relation of the higher and lower practical drives. Although Kant himself had, in the *Critique of Practical Reason*, made a strong case for keeping "the supreme principle of practical philosophy" away from anything merely "empirical" – see Kant (1956), p. 9 – there is an interesting footnote to the introduction to *CJ* (I, 16–17), where the existence of the faculty of desire in despite of its inability to produce objects is applauded as a means of our coming to consciousness of our higher powers. This is much closer to the spirit of Fichte, who is interested in articulating an epistemological version of Kant's faculty of desire, thus closing the gap between practical reason and the understanding.

The *Wissenschaftslehre* works with a dominantly twofold taxonomy of the drives (see *SK*, pp. 244, 253ff.): a "theoretical drive" (corresponding to what is here called the knowledge drive) and a "practical drive" applying, as here, to things as they ought to be, and whose "first and highest" manifestation is the *Vorstellungstrieb* or "representation drive", through which "the self first becomes an intelligence" (p. 259). In the *Sittenlehre* of 1798 yet another series of definitions appears: the "moral drive" [*sittliche Trieb*] is a "mixed" one, taking its content from the *Naturtrieb* and its form from the "pure" [*reine*] drive. It has no purpose outside itself, and it is the fine arts that function to make the transcendental point of view into the common one, bringing about instinctively and imperceptibly what philosophy can do only through rules and the expense of labour. This is a significant anticipation of Schelling: see Fichte, *SW*, IV, 152, 353ff.; translated Fichte (1907), pp. 160, 367f. Note also Fichte's comments on the relation of moral and aesthetic senses:

The aesthetic sense is not virtue, for the moral law calls for self-sufficiency according to *concepts*, whereas the former comes of itself, without any concepts. But it is a preparation for virtue, and readies the ground for it, so that when morality enters it finds half the work – the liberation from the bounds of sense – already completed.

                                                                    SW, IV, 354–5

To return to *On the Spirit and the Letter*, it seems that the relation of the practical drive to moral experience is not much explored. So when Fichte speaks of the interest of the practical drive in "qualities for the sake of qualities", he seems principally to mean empirical qualities (though as I have said he sees the one leading to the other). It should also be noted that Schiller had used a threefold model of the mind in *AE*; he identified a drive to form [*Formtrieb*], a drive to matter or content

[*Stofftrieb* or *sinnliche Trieb*], and a play-drive or aesthetic impulse [*Spieltrieb*] mediating between and reconciling the other two.

20 I.e. as modifications of the fundamental drive or *Grundkraft*, as already explained. Fichte is gradually building a synthetic model of mind in which each drive coexists with others, in act or potential. The argument here describes how what has been called the aesthetic drive is in fact implicit in *all* perceptual activity, and we can see again the way in which Fichte seeks to bring together the faculties kept apart by Kant's three *Critiques*: epistemological, moral and aesthetic.

21 The example of the magnet is a favourite one with Fichte: see also *SK*, pp. 151, 162, 178–9 etc.

22 [I.H. Fichte includes the following note from the original text of the treatise, found in *Friedrich Schiller's Remains* after the publication of his text of 1846, relating to the word *wollen*.]

"Nothing of *intelligible fatalism* is to be read into this reference. The will [der Wille] is indeed always determined by factors dominant for the subject in his present mood. But that *these* factors and not totally opposed ones predominate, and that the subject is in this particular mood and no other, is to be attributed to absolute self-activity. It is this which is the deciding factor in tipping the balance through free reflection and abstraction at the absolute beginning of each inner life-act [Lebensact], which from there on, through the many transactions of the human spirit, follows necessary laws. The drive does not impel man irresistibly, as springiness [Elasticität] governs a material body, for it is a drive directed at an independent being. Reflection on its direction is required, and this reflection is the starting point for a continuous connected process. How the disposition of the will turns out depends upon whether or not we reflect, and on how this reflection is directed, whether towards total or only partial stimulation. Therefore: the will is not free, but *man is free*. All his faculties are closely bound up with one another, and they necessarily interrelate in action. Only because it was believed that what had been taken apart arbitrarily and for the purposes of speculation was in fact really fragmented, theories arose which contradict either natural feeling [Gefühle] or reasoning; or, more correctly, both at the same time. However hard this assertion may appear to some, it is not merely the disposition of the will of the empirical individual which depends on his particular self-activity, but also his whole inner character, the way he imagines and desires, and what he finds pleasure or displeasure in. Freedom proclaimed through self-sensation [Selbstgefühl] was first related to the will, because this concludes and completes every inner life-act, which moves immediately from it to the outside world. Consequently it is at this boundary point that the difference between the free subject and the constrained object is first noticed. But exactly because it occupies the leading place in the series of mental activities [Geistesgeschäfte], the will is least of all free, for it is determined by the greater processes that have gone before it. With the will man begins a new phase in his experience of the sensible world. People have concluded that with this same will he would begin the necessarily presupposed new phase in himself; but this conclusion is false, and at the same time improbable." Compare *SK*, pp. 232n, 259. Locke had made a similar argument about the phrase "free will": see *An Essay Concerning Human Understanding*, Bk II, ch. 21.

23 The essential thing about the example of the nightingale, as it appealed to Kant, Shelley, Keats and Coleridge among others, is that it sings without self-consciousness. This is what the foregoing example of the magnet demonstrates as characteristic of the aesthetic drive.

Schiller's manuscript copy has another passage not included by I.H. Fichte but

transcribed by Lauth and Gliwitzky in Fichte (1964–), I, 6, p. 347, as concluding
the paragraph:

> ... and if we are right, then the same is recognized by the poet who, as he does so
> superbly, has his singer say:
>
> > I sing forth as the bird sings
> > Who in the branches dwelleth;
> > The song forthcoming from its throat
> > Rewards, itself rewards.

Fichte misquotes from memory from Goethe's *Wilhelm Meister*, Bk II, ch. 11, adding
the reflexive in the last line! Carlyle's translation of this stanza, beginning "I sing
but as the linnet sings", inspired Tennyson's beautiful lines in *In Memoriam*, 21.

24 The reference to "aesthetic education" specifically invokes the title and subject of
Schiller's treatise. It is not perhaps entirely fair to Schiller to see him as a naive
exponent of social renovation via the aesthetic, but Fichte wishes to make the strong
claim that the aesthetic drive may be as good as absent (i.e. repressed completely
albeit latent) in particular historical situations. Schiller's case does admit qualifications, but in general comes down more favourably for the *status quo* than Fichte
might have wished. Further, Fichte's notion of the aesthetic has less to do with the
fine arts than does Schiller's, in that he preserves its relation to ordinary experience,
though it is a constituent thereof that does not always come to self-consciousness.
The lectures had asserted the ubiquity of *Geist* even more strongly:

> Whoever experiences representations has *Geist* in the general sense, for no represen-
> tation creates others ... Thus all men have *Geist*, and to be fully without it means to
> be without consciousness – to be dead.   Fichte (1964–), II, 3, p. 317

25 Chapters 1–19 of Gibbon's great work had been translated into German in 1779,
and various excerpts were subsequently translated, including *Die Bekehrung des Kai-
sers Constantins des Grossens* (Lüneburg & Altona, 1784).

26 Goethe's *Iphigenie auf Tauris* first appeared in prose in 1779, and then later in blank
verse. The whole of the foregoing discussion about freedom and subservience should
be compared to the argument in Kant's *What is Enlightenment?* (above).

27 Compare Schiller, *AE*, p. 312, on *Liberalität*.

28 Compare the lectures, Fichte (1964–), II, 3, p. 316:

> *Geist* generally is that which is also called *productive imagination*. *Reproductive* imagina-
> tion renews what was already there in empirical consciousness ... The productive
> imagination does not renew. It is, at least for the empirical consciousness, fully
> creative, and creative out of nothing ... it is itself the creator of this consciousness.

The distinction between the two kinds of imagination is Kantian; compare *CJ*,
remark following §22.

29 What such a rule might be had been one of the basic inquiries of the *CJ*.

30 Or, a "capacity" [*Vermögen*] for the ideal. Compare Kant, *CJ*, §49.

31 [There follows another insert from the original text found after the publication of
I.H. Fichte's edition, to begin the third letter.]
  "The only thing in this whole context that has struck your neighbour – to whom,
you tell me, you communicated the contents of my previous letter – is what I said
about the obstacles which the lack of external freedom placed in the way of aesthetic
cultivation [*Bildung*]. He has hurried to apply this to his own age and fatherland,

and has found goodness knows what dangerous influences in my words. In view of his worries I want to explain myself more clearly.

In those European constitutions deriving from the Germanic – far less in the Slavonic, but am I bound to take these into account, or when I write in Germany to make sure that my words do not offend the Emperor of Morocco or the Dey of Algiers? – in the Germanic constitutions, then, it so happened that from time to time individuals among the oppressed classes stood up from under their burden, whilst individuals from the oppressing classes, whether by chance or by free choice, lost or relinquished their authority. In such cases both merged together in a happy middle class, through which the lot of the oppressed was improved in that they were given more space, whilst the worries of the oppressors were diminished in that they did not have to watch over so many people. Through this the otherwise unavoidable progression of slavery was prevented, and thanks to the room for manoeuvre that had arisen, conditions could remain more stable, as they in fact did, apart from a few intervening periods which were however followed by more auspicious ones. Any well-being that is to befall humanity must and will develop from that middle class. Anyone placed by fortune in that happy state should turn his eye inwards upon himself before he looks outwards. He should make himself free, before he wishes to free others; he should raise himself to a mode of thought which is self-contained, is true to itself, and complete in itself; one which rises above temporal ambitions and earthly fears. Then he should let the living expression of this mentality work on his contemporaries in word and deed, as best he can; and he should leave almighty nature, for which millennia are as a day, to develop and ripen the seed which he scatters. He who does not have this spirit will free neither himself nor others. He will want to overthrow tyrants only in order to take their place, albeit under the form of freedom. In fact he will simply alter the form of serfdom, whether he openly threatens the tyrants or crawls before their thrones to flatter them out of a part of their power, which he has not the courage to seek by open defiance and which, emboldened by success, he will come to desire in its entirety. Such a man is far from true freedom, for he has not yet freed himself from himself. This is my entire meaning, and I would certainly like your neighbour to be made aware of it.

In our inner selves, where, as we have just demanded, we must be at home if any one of our actions upon the outer world is to have any worth, the aesthetic sense gives us our first firm standpoint. Genius enters there etc."

32 Fichte here comes back to the question first raised by his imaginary friend's letter – how communication is possible between artist and audience. Note that the argument here seems to by-pass entirely the careful qualifications in the *CJ* about the merely assumed consensus pertaining to the aesthetic judgement.

33 Compare Kant, *CJ*, §3:

Now in the above definition the word sensation [Empfindung] is used to denote an objective representation of sense; and, to avoid continually running the risk of misinterpretation, we shall call that which must always remain purely subjective, and is absolutely incapable of forming a representation of an object, by the familiar name of feeling [Gefühl].

34 The analogy with Christ's coming into the world for the sake of mankind is presumably conscious: compare Blake (1982), p. 3: "Therefore God becomes as we are, that we may be as he is." The passage from spirit to letter is thus a fortunate fall, provided that spirit be reactivated again. For other comments on the fortunate fall, see Fichte (1847), pp. 9ff.

35 Goethe's *Torquato Tasso* appeared in 1790. See also note 26 above.

36 Perhaps a reference to Schiller's 1793 treatise *On Grace and Dignity*, in which grace, as a strictly human quality, involves a founding ingredient of morality: see Schiller (1943–), XX, 278–9. Schiller might thus have seen this passage as another attack on his social idealism. Compare also the final letter of *AE*, where Schiller speaks of the need for force [Kraft] to be bound by the graces (p. 217).

37 Schiller's manuscript copy contains the following passage, transcribed in Fichte (1964–), I, 6, p. 358:

Faust seems to me to image the passage from the last stage to the first; and in the context of the whole artistic career of the poet this piece does not seem to me as patchy and fragmentary as some believe. I see the spirit of Faust, after his unsuccessful wanderings in the world, communing with himself there to find the peace that he sought futilely outside himself; and purified by this test, passing forth again into the person of Iphigenia, according to the laws of a wonderful and yet natural metempsychosis.

The first part of *Faust* had been published in 1790.

38 Fichte may here be qualifying the formalist tendency in the argument of the *CJ*, whereby the absence of interest in the aesthetic response leads us to delight purely in the form of the object. Compare Schiller, *AE*, p. 155:

In a truly successful work of art, the contents should effect nothing, the form everything; for only through the form is the whole man affected . . . it is only from form that true aesthetic freedom can be looked for.

39 For the Pygmalion legend, see Ovid, *Metamorphoses*, X, 243ff.

40 Lauth and Gliwitzky note here a possible allusion to Jacobi's *Eduard Allwills Briefsammlung* (1792): see Fichte (1964–), I, 6, p. 360.

41 Compare the passage from the *Sittenlehre* cited above, note 19. Fichte is here arguing principally against didactic literature rather than insisting on an absolute separation between the aesthetic and the moral, though of course he has been emphatic about discriminating between them. Compare Coleridge (1954), II, 107, on how

that *negative* faith, which simply permits the images presented to work by their own force, without either denial or affirmation of their real existence by the judgement, is rendered impossible by their immediate neighbourhood to words and facts of known and absolute truth.

This in turn is behind Keats' famous views on "negative capability".

On the Nature of the Scholar, and his Manifestations in the Sphere of Freedom

1 In the fifth of the Berlin lectures of 1804–5, the series titled *The Characteristics of the Present Age* – see Fichte (1849) and *SW*, VII, 3–254 – Fichte had distinguished between "concepts" [*Begriffe*], "which come into the way of purely sensuous human nature by way of experience", and "ideas" [*Ideen*], which "kindle themselves through the in itself self-sufficient life in those who are inspired, entirely without the element of experience" (*SW*, VII, 69). This may be taken to indicate the somewhat less strict use of Kant's *Idee* in Fichte's popular writings. See, e.g., Kant, *CJ* §§17, 57 remark 1.

2 I.e. whether there is a predetermined suitability of genius to one particular expressive mode, or whether contingent experience early in life determines the form of expression that genius will follow.

3 From this point on, *Talent* (ability) and *Genie* (genius) are used as synonyms in Fichte's argument. Compare Kant, *CJ*, §46:

> *Genius* is the talent (natural endowment) which gives the rule to art. Since talent, as an innate productive faculty of the artist, belongs itself to nature, we may put it this way: *Genius* is the innate mental aptitude (*ingenium*) *through which* nature gives the rule to art.   (*CJ*, I, 168)

To avoid the implication of some sort of discrimination between a lower and a higher faculty, of the sort that Coleridge puts into play in *Biographia Literaria* and elsewhere – see Coleridge (1954), I, 153 – I have translated *Talent* as "ability".

For Fichte's insistence that he is operating in the realm of exact knowledge [*Wissenschaft*], Kant's distinction between *Wissenschaft* and *Kunst* should be consulted (*CJ*, §34).

4 Compare the opening of the third letter of *On the Spirit and the Letter*, above: "It is only the capacity for the aesthetic which gives us our first firm viewpoint for introspection . . ."

5 See the account in the general introduction of the widespread attack on *Schwärmerei*.

6 The text here reads: "daß es neu, frappant, paradox erscheinen". Given the case he was about to develop in *Addresses to the German Nation* for an authentically German language, one can imagine the venom with which this nest of foreign terms might have been delivered.

On *Besonnenheit*, see note 13 to *On the Spirit and the Letter*, above.

7 Compare Fichte (1968), p. 158; *SW*, VII, 426:

> The person who is not a scholar [Der Ungelehrte] is destined to maintain the human race at the stage of culture it has reached, the scholar to advance it further and with a clear conception and with deliberate art. The scholar with his conception [Begriff] must always be in advance of the present age, must understand the future, and be able to implant it in the present for its future development.

8 Given the general priority of the struggle against Napoleonic France this argument for the sacrifice of the part for the sake of the whole, and for the necessity of decisions on such grounds, would not have been received in the cool spirit which a modern reader might tend to bring to it. Interestingly, much the same arguments are put forward by Burke in the *Reflections on the Revolution in France* (translated into German in 1791), but in the cause of inhibiting rather than encouraging civil disobedience.

9 Thus the life of the scholar fulfils the purpose of the transcendental philosophy in general (for Fichte): to make us see beyond the life of the senses.

10 See lecture IX.

11 Because it is an important part of Fichte's case that all essential truths be self-realized, consisting as they indeed often do in the very *experience* of self-realization, then the worldly career of the scholar-teacher who is in direct contact with students must be largely a propaedeutic one, clearing the ground of errors rather than simply putting forth 'truth' in a didactic way. This avoids the paradox of the student passively receiving the incitement to self-activity. On the propaedeutic method generally – which of course has a distinguished history from at least Socrates onwards – see the prefaces to the two editions of the *Critique of Pure Reason*. Fichte's description of the two kinds of scholar-teacher should also be compared with Kant's distinction, in *What is Enlightenment?* (above), between public and private.

12 For a longer polemic against the contemporary situation, and the habits of lazy reading similarly deplored by Wordsworth and Coleridge and related by them specifically to novel reading, see Fichte (1968), p. 94f; *SW*, VII, 86f. Fichte's positioning of the book trade within the spectrum of an economy founded on luxuries and commodities taps a deep vein in eighteenth-century moral rhetoric. Fichte himself wrote a treatise *On the Closed Commercial State* (1800); see *SW*, III, 387–513.

13 This is not simply an arbitrary complaint on Fichte's part: the reliance upon a prefigured or second-hand literature is at odds with the whole imperative of *Selbstthätigkeit* in his philosophy in general.

14 Again, compare Kant in *CJ*, §34. That the aesthetic is not tied to concepts is of course the received doctrine.

15 For the full exposition of this notion of a historical evolution and a series of specific historical variants of the idea, see Fichte (1847), *The Characteristics of the Present Age*. This explains the presence of a *Weltplan*, beginning in blind instinct and moving through reason to a condition of freedom, while at the same time "these epochs and fundamental paradigms [Grundbegriffe] of different ages can only be properly understood by and through each other, realizing their connection to the whole of history". It is in this work that Fichte is closest to Hegel, whose analysis of the work of art in its relation to a historical identity is much more thorough and much more famous, and to Schelling's writings on *Mythologie*.

16 It had not, we are to recall, been beneath the dignity of those who attacked Fichte on charges of atheism during his years at Jena.

SCHELLING

System of Transcendental Idealism

1 I.e. the empirical manifestation which is the work of art. With the exception of the "intellectual intuition" (see below) Schelling uses the term *Anschauung* in the Kantian sense, specifying an empirical percept.

2 Schiller had sought to achieve a similar synthesis of freedom and nature with his model of the "beautiful soul", combining the spontaneity with the strict propriety of the moral law; but unlike Schelling here, he sought to by-pass self-consciousness. See *On Grace and Dignity*, in Schiller (1943–), XX, 287–9.

3 The agility of Schelling's argument here depends upon his discussing simultaneously both the artist's state of mind in production and that of the beholder in the productivity of response; Kant, it will be recalled, was almost exclusively interested in the second of these approaches, and we can see already how Schelling assumes an identity not to be inferred in any simple way from Kant. In the model of organic nature that is behind the above paragraph he differs from both Kant and Fichte. He differs from Kant in allowing nature a finality according to ends, which the aesthetic intuition brings from unconscious to conscious status; and from Fichte in allowing an objectivity to nature beyond what is posited by self (Fichte allowed this too, but denied that it could be *known* except under these conditions). This helps to explain how Schelling can argue for the objectivity of the aesthetic intuition, whereas for Kant it is always the limited form of the argument that is emphasized: that as individuals we are compelled to *think* it so.

4 Thus the objective world "brings forth what it generates through its own lawfulness, in complete independence of freedom, and the *freely determining element*" (1978, p. 208; *SW*, III, 599). We do not *cause* the objective world.

5 This is a summary of and agreement with Fichte's emphasis on Kant's practical faculty as characterized by longing and striving.

6 I.e. the work of art could never satisfy, never produce restful contemplation, neither in creator nor in observer.

7 Compare (1978), p. 209; *SW*, III, 600:

> This eternal unknown, which, like the everlasting sun in the realm of spirits, conceals itself behind its own unclouded light, and though never becoming an object, impresses its identity upon all free actions, is simultaneously the same for all intelligences, the invisible root of which all intelligences are but powers [Potenzen], and the eternal mediator between the self-determining subjective within us, and the objective or intuitant; at once the ground of lawfulness in freedom, and of freedom in the lawfulness of the objective.

8 Compare the *Philosophy of Art*, *SW*, V, 460: "[Genius] is so to speak a portion of the absoluteness of God. Thus each artist can only produce as much as accords with the degree of unity of his own being with the eternal concept in God."

9 "I suffer (am the vehicle of) the God." I have been unable to trace a source for this precise wording, but similar expressions are commonplace among classical writers, and indeed their tragic protagonists.

10 *Poesie* here seems to play a role similar to that of Fichte's *Geist*: not just the literary genre narrowly defined, but the essential element in all creative activity. Compare Shelley's use of "poetry" in *A Defence of Poetry*.

11 Schelling intends here the more commonplace use of *Kunst* – technical ability to fashion something. Compare Fichte's argument on the relation between talent and industry in *On the Nature of the Scholar* (see above, pp. 97f.), and Kant's remarks on the subservience of genius to understanding in the best works of art (*CJ*, §50).

12 On *Besonnenheit*, see note 13 to Fichte, *On the Spirit and the Letter in Philosophy*.

13 In 1795 Schelling had published *On the Ego as the Principle of Philosophy; or, on the Unconditioned in Human Knowledge*, in which the ego is the locus of the representation through which subject and object mutually and necessarily condition one another.

14 This simulation might describe either the mere imitation or the merely didactic work of art whose effect is limited by the conscious intentions of its creator.

15 It is hard not to infer the presence of the Laocoön behind this remark. The sculpture was a kind of touchstone for eighteenth-century aesthetic theorists, and was written about by Winckelmann, Lessing, Goethe and others. Winckelmann had set forth the terms of the argument about the reasons for Laocoön's apparent quietude:

> Laocoön suffers, but he suffers like Sophocles' Philoctetes. His suffering goes right to our souls, but we would like to be able to suffer as this great man does . . . .
> Howard (1910), p. 27

He "raises no terrible cry . . . the opening of the mouth does not suggest this: it is rather an anxious and suffocating sigh . . .". The discussion is taken up again by Schopenhauer (see below).

16 For a longer account of the differences between and synthesis of the beautiful and the sublime, see the *Philosophy of Art*, *SW*, V, 461–70. Schelling's use of the various meanings and compounds of the verb *aufheben* prefigures Hegel.

17 Schelling is implicitly inverting the *ut pictura poesis* formula (Horace, *Ars Poetica*, l. 361), usually misunderstood as demanding that art imitate nature. Here, we take pleasure at natural beauty because it seems to imitate art.

18 On the debate between *Kunst* and *Wissenschaft*, see Kant, *CJ*, §§43–7, from whence the example of Newton (in the following paragraph) is taken. See also Fichte's remarks in lectures III and X of *On the Nature of the Scholar*. Kant had maintained that "there is no science of the beautiful, but only a Critique" (*CJ*, I, 165), though we must remember that this critique itself has the status of exact or "scientific" knowledge, precisely as it proves the impossibility of there being a "science" of the beautiful: see *CJ*, §34.

19 Compare Wordsworth (1974), I, 141: "Poetry is the breath and finer spirit of all knowledge; it is the impassioned expression which is the countenance of all Science." Wordsworth does go on to speak of science in some sense anticipating poetry (as it had done for much of the preceding century), which may be why Shelley(1977), p. 503, makes the case even stronger in calling poetry (in his expanded sense of the word) "at once the centre and circumference of knowledge; it is that which comprehends all science, and that to which all science must be referred".

20 Schelling here differentiates the two terms reunited by Fichte in 1805; see note 3 to *On the Nature of the Scholar*.

21 "Philosophy as a whole proceeds, and must proceed, from a principle that, as the absolute principle, is also at the same time the simply identical. An absolutely simple, identical entity cannot be apprehended or communicated by description or, in general, by concepts. It can only be intuited. Such an intuition is the organ of all philosophy. But this intuition, which is not sensuous but intellectual and which has for its object not the objective or the subjective but the absolutely identical, the in-itself neither subjective nor objective, is itself merely something inward which cannot again become objective for itself: it can become objective only through a second intuition. This second intuition is aesthetic intuition." [Alternate version by Schelling.] At this point Schelling's argument becomes very hard to follow without some account of his placing of the "intellectual intuition" [intellektuelle Anschauung]. Despite hints to the contrary, Kant had not favoured this term, limiting all intuitions to sensible ones, whether pure (mere space and time) or empirical: see Kant (1933), B 147f. This did not of course interfere with the necessary appending of the 'I think' to all representations, and the deduction of the transcendental unity of self-consciousness (B 131ff.; see also A 287ff.). It is the discussion of the noumenon, or thing as thought in itself (see A 287f., and *CJ*, §77), which as it were opens the field for Fichte, whose use of the term in the *Wissenschaftslehre* never entirely loses the Kantian restraint: intellectual intuition is "the immediate consciousness that I act, and what I enact: it is that whereby I know something because I do it". It can never be apprehended in isolation, but is "an inference from the obvious facts of consciousness" (*SK*, pp. 38–9). Schelling takes the case much further, and regarded Fichte as having stopped short, owing to the limits of his method, sooner than he need have. For Schelling, at this stage of his career, intellectual intuition is still partial, still too dialectically unresolved, and not yet totally objective, shifting between freedom and necessity. It is "the organ of all transcendental thinking" (1978, p. 27), without which all philosophy would be unintelligible, but requires the aesthetic intuition for its final expression: see the "General Observation" below. Harris and Cerf give useful accounts of the whole controversy over the "intellectual intuition", and its place in the development of Idealism, in Hegel (1977), pp. xxv–xxxv, 11–12, 69 n. 32. Hegel later attacked this entire terminology in his predecessors, though the grounds for this attack have themselves been queried (see Esposito (1977), pp. 175–8).

22 "Potency" is a (necessarily) ungainly translation of Schelling's *Potenz*, one of the key terms in his vocabulary. He worked with a model of three *Potenzen*, each embodying

an ideal stage in the development of the absolute, which is the totality of all three. The clearest account of the *Potenzen* is in the introduction to the *Philosophy of Art* (*SW*, V, 366f.), the leading points of which are translated in Hegel (1977), pp. 53–4. There is also a useful schema in Engell (1981), pp. 307–8, where the three stages are related to the empirical, the productive (leading to the intellectual) and the aesthetic intuitions.

23 Schelling would seem to be the source for Coleridge's fascination with this word and its cognates, taking it as he does much further than Kant had in his predominantly normative epistemology. See *SW*, V, 386:

Through art the divine creation comes to be presented objectively, for it devolves through the same synthesis [Einbildung] of the infinite ideality into reality as does art. The excellent German word "Einbildungskraft" actually signifies the force of *making into one* [*Ineinsbildung*], upon which in fact all creation depends. It is the force whereby an ideal is similarly a reality, and the soul is a body; the force of individuation, which is the truly creative principle.

There is an important note some pages later (V, 395):

In relation to *Phantasie* I define *Einbildungskraft* as that wherein the products of art are conceived and brought forth; *Phantasie* is that which intuits them outwardly, works them out of itself, so to speak, and thus presents them. In reason, and from its material, as it were, ideas [Ideen] are formed; the intellectual intuition is the inner presentational faculty. *Phantasie* is then the intellectual intuition in art.

24 One may suspect here another comment on the popularity of the aphoristic mode among the Romantic ironists.

25 The arguments and imagery of the two preceding paragraphs are very close to those of Shelley in *A Defence of Poetry*. For a different emphasis of the relation between philosophy and art, see (1966), p. 147: "because both are absolute, each can be the archetype of the other". The *Philosophy of Art*, written two years later than the *System*, is also less rhapsodic about the primacy of art over philosophy: see *SW*, V, 364f.

Given that art is here the most complete "objectivation" of philosophy, which is itself "a progressive history of self-consciousness" (1978, p. 2), we can see the potential in Schelling's system for a historical analysis of art as an index of the genetic development of the absolute – the kind of analysis made famous by Hegel. In the *Philosophy of Art* Schelling defines *Mythologie* as the "necessary condition and primary material of all art" (*SW*, V, 405), and it is the Greeks who provide the exemplary case. In his later writing on "mythology" Schelling employs the term to define religious doctrines prior to revelation – necessary to such revelation but superseded by it. Here, as in the essay on Dante and the comments on Shakespeare (see below), the word seems to suggest a unifying body of representations held in common by an artist, his public, and the idea which he objectifies; i.e. a body of material from which art may emerge and in whose terms it may be understood.

26 Compare *CJ*, §65, on "organization".

27 Schelling's exposition seems confused here because the other models of the *Potenzen* (see note 22 above) include only three stages. It might be pointed out that in this case simple sensation is the second stage, preceded (for the philosophical consciousness only) by an act of uncontingent self-intuition; and that the third stage includes the other two and yet another, which leads into the fourth stage, the union of the purposive and the unconscious. Schelling goes on to describe the importance of the recognition of other persons in a way clearly important for Hegel, and for the

general passage of Idealist epistemology out of its Kantian focus on a single exemplary subjectivity operating with objects in the world.

28 The categorical imperative is the famous centrepiece to Kant's second *Critique* (1956), p. 30: "So act that the maxim of your will could always hold at the same time as a principle establishing universal law." Schelling (1978), p. 188, puts it slightly differently: "thou shalt will only what all intelligences are able to will".

On Modern Dramatic Poetry

1 I.e. an opposition or indifference not reconciled, not sublimated into a higher unity.

2 Schelling is here noticeably at odds with the notion of Shakespeare as a wild and untutored genius transforming everything he touches into things rich and strange; this may be a reaction to *Sturm und Drang* priorities.

3 In his explanation of the famous ἁμαρτία or "mistake" in Aristotle's *Poetics* (1453a) Schelling shows himself to be at one with more recent scholarship, which emphasizes the irrelevance of meditated and conscious decisions emanating from free will. Philoctetes, for example, wanders unknowingly into a forbidden place, making no decision of his own to do so.

4 Compare the extended comparison of the Greek and Christian worlds pursued earlier in the lectures, *SW*, V, 430–57. Among Christian cultures, "only Catholicism lives in a mythological world" (p. 443), but it can never achieve totality therein: "Catholicism is a necessary element of all modern poetry and mythology, but it is not the whole of it, and in the purpose of the world spirit [Weltgeist] it can doubtless only be a part thereof" (p. 442).

5 *Poetics*, 1452b–1453a.

6 *King Lear*, IV, ii, 40–, or so I assume. Schelling's prose rendering of this passage is a long way from Shakespeare's verse, and seems to conflate various images from Albany's speech, the end of which I quote: "Wenn die Tiger des Waldes oder die Ungeheuer der See aus der Dumpfheit heausträten, so würden sie auf solche Weise wirken." There were several extant translations or adaptations of the play from which Schelling might have drawn: see Price (1934), pp. 209–10.

7 *Henry VI, Part II*, IV, iv.

8 *Richard III*, V, iv, 7.

9 The identification of the modern with the fragmentary was a commonplace in Romantic thought and is explored elsewhere in Schelling, for example in the essay on Dante (below). Elsewhere in the lectures he comments that "the modern world generally can be called a world of individuals: the ancient world a world of species" (*SW*, V, 444); "*Originality* is the fundamental law of modern poetry . . . each truly creative individual has to create his own mythology" (p. 446). Protestantism is the symptom and analogue of this fact, and it is from Protestantism that Shakespeare's art emanates. Christianity as a whole had already broken apart the unity of the finite and the infinite by its preoccupation with the ideal at the expense of the mundane; Protestantism, being "essentially anti-universal", carries this trend even further. See Schelling (1966), pp. 89, 98. Compare p. 66:

The modern world is in general a world of antitheses, whereas in antiquity, except for individual stirrings, the finite and the infinite were united under a common veil. The spirit of the modern era tore this veil and showed the one in absolute opposition to the other.

It is central to Schelling's reasoning here that the Greek gods easily and frequently took on human form.

10 Pythagoras was said to have deduced all the ratios of the octave as recognized by the Greeks in relation to a series of numbers from 1 to 4.

11 In the *Letters on Shakespeare* (1800), Tieck speaks of "a whole gallery of English commentators, whom perhaps one ought rather to pass over, since when I read Shakespeare and from time to time chance to cast an eye over the notes, then I am in exactly the same spirits as if, journeying through a beautiful romantic landscape, one were to go by a tavern in which drunken peasants were bickering and fighting". See Tieck (1848–52), I, 147. Tieck's residence in England seems to have left him with an abiding disrespect for the English common man.

12 Perhaps a reference to Pope's remark about a "fluent Shakespear" who "scarce effac'd a line" ('Imitations of Horace', Ep. II, i, 279), or to his contrast of "Shakespear's nature" with "Johnson's art" (*The Dunciad*, Bk II, A 216, B 224). For Pope, the whole case for the spontaneity of Shakespeare as against any element of premeditation was evidence to be adduced in the quarrel between the ancients and the moderns, and in the support of his particular polemic against Theobald and other 'learned' editors.

13 Schelling means to rescue not only the mature Shakespeare, for whose mediated and derivative genius he has already argued, but also the youthful poet from the *Sturm und Drang* image of him as the vehicle of an unconscious emotional outpouring.

14 By "sinful" Schelling presumably means an art not based on recognition of or reconciliation with the gods; "unboundedness" is in this sense not a positive quality, and it is Sophocles who is for him the pinnacle of the dramatic art. The "less well-known source" is Spain, and it is Calderón (whom Schelling knew in A.W. Schlegel's translation) especially who is, so to speak, the "Catholic Shakespeare" (V, 726), and who has less need of the "characteristic" because he can deploy a "true fate" (p. 729): "this highest and absolute composure [Besonnenheit], this ultimate indifference of intention and necessity, is achieved in such a way by Calderón alone among the moderns" (p. 729).

On Dante in Relation to Philosophy

1 This recapitulates the end of the argument of the *System of Transcendental Idealism* (1800), where art is presented as the consummation of philosophy, each being the complement of the other. The lectures on the *Philosophy of Art* (1802–3) had made poetry the highest among the arts:

> Poetry . . . permits the absolute act of cognition [Erkenntnißakt] to appear immediately as an act of cognition, and is thus the highest potency [Potenz] of the plastic arts, as it maintains in synthesis both nature and the character of the ideal, of essence, of the universal. That through which plastic art expresses its ideas is something in itself concrete; the speaking art does it through something in itself *universal*, namely language.   (*SW*, V, 631)

2 Schelling elsewhere defines the epic as the unity of freedom and necessity without any opposition between finite and infinite. Its action is "timeless" because it does not involve the difference between possibility and actuality which is the basis of time. See *SW*, V, 646, 648.

3 Compare *SW*, V, 554–5:

> An image is *symbolic* when its object not only signifies the idea, but *itself* is the idea, . . . the most completely symbolic representation is afforded by the static and inde-

pendent poetic form of a particular *mythology*. So St Mary Magdalene not only *signifies* repentance, but she is herself living repentance.

4 Nor, indeed, was it necessary, Schelling means to imply.

5 See also the discussion of *Faust* in *SW*, V, 731–4.

6 For an account of the limited number of Aristotle's texts available to mediaeval scholars, and the consequent Platonized versions of this thought in circulation, see Edwards (1967), article "Aristotelianism".

7 The history of the birth of the soul is recounted by Statius in *Purgatorio*, XXV, 52ff.

8 The aphelion is that part of a planet's orbit when it is furthest from the sun.

9 This reference is something of a puzzle, in that there seems to be no single line which satisfies all the terms of Schelling's description here, at least in the literal sense. Ronald Martinez has offered me (in correspondence) considerable assistance here, and I cite one of his suggestions as follows, making a case for *Purgatorio*, VI, 45, a line referring to she (Beatrice) "who shall be a light between truth and intellect":

There is no direct mention of *occhi*, though if we consider the attributes usually assigned to Beatrice then we could argue that the *lume* mentioned in the line is related to her eyes as effect to cause. Nor is there any direct mention of elevation, though philosophically speaking the trajectory between the intellect and the truth can be nothing if not an ascent. And the verse also responds to Schelling's interpolated clause, "through which the divine force so to speak transmitted itself to him", because the relation of truth to the human intellect is a directly informing one. In fact the verse is particularly satisfactory because of its distinctly philosophical, Neoplatonic density of meaning, diagramming the hierarchy of grace with Beatrice as mediator.

Professor Martinez also notes that a reference to the *Purgatorio* would accord with the structure of the paragraph, and the paragraph before it, where references to all three books of the *Comedy* appear in order; and he further suggests that Schelling might have in mind (or indeed even intend reference to) various passages from the *Paradiso*, e.g. I, 46–64, XIV, 82–4, and XVII, 112–14. The latter is especially significant in occurring in the central canto of the book, and in standing as a summary of the narrative so far.

Another hypothesis might attend to the fact that *Paradiso*, I, 46–64, would have been available to Schelling in A.W. Schlegel's translation, e.g. l. 53: "Frei schaut' ich in den Sonnenball, wie sie."

10 *Paradiso*, II, 34f.

11 Presumably in the first canto of the *Purgatorio*, describing the ascent out of hell. Schlegel translated ll. 1–28.

12 Schelling himself repeats this view in *SW*, V, 644.

13 *Paradiso*, XXV, 1–9. I cite from Henry Cary's translation (1805–6, reprinted 1814), which became the one most familiar to nineteenth-century English readers.

14 *Inferno*, XXIX, 1–8.

15 Schelling may have in mind the famous meeting with Paolo and Francesca in *Inferno*, V, or perhaps the wood of the suicides, where men have become trees (*Inferno*, XIII).

16 *Purgatorio*, III–XXVII.

17 *Purgatorio*, XXV.

18 *Paradiso*, III, 88–90.

19 *Inferno*, III, 9.

Concerning the Relation of the Plastic Arts to Nature

1 Delivered on 12 October 1807, at Munich. Schelling's footnotes were added for the version published in volume one of the *Philosophical Papers* (1809).

2 This synthesis of the *Kraft* of nature with that of our spirit is a rhapsodic version of the argument of the end of the *System* (1800).

3 I have generally altered Bullock's translation so that *Begriff* tends to appear as 'concept' rather than as 'idea' or 'notion'. While taking the point that Schelling may mean to invoke less technical meanings of the word, it seems important to avoid 'idea' for reasons relating to Schelling's own vocabulary, and 'notion' because of its existence in now outdated translations of Hegel. It seems to me important to render the dynamic function Schelling attributes to the Kantian term *Begriff*.

4 Again, compare the concluding sections to the *System*.

5 Given Schelling's emphasis on the unity of the human and the natural world recognized in the workings of the absolute Idea (or, as here, its *Kraft*) in each, any assumption of a basic difference between the two would be out of place.

6 I have not been able to discover a precise source for this familiar idea, but there is a very similar statement in section III of Lessing's *Laokoon*. What Schelling says here is also much in the spirit of Goethe's *Diderots Versuch über die Malerie* (1798), as of Aristotle's *De Generatione et Corruptione*!

7 This is what Coleridge, among others, calls "organic form". Compare Kant's more limiting arguments in the 'Critique of Teleological Judgement'.

8 I.e. in the representation of particular, individuated forms, which Schelling calls "characteristic". In the remarks on Shakespeare (see above) he had related such individuation to the Protestant ethos, essentially anti-universal. Significantly, this oration speaks for the acceptance and even celebration of this obligatory singleness of form as a determinate moment on the way toward synthesis with the absolute. In this sense it is an important document in the central romantic preoccupation with the paradigm of the fortunate fall.

9 Schelling's word *Geschöpf* can refer to a creature or a created thing; thus it presents art and nature as equally organic.

10 This is another reference to Schiller's essay on the subject of grace; see note 27 to the *Critique of Judgement*.

11 Behind this section of the exposition is Schelling's conviction about the essential relation of particular art-forms to their historical circumstances, their "mythologies" (if any). Thus, in general, Christian art is committed to the isolation of the spiritual from the material, and will naturally tend to privilege those art forms serving this end, in this case (for poetry is not under discussion here) painting. Sculpture always remains more fully materialized. Many of Hegel's later arguments on the subject are anticipated here.

12 "As a matter of fact, the assertion that monuments of ancient art were available to the originators of the newer school of painting cannot be made in respect of the first or earliest of them. For, as the worthy *Fiorillo* expressly remarks in his *History of the Graphic Arts*, Vol. I, p. 69, no ancient paintings and statues had yet been discovered at the time of Cimabue and Giotto; they lay neglected beneath the ground. [Johann Dominik Fiorillo, *Geschichte der zeichnenden Künste von ihrer Wiederauflebung bis auf die neuesten Zeiten*, 5 vols. (1796).] 'Hence no-one could think of training himself after the patterns bequeathed us by the ancients, and the sole object of study for painters was nature. One notices in the works of Giotto, a pupil of Cimabue, that he had already diligently consulted it.' Following his example, this path, which was able to

prepare the way for and lead closer to the antique, was pursued until, as the same historian notes on p. 286, the house of Medici (namely with Cosimo) began to search for monuments of ancient art. 'Hitherto, artists had to content themselves with the beauties offered them by nature; nevertheless this assiduous observation had the advantage of preparing the way for a more scientific elaboration of art, and the subsequent philosophic artists, such as da Vinci and Michelangelo, began to investigate the fixed laws underlying natural phenomena.' But even the re-discovery of ancient works of art during the time of these masters and that of Raphael in no way gave rise to their imitation in the sense that arose only at a later period. Art remained true to the path upon which it had embarked and reached consummation entirely out of itself; absorbing nothing from outside itself, but striving in its own particular way toward the goal of those prototypes, and only meeting with them at the ultimate point of consummation. Not until the time of the *Caracci* did imitation of the antique, which means something quite different to forming one's *own* taste according to its spirit, become an established principle and pass, particularly through *Poussin*, into the art theory of the French, who have an exclusively literal understanding of almost all the more exalted subjects. Thereupon the same practice became indigenous to us through Mengs and the mis-interpretation of Winckelmann's ideas, bringing upon German art of the middle of the last century such dullness and lack of spirit, with such forgetfulness of its original meaning, that even individual rebellions against it were mostly no more than misconceived emotion that led from one imitative mania to another worse one. Who can deny that a far freer and more original taste has recently shown itself again in German art, which, if all else conformed to it, would give grounds for great hopes and perhaps allow us to await the spirit which will open up in art the same lofty and free path that has been trodden in poetry and the sciences, and which alone could give rise to an art that we could truly call *ours*, i.e. an art of the spirit and of the energies of *our* nation and our *age*." [Schelling's own note.]

SCHOPENHAUER

The World as Will and Representation

[Payne's notes are indicated by the initial P.]

1 For Schopenhauer's particular formulation of the relation between concepts and ideas, see below, §49. For the moment it is enough to say that he regards art as capable of expressing (his version of) the Platonic Idea: that which is essential, eternal, archetypal. His first published work of 1813, *On the Fourfold Root of the Principle of Sufficient Reason* (see 1974b), had taken up the exposition of the inherited maxim or principle of sufficient reason (found in Leibniz among others), that "nothing is without a reason why it is thus and not otherwise"; i.e. everything that there is can be explained by reference to its relation to other things. The fourfold division of the principle covers, for Schopenhauer, all empirical phenomena. Schopenhauer often demanded that all his works be read as a whole, and he here presumes acquaintance with this earlier work.

2 One of the hallmarks of Schopenhauer's style is his frequent use of words of English or French origin (he did briefly attend school in London), e.g. "Inspiration", "Motivation". Sometimes the foreign word and the German word alternate with apparent synonymity, e.g. "Kontemplation" will alternate with "Betrachtung".

One can sense here a conscious campaign against the ideas expressed in Fichte and Hegel about the need to produce an authentic German Language in philosophy (not that they always obeyed the rule themselves).

3 Schopenhauer does intend to preserve the Kantian use of *Anschauung* and its compounds, as referring to an empirical experience, and the translation "intuition" which I have generally adopted throughout this anthology is admitted by Payne (1969, I, viii-ix) as a possible alternative.

4 Goethe's *Faust*, Bayard Taylor's translation [P]. The citation is from the end of the prologue in heaven (*Faust*, Pt. I). God is addressing the archangels, and bestowing creative power upon them.

On *Besonnenheit*, see note 13 to Fichte, *On the Spirit and the Letter in Philosophy*.

5 Kant had defined both an empirical and a transcendental "apperception" as making possible the synthesis that constitutes experience.

6 I.e. Bk. II, the selections here being taken from Bk. III. The idea of art going beyond nature, and perfecting what nature alone can never perfect because it is the forum of the various struggles of objectified will, is a point of contrast between Schopenhauer and Schelling.

7 The word used by Schopenhauer is *gemütlich* [P]. In his remarks on the imagination [Phantasie] Schopenhauer does not invoke the Kantian *Einbildungskraft*, which is the connective principle in ordinary perception, but refers to the distinction between true perception of the Idea and mere loose association or interest-dominated representation. See below.

8 For Schopenhauer, the whole physical form of a person is the expression of the will, and this leads him at times to a completely 'scientific' model of the relation between human organs and the kind of will they express. Thus

it must really be possible to understand and deduce not only the nature of his intellect from that of his brain and from the blood-flow that excites this, but also the whole of his moral character with all its traits and peculiarities from the more specific nature of all the rest of his corporization, thus from the texture, size, quality, and mutual relation of heart, liver, lungs, spleen, kidneys, and so on, although, of course, we shall never succeed in actually achieving this. But the possibility of doing this must exist objectively.   (1974a), II, 176

Speculations about the scientific credibility of phrenology and physiognomy were widespread in the eighteenth and nineteenth centuries. Compare Schiller's case for the outward visibility of inner moral identity in *On Grace and Dignity* (1943–), XX, 251f.

9 Compare Shelley (1977), p. 507:

But in the intervals of inspiration, and they may be frequent without being durable, a poet becomes a man, and is abandoned to the sudden reflux of the influences under which others habitually live.

10 One of Schopenhauer's earlier works, *On Vision and Colours* (1816), was a defence of Goethe's theory of colours against the Newtonian tradition; see also (1974a), II, 177–200. The argument about the applicability of a notion of genius to the sciences or to mathematics recalls Schelling in the *System* (see above, pp. 126–7). It might also be noted that Kant had seen mathematics as offering important evidence for the deduction of synthetic *a priori* propositions (then as now the subject of debate), i.e. as independent of and prior to the recombination of memorized or previously experienced data.

11 "What does all that prove?" [P].

12 I.e. by the principle of sufficient reason [Satz vom Grunde]. Schopenhauer's 'proof' of the relation between genius and madness, and his argument for the necessary eccentricity of the genius, would not have pleased those of his predecessors who were concerned, as Kant had been, to regulate the energies of genius by the rules of the understanding, without which no shared experience could occur.

13 "There has been no great mind without an admixture of madness" [P].

14 "For Democritus asserts that there can be no great poet without madness, and Plato says the same thing" [P].

15 From Dryden's *Absalom and Achitophel*, I, 163; not from Pope as attributed by Schopenhauer [P]. Schopenhauer quotes in English.

16 Compare vol. II, ch. 31 [P].

17 This is a looser usage of *Ideen* than Schopenhauer usually conveys – perhaps *fixen Ideen* is to be recognized as a direct adaptation of the French or English.

18 I.e. Sophocles' *Ajax*, and, of course, Shakespeare.

19 Compare vol. II, ch. 32 [P].

20 It is worth pointing out how much of Schopenhauer's exposition so far has concentrated on the artist, the man of genius. Kant's priority had always been the analysis of the aesthetic *response* and of the judgement involved therein.

21 Compare (1974a), I, 317:

Differences of rank and wealth give everyone his part to play, but there is certainly not an internal difference of happiness and satisfaction that corresponds to that role. On the contrary, here too there is in everyone the same poor wretch with his worries and wants. Materially these may be different in everyone, but in form and thus in their essential nature they are pretty much the same in all, although with differences of degree which do not by any means correspond to position and wealth . . .

22 I.e. of particular kinds of art and objects.

23 The two polar principles of the Zoroastrian religion, always at war with one another until the eventual expulsion of the evil by the good (but Schopenhauer would not have gone this far!).

  The relation between light and spirituality (see also (1969), I, 216) was of course traditional and commonplace, but it was also of special interest to the Romantic generation. Schelling, in the *Philosophy of Art* (*SW*, V, 507), declares that "Light is the ideal appearing in nature, the first breakthrough of idealism. The *idea itself* is light, but *absolute* light."

24 In the *Anthropology*; see (1974), pp. 33f. (§16). See also Hegel's remarks in the *Aesthetics* (*SW*, XII, 67–8), below.

25 Compare vol. II, ch. 33 [P].

26 "I am now all the more delighted and surprised, forty years after advancing this thought so timidly and hesitatingly, to discover that St Augustine had already expressed it: 'Arbusta formas suas varias, quibus mundi hujus visibilis structura formosa est, sentiendas sensibus praebent; ut, pro eo quod NOSSE non possunt, quasi INNOTESCERE velle videantur.' (*De Civitate Dei*, xi, 27.)" [Schopenhauer's own note.] "The trees offer to the senses for perception the many different forms by which the structure of this visible world is adorned, so that, because they are unable to *know*, they may appear, as it were, to want to *be known*" [P]. Since the perfection of plant forms cannot be attributed to an active intelligence contemplating itself, an extrinsic intelligence (in the beholder) is required for these forms to appear as representations. Compare §42 below.

27 This dualism is characteristic of Schopenhauer's generally pessimistic view of the relations between the sexes; see (1969), II, 531ff. The events of Hardy's *Jude the Obscure* may be seen in the light of this logic.

28 These extreme examples are closest to the ones Kant gives from the first as typical of the sublime (*CJ*, §28); we can see here how much less emphatic Schopenhauer intends to be about the difference between the sublime and the beautiful.

29 For Kant's relation of morality and the sublime, see *CJ*, §29, and my remarks in the general introduction. The reference to scholasticism may be in reaction to Kant's use of the distinction between *apprehensio* and *comprehensio* (*CJ*, §26f.). See also note 31, below.

30 "I am all this creation collectively, and besides me there exists no other being" [P].

31 This may be a reference to Kant's famous declaration at the end of the *Critique of Practical Reason*: "Two things fill the mind with ever increasing admiration and awe, the oftener and more steadily that we reflect on them: the starry heavens above me and the moral law within me" ((1956), p. 166; *Ak.*, V, 161–2).

32 Schopenhauer quotes in English.

33 "In accordance with nature" [P]. On the tradition of argument about the Laocoön group, see note 15 to Schelling, *System of Transcendental Idealism*.

34 The reference is presumably to *Werke*, ed. C.L. Fernow *et al.*, 11 vols. (Dresden and Berlin, 1808–25).

35 For the 1799 translation of Goethe's essay into English, see Goethe (1980), pp. 78–88. He refers to the group as "a flash of lightning fixed, a wave petrified at the instant when it is approaching the shore" (p. 81). His own reading of the sculpture also stresses the physiological approach: the energy required to fight the snake, and the recoil from its bite, are what prevent Laocoön from crying out (p. 77).

36 Alois Hirt's essay on the Laocoön appeared in *Die Horen*, 1797, tenth part, pp. 1–26.

37 Carl Ludwig Fernow, *Römische Studien*, 3 parts (Zürich, 1806–8).

38 Virgil, *Aeneid*, II, 774; III, 48. It is actually Aeneas who is thus described, not Laocoön.

39 Schopenhauer uses the Latin names of Ares and Athene. Virgil's account of Laocoön occurs in *Aeneid*, II, 199ff.

40 Kotzebue's play of 1796, *Die Spanier in Peru, oder Rollas Tod*, had been translated into English no less than seven times by 1800. Sheridan's 1799 translation bore the title *Pizarro*.

41 Goethe (1980), p. 11, does generally condemn the mixing-up of separate art-forms, and refers elsewhere to the painted figures on the walls of the opera house, though not pejoratively ((1980), pp. 25–30). I can find no specific mention of "painted music", although A.W. Schlegel does defend such a thing ((1962–74), II, 197), as does Friedrich Schlegel in his discussion of Correggio as a "musical painter" ((1849), p. 11).

42 "This episode has its supplement in chapter 36 of volume II." [Schopenhauer's own note.]

43 On the relation of naked to clothed form, see Kant, *CJ*, §§14, 41; and Hegel's *Aesthetics* (1975), pp. 742–50. Throughout the eighteenth century there had been an important debate about the cultural and ethical implications of nakedness and clothing, the primitive and the civilized, with frequent reference to the example of Sparta.

44 See §§30–5 on the Idea, and the early sections of the work for the explanation of the concept. The argument is briefly summarized in what follows.

45 I.e. "unity after the fact" and "unity before the fact".

46 The distinction between analytical and synthetic is a Kantian one; see Kant (1933), pp. 48ff. (A 7f., B 11f.).

47 "Imitators, the slavish mob" [P]. Horace, *Epist.*, I, xix, 19.

48 *Apparent rari, nantes in gurgite vasto.* [Schopenhauer's own note.] "Singly they appear, swimming by in the vast waste of waves." Virgil, *Aeneid*, I, 118 [P]. Appropriately, given Schopenhauer's view of the fate of excellence, the reference is to the wreck of Aeneas' ships and to the sight of his crew trying to save themselves from drowning.

49 Compare vol. II, ch. 34 [P].

50 "It goes without saying that everywhere I speak exclusively of the great and genuine poet, who is so rare. I mean no one else; least of all that dull and shallow race of mediocre poets, rhymesters, and devisers of fables which flourishes so luxuriantly, especially in Germany at the present time; but we ought to shout incessantly in their ears from all sides:

> Mediocribus esse poetis
> Non homines, non Di, non concessere columnae.

["Neither Gods, nor men, nor even advertising pillars permit the poet to be a mediocrity." Horace, *Ars Poetica*, l. 372–3. [P].] It is worth serious consideration how great an amount of time – their own and other people's – and of paper is wasted by this swarm of mediocre poets, and how injurious their influence is. For the public always seizes on what is new, and shows even more inclination to what is perverse and dull, as being akin to its own nature. These works of the mediocre, therefore, draw the public away and hold it back from genuine masterpieces, and from the education they afford. Thus they work directly against the benign influence of genius, ruin taste more and more, and so arrest the progress of the age. Therefore criticism and satire should scourge mediocre poets without pity or sympathy, until they are induced for their own good to apply their muse rather to read what is good than to write what is bad. For if the bungling of the meddlers put even the god of the Muses in such a rage that he could flay Marsyas, I do not see on what mediocre poetry would base its claims to tolerance." [Schopenhauer's own note.] Marsyas challenged Apollo to a musical contest. Having lost, he was flayed alive as punishment for his presumption. See Ovid, *Metamorphoses*, VI, 382ff.

51 *Des Knaben Wunderhorn* was a collection of old German songs, published in 1805 by Clemens Brentano and Achim von Arnim.

52 Anacreon, a Greek lyric poet of the 6th century B.C., whose works survive only in fragments; Angelus Silesius was the name taken by the German philosophical poet Johannes Scheffler (1624–77).

53 Again, Schopenhauer quotes in English.

HEGEL

On Classical Studies

1 In other words the ancients should not be identified with any primitive state of mere innocence.

2 See note 13 to Fichte, *On the Spirit and the Letter in Philosophy*.

3 See also the argument in Schiller's *On Naive and Sentimental Poetry* about the difference between passive imitation and the active recreation of inherited prototypes.

4 There is an implicit reference here to the famous "unhappy consciousness" dis-

cussed in the *Phenomenology*, paragraphs 206ff., as central to the Judeo-Christian world-view as well as to the individual's coming to self-consciousness within it. The classical world did not demand this specific form of alienation; consequently the merely "theoretical" alienation involved in learning its languages may result in the discovery of an alternative to the inherited social–moral anxieties. Nietzsche and Arnold, in their different ways, were both interested in the classics from this point of view. See Taylor (1975), pp. 57–9, 159–61, 206–8, 498.

5 See note 23 to Kant, *CJ*.

6 Compare Schelling (1966), pp. 39–40:

Language in itself, even considered from a grammatical point of view, is a continuously applied logic ... Nothing forms the intellect so effectively as learning to recognize the living spirit of a language dead to us. To be able to do this is no whit different from what the natural philosopher does when he addresses himself to nature.

Aesthetics: Lectures on Fine Art

[Knox's notes are indicated by the initial K.]

1 By "theoretical" and "practical" Hegel does not invoke the strict Kantian use of the terms, where they would correspond respectively to the laws of the empirical understanding and of the moral faculty. His idea of the "practical" would seem to include the modifications wrought by Fichte in connecting ordinary purposive activity or mere appetite with the higher faculty of desire, the one preparing the way for the other. The "theoretical" activity is, roughly, contemplative activity. See *SW*, XII, 65 (below):

The theoretical study of things is not interested in consuming them in their individuality and satisfying itself and maintaining itself sensuously by means of them, but in coming to know them in their *universality*, finding their inner essence and law, and conceiving them in accordance with their concept.

Hegel's *Begriff* (concept) is also much more active than Kant's, and should be thought of as a necessary principle actually bringing into being that in which it is perceived or thought.

2 See also Kant, *CJ*, §41. Hegel makes clear his negative attitude toward an undifferentiated primitive condition, and his conviction that the development of socially implicated forms of self-representation (the recognition of self as and through other) is a necessary step beyond it. This process may however involve perverse forms and is not always instinct with *Geist*. On *Bildung*, see Gadamer (1975), pp. 10–19.

3 See, for example, *Briefe über die Empfindungen* (1755), or *Betrachtungen über die Quellen und die Verbindungen der schönen Künste und Wissenschaften* (1757) [K]. The following remarks against the aesthetics of mere "feeling" had been paralleled in Britain by the arguments of the Romantic generation against the literature of "sensibility".

4 See *Aesthetics* (1975), pp. 16ff. [K].

5 See *Aesthetics* (1975), pp. 14f. [K].

6 Hegel's use of *Objekt* and *Gegenstand* here would seem to be symmetrical with Kant's: see note 2 to *CJ*.

7 On this division of the senses, see Kant, *Anthropology*, §15f. The status of art as appearance [*Schein*] had been important to Kant, and also to Schiller, for example

in *AE*. For Hegel's general placing of *Schein*, see *Phenomenology*, paragraphs 132f.; *Science of Logic* (1969), pp. 394–408; *Encyclopaedia*, §§131ff. See also Taylor (1975), pp. 273–9, and compare *SW*, XII, 78–9 (below). *Schein* has an integral status but one which is yet recognized and thought beyond. Unlike Schelling, who had dignified both mind and nature as instinct with spirit and with the ideal, and who could celebrate art precisely because it fuses the two together, Hegel operates with a model of the evolution of spirit *from* nature and matter.

8 Or, roughly, ideal prototypes to which actual objects never precisely correspond. For the technical functions of schemata in Kant, not very specifically invoked here, see Kant (1933), A 137ff, B 176ff.

9 *SW*, XII, 70, reads "als bewußtes Wirken", which makes no sense; Hotho and other reprints of his text read "bewußtloses", i.e. "unconscious". There had been much speculation on the presence or absence of genius in scientific investigation: see note 10 to Schopenhauer, *The World as Will and Representation*; and Fichte, *On the Nature of the Scholar*, lecture III (above).

10 Knox notes the apparent contradiction with *Aesthetics*, p. 28:

> In poetry ... the spirit and heart must be richly and deeply educated by life, experience, and reflection before genius can bring into being anything mature, of sterling worth, and complete in itself. The first productions of Goethe and Schiller are of an immaturity, yes even of a crudity and barbarity, that can be terrifying.

> But Hegel is not necessarily implying here that youthful energies produce works of genius – just that they forecast its development.

11 *Aesthetics*, p. 25 [K].

12 *Travels to Discover the Source of the Nile*, 3rd edn (London, 1813), VI, 526–7. Hegel quotes from memory, and usually inaccurately, but here he has given the gist of the story accurately enough for his purposes [K]. The first edition of Bruce's work had been translated into German, at Leipzig, in 5 volumes (1790).

13 The Sunna is a body of traditions incorporating the history of Mahomet's life and so is a sort of supplement to the Koran [K].

14 For Zeuxis, see e.g. Pliny, *Natural History*, XXXV, 36. J.F. Blumenbach told a story of an old fellow-student of Linnaeus called Büttner [?C.W., 1716–81, professor at Göttingen], who put all his money into books and acquired a copy of Rösel's book (published 1746–55) with coloured plates [K]. Both these examples of the deceptive power of art are cited within a few lines of each other by Goethe in his dialogue "On Truth and Probability in Works of Art", *Propyläen*, I, ii (1798). See Goethe (1980), p. 29.

15 *CJ*, §42 [K]. See also the remark following §22 (*CJ*, I, 89).

16 I have been unable to trace the source of this story [K].

17 Terence, *Heauton Timorumenos*, I, i, 25. "I count nothing human indifferent to me." As usual Hegel quotes inaccurately [K].

18 Hegel uses the French word, and presumably means to invoke the achievement of the French Enlightenment in removing superstition, and this in both positive and negative moments. See the discussion in *Phenomenology*, paragraphs 538ff. While clearing the ground of prejudices and mysteries, the Enlightenment still bears within it "the blemish of an unsatisfied yearning" (paragraph 573).

19 "The story teaches." *Aesthetics*, p. 385, shows that Hegel regarded these words in the Greek text of Aesop's fables (ὁ μῦθος δηλοῖ) as a corrupt, later addition.

20 "Poets wish alike to benefit and to please"; *Ars Poetica*, l. 333 [K].

21 I have not been able to discover a precise source for this view, which is yet frustra-

tingly familiar. The reference is most probably to a comment made about Correggio's Dresden Magdalene, to which Hegel himself alludes (*Aesthetics*, p. 868; cf. pp. 549–50). The inherent graciousness and beauty of the painting had often been noted, e.g. by Raphael Mengs and by Friedrich Schlegel (1849), p. 24. But there were also many seventeenth-century versions of the subject, any one of which might have inspired this ironic remark.

22 Hegel makes a clear distinction between *Sittlichkeit* and *Moralität*. The former indicates the conventional values of a community, to which we owe allegiance as its members (the other meaning of *sittlich* is thus "customary"). *Moralität* is that which pertains to us as universal, independent rational wills, rather in the spirit of the Kantian categorical imperative. See Taylor (1975), pp. 365–88.

23 This is a restatement (further expounded in the next two paragraphs) of Hegel's view of the effects of Kant's system on the ethical thinking of his generation, instituting a radical separation or strife between the empirical and the moral will. Hegel generally regarded Kant as having bequeathed a series of unfortunate dualisms to philosophy; but he also saw these divisions as a necessary historical moment, an expression of the spirit of the late Enlightenment. Like Fichte and Schelling before him, Hegel saw his own function to be the reconciliation of these divisions between ideal and empirical, noumena and phenomena, independent selfhood and wider community. Alienation has a central and inevitable place, but through time it can prospectively be overcome. In what follows, Hegel declares for the truthfulness of Kant's claim for art as standing outside didactic limitations, but insists that it has an essential content in itself: the setting forth of the reconciled opposition between spirit and nature. For Hegel on Kant and the Kantian inheritance, see *Aesthetics*, pp. 56–61; *Encyclopaedia*, §§40ff.; Hegel (1892), III, 423ff.; and Taylor (1975), pp. 29–36.

24 With this discussion we rejoin the lectures after Hegel has been through not only the theoretical analysis of the aesthetic but also the various (roughly) historical genres of art: the symbolic (early, pre-classical and oriental art), the classical, and the romantic, which begins in the middle ages (as it had for Schelling and others). This evolution is summarized in the following paragraph, and Hegel then goes on to describe the contemporary situation.

25 This is an important statement of the relation of the artist to his *Weltanschauung*. The standard translation of this term, as "world-view", unfortunately loses the foothold that Hegel's use of *Anschauung* always has in its Kantian context: it signifies an embodied, empirical intuition. This is why the artist, when in earnest, is at one with the actuality of this world-view; he *is* its empirical expression. This actualized intuition also explains why art is understood as significant by its wider community. Schelling's idea of *Mythologie* should be compared here.

26 Schiller and Schelling, among others, had also insisted on the futility of merely reproducing or copying rather than in some way recreating the spirit of ancient art, or of any art of the past. Behind the whole discussion we may sense the spectre of Winckelmann, who had declared ((1765), p. 2) that "There is but one way for the moderns to become great, and perhaps unequalled; I mean, by imitating the antients."

27 Consequently for Hegel, unlike Schelling in the *System*, a further stage is necessary in which release from the 'natural side' may take place. As Hegel goes on to explain, it is this longing which Romantic art dramatizes, signalling as it does so the imminent end of all art and the passage into pure thought, or philosophy (Romantic art being itself the expression of a religious world-view, as it is religion which precedes the emergence of philosophy in Hegel's scheme).

28 It would seem to follow from this that, whatever the relative status of art as a whole (highest in classical civilization), the individual artist is yet the most sensitive barometer of the changes happening or about to happen in the world-view. Similarly for Shelley (1978), p. 508, poets are "the mirrors of the gigantic shadows which futurity casts upon the present". Shelley does however accord the poetic more formative power than does Hegel, for whom the whole relation of the artist to his times is more potentially disjunctive or tragical.

29 Kant and his followers were often spoken of as the exponents of the "critical philosophy", and Kant himself had stressed the nature of the *Kritik* as a 'negative' analysis, narrowing the limits of what can properly be thought or argued by exposing what cannot be so thought or argued.

30 There had been a widespread fashion for Catholicism during the early years of the nineteenth century. The most famous conversion was that of Friedrich Schlegel, who began as the exponent of Romantic irony, seeking to avoid (in Hegel's eyes) all accountable relations to any form of worldly engagement or dogma, and then went through a period of pantheist idealism (around 1804–6) before declaring for Catholicism in 1808.

31 See note 24 to Kant, *CJ*.

32 See note 17, above.

33 See *Aesthetics* (1975), pp. 421ff.

34 *Witz* and *Phantasie* were among the major conceptual terms in Solger's *Vorlesungen über Aesthetik* (Leipzig, 1829), first delivered in 1819. It is not clear that a direct allusion is intended, and the terms are certainly common elsewhere; but Hegel did respect Solger as a serious exponent of the spirit of the age, and gave him much more credit than he extended to other theorists of irony. For Hegel's views on irony, see *Aesthetics*, pp. 64–9; Hegel (1967), pp. 101–2; and the review of Solger in Hegel (1956), pp. 155ff.

35 In *Die künftige Geliebte* (*The Future Sweetheart*), 1747 [K].

36 Goethe's *West-östliche Divan*, composed under the inspiration of the very Persian and Arabic poetry just commended by Hegel, was begun in 1814 when the poet was sixty-five.

37 This is another summary of the evolution of art through history, and it conflates the formal or theoretical sequence (symbolic–classical–romantic) with particular art forms (architecture–sculpture–painting). This relation of the historical and the generic has caused some debate. Karelis (1979), pp. lxi–lxiii, xlviii–xlix, has argued (following R.S. Lucas) for an 'affinity thesis' in which specific art forms correspond significantly to the historical trichotomy, but do not exhaust it, nor are they exclusively determined by it. Thus architecture is predominantly related to the symbolic, sculpture to the classical, and painting, music and poetry to the romantic; though there obviously can be and has been a classical poetry or a romantic architecture, and so forth, the point is that certain art forms best express the major moments in the evolution of *Geist*. See Hegel's own explanation; *SW*, XIV, 230, below. In what follows, it should be understood that poetry inaugurates the final stage in romantic art as it tends toward its own dissolution.

38 Unlike Schopenhauer, who was ready to define music as the highest of the arts because it is the pure expression of will, not limited by embodiment in an Idea, Hegel insists on the relation of art to self-consciousness. Thus, because of its existence in language, the most appropriate medium of self-consciousness, poetry is the genre through which art most efficiently cancels itself. Music does not provide any material for self-consciousness; thus Kant had remarked that by music, "all said and done, nothing is thought" (*CJ*, §54; compare *Anthropology*, §71).

39 Hegel carries his case for the importance of the (spiritual) content of poetry so far as to suggest that it can even survive translation – not a view shared by many Romantic critics or writers, even where they accept some unifying principle for poetry and prose, as Wordsworth and Shelley do. Indeed, for Hegel, the self-consciousness of spirit achieved in poetry could be said to be already translating itself into the prose of thought, which (as incorporating revealed religion) is the goal of his system.

The Philosophy of Spirit

1 I.e. in classical civilization. In §§503–51, immediately preceding the final chapter, Hegel has been expounding the relation of the moral law to conscience and to social ethics; the function of the argument is to demonstrate the presence of objective *Geist*, and this is why it appears under the title of a *philosophy* rather than a *phenomenology*, which Hegel had come to see as a Kantian mode now left behind. Compare §562 below. Being pagans, the Greeks did not have the "subjective inwardness of conscience" as we know it – a fact which Nietzsche was to celebrate – and could thus allow art to develop without its being obliged to demonstrate its own decline and displacement. Hegel (1975) notes that the Greeks had "no concept of universal freedom . . . no real morality or conscience . . . morality . . . dates only from the time of Socrates" (p. 62).

   Taylor (1975), p. 204, offers a definition of *Cultus*: "Cult is that dimension whereby men strive to become one with God. For all religion contains some inkling that it is the self-consciousness of universal *Geist*, hence that the finite consciousness is both separate from and at one with the infinite one it worships. Hence the necessity of overcoming the separation and returning to the underlying unity. This is the role of cult." The term is also used by Schelling (*SW*, V, 435) to describe the unifying ideal of the Christian church.

   When Hegel speaks of the "religion of fine art" we have to register a double reading of *schöne Kunst* as both "fine art" and, specifically, the art of the beautiful. See Karelis (1979), pp. xlix–l.

2 Behind this paragraph we may sense: (i) that artistic inspiration is often attributed to a visitation from above, or, as Shelley (1977) put it, "the interpenetration of a diviner nature through our own" (p. 504) (this idea is common among the Greeks); (ii) that because the artist (implicitly the Greek sculptor) is able to embody the god in marble he is, through his technique, the master of the god who masters him.

3 On the symbolic and the romantic, see e.g. notes 24 and 37 to *Aesthetics*, above. The cheerfulness of the Greeks and its relation to the absence of certain forms of self-consciousness was to appeal strongly to later thinkers, Nietzsche and Arnold among them.

4 It is romantic art that, as the expression of the Christian world-view, brings fully into the open the status of art as *Schein*, mere appearance.

5 Hegel here suggests that he finds the philosophy of religion (itself the subject of another of his lecture courses) a more unifying and representative inquiry than the philosophy of art, in terms of its ability to project cultural and historical forms. Hegel's later thought does tend to emphasize that art should be subsumed within religion if its whole significance is to be understood – not the other way round.

6 I.e. despite the enormous gap between the Greek statues and the idols and fetishes of primitive cultures, they are yet extremes of the same scale, within which art is the spirit's primary means of self-apprehension. The idol begins the sequence which the statue completes; thus the statues of the Greeks also point to a new system incipient in their own fullness of expression.

Bibliography

Abrams, M.H. 1953. *The Mirror and the Lamp: Romantic Theory and the Critical Tradition.* London, Oxford, New York, Oxford University Press.

1971. *Natural Supernaturalism: Tradition and Revolution in Romantic Literature.* New York, W.W. Norton & Co.

Arnold, Matthew. 1960–78. *The Complete Prose Works of Matthew Arnold.* Ed. R.H. Super. 11 vols. Ann Arbor, University of Michigan Press.

Ashton, Rosemary. 1980. *The German Idea: Four English Writers and the Reception of German Thought, 1800–1860.* Cambridge, Cambridge University Press.

Baumgarten, Alexander. 1964. *Reflections on Poetry. A.G. Baumgarten's 'Meditationes philosophicae de nonnullis ad poema pertinentibus'.* Trans. and ed. Karl Aschenbrenner and William B. Holther. Berkeley and Los Angeles, University of California Press.

1973. Hans-Rudolf Schweizer. *Ästhetik als Philosophie der sinnlichen Erkenntnis.* An interpretation of Baumgarten's *Aesthetica,* with Latin and German texts. Basel and Stuttgart, Schwabe.

Baumgartner, Hans Michael and Jacobs, Wilhelm G. 1968. *J.G. Fichte-Bibliographie.* Stuttgart–Bad Canstatt, Frommann-Holzboog.

Bennett, Jonathan. 1966. *Kant's Analytic.* Cambridge, Cambridge University Press.

1974. *Kant's Dialectic.* Cambridge, Cambridge University Press.

Blackall, Eric A. 1959. *The Emergence of German as a Literary Language, 1700–1775.* Cambridge, Cambridge University Press.

Blake, William. 1982. *The Complete Poetry and Prose of William Blake.* Ed. David V. Erdman. Newly revised edition. Berkeley and Los Angeles, University of California Press.

Boswell, James. 1970. *Life of Johnson.* Ed. R.W. Chapman, corrected ed. J.D. Fleeman. London, Oxford University Press.

Brown, Marshall. 1979. *The Shape of German Romanticism.* Ithaca and London, Cornell University Press.

Brown, Robert F. 1977. *The Later Philosophy of Schelling: The Influence of Boehme on the Works of 1809–15.* Lewisburg and London, Bucknell University Press & Associated University Presses.

Bruford, W.H. 1935. *Germany in the Eighteenth Century.* Cambridge, Cambridge University Press.

1962. *Culture and Society in Classical Weimar, 1775–1806.* Cambridge, Cambridge University Press.

Burke, Edmund. 1759. *A Philosophical Enquiry into the Origin of our Ideas of the Sublime and Beautiful.* 2nd edn., London.

Cassirer, Ernst. 1945. *Rousseau, Kant, Goethe.* Trans. James Gutmann, Paul Oskar Kristeller, and John Herman Randall Jr. Princeton, Princeton University Press.

1951. *The Philosophy of the Enlightenment*. Trans. F.C.A. Koelln and J.P. Pettegrove. Princeton, Princeton University Press.

1953–57. *The Philosophy of Symbolic Forms*. Trans. Ralph Manheim. Introduction by Charles Hendel. 3 vols. New Haven, Yale University Press.

1981. *Kant's Life and Thought*. Trans. James Haden. Introduction by Stephan Körner. New Haven and London, Yale University Press.

Cassirer, H.W. 1938. *A Commentary on Kant's 'Critique of Judgement'*. London, Methuen.

Clark, R.T. 1942. "Herder's Conception of *Kraft*". *PMLA*, 57, 737–52.

Coleman, Francis X.J. 1974. *The Harmony of Reason: A Study in Kant's Aesthetics*. Pittsburgh, University of Pittsburgh Press.

Coleridge, Samuel Taylor. 1954. *Biographia Literaria*. Ed. John Shawcross. Corrected reprint. 2 vols. London, Oxford University Press.

1972. *Lay Sermons*. Ed. R.J. White. The Bollingen Edition of the Collected Works of Samuel Taylor Coleridge. Vol. VI. London and Princeton, Routledge & Kegan Paul and Princeton University Press.

Copleston, Frederick, S.J. 1964a. *A History of Philosophy. Vol. VI, Pt 1: The French Enlightenment to Kant*. Garden City, N.Y., Doubleday.

1964b. *A History of Philosophy. Vol. VI, Pt 2: Kant*. Garden City, N.Y., Doubleday.

1965a. *A History of Philosophy. Vol. VII, Pt 1: Fichte to Hegel*. Garden City, N.Y., Doubleday.

1965b. *A History of Philosophy. Vol. VII, Pt 2: Schopenhauer to Nietzsche*. Garden City, N.Y., Doubleday.

Crawford, Donald W. 1974. *Kant's Aesthetic Theory*. Madison and London, University of Wisconsin Press.

Dante Alighieri. 1908. *The Divine Comedy*. Trans. Henry Cary. Ed. Edmund Gardner. London and New York, Dent & Dutton.

De Quincey, Thomas. 1889–90. *The Collected Writings of Thomas de Quincey*. Ed. David Masson. New and enlarged ed. 14 vols. Edinburgh, A. & C. Black.

Drummond, Rt Hon. William. 1805. *Academical Questions. Volume One*. London.

Edwards, Paul, ed. 1967. *The Encyclopaedia of Philosophy*. London and New York, Macmillan and The Free Press.

Eisler, Rudolf. 1961. *Kant-Lexicon*. 1930; rpt. Hildesheim, Georg Olms.

Engelbrecht, H.C. 1933. *Johann Gottlieb Fichte: A Study of his Political Writings with special reference to his Nationalism*. New York, Columbia University Press.

Engell, James. 1981. *The Creative Imagination: Enlightenment to Romanticism*. Cambridge, Mass. and London, Harvard University Press.

Esposito, Joseph L. 1977. *Schelling's Idealism and Philosophy of Nature*. Lewisburg and London, Bucknell University Press and Associated University Presses.

Fackenheim, Emil L. 1954. "Schelling's Philosophy of the Literary Arts". *Philosophical Quarterly*, 4, 310–26.

Fichte, Johann Gottlieb. 1845. *Johann Gottlieb Fichtes sämmtliche Werke*. Ed. I.H. Fichte. 8 vols. Berlin.

1847. *The Characteristics of the Present Age*. Trans. William Smith. London, John Chapman.

1889a. *The Popular Works of Johann Gottlieb Fichte*. Trans. William Smith. 4th ed. 2 vols. London, Trübner & Co.

1889b. *The Science of Rights*. Trans. A.E. Kroeger. Preface by William T. Harris. London, Trübner & Co.

1907. *The Science of Ethics as Based on the Science of Knowledge*. Trans. A.E. Kroeger. Ed. W.T. Harris. London, Kegan Paul, Trench & Trübner.

1956. *The Vocation of Man.* Ed. Roderick M. Chisholm. Indianapolis and New York, Bobbs-Merrill.

1964–. *J.G. Fichte: Gesamtausgabe der Bayerischen Akademie der Wissenschaften.* Ed. Reinhard Lauth, Hans Jacob, Hans Gliwitzky etc. In progress. Stuttgart and Bad Canstatt, Frommann–Holzboog.

1967. *J.G. Fichte: Briefwechsel.* Ed. Hans Schulz. 2 vols. Hildesheim, Georg Olms.

1968. *Addresses to the German Nation.* Trans. R.F. Jones & G.H. Turnbull. Ed. and revised George Armstrong Kelly. New York and Evanston, Harper & Row, 1968.

1970. *Fichte: 'Science of Knowledge' (Wissenschaftslehre).* Ed. and trans. Peter Heath and John Lachs. New York, Meredith Corporation.

1978. *Attempt at a Critique of all Revelation.* Trans. Garrett Green. Cambridge, Cambridge University Press.

Frei, Hans W. 1974. *The Eclipse of Biblical Narrative: A study of Eighteenth and Nineteenth Century Hermeneutics.* New Haven and London, Yale University Press.

Gadamer, Hans-Georg. 1975. *Truth and Method.* Translation ed. by Garrett Barden and John Cumming. New York, Seabury Press.

Gay, Peter. 1966. *The Enlightenment: An Interpretation. Volume I: The Rise of Modern Paganism.* New York, Alfred Knopf.

1969. *The Enlightenment: An Interpretation. Volume II: The Science of Freedom.* New York, Alfred Knopf.

Gibelin, Jean. 1933. *L'esthétique de Schelling d'après la 'Philosophie de l'Art'.* Paris.

Glockner, Herman. 1957. *Hegel-Lexicon.* 2nd (revised) ed. 2 vols. Stuttgart, Frommanns Verlag.

Goethe, J.W. von. 1974. *The Autobiography of Johann Wolfgang von Goethe.* Trans. John Oxenford. Introduction by Karl J. Weintraub. 2 vols. Chicago and London, University of Chicago Press, 1974.

1980. *Goethe on Art.* Ed. John Gage. Berkeley and Los Angeles, University of California Press.

Guéroult, Martial. 1930. *L'évolution et la structure de la doctrine de la science chez Fichte.* 2 vols. Paris.

Guyer, Paul. 1979. *Kant and the Claims of Taste.* Cambridge, Mass., and London, Harvard University Press.

Hamlyn, D.W. 1980. *Schopenhauer. The Arguments of the Philosophers.* London, Boston, Henley, Routledge & Kegan Paul.

Hatfield, Henry. 1964. *Aesthetic Paganism in German Literature from Winckelmann to the Death of Goethe.* Cambridge, Mass., Harvard University Press.

Hazlitt, William. 1930–4. *The Complete Works of William Hazlitt.* Ed. P.P. Howe. 21 vols. London and Toronto, J.M. Dent.

Hegel, Georg Wilhelm Friedrich. 1834. *G.W.F. Hegels Werke.* Vollständige Ausgabe. Vol. XVI. Berlin.

1892. *Hegel's Lectures on the History of Philosophy.* Trans. E.S. Haldane. 3 vols. rpt. London and New York, Routledge & Kegan Paul and The Humanities Press, 1963.

1948. *Hegel: Early Theological Writings.* Trans. T.M. Knox and Richard Kroner; rpt. Philadelphia, University of Pennsylvania Press, 1971.

1949–59. *Sämtliche Werke.* Jubiläumsausgabe in 20 vols. 3rd printing. Ed. Ludwig Boumann etc., newly arranged by Herman Glockner. Stuttgart, Frommanns Verlag.

1956. *Berliner Schriften, 1818–31.* Ed. J. Hoffmeister. Hamburg, F. Meiner.

1967. *Hegel's Philosophy of Right.* Trans. T.M. Knox. 1952; rpt. Oxford, London, New York, Oxford University Press.

1969. *Hegel's Science of Logic*. Trans. A.V. Miller. Introduction by J.N. Findlay. London and New York, George Allen & Unwin and The Humanities Press.

1971. *Hegel's Philosophy of Mind*. Trans. William Wallace. Oxford, Clarendon Press.

1975. *Hegel's Aesthetics: Lectures on Fine Art*. Trans. T.M. Knox. 2 vols. continuously paginated. Oxford, Clarendon Press.

1977. *The Difference Between Fichte's and Schelling's System of Philosophy*. Trans. H.S. Harris and Walter Cerf. Albany, State University of New York Press.

1979. *Phenomenology of Spirit*. Trans. A.V. Miller. Introduction by J.N. Findlay. Oxford, Clarendon Press.

1980. *Lectures on the Philosophy of World History. Introduction: Reason in History*. Trans. H.B. Nisbet. Introduction by Duncan Forbes. Cambridge, Cambridge University Press.

Hettner, Hermann. 1961. *Geschichte der deutschen Literatur im achtzehnten Jahrhundert*. 2 vols. Berlin, Aufbau-Verlag.

Hipple, W.J. 1957. *The Beautiful, the Sublime and the Picturesque in Eighteenth-Century British Aesthetic Theory*. Carbondale, Southern Illinois University Press.

Hirsch, E.D., Jr. 1960. *Wordsworth and Schelling: A Typological Study of Romanticism*. New Haven, Yale University Press.

Hofstadter, Albert, and Kuhns, Richard. 1964. Eds. *Philosophies of Art and Beauty: Selected Readings in Aesthetics from Plato to Heidegger*; rpt. Chicago, University of Chicago Press, 1976.

Howard, William Guild, ed. 1910. *'Laokoon': Lessing, Goethe, Herder*. New York, Henry Holt & Co.

Hübscher, Arthur. 1981. *Schopenhauer-Bibliographie*. Stuttgart–Bad Canstatt, Frommann–Holzboog.

Hume, David. 1912. *Essays Moral, Political, and Literary*. Ed. T.H. Green and T.H. Grose. 2 vols. London, Longman's, Green & Co.

Kaminsky, Jack. 1962. *Hegel on Art: An Interpretation of Hegel's Aesthetics*. New York, State University of New York Press.

Kant, Immanuel. 1900–42. *Kants gesammelte Schriften*. Published by the Königlich Preussische Akademie der Wissenschaften. 22 vols. Berlin.

1933. *Immanuel Kant's Critique of Pure Reason*. Trans. Norman Kemp Smith. 2nd impression with corrections. London, Macmillan.

1935. *Immanuel Kant on Philosophy in General*. Trans. Humayun Kabir. Calcutta, University of Calcutta Press.

1952. *The Critique of Judgement*. Trans. James Creed Meredith. Two parts in one volume. Oxford, Clarendon Press.

1956. *Critique of Practical Reason*. Trans. Lewis White Beck. Indianapolis and New York, Bobbs-Merrill.

1960. *Observations on the Feeling of the Beautiful and Sublime*. Trans. John T. Goldthwait. Berkeley and Los Angeles, University of California Press.

1963. *Kant on History*. Trans. Lewis White Beck. Indianapolis and New York, Bobbs-Merrill.

1974. *Anthropology from a Practical Point of View*. Trans. Mary J. Gregor. The Hague, Martinus Nijhoff.

Karelis, Charles. 1979. *Hegel's Introduction to Aesthetics*. Trans. T.M. Knox. Ed. with an interpretative essay by Charles Karelis. Oxford, Clarendon Press.

Kemp Smith, Norman. 1923. *A Commentary to Kant's 'Critique of Pure Reason'*. 2nd (revised) ed. New York, The Humanities Press.

Klapper, M. Roxana. 1975. *The German Literary Influence on Shelley*. Salzburg Studies in English Literature: Romantic Reassessment. Salzburg, Institut für englische Sprache und Literatur.

Knox, Israel. 1936. *The Aesthetic Theories of Kant, Hegel, and Schopenhauer*. New York, Columbia University Press.

Kohlschmidt, Werner. 1975. *A History of German Literature, 1760–1805*. Trans. Ian Hilton. London, Macmillan.

Korff, H.A. 1923–57. *Geist der Goethezeit: Versuch einer ideellen Entwicklung der klassisch-romantischen Literaturgeschichte*. 5 vols. Leipzig.

Körner, Stephan. 1955. *Kant*. Harmondsworth, Middx., Penguin.

Léon, Xavier. 1922–7. *Fichte et son temps*. 2 parts in 3 vols. Paris.

Lewes, George Henry. 1857. *The Biographical History of Philosophy, from its Origins in Greece down to the Present Day*. Revised ed. London, John Parker & Son.

McFarland, Thomas. 1969. *Coleridge and the Pantheist Tradition*. Oxford, Clarendon Press.

Menhennet, A. 1973. *Order and Freedom: German Literature and Society, 1720–1805*. London, Weidenfeld & Nicolson.

Meredith, James Creed. 1911. *Kant's Critique of Aesthetic Judgement*. Oxford, Clarendon Press.

1928. *Kant's Critique of Teleological Judgement*. Oxford, Clarendon Press.

Molnár, Géza von. 1981–2. "Goethe's Reading of Kant's 'Critique of Esthetic Judgement': A Referential Guide for Wilhelm Meister's Aesthetic Education." *Eighteenth Century Studies*, 15, 402–20.

Monk, Samuel Holt. 1935. *The Sublime. A Study of Critical Theories in Eighteenth Century England*. New York, Modern Language Association of America.

Muirhead, J.H. 1927. "How Hegel Came to England." *Mind*, 36, 423–47.

Nauern, Franz-Gabriel. 1971. *Revolution, Idealism and Human Freedom: Schelling, Hölderlin and Hegel and the Crisis of Early German Idealism*. The Hague, Martinus Nijhoff.

Nivelle, Armand. 1955. *Les théories esthétiques en Allemagne de Baumgarten à Kant*. Bibliothèque de la Faculté de Philosophie et Lettres de l'Université de Liège. Fascicule CXXXIV. Paris.

Ogden, C.K., & Richards, I.A. 1923. *The Meaning of Meaning*. 10th ed., London, Routledge & Kegan Paul, 1949.

Orsini, Gian N.G. 1969. *Coleridge and German Idealism: A Study in the History of Philosophy, with unpublished materials from Coleridge's Notebooks*. Carbondale, Illinois, Southern Illinois University Press.

Pascal, Roy. 1937. *Shakespeare in Germany, 1740–1815*. Cambridge, Cambridge University Press.

Pochmann, Henry A. 1957. *German Culture in America*. Madison, University of Wisconsin Press.

Prang, Helmut. 1972. *Die romantische Ironie*. Darmstadt, Wissenschaftliche Buchgesellschaft.

Price, Mary Bell and Lawrence Marsden. 1934. *The Publication of English Literature in Germany in the Eighteenth Century*. Berkeley, University of California Press.

1955. *The Publication of English Humaniora in Germany in the Eighteenth Century*. Berkeley and Los Angeles, University of California Press.

Ralli, Augustus. 1932. *A History of Shakespearean Criticism*. 2 vols. London, Oxford University Press.

Read, Herbert, 1947. Ed. *The True Voice of Feeling: Studies in English Romantic Poetry* rpt. London, Faber & Faber, 1968.

Robinson, Henry Crabb. 1869. *Diary, Reminiscences, and Correspondence of Henry Crabb Robinson*. Ed. Thomas Sadler. 3 vols. London, Macmillan.

1929. *Crabb Robinson in Germany, 1800–1805*. Extracts from his correspondence. Ed. Edith J. Morley. London, Oxford University Press.

Rousseau, Jean Jacques. 1767. *The Miscellaneous Works of Mr. J.J. Rousseau*. 5 vols. London.

Schelling, Friedrich Wilhelm Joseph von. 1856–61. *Sämmtliche Werke*. Ed. K.F.A. von Schelling. 14 vols. Stuttgart and Augsburg.

1936. *Of Human Freedom*. Trans. James Gutman. Chicago, Open Court.

1966. *On University Studies*. Trans. E.S. Morgan. Ed. Norbert Guterman. Athens, Ohio, Ohio University Press.

1967. *The Ages of the World*. Trans. Frederick de Wolfe Bolman Jr., 1942, rpt. New York, AMS Press.

1974. *Schelling's Treatise on 'The Deities of Samothrace'*. Trans. Robert F. Brown. American Academy of Religion, Studies in Religion. Missoula, Montana, Scholars' Press.

1978. *System of Transcendental Idealism (1800)*. Trans. Peter Heath. Introduction by Michael Vater. Charlottesville, University of Virginia Press.

1980. *The Unconditional in Human Knowledge: Four Early Essays (1794–96)*. Trans. Fritz Marti. Lewisburg and London, Bucknell University Press and Associated University Presses.

Schiller, Johann Christoph Friedrich von. 1943–. *Schillers Werke*. Nationalausgabe. Ed. Julius Petersen, Gerhard Fricke, Liselotte Blumenthal, Benno von Wiese etc. In progress. Weimar, H. Bohlaus.

1967. *On the Aesthetic Education of Man, in a Series of Letters*. Ed. and trans. Elizabeth M. Wilkinson and L.A. Willoughby. Oxford, Clarendon Press.

Schlegel, August Wilhelm. 1962–74. *Kritische Schriften und Briefe*. Ed. E. Lohner. 7 vols. Stuttgart, W. Kohlhammer.

Schlegel, Friedrich. 1849. *The Aesthetic and Miscellaneous Works of Friedrich von Schlegel*. Trans. E.J. Millington. London, Henry Bohn.

1971. *Friedrich Schlegel's 'Lucinde' and the Fragments*. Trans. Peter Firchow. Minneapolis, University of Minnesota Press.

Schleiermacher, Friedrich Ernst Daniel. 1834–64. *Friedrich Schleiermacher's sämmtliche Werke*. 32 vols. Berlin.

1926. *Schleiermacher's Soliloquies*. Trans. Horace Leland Friess. Chicago, Open Court.

1928. *The Christian Faith*. Trans. from the 2nd German edition by H.R. Mackintosh and J.S. Stewart. Edinburgh, T.& T. Clark.

1958. *On Religion: Speeches to its Cultured Despisers*. Trans. John Oman. New York, Harper & Row.

1977. *Hermeneutics: the Handwritten Manuscripts*. Ed. Heinz Kimmerle. Trans. James Duke and Jack Forstman. American Academy of Religion, Texts and Translation Series 1. Missoula, Montana, Scholars' Press.

Schneeberger, Guido. 1954. *Frans Wilhelm Josef Schelling: eine Bibliographie*. Bern, Francke Verlag.

Schopenhauer, Arthur. 1911. *Arthur Schopenhauers sämtliche Werke*. Vol. 1. Ed. Paul Deussen. Munich.

1969. *The World as Will and Representation*. Trans. E.F.J. Payne. 2 vols. 1958; rpt. New York, Dover Publications.

1974a. *Parerga and Paralipomena*. Trans. E.F.J. Payne. 2 vols. Oxford, Clarendon Press.

1974b. *On the Fourfold Principle of Sufficient Reason*. Trans. E.F.J. Payne. Introduction by Richard Howard. La Salle, Illinois, Open Court.

Seidel, George J. 1976. *Activity and Ground: Fichte, Schelling and Hegel*. Hildesheim & New York, Georg Olms.

Shaffer, Elinor S. 1975. *'Kubla Khan' and the Fall of Jerusalem*. Cambridge, Cambridge University Press.

Shaper, Eva. 1979. *Studies in Kant's Aesthetics*. Edinburgh, Edinburgh University Press.

Shelley, Percy Bysshe. 1977. *Shelley's Poetry and Prose*. Ed. Donald H. Reiman and Sharon B. Powers. New York and London, W.W. Norton & Co.

Simpson, David. 1982a. *Wordsworth and the Figurings of the Real*. London and Atlantic Highlands, N.J., Macmillan and The Humanities Press.

1982b. *Fetishism and Imagination: Melville, Dickens, Conrad*. Baltimore and London, The Johns Hopkins University Press.

Sorg, Bernhard. 1975. *Zur literarischen Schopenhauer-Rezeption im 19. Jahrhundert*. Heidelberg, Carl Winter.

Staël, Madame de (Baroness de Staël-Holstein). 1813. *Germany*. 3 vols. London, John Murray.

Stahl, Ernest L. 1947. *Shakespeare und das deutsche Theater*. Stuttgart, W. Kohlhammer.

Steinhauer, Kurt. 1980. *Hegel Bibliography-Bibliographie*. Background Material on the International Reception of Hegel within the context of the History of Philosophy. München, New York, London, Paris, K.G. Saur.

Stewart, Dugald. 1854. *The Collected Works of Dugald Stewart*. Ed. Sir William Hamilton. 11 vols. Edinburgh, Thomas Constable.

Stokoe, F.W. 1926. *German Influence in the English Romantic Period, 1788–1818*. Cambridge, Cambridge University Press.

Strawson, P.F. 1966. *The Bounds of Sense*. London, Methuen.

Strohschneider-Kohrs, Ingrid. 1960. *Die Romantische Ironie im Theorie und Gestaltung*. Tübingen, Max Niemeyer.

Taylor, Charles. 1975. *Hegel*. Cambridge, Cambridge University Press.

Tieck, Ludwig. 1848–52. *Kritische Schriften*. 4 vols. Leipzig.

Todorov, Tzvetan. 1982. *Theories of the Symbol*. Trans. Catherine Porter. Ithaca, N.Y., Cornell University Press.

Vogel, Stanley M. 1955. *German Literary Influences on the American Transcendentalists*. New Haven, Yale University Press.

Weiskel, Thomas. 1976. *The Romantic Sublime: Studies in the Structure and Psychology of Transcendence*. Baltimore and London, The Johns Hopkins University Press.

Wellek, René. 1931. *Immanuel Kant in England, 1793–1838*. Princeton, Princeton University Press.

1955. *A History of Modern Criticism, 1750–1955*. 4 vols. New Haven, Yale University Press.

1965. *Confrontations: Studies in the Intellectual and Literary Relations between Germany, England and the United States during the Nineteenth Century*. Princeton, Princeton University Press.

Wheeler, Kathleen M. 1980. *Sources, Processes and Methods in Coleridge's 'Biographia Literaria'*. Cambridge, Cambridge University Press.

Winckelmann, Johann Joachim. 1765. *Reflections on the Painting and Sculpture of the Greeks*. Trans. Henry Fuseli. London.

Wordsworth, William. 1967. *The Letters of William and Dorothy Wordsworth: The Early Years, 1787–1805*. Ed. E. de Selincourt. 2nd ed. rev. Chester L. Shaver. Oxford, Clarendon Press.

1974. *The Prose Works of William Wordsworth*. Ed. W.J.B. Owen and Jane Worthington Smyser. 3 vols. Oxford, Clarendon Press.

Index

Note: in the interests of space, cross referencing is not complete in this index. Both author and topic entries should therefore be consulted.